ETHNO Autobiography

Ethnoautobiography

Stories and Practices for
Unlearning Whiteness
Decolonization
Uncovering Ethnicities

Jürgen Werner Kremer

&

R Jackson-Paton

ReVision Publishing

Sebastopol, California

Library of Congress Cataloging–in–Publication Data
Kremer, Jürgen W., 1949–
Jackson–Paton, R, 1968–

Ethnoautobiography: Stories and Practices for Unlearning Whiteness,
Decolonization, Uncovering Ethnicities / Jürgen W. Kremer and
R Jackson–Paton

Includes index.
p. cm.
includes bibliographical references

ISBN 9780981970660

1. Identity – psychological aspects – autobiography
2. Identity – social aspects – autobiography
3. Multiculturalism – ethnicity
4. Ethics – moral aspects
5. Indigenous peoples – social life and customs
6. Postcolonialism – history or historical aspects
7. Decolonization – United States

Designed by Paula Kline using Adobe® InDesign.®
The typefaces used are Comic Sans for Title Page,
Palantino Linotype, and Calibri for body text.

We dedicate this book
To the memory of Biret Máret Kallio,
Teacher extraordinaire and magician of languages

Jürgen:
To Ursula Bear, tireless fellow traveler and inspiratrix and
To Freyja who carries cultural memory into the future
through dance and song

R:
To Jenny, Malaya and Fenua with
gratitude for all the teachings

CONTENTS

LIST OF RIFFS

LIST OF ACTIVITIES

List of Figures and Tables

List of Tables

LIST OF ILLUSTRATIONS

Special Thanks

The first round of thanks goes to all students, past and present, who have tirelessly support-ed this project through their feedback, suggestions, encouragement, supportive hands–on work, and admirable engagement with the process of ethnoautobiography. You have been instrumental for our stamina and persistence. Without you the project would not be what it is now. While we cannot name you all, we appreciate each of your contributions!

Paula Kline exhibited a determined, patient, feisty, organized and faithful hand in helping to bring this book to reality. You would not be reading this if not for Paula. We are so very grateful for her tireless work, not only in providing us with the book design and layout, but also in her careful and thorough attention to detail, in helping with copy editing, in assisting with research when needed, and in making sure we had the index that we felt was essential for the needs of our students. As a result, we feel that she should rightfully be called the midwife of this process. Her never–ending encouragement, humor, and enthusiasm for the project helped us get to the finish line. Thank you, Paula, for your dedicated work!

Chris Boyd made numerous contributions to this book including graphics design as well as some writing (you'll notice some riffs with CB).

Karen Jaenke has generously given us permission to use her instructions for dreamwork in this book (pp. 116–117 and pp. 334–339 in this book). Her work can be accessed via www. dreamhut.org.

We appreciate Elenita Strobel's contributions to Chapter 6 (pp. 182 – 186 in this book).

Many thanks to Inga–Maria Mulk for permission to reproduce the graphic in Mulk & Bayliss–Smith (2006) (page 120 in this book).

Carla Rudiger has been teaching R about embodiment for about three years and has deeply influenced this work.

Melissa Weiss gave some of her precious summer to proofread and offer much needed encouragement.

Jenny Jackson–Paton has been a patient and loving proofreader, supporter, and brainstormer.

Undoubtedly there are others who should be named and who have slipped our minds — our apologies to all those whom we have forgotten at this moment.

Ethnoautobiography: A Map to Decolonization and Indigenization

Foreword

A long–time colleague asked me, for the first time, the other day: *When did you become interested in the Indigenous?* My answer was an academic one: *When I started doing research on Filipino Indigenous Knowledge Systems and Practices.*

What I really wanted to say was: *I have always been interested in the Indigenous worldview; it's what my bones know and what my soul sings.*

I have been teaching whiteness studies for a long time. My first entry into this emergent field was decades ago when authors like Gloria Anzaldua, Cherrie Moraga, Audre Lorde, and bell hooks were writing about the colonized subject's archeological project of unearthing the buried bones and memories of the colonized psyche. In my own work I write about undoing the colonial gaze, taking off my colonial jacket, and remembering the messages I received from the dream world that I should keep my homeland on the map of Memory and Place.

Whiteness, I realized, was one of those constructs that I had to reckon and wrestle with as it became clear, the deeper I went into my work, that I had to learn how to let go of its hold in my life. In the letting go and in being emptied of colonial projections, I needed to find another toehold that would ground my being. I found my way back into my own Indigenous roots.

In my multicultural studies courses, I always include the topic of White privilege and its intersection with class and gender. Over the years I've seen my students become more and more receptive to the concept of privilege but most of the discourse on White privilege always stopped short of offering students a process on how to decolonize European colonial thinking and how to end whiteness.

So I was very glad when I met Jürgen Kremer and read his work on Ethnoautobiography. I realized that I could have summed up my own process of decolonization and Indigenization with this concept. Our conversations led to the idea of a workbook that undergraduates can use that will offer a pathway out of whiteness and White privilege, out of the masterful (but empty) self constructed by modernity.

In the three consecutive semesters that I have piloted this workbook in one of my courses, the students are appreciative of the process that teaches them how to deal with the shadow material of history, how to rediscover their ancestral roots, how to connect with myths, storytelling, dreams, spirituality. As one student said: *This process gave me a more expansive sense of self and a more solid ground to stand on. I'm no longer afraid of letting go of my White privilege.*

This is the book in your hands. May you, likewise, benefit from the power of the Indigenous paradigm to help us decolonize and to find the gems hidden in the shadows of our modern lives.

Leny Mendoza Strobel, December 8, 2012
Professor, American Multicultural Studies Department, Sonoma State University

The Ceremonial Stepping–Stones of Ethnoautobiography

Foreword

When you see the term "ethnoautobiography" you may think of it as a term from the field of psychology or anthropology. In fact, ethnoautobiography is a ceremony laid out step by step with clear definitions. The work of ethnoautobiography can be done individually, however, doing it as part of a learning community enhances and accelerates the process since the group provides multiples mirrors.

Each of the elements of ethnoautobiography represents stepping–stones or points of reflection mirroring the workings of our minds with the capacity to identify distortions. Each term or dimension is a teaching. When we hold that teaching before the light of Indigenous mind it helps us to free ourselves from the torment of being separated from the source of our being, the source of our power, and it helps us develop the capacity to experience life in all its vitality. In so doing, even just a moment of immersion in this ceremony points the way out of the disasters our rational mind has created by rejecting its ethnoautobiographical grounding.

The terms and stories in this workbook help us to make our inner voices for peace audible, to hear the voices of our ancestors, to offer forgiveness for the traumas of our histories, and to reconcile with our natural born inheritance, our Indigenous mind.

For too long White people have been beggars at the doors of native ceremonies longing to be included. With their arrogance and sense of entitlement in place they refuse to investigate their Indigenous roots. Working through the ceremonial steps of ethnoautobiography makes participation in native ceremonies part of a healing.

Once we know who we are we can contribute to the ceremony of life. Through the process of ethnoautobiography we can become full participants around the sacred fire of Indigenous spirituality. Thus we are able not only to fulfill the responsibilities to ourselves, our loved ones, our people, Earth and life past and present — we find reality.

Apela Colorado, February 17, 2013
Founder, Worldwide Indigenous Science Network

Truth Makes Us Free, but First We Have to Free Truth

Foreword

One question that shamans, and native people in general, often ask is: "Who are you?" "Well, I am Stanley Krippner" or "I am Jürgen Kremer" is not the answer they are looking for. Native people are looking for an answer with a point of view that extends across generations, an answer that looks at one's roots. Answering the question "Who are you?" in this way cannot only answer a question, it can help to ground a person's sense of being.

I have engaged in genealogical research to determine where my grandparents came from. My maternal grandfather was born in Norway and immigrated when he was a boy. My maternal grandmother was the daughter of Norwegian immigrants. My paternal grandmother's side of the family hailed from Northern Ireland. My paternal grandfather's side leads back to Bavaria, which I have visited several times. One of these ancestors crossed the border in order to avoid military service in what is now the Czech Republic. In German, the name Krippner literally translates as "cradle maker". The Krippners were Protestant, and thus a bit out of place in Catholic Bavaria; they left for the United States and eventually ended up in Wisconsin.

The concept of the "long body" is useful for ethnoautobiography. In Haudenosaunee (Iroquois) tradition, family members are taught to plan for the next seven generations, and they also are instructed to look seven generations back. Talking and thinking about the future leads to planning; talking and thinking about the past helps one to understand one's personal identity. One's "long body" reaches beyond one's psyche, beyond one's skin, and is capable of reaching into other realms. Today, people easily identify with a particular political party, sports team, ethnic group, or institutionalized religion; however, Indigenous identity has a broader sweep. It extends to other forms of nature, such as the "four legged ones" or the "standing nations" (animals and trees). These are both seen as relatives and are part of the "long body" concept.

I have never been particularly comfortable with the term "humanistic" in humanistic psychology. Psychology is disciplined inquiry into behavior and experience. But it is not just humans who behave and experience, other animals do so as well. A term that restricts psychology to humans does not make sense and is too restrictive. Hence, ecopsychology should be an important part of humanistic psychology (Krippner, 2002).

Transpersonal psychology emphasizes shifts in consciousness that extend beyond one's skin and body. This includes transcendental aspects of the cosmos such as feelings of union with Nature. Such unitive processes put people in touch with other forms of Nature and, for some, may provide the motivation to become an environmental activist. Humanistic and transpersonal psychology could make a greater effort to include the Natural as well as the Supernatural in their perspectives and practices.

How does this discussion relate to ethnoautobiography? When people see themselves as part of Earth, they realize that they are not merely inhabitants and caretakers, they are part of the very cosmos they spend their time studying. The perspectives contained in ethnoautobiography often awaken people to their connections with Nature. This is the position taken by Metzner (1994) in *The Well of Remembrance.*

Carl Gustav Jung used the term "personal myth" (1965, p. 3). In my book with David Feinstein (2008), we linked our readers with past generations and helped them to accept or reject the myths of their parents and grandparents. It is important to keep in mind that even if they reject parental myths, such as racism, they still need to acknowledge these mythologies as part of their history.

It is somewhat amusing when people say, "I am starting fresh," implying they have no need for knowledge of their ancestral lineage. But even if one is a "born again" Christian or a newly "enlightened" Buddhist, one still needs to acknowledge the links with one's past, even if one no longer identifies with them. People cannot renounce their heritage without losing parts of their psyche. Albert Ellis stressed the importance of accepting oneself unconditionally. This means that people also have to accept their past unconditionally.

Like it or not, the past is still a part of the "long body." And one cannot neglect dysfunctional family myths, which are also part of that "long body."

I define myths as imaginative statements or stories about important existential human issues, narratives that have behavioral consequences. The word "imaginative" is important. It is not life events themselves that are ultimately important, but how people react to those events. One's reactions to life's events display imagination, attribution, and personal construction at work. The human brain did not evolve to impart truth but to impart meaning.

When people make and apply meaning to an event they are trying to cope with their understanding of that event or the lack thereof. When a myth becomes outmoded, there is a need to determine where that understanding went astray. If planting crops during the full moon does not succeed, farmers may have to research and understand the role played by other variables such as drought, climate change, and seasonal variations. Earlier, less dependable, beliefs can be relegated to folklore. When myths have become dysfunctional, people need to find new myths. If a myth is no longer based on consensual reality and/or empirical data, then a new myth needs to be found that is better grounded. Personal myths can lead to disastrous or beneficial results, as can cultural myths.

An ethnoautobiographical approach, for example, can reveal what previous generations thought about myths related to psychosexual development in child rearing practices. Psychohistorians have pointed out how frequently children were abused throughout European history. Western cultures, according to many psychohistorians, need to confront their dark history of child abuse and neglect.

Similarly, the study of transgenerational trauma emerged when the effects of the Nazi Holocaust were observed not only in survivors but in their children too. It seems that the "long bodies" of earlier survivors of genocides bear the scars of additional horrors. Is it any wonder that many Native Americans whose forebears survived the European invasion (with all of its weapons and microbes of mass destruction) and the descendants of slaves (brought against their will to the New World from Africa) have been troubled by domestic abuse, alcoholism, substance abuse, and other maladies? Transgenerational trauma requires transgenerational repair.

Postmodernists and other skeptical writers make a practice of questioning authoritative statements, even those that have been considered venerable and reliable for generations. The postmodern literature can be helpful for ethnoautobiographical studies, assisting humanity's search for both truth and meaning. Postmodernity questions the sources of authority that have been taken for granted, whether literary or scientific. It also points out the ubiquitous use of power in the enforcement of mainstream authority, whether scientific, political, or religious. On the positive side, Western science has disabused humanity of much outmoded dogma. But on the negative side it has frequently used its power to label and describe phenomena that could be just as accurately constructed by other ways of knowing. Postmodernists have turned mainstream ideology on its head: Yes, truth empowers — but all too often power determines what is held to be true.

As Jürgen Kremer and R Jackson–Paton remind us in this admirable book on the topic, students of ethnoautobiography cannot take for granted what they have been told about their forebears. They need to look critically at how their family myths may have been socially constructed and manufactured. This is why ethnoautobiographers need to question their sources and use multiple references whenever possible.

Ethnoautobiography asks pertinent questions and presents methods by which these questions can be answered. These methods help them sift and winnow data as to what is verifiable. This process, when successful, can provide insight into one's genetic heritage. When seeking answers to the question "Who are you?" contemporary humans, like Indigenous peoples, need to go back several generations. Truth makes us free, but first we have to free truth.

Stanley Krippner, PhD August 25, 2013
Professor of Psychology and Integrative Inquiry, Saybrook University

Preface

This is a book of hope in the face of profound personal, cultural, and environmental challenges. Such hope is not the shallow optimism that has been invoked again and again in recent years. Our hope is much more radical; it reaches toward something that we have yet to understand fully. It is a radical hope that anticipates something good that we can't quite put in words yet (Lear, 2006). This stems from the potential that we humans can remember and work with ancient capacities built into each of us. We each carry the means to overcome individualistically driven crisis responses by accessing and appreciating sources beyond the small selves of our personhood. From this rich and creative well at the roots of who we are hope and inspiration for the future may arise. Expanding or deepening our sense of self is our hope for the future, our hope for the resolution of our current crises. It is an active hope, to use Joanna Macy's phrase (Macy & Johnstone, 2012).

Ethnoautobiography is an invitation to envision, self–reflect and renew. It has been our experience that readers from a spectrum of disciplines (from accounting and computer sciences to the social sciences) as well as a variety of spiritual and (non)-religious backgrounds have found the ethnoautobiographical process enriching. These stories and practices are an invitation to strengthen your own voice, whatever your background and beliefs, and to reinforce a participatory sense of presence in the world.

We acknowledge that we write from White experience and offer ethnoautobiography especially for White people. That said, these practices can assist many other survivors of colonization — having internalized aspects of White mind — with decolonizing self and society. We are offering a *process* that allows you to find your own answers and resolutions to our contemporary confusions and challenges, whether obvious or more hidden. This workbook is therefore both *call* and *response*.

It is a *call* for all people and peoples to engage anew with the thorny, complicated issues of personal and cultural identity, and how it relates to our relationships with other people and the places we live. Whether recent settlers, whether our family has been settled for many generations on the North American continent — often called Turtle Island by Native Americans — we want to do this work with integrity and creativity. We want to dig deeper than our family tree and branch out into the complex weave of roots and what nurtures our roots. Integrity and depth in the work of ethnoautobiography is nurtured by investigating the issues that are so often denied in our society: cultural shadow issues such as the history of Native American genocide or the slave trade. While these are difficult and shameful topics, confronting them leads to inspiration and creativity to work through challenging issues and discover new possibilities.

This book is also a *response* to this time of crisis. Maybe every generation has its crisis, yet our present–day crisis seems to involve factors that increase the level of challenge. Responding with panic oftentimes does not invoke the most mindful responses. And yet, thoughtful responses to support our wellbeing, and the wellbeing of future generations, must be found. There can be no denying the ecological, political, and economic crises sweeping the world on any given day. Some of these seem to cause anxiety that is difficult to voice — a sense of something unknown and incomprehensible looming just beyond the horizon. At times the complexity of a particular crisis seems to be well above our heads. Importantly, our current crises are not just 'out there', they are also inside of us, inside our selves, inside the very way we experience and think about our personal and cultural identity.

This is also a time of tremendous potential. As life expectancy increases, as our world becomes increasingly computer–based, as multiple technologies change our world, as media changes dramatically beyond books, and as global interconnectivity continues to increase, we are challenged to respond. Further, our global economy is becoming ever more deeply intertwined, and biological, biochemical, and genetic sciences impact the very fabric of life itself. We have to confront economic growth that is unsustainable and question our relationship with our ecosystems and the use of energy (Davis, Fidler & Gorbis, 2011; Gore, 2013; Lovins, 2011). Of course, these and other trends impact our sense of who we are and the skills and capacities we acquire to live and to live well. It is our contention that we will be able to respond constructively and with life affirming creativity when we are in an organic process of our networked sense of self, our natural embeddedness in where we come from and where we are.

Several assumptions are at the core of this workbook. First, individualism, the primary concern in the West with individual rights, self worth, and personal achievements, is not only a pernicious threat to much that we hold dear, it also prevents us from accessing the sources in each person that can be helpful in developing responses to the crises we are facing. In fact, individualism cuts us off from deep sources of cultural renewal. Each individual is so much more than what individualism permits. Ethnoautobiography suggests that we are complex webs of place, history, gender, ancestry, ever growing and changing. In an individualistic paradigm we are in denial about these tremendous sources of inspiration, even though they are still available to all of us.

Individualism is a reflection of colonialism and a colonial mindset. Remembering the fluidity of our embedded selves, selves woven into what is around us, brings us to the next ingredient: ethnoautobiography is fundamentally anti–colonial. This may seem anachronistic — who talks about colonialism in the 2010's? And while the historical time period of explicit colonization may be in the past, Indigenous peoples (among others) are quick to point out that we are far from a postcolonial age. External colonial moves continue, albeit under different names (such as globalization or free trade).

At the same time, the external colonial moves of the past now also reside in the internal mindset of objectifying the world around us. Individualism as personality structure is inherently colonial in its view not only of the external world, but also the physical body in which the self makes its home with the airs of a master. Our bodies are viewed with distance, at best, disdain, at worst, ruled by the mind from above. White privilege that fuels political distrust and endangers the well being of communities is another exemplary part of the individualistic perspective. The dysfunctional attitudes toward the ecologies we are a part of and from which we continue to "harvest" resources without regard for any future is another.

Both authors were raised in a culture of whiteness (one of us in Germany, the other in the U.S.). Yet, we would not be who we are and where we are today if not for the rich and varied inspiration of Indigenous models. Indigenous worldviews did not come abstractly, they came through numerous Indigenous friends, colleagues, ceremonialists, and teachers who opened our eyes and continue to do so. All of this took many forms: exposure to diverse storytelling traditions, appreciating cultural survival, or survivance, engaging in ceremonial approaches to community and identity, and listening to the never–ending call for decolonization. We are grateful for the land we live on, to the spirits of the places where we live, and also for all of the teachings about how to live in a good way and with a good mind, how to live with an eye on balance rather than merely progress. Accordingly, the context out of which this book arose reflects the decolonization practices demanded by Indigenous peoples.

This book has its origins in an article which Jürgen published in 2004, entitled "Ethnoautobiography as Practice of Radical Presence — Storying the Self in Participatory Visions" (Kremer, 2004). This scholarly essay was dense and in need of elaboration. With Leny Strobel's encouragement Jürgen began to break the article into chapters. He then was fortunate to find a willing and inspiring contributor and collaborator in R. Yet, none of this would have happened without three women.

Three Indigenous women activists, in particular, are responsible for supporting and encouraging the transformative work before you. Of course, they are not responsible for our mis–steps and failings, but it is safe to say that most likely none of this would exist if not for the passionate, spirited, and compassionately challenging presence of Apela Colorado, the late Biret Máret Kallio, and Leny Strobel. Apela challenged us to explore our Indigenous roots and opened new vistas beyond shame and forgetting. It was her persistence that first led Jürgen, finally, to take the trip to Sápmi he had originally planned as an adolescent; later R and Jürgen spent time together with our Sámi friend and colleague Biret Máret. She confronted us ruthlessly when our whiteness got the better of us and she showed us connections we had not seen before. And Leny was the generously supportive and patient midwife of this project — without her willingness to try out the book in her seminars and her invitations to discuss the material with students the book would not be what it is. Our gratitude goes to the three women who stand at the birth of this book.

In the Old Norse universe three women around the well lift the fertile clay "to dabble the dales", to create new life in the world: the woman of memory (*Urðr*), the woman becoming (*Verðandi*), and the woman of obligation (*Skuld*). It is through the labors of these three women that life is renewed and birth becomes fateful. Similarly, we find a central image of three women among the Sámi peoples: *Sáráhkká*, the mother of creation, who brings new life into the mother's womb and who lives under the fire place; the midwife, *Juoksáhkká*, who is responsible for the child's gender; and *Uksáhkká*, who protects the nearest environment and takes care of mother and child after birth. Sápmi, the land of the Sámi peoples has figured centrally in our own ethnoautobiographical process since it is here that we found the Indigenous neighbors closest to our own ancestries.

We are also deeply grateful to all of those who have given us feedback and support along the way, most especially our spouses Ursula and Jenny. Additional colleagues and friends who believed in the project include Melissa, Susan, Chris, Mary Gomes, Elenita Strobel, and even Shadow. We are also deeply indebted to the innumerable students who provided rich feedback on the various drafts of the book.

We have designed the book to serve both as tool for personal reflection and as textbook for college and university classes (such as American Multicultural Values and Ethics or Psychology of Identity). The first six chapters provide an overview map of the territory the reader will encounter. The subsequent ten chapters (6 – 15) explore in detail the different dimensions that define ethnoautobiography. The final two chapters (16 & 17) bring us back to a look at the territory explored and encourage the continuation of the work to look at ourselves with different eyes.

What we present here is a workbook to guide personal inquiry. The importance of autobiographical writing as research method is increasingly recognized (see Denzin & Lincoln, 1994). The inquiry we are describing here can be seen as specific application of what is established as autoethnography (Chang, 2008), which "combines cultural analysis and interpretation with narrative details" (p. 46), as well as critical, Indigenous inquiry (Denzin, Lincoln, & Smith, 2008). It can thus be applied to personal process work as well as academic research. Accordingly, we have included a brief appendix about ethnoautobiography as research methodology.

As the title of this book makes clear, it is a workbook with activities, readings and various voices and threads. It is a both a journey and a destination. It is about learning how to change and about changing how we learn. Whether we look at our personal stories, our family history or the narrative we tell about where we live and what happened to get us there, all of these are vital elements to explore with caring attention and an embodied sense of purpose. The book is designed to explore what is not only up front in our minds, but also the depth of what we might call our 'second nature', our unconscious way of being in the world. Out of this storytelling will emerge, we hope, new stories and visions that help us address our contemporary challenges.

Jürgen Werner Kremer
R Jackson–Paton

Chapter 0
Let's Have a Conversation

Riff

So You Really Want to Know Who I Am?

So you want to know who I am?
I used to have an easy answer
Simple and straightforward
Name and profession

Now there are complications
Stories
Memories
And then there is ancestry.com
And the National Geographic Geno kit

Now there are the names
Of my mother and father
My grandmothers and grandfathers
And great–grandmothers and great–grandfathers
And on
Their places
Along the Baltic
Towns, villages, shtetls
Along the River Rhine
Into Alsace–Lorraine
Into the hinterlands of yore
Where you can change your identity
From Jew to Gentile
And on go the names

Now there are my memories
Of places I have lived and traveled
Germany, Iceland, Scandinavia, Poland
The land of the eagle, North America
The land of the condor, South America
Africa
And on into the histories
Of these places, their memories
Of the places where I go
To chant and talk to presences
Waltoykewel, Nomlaki land
Northern California

So you really want to know who I am?
Beware
When you listen to my response
Your straightforward answers
May turn into stories and
May dissolve under the force of memory and imagination

JWK

Conversation Pieces

Many ancient traditions contain stories in which animals can speak just like humans. Listen in on this conversation between two animal companions of the authors (fárrosaš or fetch are words for animal companion in two of our ancestral languages).

Salmon: Let's start out with the most obvious: Why would the authors start with Chapter Zero? *Zero?* Really?

Raven: Well, I can go mathematical on you, dear Salmon, and say: G. Spencer–Brown (1969) argues that the first cardinal number is actually not one, but zero. I know that 'one' becomes 'first' when it changes from ordinal to cardinal, but I don't quite know how to do it with 'zero'. So *there* is that question: zeroth chapter?

Salmon: Being a swimmer I find the real lack of elegance very challenging.

Raven: Have no fear. Beyond this mathematical point there is a more philosophical one. Building on the Buddhist traditions we can say: Zero is emptiness and nothingness and thus the fullness of being and potential. It is a paradox and so much of this book examines paradoxes and contemporary conundrums. Issues where there aren't easy answers, where the authors have to say: 'both/and' or 'neither/nor'. What we'll do here is mention a few key terms where there aren't straightforward

answers. Then we have to delve into the fullness of the zero, the ambiguity of not knowing or no longer knowing or not yet knowing. For me the zero is excitement, it contains surprises, it puts me on edge. Of course, as Raven I love the play of chance, trickery, and creation. So, how do you account for being here in these latitudes?

Salmon: My natural response is a riff …

Raven: Hold it right there — riff? You are going to make music?

Salmon: I fluidly apply this musical term to an evocation of thoughts to conjure melodies of the mind. My pleasure is to create catchy rhythmic figures that make the imagination dance and help me come to presence. The repetition and the improvisation get me into "thriving on a riff", as Charlie Parker would have it. My riffs are music of the mind.

Raven: All very well, but I think you are avoiding an answer to my question "how do you account for being here in these latitudes?"

Salmon: My account, my story …

Raven: I'm not sure if we have enough time for all of that.

Salmon: Well, in keeping with your love of ambiguity and potentiality, my arrival here has been in the works for some time. It would seem that these accounts or stories are long overdue. Ultimately, my presence here is initiated by these very stories told. Place, ancestry, history are all woven into the accounts we tell, and as you appreciate trickery, I embrace memory. Besides, this is difficult work that will take time and perseverance.

Raven: That once again fits with the purposes of this book, where we might be able to remember better if only we had some recognition of what got us here. So this zeroth chapter is intended as a conversation between us to account for what key terms might need some clarity in order to talk honestly about where we have been. This will help us remember. Of course, others are invited to the conversation also! The more, the richer!

Salmon: Are we going to begin? I have a few terms that we've already used that I'd like to talk to you about.

Raven: Well, before we begin, let me make an important point: The way the authors use the term Whiteness is a state of consciousness and a way of being in the world. It is not something people are condemned to either by force of genetics or by social factors. On the contrary, it's something that can be changed and changing it may break down the dams and open big reservoirs of creativity and imagination.

Salmon: Which, as you might expect, we salmon will only be happy about.

Raven: Let's not get too distracted here into a discussion of salmon runs. You said you had some terms you want to talk about. But I must warn you: I have barely warmed up.

Salmon: I wish to begin with account, or accounting. I encountered this word used by White ecologist Wes Jackson in his 1996, *Becoming Native to This Place*. He uses the terms in reference to a more detailed story of place, where a kind of accountant's book is created in order to know who has lived in certain places, who owned homes, what companies have come and gone, what the ecology was like in a place, and so on.

Raven: That word is perfect for me, and my love of both/and. Because we are talking about an account, as in a story told about places, as well as the accountant's version where we are tracking inputs and outputs. I prefer the story version, being something of a narrator myself.

Salmon: Well, yes, and I feel it's important to move away from an accountant's balance sheet to the world of story. Many suggest that it's turning everything into a cash commodity that has gotten us into so much trouble in the first place. And once more, to tell a good story helps us remember.

Raven: And that's what is being attempted in this book, enlarging our stories so they are fuller, richer, with more potential. The way I like it. Ethno, as in 'tribe'. So then we're talking about ethno-accounting or ethno–accounts, right?

Salmon: Absolutely. We put together these accounts, or stories told, with the Indigenous sense of *ethno–*. It's funny, isn't it, to see two–legged creatures work at accounting for everything they are, while we don't have any way around it? From my perspective as a swimmer this ethno– is such a ridiculous necessity. What is obvious to us has to be emphasized for the two–leggeds.

Raven: I like your words 'ridiculous necessity'! Reminds me of critical humility and compassionate ruthlessness that I've heard used. These appeal to the both/and lover in me, as you well know.

Salmon: Since you like them so much, explain them to me.

Raven: Compassionate ruthlessness is the way I play with humans, stealing things to teach lessons, playing tricks

that teach. It means being gentle while having very high expectations, like an elder, I suppose. As *Muninn*, the raven of memory, I ruthlessly foster remembering, as *Huginn*, the raven of intent, compassion pervades my consciousness and intentions. The task is challenging! Critical humility was coined by the Euro–American Collaborative Challenging Whiteness (2010) to explain their experience of confronting inequality, racism and White supremacy, and doing so in a fashion that doesn't come across as being arrogant, or condescending. Rather they say, "Critical humility embodies a delicate and demanding balance of speaking out for social justice while at the same time remaining aware that our knowledge is partial and evolving" (p. 147). I just love paradoxes! We speak on behalf of justice, yet we know so little how to work on behalf of justice.

Salmon: That's like I was just saying about the prefix ethno– they keep using. It's a paradox to attempt to make something demanding, challenging, and necessary, then have it become automatic and almost forgotten. Not really though, because I'd never support forgetting.

Raven: Because forgetting is so much part–and–parcel of where Eurocentered or White society has gone wrong. Isn't it ironic that the arrogance and condescension I was just speaking of, co–exists, and actually thrives amidst such forgetting?

Salmon: Well, that is Eurocentered or White society exactly. Returning to the math that you started with, we might suggest an equation to establish the relationship between forgetting and arrogance: the more forgetting the more hubris?

Raven: That is only one aspect of Eurocentrism, of course. However, the other aspects all mutually reinforce each other. Christianity, for example: on the one wing, forgetting about other spiritual traditions, about its broad heritage in the teachings of Jesus, his shamanic side, the Black Madonna; and on the other wing, behaving as if it is the one true religion.

Salmon: Right. It's no accident that patriarchy goes hand in hand with Christian domination, not to mention White supremacy, and its offspring Whiteness. Of course, most pressing to us, and everyone actually, in these times of climate change, is the objectification and commodification of nature. Everything is in danger of being reduced to something that can be bought or sold. It's wonderfully ironic to have this conversation with you: in this one small act we are resisting the ridiculous notion that the world is devoid of spirit, presence and intelligence.

Raven: Indeed, one more act of resistance, or survivance. And that is why forgetting becomes so crucial to maintaining Eurocentrism. If people really began to take account of all of this, Eurocentrism would collapse on the weight of it's own many contradictions.

Salmon: Again, that is why this book is practicing remembrance. You carry memory well, I realize, but everyone knows that I return to my origins before I leave this world, so memory is very important to me, as well. I feel this book is building an integrated sense of remembrance, where people can better remember about themselves, about others, and about the relationship between self and other.

Raven: Yes, and such remembrance helps to grapple with all of the horrible losses that have occurred and, at the same time, creates things worth celebrating. I would imagine jumping up waterfalls for you is both hard work and full of joy, challenging and rewarding. It's a joyous contradiction again, remembering what has been lost, in order to interrupt the forgetting — now that's something to enjoy!

Salmon: And it also takes imagination, what they're calling genealogical imagination. Inspired by the Irish poet laurete Seamus Heaney, genealogical imagination is the idea of remembering ancestral ties and relationships, while also being aware that many of them dwell in the imaginal realms, in the places of possibility. Like these conversation pieces...

Raven: Oh, yes. And I really like the way the authors are connecting this idea with genealogy itself, in order to break out of the rigid, linear sense of family ties, to an integrated, organic sense of relationship with all things. That is my kind of genealogy. Especially since even famous academics such as Michel Foucault have written about genealogy, with laudatory intent, of course, yet he has taken much of the wonder and creativity out of it. We need more wonder, not less, especially these days.

Salmon: Isn't that the truth? When I ponder genealogy I include all manner of things that participate in my existence. There are the ancestral lineages, the places lived, there is the influence of others.

Raven: Yes, it gets back to the prefix ethno– the authors use. In this Indigenous sense ethno refers to the seasonal cycles, nature, ancestry, dreams — all these are included in a genealogy.

Salmon: That's what they call radical, or Indigenous presence. It's the reality of an existence that is fully integrated, and does not have to work at being so.

Again the irony, or contradiction, is that these ways of being require much work as two–leggeds emerge from White mind, to break the hall of mirrors contemporary life is caught in. The goal is to have it become a natural way of being, without having to think about it.

Raven: Well, of course we encourage them to stop thinking so much, since rationality has become one more part of the challenge before us. Rather, radical presence is another way of describing being embodied, using natural reason, like us wild things!

Salmon: Oh, say more...

Raven: This notion of ethno– reconnects people with the genealogies that are already there, they have only been forgotten. That reconnection catalyzes radical presence, and it brings all of the genealogical elements to bear on a person. In that way they become embodied, fully present in their body, their ancestry, dreams, the places they live, and so on. Now we can make good use of reason, instead of flattening it into one-dimensional rationality.

Salmon: That sounds like you are describing decolonization. The process of deconstructing ourselves, as the postmoderns like to say, and doing so in a way that leads to connection and wholeness, rather than more fragmentation. This breaks the imaginary shell of the self. Imaginary, since we are always connected, we are just not always aware of our connectedness.

Raven: This journey of self– and collective discovery, what the authors are calling decolonization, is about remembering connection and relationship, knowing that this is an ongoing process of *be(com)ing*.

Salmon: Now you have done it, Raven, with your both/and! Tell me about be(com)ing.

Raven: It's simple, really. Be(com)ing the both/and of being and accepting that we all become something else. It's allowing change to occur, knowing that things change, grow, and decay. Rather than seeing this as discouraging, such an integrated process of being and becoming, or be(com)ing, is a mark of decolonization. This may sound scary, especially since shadows are always looming, yet it is burgeoning with potential of renewal.

Salmon: It sounds very familiar, the act of being present *now* in order to have something become in the future. Like swimming upstream.

Raven: And perhaps that's a good place to pause in this conversation, because much of this work, though rewarding, can feel like swimming upstream.

Salmon: Especially when surrounded by a society that actively opposes, or at least is threatened by such work. In my experience it's like facing dams as I attempt to move up the waters. And yet it is so worth it. And not only can it be rewarding, it can be fun!

Raven: There has to be fun, laughter, and play for growth and learning to occur. That's why I play as many tricks as I can. Well and partly because humans are such easy prey. They just can't help themselves sometimes…

Inspirations for Further Conversations

The conversation Raven and Salmon began is one to be continued, naturally. There are many other concepts that can be considered. The following list provides a number of terms that are in the glossary. They provide beginning points to continue the conversation. Choose ones that interest you or that you have questions about. You will glean deeper meanings in each of the chapters where your encounter these terms. A conversation is a process in the same way that ethnoautobiography is — a meandering, spiraling, circuitous exploration. This form of questioning and inquiring in an autobiographical fashion is process–oriented. Thus, this workbook is not about answers, per se, rather the intention is to help find answers through profound questioning of self, society, and place. These conversation pieces are one way of starting your self–reflection.

Accounting	Genealogical imagination	Restor(y)ing
Amer–european	Genealogy	Rituals of reconciliation
Critical humility	Genocide	Settlement privilege
Critical, Indigenous inquiry	Groundwork	Settler
Cultural ecology	Indigenous	Storytelling
Decolonization	Indigenous presence	Survivance
Embodiment	Initiation	White
Environmentalism	Playing Indian	White mind
Ethno–	Radical presence	White privilege
Ethno–accounting	Recovery of Indigenous mind	Whiteness
Ethnoautobiographical riffs	Relationship	Witchery
Ethnoautobiography	Remembrance	
Eurocentered	(Re)placing	

Reflecting on an Issue

Identify an issue in our society that you think needs (more) attention.

Choose an issue that is meaningful to you in your personal life. This can be a new perspective on a current issue, or simply the need to further address something that you think needs more attention. For example, gun control, affordable education, or climate change all are in the news, but perhaps the degree of investigation is superficial or you have a particular aspect that you wish to address further. Of course, there may be issues of concern that are less publicized which are important to you, such as cross–cultural reconciliation projects, arts education with youth, and so on.

The assignment may be a written response or a collage with a brief narrative explanation.

Riff

Boundaries

Images
Handprints
Cave walls
In Argentina
In France
In the Yucatan
And elsewhere
This motif appears
Around the world
There are many suggestions
About what these images might mean

Certainly the hand
Is in keeping with what
Ethnoautobiography suggests
Deeply personal, articulate, deft
Integral to all we do
Hands and stories
Go together

We feel drawn to the idea
That these hand prints
Mark the boundary between
This world and the underworld
As scholars and shamans suggest

The ancients marked the spot
Whether in trance
Enlightenment
Or some other state of heightened
Awareness
Where they saw themselves
At the boundary
Between this world and
The world of spirit

The work before us now
Touches boundaries
This work
Is a rite of passage
So often an underworld journey
Moving from this world
Into the places of shadow
Spirit
Transformation

Especially when people suggest
These ancient marks on sacred walls
In caves deep in the earth
Might be acknowledgments
That people had touched
Boundaries between worlds
It might be that they outlined
Their hand
As if to say
They had touched the
Boundary
Between the worlds
And come back to tell
Stories of wonder

That they had been in contact
With this boundary
Between self and cosmos
Ordinary and magical
Between one place and all others
In between light and shadow
All present in one hand print
Perhaps like those
Ancient ones
Whose presence in this world
Was grounded with a connection
To the other
So too is our well being
Connected to the relationships
Between body and mind
Between self and other
Between the known and the unknown

Maybe the descent into the
Underworlds of this work
Of Ethnoautobiography
Is just one more aspect
Of a life's journey
Healing ruptures
Making connections
Touching shadows
RJP

NOTES

Chapter 1
Who Am I?

Riff

No Longer a Teen

As a young adult
No longer a teen
I thought that adolescence
Was the time when
I had developed my answers to
"Who am I?"
Distinguishing myself
From who I thought my parents were
From how I saw my parents

As a young adult
I thought that adolescence
Was the time when I was lost
Lost in dark valleys of confusion
And on peaks of enthusiasms and obsessions
My sense and boundaries of ego
Stretched like an amoeba moving
Worried about who others think I am
Worried about who I am
Experimenting with the roles of
Poet, provocateur, artist
Researcher, scholar, biologist
Activist, believer, and more

As a young adult
No longer a teen
I thought that adolescence
Was the time when I had
Tried to clarify for myself
What I am committed to
My beliefs and values
In the likeness of my parents
In contradistinction to my parents
The time when I was seeking models to inspire the
Settling of my ego
What I am identifying with
What I want to be identified with

As a young adult
No longer a teen
I thought that adolescence
Was the time
To build a clear structure
That I would live out
As I moved through adulthood

As it turned out
I had bought into an illusion
Of Western thought and psychology
The persona of *Western Man*

As it turned out
My answers to
"Who am I?"
Had only scratched the surface
And there were deeper valleys
And deeper shadows to explore
More challenging places
To get lost in

As it turned out
The comfort of my answers
Dissolved into a weave of
Stories
Histories
Associations
Rhizomes
Migrations
Memories
Images

As it turned out
I had to unsettle
My persona of *Western Man*
And regenerate myself
In the image of
Indigenous transmotion and sovereignty
In the image
Of presence in place and history

As it turned out
I had to go play with trickster
To shake up the constructs and scaffoldings
I had created for myself

As it turned out
It was dark and humorous
Illuminating and endarkening
It was
It turned out
Rewarding
And real

JWK

Chapter Outline	Core Concepts	Ethnoautobiographical Perspectives	Expected Outcomes
No longer a teen	Our sense of identity keeps developing until we die	Though psychology was primarily concerned with childhood & adolescent development, research shows we develop throughout our life	Opening to ways of investigating our own sense of identity
Who am I?	There are different culturally expected answers to this question	Being aware of cultural context helps us be aware of our own sense of self and the sense of self of others	Question the nature of the personal self or identity
How all this got started	Challenging a sense of individualism	Healing history means finding a different relationship with colonized peoples and feeling a more complex sense of personal identity	Understand the role of culture, history and place in the formation of self and identity
I am R	Acknowledging ancestors	Telling our story allows for completion and healing	Appreciate an example of ethnoauto–biography
I am Jürgen	Acknowledging ancient stories and the power of our imagination	Denied or shadow parts of ourselves and our culture are still present in our selves	Develop a sense of the power of cultural shadow material
Varieties of ethnoauto–biography	Ethnoauto-biography is a creative endeavor	When we acknowledge the stories of our roots, it deepens our creativity and imagination	Appreciate the varieties of ethnoauto-biographies

```
┌─────────────────────────────────────┐
│          Key Terms                  │
└─────────────────────────────────────┘
```

Colonial thinking
Indigenous transmotion
Modernity or modern
Normative dissociation
Sovereignty
Transpersonal
Trickster
White mind
Whiteness

Note: All key terms in this textbook are highlighted in bold and can be found in the Glossary at the end of the book.

Resources Alongside This Chapter

Allen, P. G. (1998). *Off the reservation* (pp. 181–192). Boston, MA: Beacon.

Anzaldúa, G. (1987). *Borderlands/la frontera: The new mestiza* (pp. 15–23). San Francisco, CA: Aunt Lute.

Cixous, H., & Calle–Gruber, M. (1997). *Hélene Cixous, rootprints: Memory and life writing* (pp. 187–205). London, England: Routledge.

Moyers, B. (2013, June 3). *Sherman Alexie's favorite films about Native Americans.* Retrieved from http://billmoyers.com/content/sherman–alexies–favorite–films–about–native–americans

Native American films. (n.d.). *Independent Lens.* Public Broadcasting Service. Retrieved from http://www.pbs.org/independentlens/films/native–american/

Who Am I? Who Are You?

The standard answers to these questions are, of course, name, profession, where we grew up, where we live, our nationality. Maybe we also talk about our education, the different places we have lived, maybe even who our parents are. This workbook suggests that there are questions and answers beyond these categories. In a sense one could say that these are the critical questions of our times and finding answers is equally important. Examples of such questions are: How did I come to be here on this continent? How did my ancestors get here? Why? What is the history of the place where I am living? And even, more specifically: Do my answers to the question "Who am I?" create an "us vs. them"? Do my answers address or confront the challenges and trends in contemporary society?

Our sense of self is deep seated, and is our 'second nature', a habitual way of being in the world (by contrast to our somatic or biological nature). The self includes things we are not aware of, including our unconscious, habits we may not be aware of, judgments and responses that are made in split seconds. This sense of self is the place of our values and morals that determine in profound ways how we approach the world and also how we are approached by the world around us. It is the lens with which we perceive the world and our self in the world; our tool for inquiry and learning. The sense of self determines how we engage with each other, what we see and don't see, what we think is important and unimportant.

The self, of course, is not a thing, rather, it is a process that has labels attached to it. These become easily visible when we tell stories about ourselves. It also becomes visible in the projections, attributions, and perceptions of others. These parts of the self that are our 'second nature' are generally slow to change, while our conscious, rational mind can make certain types of changes more rapidly. When we think of our self as a thing, as something that is complete and relatively immutable once we are adults, we deceive ourselves. Psychological research shows that we go through phases or stages all our life, including adulthood (there is an increasing literature on adult development, beginning with Erickson, 1959). As glimpsed in the above riff, there can only be gains if we become more aware of our self in process, if we increase our self–reflectiveness, if we enlarge the self-process to include more of the world, of our body, and our 'second nature'. This is the purpose of this workbook.

How this all got started – Jürgen's story

"Who are you?" This question by a Native American colleague, Apela Colorado, to me, Jürgen, sent me on a journey. Apela and I were beginning to work together with Native American students. Who was I going to be in that program? A White guy teaching Natives in the European academic framework that I was trained in? Was there even another possibility?

"Who are you?" It was a challenge to find answers from within an *Indigenous* paradigm, from within the paradigm Apela was living and teaching in, from within the worldviews that native or aboriginal people take for granted. The question was very unsettling. I did not have a tribe, clan or totem for an answer, and I barely knew my ancestors beyond the generation of my grandparents. My place of birth in Germany seemed rather remote.

"Who are you?" The question spawned inquires and self–reflections that have resulted in the practice of "ethnoauto-biography." Apela's question, of course, did not aim for my curriculum vitae or resume; neither did she ask for an account of the road I saw myself on, or where I thought my destination was. It actually was an attempt to probe the cracks of my **White mind**, the mindset I was trained in from birth as I was growing up in one of the Western cultures.

As we developed a **decolonizing** framework for teaching Native students, I wanted to be certain that I did not perpetuate conscious or unconscious supremacy, **Whiteness**, or **colonial thinking**. Her simple question, a challenge, for sure, threw me into an internal abyss. Ethnoautobiography has been my way to climb out of a cultural chasm that has led to a renewed and inspiring sense of self. It has been tremendously enriching and healing. The sense of who I am is richer, more complex. I have a more integrated sense of the stories that are woven into me.

I pursued my answers as Apela persevered in confronting me with the internal and external losses I felt. What were these losses? There was my loss of connection with nature: Did I know the ecology I lived in well enough to know what's edible and inedible? Could I survive on my own in nature near where I live for a week or two?

Another loss I confronted was my dearth of spiritual experiences, whether in nature or in community with others. As a child I would go out on frosty nights to enjoy the bright sparkle of the stars and I listened to Beethoven — all spiritual experiences, for sure. But I was lacking a context, a container to hold it all. There was no continuity, no stories, there were no rituals attached. I had read any number of novels growing up, but where were the older stories? Where were the oldest mythic stories of my culture? What could they mean to me today? I had no idea. Hitler had abused these stories to pursue his genocidal aims; Wagner was a rampant anti–Semite who powerfully set German myths to music. And the Vikings? Raping and pillaging as rite of initiation? As I reflected on my situation I began to see it as disengagement or dissociation from realms that are a natural part of Indigenous selves. I began to understand it as **normative dissociation** in individualistic cultures. My self was closed off from deep intimacy with nature, ongoing experiences of spirituality, deep storied connections with history, and other aspects of life that I saw as 'out there'. The self I grew up with was thickly boundaried and created a profound split between inside and outside, rather than facilitating a fluid movement.

The viewpoint of individualism or Western **modernity**, the way I was raised, is an imperial gaze. It is the distancing inspection of people and nature; that we find commonly in anthropology and psychology. Such a worldview has its origins in a dissociative and objectifying understanding of self and reality. According to this modernist worldview, the individual is to be (self) controlled, and the world is there for the taking. This all takes place at the whim of governing *masterful* selves who are in charge. Inevitably, this furthers the colonization of peoples, nature and spirituality, while advancing notions of individualism, natural resources, **sovereignty** that only serve the measures of commerce, and the elevation of profit as the ultimate answer.

For me, these losses of connections to nature, community, ceremony, the stars, mythic stories, and other aspects of my self and my surroundings became increasingly painful and motivated me to enlarge my sense of self. I felt starved and yearned for re–connection in a living web of connections. Confronting this

lack spawned ethnoautobiographical questioning and storytelling. My answers to the question "who are you?" have evolved over the years. I have gradually learned more and more about the northerly **Indo–European** peoples, my ancestral realms of the peoples of Germany, Denmark, Sweden, etc., and their cultural and political histories and interactions with neighboring Sámi, Finnish, and other nations of the **Finno–Ugric** peoples. I have also deepened my understanding of contemporary contexts and need to provide answers outside of the framework of West–ern **modernity**.

I write as a person of European and Germanic ancestries, a White man who has settled rather recently on Native American lands. We as authors of this workbook do not claim to speak outside of these boundaries of Eurocentrism, rather we self–consciously speak through them. R's and my concern is the **White** or **Eurocentered mind** and its experiences and descriptions of personal and **transpersonal** events. And, importantly, its impact in the world. This is an invitation to examine our sense of self and work with our imagination to contribute to constructive responses to the challenges in front of us.

The rock carving image from Scandinavia at the beginning of this chapter can be seen to represent the track of our ancestors, tracks which we think are significant for today. We can think of them as tracks of migrations or generational tracks. The dots are so–called fairy mills in which offerings to the spirits were made, a practice that continued in Sweden into the 20th century in places. Ethnoautobiography supports such practices, and indeed we consider this work to be such an offering.

Who are you?

"Who are you?" One strand of answers and inspirations emerges out of the shambles of **modernity**. Growing up we were impressed by our scientific and technological capabilities, but dismayed by pervasive inequities and unnecessary suffering in the world. The emancipatory power of the enlightenment and its manifestations in terms of science, religious freedom, and civil societies held such great promise. Yet, how do we come to terms with the incredible number of children dying every day needlessly or the levels of poverty even in countries like the U.S. or the lack of access to education for millions of people?

The many contradictions felt in terms of personal identity (such as that expressed in this chapter's riff), or being trained to think critically in academia, or taking action to change the world only made the shambles of **modernity** more stark. Further questions emerged: Who are we as the individuals who need to hold all this change and questioning? Where can we ground ourselves? Where is our source of inspiration, nurture, and healing?

"Who are you?" Other parallel responses emerge from questioning certainties about personal and **trans-personal** identities: Who are we in relation to the divine? What do we believe? What is our relationship with nature (Does it matter when species go extinct? Is it okay to destroy nature for resource use?) And what about scientific inquiry? (What is truth?) And then there are questions like: How big is our carbon footprint? Does it really matter? And what about the electronics, the t–shirts, or the sneakers that come from places where labor is very cheap and workers are not protected by laws similar to the U.S.? Should we care? **Modernity** has left many questions unanswered, whether scientific, philosophical, or ethical, which has led to deep, and at times cynical, questioning characteristic of **postmodernity.**

The ferment of this **postmodern** breakdown can provide a release from certain limitations and facilitates the emergence of a playful freedom. But what are the boundaries of this freedom? Should there even be any? Anything goes now. Whites can dress as Native Americans; individuals self–proclaim as gurus. It seems that whatever the market carries, and whatever gets ap-proval, goes. Underneath all of this we may discover cynicism that dismisses anything that is not pushing the edge, that doesn't have an outrageous or narcissistic flavor, and that is connected with traditional values. Such cynicism seems to arise from a lack of guiding values and principles and self–centered ungrounded–ness, whether in **New Age** gurus or artistic self–importance which focuses primarily on the experience of self worth. This **postmodern** breakdown without the **postmodern** condition (Vizenor, 1989). If this is indeed the case, then there is reason to hope for working our way out of our dilemmas and challenges., It means not to look at tribal peoples as primitive and to hold inflexible and static representations of their traditions in mind. Indeed, it means looking at these cultures as contemporary and changing to this

> I did not have a tribe, clan or totem for an answer, and I barely knew my ancestors beyond the generation of my grandparents and my place of birth seemed remote.

also has the positive potential of the renewal of traditions and imaginative responses that heal our cultural stories.

What is a way to expand and ground our imagination and creativity both individually and socially? If neither **modernism** nor **postmodern** cynicism provide sufficient answers, then what might be a third way? Thus, the *second strand of answers* emerges out of Indigenous contexts that define a vision of grounded presence in nature; a Native vision of **sovereignty** that internally and externally connects with place, history, and community. This nourishing sense of natural connections, ceremony, and mythic stories can feed our creation of imaginative identities. This is the positive potential of both the **post-modern** questioning of traditions and the rapid development of technologies.

The argument has been made that Indigenous traditions have never been day. This also undermines **New Age** fantasies of Indigenous traditions as a state of paradise, as well as idolatrous, romantic, or dogmatic notions of any tradition. Looking at Indigenous cultures can also break open the **modern** individualistic senses of a well–boundaried and defended self that sees itself in opposition to and separate from community and nature, for example. What emerges then is our ancient potential of profound engagement with story, place, and community. Activating these possibilities may be exactly what we need in order to find solutions for the numerous challenges and crises we presently face. Ethnoautobiography is the practice of developing stories that help us unlearn patterns and assumptions that stand in the way (such as "**Whiteness**") and to appreciate an Indigenous sense of being in the world that is part of all our ancestries.

With inquiry based in an Indigenous paradigm, we inevitably must make these ventures and adventures a critique, and begin with the question of how we have lost and abandoned our own Indigenous roots. This becomes a critique of where we are today as societies (whether we think of privilege and dramatic economic inequities or of global warming) and an invocation of where we could be (the potential of our rich traditions, science, and art). Imagining our selves through deep connection with place; confronting dark aspects of history; engaging ritually

mean (whether you think of robotics, gene sequencing, cloning, surveillance, or cryonics, to mention just a few developments). The fear of the unknown potential of these rapid developments may tempt us to seek a community or culture that appears whole in an attempt to shield ourselves from the forces unleashed (whether religious or Indigenous in flavor). Or we may put all our faith into science and technology, hoping that is will eventually provide sufficient answers and leave questions of values and morals largely aside. Or we may decide on a particular religious or political or other dogma that gives us comfort and allows us to

> ## Anglo–Americans have failed to create a satisfactory identity for themselves.
>
> ### Silko (1979, p. 213)

and ceremonially with the world; and exploring and dialoging in a learning community is inevitably an invitation to stretch toward what could be (and thus be critical of what is). Ethnoautobiography suggests the riches we all carry and can realize individually and together.

Our **postmodern** challenges may induce fear and insecurity since we can't quite see beyond the horizon to determine what will emerge. It appears that our sense of the future is changing as we have unleashed a tremendous potential without knowing what it will

override the concerns created by science, technology, and ethics (scientology or political ideologies of various shades are examples). It takes courage to acknowledge the fear and pain and to seek inspiration and vision in this darkness.

Decolonizing is about changing our appropriative and imperial stance toward the world, and is thus not just the recovery of the memory traces of Indigenous presences in all of us, but a creative psycho–spiritual, moral, political and activist endeavor. It doesn't just join 'the other' ("the natives," the "Third World," "the poor," etc.) in their struggles of **decolonization**. First and foremost, decolonization turns its gaze to the center of colonial processes — Europe, "the West," and its allies — and their process of self-colonization, that is, the denial of rich interconnections and sources of balances inside of ourselves, the denial of the meaning of our origins for the future.

Leslie Marmon Silko (1979, p. 213) has pointed out that when Whites "attempt to cast off their Anglo–American values, their Anglo–American origins, they violate a fundamental belief held by the tribal people they desire to emulate: they deny the truth; they deny their history, their very origins. The writing of imitation 'Indian' poems then, is pathetic evidence that in more than two

us. This doesn't mean returning to some form of traditional society, but using the inspiration from our work of memory to create our future. Diamond (2012) has provided an analysis of what traditional and **modern** worlds have to offer and what their limitations are. Using an ethnoautobiographical approach may allow us to find our personal answers to integrate what we have learned from our remembrance. This may lead us to use computer skills in a way that is very different from what is envisioned right now. For example, they might be used for the benefit of ecological healing or imaginative forms of networking that are liberating or create multimedia presentations that include vision, body, memory, play, emotion, dream, and other aspects of ourselves. Or this may lead to a commitment to community work to heal

> **Whites violate a fundamental belief held by the tribal people they desire to emulate: they deny the truth; they deny their history, their very origins.**
>
> Silko (1979, p. 213)

hundred years, Anglo–Americans have failed to create a satisfactory identity for themselves."

Silko's critique cuts to the quick. What we offer here is a positive response where we imagine a remembered sense of Indigenous presence that looks forward and that is aware of our interconnectivity and embeddedness in the world around

local history and to strengthen community. The answers we find build on our given talents, whether that is computer skills, acting, organizing, speaking, accounting, critical analysis, bodywork, or something else. Ethnoautobiography is a way to contextualize our given talents and skills and to enrich them for the sake of our future.

When we look at ourselves within an Indigenous context and acknowledge history and origins, it is not for the sake of guilt, but for the sake of making ourselves whole again. While we may experience guilt or shame along the way, the goal is healing, taking responsibility, and releasing our visionary potential for the future.

Who Am I? Who is Jürgen? Who is R? Let us give some examples of the beginnings of ethnoautobiographical storytelling.

> This ethnoautobiographical introduction is a beginning, about my beginnings. But rather than make no attempt, because it will be somehow incomplete, or inaccurate, I begin with what I have, knowing that there will always be "something left unfinished."

I am R

I am R. I was born in Philadelphia, Pennsylvania, in August 1968, the third child of a heterosexual couple. My ancestry is Celtic (English–Irish–Scottish), but my more recent Christian lineage is predominantly Anglo–Irish Quaker. My Quaker ancestors have been present in North America since the late 17th century.

I am the child of James Paton and Marjorie Pickett. I am the grandchild of Russell Paton and Linda Chandler, Ernest Pickett and Pauline Hudelson. I am the great–grandchild of James Paton and Agnes Singer, Warren Chandler and Ada Graham Meehan, Howard Pickett and Bertha Pitts, Chester Hudelson and Edna Frazer. My ancestors have lived in North Carolina, Indiana, Ontario, Canada, and throughout Philadelphia, and the Delaware Valley. Coaquannok is the Lene Lenape name for where I was born: "the place of the long trees." I came of age on Huichon Ohlone land in the San Francisco Bay Area, and began to learn how to "see" the land more deeply at Wy'east, near Portland, Oregon and at Timbisha, or Death Valley. I now live in Dallas, Texas — Comancheria — in the shadow of the famed warrior–turned–diplomat Quanah Parker and his White mother Cynthia Ann Parker.

This is not, and cannot, be a definitive introduction. It is a beginning, about my beginnings. But rather than make no attempt, because it will be somehow incomplete, or inaccurate, I begin with what I have, knowing that there will always be "something left unfinished" (Santos, 1999).

Now that I have given a brief introduction of myself, I must also introduce one of the cultural guides through my landscapes: Oisin. In fact, as a teacher he has an honored place on my license plate: O, I, S, I, N. I first met Oisin in a theater performance entitled "The Tales of Oisin," based on the writings of Scottish Romantic James Macpherson. Perhaps most in the audience experienced Oisin as a puppet, though full of spirit for me. As the years have gone by, I have learned more about his gifts. Suffice it to say, his first lesson was an invitation to participate in his story and that is one that I extend, as well. Oisin is a Celtic mythic figure who falls in love with a fairy and travels across the sea to live in the fairy world. When he longs to see his home again, what seemed like a short time, centuries had passed and all his family and friends are but distant memories.

My narrative is one of finding stories of renewal for myself, in addition to my broader community; you might say, the White culture to which I belong. Laguna writer Leslie Marmon Silko, among others, believes that story, in itself, is ceremony. So while this is a story with something of a goal in mind, it is also explicitly a process. One of the challenges I repeatedly face whenever I want to tell my story is that I never know for certain where to begin. Some years ago I read a book entitled *Places Left Unfinished at the Time of Creation* (Santos, 1999). That phrase and sentiment remains with me as I continue to learn how to tell my story. What is unfinished in my creation story, and how does that impact upon who I am?

As I said before, I was born in, Coaquannok, roughly "the place of the long trees," Philadelphia. With both sides of my ancestry being Quaker, those long trees in Coaquannok became the long benches of Quaker meetinghouses my ancestors sat on. There are contradictory stories of the relationships between Quakers and the Lenapes. Similarly, there are conflicting reports as to the debates about enslaving Africans that took place on those benches, too. Some reports suggest William Penn wanted to treat the Lenape fairly, yet within a generation all Lenape land in eastern Pennsylvania was in European control. Similarly, concerning the enslavement of Africans; the earliest written anti–slavery protest was written by Quakers in 1682. And at the same time, many Quakers were thoroughly entrenched in the trade in enslaved humans.

My creation story—dare I say the creation of White settlers (we still are settlers, aren't we?) — is bound up with these stories of history, culture, and place. It is the story of the creation of settlers, of settler ancestries, and ongoing settler stories. Thus, my creation is ripe with conflict and discord. These foundations include land that was literally stolen, through open war or deceit, a story that continues in ways which are hidden from easy view. My beginnings are bonded to an economy born of enslavement and the Middle Passage. In the process so much has been lost, the landscape is so full of ghosts of what has been left behind.

Given these origins, is it any wonder that my ancestors continued the migrations? This pattern even persisted into my own life, having lived in at least seven places before I was eighteen. Perhaps this roaming was the lingering effects of a haunted past. I found myself asking, what was I looking for? Eventually, I had to ask, what was I also running from? I believe we are doing both: looking for and running from something, simultaneously.

This is where I wish to return to my cultural guide, Oisin. He was a warrior of the Fianna, but he was also a poet. He fell in love with a fairy and went off over the seas to Tir na Nog, to live happily ever after. However, when he left Ireland for the fairy world his sense of time was thrown askew, so when he returned to visit his beloved country, family and friends, hundreds of years had passed, and they were but a memory. Then, through a simple error, the spell was broken and he instantly became a wizened old man, not able to return to the land of the fairies ever again. Grieving for the loss of his family, ancestry and his love, he had only his poetry left to offer. In his vulnerability, he became a poet and bard, narrating a middle ground. Oisin was stranded between two worlds, that of his fairy love, and that of his family and friends long since past. His place was a borderland between love and longing, hope and loss, sadness and redemption.

Similarly, then, the warriors among Whites need to give way to the poets. Certainly, the desire for justice, reparation, and reconciliation comes from the colonized. But I offer that it must come even more from the colonizer — White settlers — as well. This is not simply because it is the right thing to do, which it is, of course. But our healing, my healing, is necessary, too. There need

to be conversation, dialogue, and rituals of reconciliation. We — I mean White settler folks — need to talk amongst ourselves about what this means. We don't need answers (we come from a long line of folks who thought they knew the answers!). Colonization emerged from a mind out of balance, it is a virus, and is in need of healing. We could use some confusion, guilt, shame, sadness, and grief. It would be good to face the haunted landscapes and the shadows of genocide and slavery. Grieving what has been lost is really important. Out of it will emerge answers we can't yet imagine.

Healing these stories on our own is not recommended or possible. Healing ceremonies, like all stories, have to be shared. Ceremonies are about connection and relationships, with other humans, with place, and with the world of the spirits, certainly. To connect with spirit, and communicate with them, to awaken relationship all people have (or had) maintained is one purpose of shamanism. Shamanism demands relationship; there is no place for one–sidedness. The worlds are fluid, dynamic, and malleable. Shamanism also means healing, balancing and renewal, all ultimately transformative. These characteristics also describe reconciliation. Rituals of reconciliation are something that will help me cope—like Oisin—with the mourning for what has been lost. It is my hope that it will help others as well.

I am Jürgen — I am Raven

Here is one way in which Jürgen introduces himself. He uses the voice of raven, a bird he has had frequent intimate encounters with. His connection with this bird is shamanic or ceremonial. At the beginning of the relationship with this amazing black bird was a ceremony in which Jürgen fasted for raven in order to develop a deeper connection. The following self–introduction is poetic and imaginative in character. It is an example of the creative writing which ethno-autobiography invites.

I am the dark cross of memory. I am Raven, black feathers glistening in the sun. My wings carry vision, bring knowledge from afar.

Raven they call me, *Rabe* and *hrafn* in Icelandic, they call me *gáranas* in the language of the Sámi people. By many names I go, and many tales are told about me. I am known as *Big–Raven*, as *Raven Man*, as *Yetl, Nankilslas, Txamsem, Kurkyl, Kutqu,* and *Quiknnaqu* in Native traditions. The people of the northern part of this earth, they see me in multiple ways, as creator and transformer, as trickster, and as hero who brings new things into the world. Some talk of how I was white once, in the long–ago, and how I was blackened with smoke and soot. Other stories speak of the dark times when light was kept hidden away by possessive beings; so they tell how I liberated the light, they talk of my theft so that sun, moon and stars would shine again; and they tell tales of how I stole fresh waters so that there would be rivers and streams on earth. There are stories of how I tricked salmon and bear and cormorant, there are stories of how I changed from man into woman.

My name is different in different places. So often I helped people with their far sight and visions, with divination, and a deeper knowing of the times.

I am the black one, as big as a hawk. "*Kolk*," I croak in German, and "*ruŋk*," I speak in Sámi. I sound low and high, and my beak can peck into wakefulness what fearful humans would rather forget. I croak and croak until I get their attention. And I circle and scout to bring awareness and the arrow of intent. *Huginn* and *Muninn* are among my names in Icelandic, as *Ravenmind* I am known, and *Ravenmemory* also.

My adventures have been many. The Native American Tlingit, Tsimshian, and Haida, the Siberian Chukchi and Koryak recount them, and so do many others. I have been there in mythic times of the great deluge, I kicked the waters until they receded, I scouted for dry lands. And I have kept the company of the earthdiver, the loon, who brought up the lands from the water. I have served as totem for many. I have been a sign of lineage and relation. Gratefully I have received the offerings of those who honor my presence.

Many transformations have resulted from my flights. And I have been transformed by my human company—what I was in ancient times I no longer am. Once I was creator, trickster of change, visionary ally, and power animal to the shamans of old. Then the Christian church arose and many would see my powers as evil. They would cast dispersions upon my name. In many lands they would hunt me close to extinction.

In the long–ago I would be seen sitting on the shoulders of the women and men of seeing. I was of the sun and the fire, of water and rain. I served as spirit guide and messenger to those who kept my relation in the proper way of imaginative attention. I lived with the shamans, the healers, and visionaries. In those times I was honored as helper and in certain places even as supreme spirit and creator.

With Greek Apollo, Athena, and Hera; with Cuchulain, Bran, and Lug of Celtic traditions I flew; I kept the company of Nergal in Sumer, with Mithra I was in ancient Persia and beyond, and with so many others. The Celtic Mabinogion tells of me, and Horace sees me as rising sun and bringer of rain. Shakespeare wrote, *Swift, swift, you dragons of the night, that dawning may bear the raven's eye*! There are so many stories, some short, some epic, that tell adventures of mine.

Some people, they don't know the difference between my cousin crow and myself. To others this difference does not matter at all: Ravenbird, crowbird — it's all the same to them.

As times changed, greed began to move voraciously across the earth from place to place. People now began to see me with different eyes. In the north of Europe my name turned bad and I was hunted as bird of ill omen. The village shaman had been pushed aside by jarls or earls or even kings of saga fame. Women were dishonored during these times, and, later, they were persecuted for their visionary sight, and for their healing powers. Now I was seen as sitting on the shoulders of Wotan or Odin in the world of the Old Norse; the grim master with one eye who had usurped what once was shaman's privilege, the place of women and men of seeing. He was used to justify so many atrocities, hangings, drownings, and more. People no longer knew what it meant to be in good relation with all they are a part of and all that is a part of them, how to bring mindfulness to the lands inside with imaginative reason. And then there were those who did not follow the revolutionary impulse of the Jew Jesus; his visionary original instructions were spoken words, not scriptures. Instead, they created the Christian churches and stilled the liberation in words. Their missionaries and priests, they saw my power of old, and called me evil. They did not want me as helper and midwife, as healer and messenger.

So here I fly, dark cross of memory. Scout for memory shards as I help this man see how he walked as a child in Germany, how he always walked with his ancestors, shrouded in stories, how he received calls from the far north, the arctic. He wants to see me, yet the veils of his culture have constricted his sight, have shrunken his imagination and vision. I was his company then, as I am now. He moved from Hamburg to Native American lands to learn the ways of vision balancing. He suffered his people's memory losses, the storylines dropped, the denials of who I, Raven, can be; the ways in which they had made me an accomplice in the use of bad medicine, of evil; an accomplice in greed, death, and destruction. He gives away food in my honor, he fasts, and now he can see a little better; he discerns me past the distortions that have perverted my name. Now he remembers his obligation to be present to me, to talk with bear and ancestors. He remembers his duty to purify the roots that have been abused to justify so much destruction. Storysherds are revisioned as he nurtures this compulsion to trace erasures, as he tracks what many think has been lost forever. I help him remember his ties to a conversation that works to honor and nurture all beings about him. I watch him turn around, facing away from Native American traditions that had helped him out so many times, facing toward his own ancestors now, and the people they once traded with in a respectful way, the Sámit, the Lapps. That was in the long-ago, before Odin

and church, before missionaries and willful taxation. As a child he had felt that call, that yearning for travel to Kirkenes in northernmost Norway, in Sápmi, to be with reindeer and plover, to be in the tundra. I am his company as he seeks the trade of old, as he works to be in the balancing mind of his ancestors of ancestors of ancestors. I help him drink the dark milk of daybreak and I carry his black cross of memory on my wings. I dunk him into his romanticism and the idealizations and betrayals it invites. I give him vision to walk on the Native American lands as a White man, now with some color in his face. I help him stand where different circles of memory and knowing meet inside him. With the persistence of memory, its force and persuasiveness today, and the desires and needs that modify memory, with all this I help him out. In my beak I carry deliverance from the enslave–ment of forgetting and denial.

What I was in ancient times I no longer am nor can be. But if truths are spoken, then the awareness I carry can arise from the knowledge of old, now richer for today, for the future. Stories renewed.

I am raven and Raven, I am white feathered and black feathered, as much bird as a figure of speech, as much feathery flight as the twist of imagination.

I am the opener. Gently I unlatch the portal. It is made from leaf of the lindentree. It is a place of vulnerability.

I work the soft spot on his back so that memory may enter, so that the story may be recounted. I, Ravenmemory, and my twin, Ravenmind, we help to lift the fateful words from the well of memory and renewal.

Varieties of Ethnoautobiography

By now you will probably suspect that there are many ways to write ethnoautobiographies; indeed, there isn't one right way. Finding your own voice, your own *creative* voice, is critical. You will know, both on a gut level and the mind level, when you hit your stride. When you follow that rhythm you may develop a sense of flow and get fully absorbed in your story.

Autobiographical explorations with awareness of ethnicity, class, gender, place, and history can be conducted in many different ways and there is no limit to the format and approach. For each one of us the starting place will be different. It all depends on our autobiography, on the experiences we carry. Look at the examples by Helene Cixous (1997), Gloria Anzaldua (1987), Gerald Vizenor (1987), Elenita Strobel (2005), and Paula Gunn Allen (1998). Look at the readers of native autobiographies (Krupat, 2000; Krupat & Swann, 2000; Swann & Krupat, 1987). These pieces were not written in the framework of ethnoautobiography, but they fit the definitions we use in this workbook. The voice and focus in each of these pieces is different and unique. Part of the ethnoautobiographical process is finding your own voice and then giving it expression.

Activity

Self Introduction

Develop your own self–introduction. Who are you, culturally speaking? Who are your ancestors? How did you come to live where you live? How would you introduce yourself in a class in 5 minutes? In 10 minutes? How would you do it in writing (1,000 – 1,500 words)?

Note: If you are completing these activities on your own, and do not have an organized group to do oral presentations for (such as in a classroom, community organization and so on), it is encouraged that you present the work you are doing to a friend, family member or spouse to experience sharing your process in oral form.

Chapter Summary

Personal identity develops until we die, with culturally varied answers to the question of who we are. Ethnoautobiography is a creative endeavor emerging from a multiplicity of factors, but especially an acknowledgment of ancestry, ancient stories and the power of our imagination.

Concept Check

What was the outcome of Apela asking Jürgen "who are you?"

If **decolonizing** is not just the recovery of memory traces of **Indigenous presence**, what else is it?

What is included in R's ethnoautobiographical creation story?

Describe how the **trickster** Raven assists Jürgen in facing **cultural shadow**.

Though many narratives are not explicitly created as ethnoautobiography, what is a critical ingredient in various examples?

NOTES

Chapter 2
The Self — Now Larger, Now Smaller

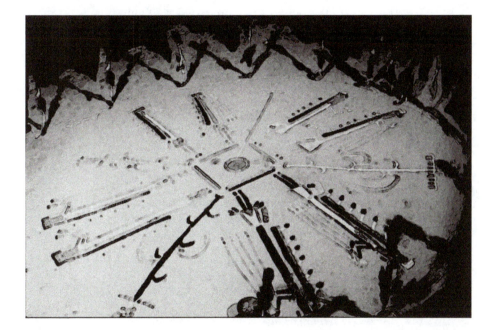

Riff

Circles

The scene is ancient
But the time is today:

In the center of the circle
In the middle of the sandpainting
Sits the Navajo Indian patient
Right by the place of emergence
Ready to be re–created from the beginning point
The place of emergence
The circle of the rainbow person in pink and light blue
All around him
Holding him in this circle
Prayer sticks placed all around
Intentions for healing
Thirteen standing–up prayer sticks with feathers
In each direction a pair of gods
Between them a corn plant
Four corn plants in different colors
I see the Navajo cosmos
The patient placed in ceremony in a balanced world
So that it may shift his imbalance, his illness

The Navajo patient sits at the center of his cosmos
His self held by the powers of the four directions
By the powers of the four sacred mountains
The four–leggeds in the mountains
The winged ones
The plants of the mountains
The self a circle that is part of the Navajo cosmos

With the Sons of Sun, he is moving.
With the Sons of White Corn Girl, he is moving.
With Dark Cattails on top, he is moving.
With the Flash of Lightning, he is moving.
With the Black–blossomed Plant, he is moving.

The Navajo patient sits
In a large circle of self

The White Corn Boy, it is I walking.
Beneath the Two Rising, on White Mountain, it is I walking.
The Yellow Corn Boy, it is I walking.
Beneath the Two Setting, on Yellow Mountain, it is I walking.
The Blue Corn, it is I walking.
Beneath the Two, on Blue Mountain, it is I walking.
The Black Corn, it is I walking.
Beneath where Big Dipper turns, it is I walking.
With Pollen it is I walking.
Happiness before me, it is I walking.
Happiness behind me, it is I walking.

I remember myself
Walking on Navajo land
Alone
Not knowing the mountains
The spirits inhabiting the mountains
A song came to me as I walk
I start chanting
A thread from beyond my self enters
Walking alone
A thread to my heart
A thread from my heart

My small circle of self pierced by the spirit of song
I remember myself
Walking alone
In the soggy river marsh by my home
The air filled with dampness
My boots getting heavy with mud
I did not know the circle of old
I did not know the offerings
I was walking alone in my small circle
The song of the curlew rising mellifluously
The soft whistle of the killdeer running in front of me
The scream of the hawk a lament in the sky
My small circle pierced by birds
I dream with them

JWK

Chapter Outline	Core Concepts	Ethnoautobiographical Perspectives	Expected Outcomes
Circles	The sense of self in different cultures may have a different "circumference"	The boundaries of the self vary	Consider the option of seeing & experiencing your self differently
Early beginnings	Core assumptions about the self are learned very early	Allows for a deconstruction of old patterns of the self	Understand the earliest roots of the self
Cultural differences in self	Different cultures understand self or personality in different ways, through independent &/or interdependent views	Different senses of self provide options and alternatives for self identity	Distinguish between different qualities of self–narration or construction in different cultures
Three qualities of self	Individualism, collectivism, & Indigenism	By seeing these versions of the self we begin to see more of our selves	Understand three basic ways of narrating the self: modern individualistic, interdependent and Indigenous
The WEIRD cultures (Western, educated, industrialized, rich, democratic)	The modern western self is an outlier	Addressing this unusual self begins to transform the WEIRD self	Understand how unusual the Western self understanding is in the world
Sociocentric cultures	Understanding the self in terms of the group	Reconnecting with community builds richer identity in relation to people	Appreciate interdependent interconnectivity
Indigenist cultures	Understanding the self in terms of the group, place, ritual & story	An embedded self provides a complex self identity	Envision a self that reaches beyond human boundaries

Key Terms

Collectivism
Indigenism, or Indigenist
Individualistic, or individualism
Sociocentric
WEIRD

Note: All key terms in this textbook are highlighted in bold and can be found in the Glossary at the end of the book.

Resources Alongside This Chapter

Bastien, B. (2004). *Blackfoot ways of knowing – The worldview of the Siksikaitsitapi*. Calgary, Canada: University of Calgary Press.

Beck, P. W., & Walters, A. L. (1976). *The sacred: Ways of knowledge sources of life*. Tsaile, AZ: Navajo Community College Press.

Liu, Y. (n.d.). http://blog.nationmultimedia.com/print.php?id=1748

Nisbett, R. E. (2003). *The geography of thought*. New York, NY: The Free Press.

Early beginnings

The origins of our sense of self begin very early in life. In fact, Damasio (2010) shows that its origins can be found in our brainstem, a very old structure in our brain (a structure also found in reptiles). The earliest development of the self is impacted by critical nonverbal experiences, such as physical touch, being fed, diapers getting changed, etc. These are the earliest experiences of being cared for, are somatic in nature, and form part of our core identity. Such early nonverbal programming is not easily accessed verbally since it is literally very deeply ingrained inside of us, in our oldest brain structures as well as in our soma, or 'body'. When talking about cultural differences in sense of self, we are not only talking about differences in cognition or attitudes (which are accessible in words), we are also talking about differences that were learned very early and that are not so easily accessed verbally. Such early learning makes our sense of self seem natural and given. It also makes it more challenging to see the world through the eyes of another cultural worldview. This is important to keep in mind when reading the rest of this chapter, as well as when we deepen our ethnoautobiographical work.

Cultural differences in self

How do we define the self? How do we know ourselves? What guides our self awareness? "Who am I?" These are, of course, central questions as we grow up, especially during adolescence. There are two major perspectives that are commonly defined in the field of social psychology:

- The *independent* or **individualistic** view of the self vs.
- the *interdependent* or **sociocentric** view of the self.

In the **independent** view, we define ourselves primarily in terms of our own thoughts, feelings, and actions, but not to any significant degree in terms of the thoughts, feelings, and actions of others. As Westerners we define ourselves as clearly separate from other people: uniqueness, independence, and individual achievement are most important. By contrast, in the **interdependent** view we define ourselves in relationship to others, we recognize that our behavior is often determined by the thoughts, feelings, and actions of other people. Independence and uniqueness are seen as problematic (from the perspective of interdependence), while connectedness is valued. In Asian cultures we find more frequent references to families and various social groups in response to the question "who am I?" than in Western cultures (Aronson, Wilson, & Akert, 2010).

While in the independent view a person might feel comfortable being singled out for praise, this might lead to discomfort in cultures with an interdependent view of the self. Western persons are more likely to say "no!" to the question whether their happiness depends on those around them, while an Asian person would likely answer "yes!" These differences are foundational to such an extent that for Western persons it is difficult to imagine themselves participating in an **interdependent** cultural view. Here are a few more questions to ponder:

- My close relationships are an important reflection of who I am.
- I usually feel a strong sense of pride when someone close to me has an important accomplishment.
- If a person hurts someone close to me, I feel personally hurt as well.
- My sense of pride comes from knowing who I have as close friends.
- When I think of myself, I often think of my close friends or family also.
- Overall, my close relationships have very little to do with how I feel about myself.

The perspective illustrated by each statement is probably self–evident.

Clifford Geertz has noted how unusual, even "peculiar" Western individuals' thinking about themselves is: "The Western conception of the person as a bounded, unique, more or less integrated motivational and cognitive universe, a dynamic center of awareness, emotion, judgment, and action organized into a distinctive whole and set contrastively both against other such wholes and against its social and natural background, is, however incorrigible it may seem to us, a rather peculiar idea with the context of the world's cultures" (1984, p. 126). Most societies have developed an **interdependent** or **sociocentric** view where the needs of groups and social institutions come first and the individual second. This is different from the description of Western personality just given by Geertz where the individual is placed front and center and groups and social institutions serve the individual.

Three qualities of self

Incorporating such dimensions as place and ritual to the sense of **individualism** vs. community connection, we can distinguish three different qualities of self that we find fostered in different cultures:

Individualism: Defining the self in terms of personal traits and giving priority to self goals. This is the normative sense of self in Western, Westernized, or Eurocentered cultures. This sense of self is well boundaried and masterful (in charge), it wants to be distinctive and feel good about itself, and sees itself in control of its behavior. These assumptions look obvious to most Westerners.

Collectivism: Defining the self in terms of relationships to other people and groups and giving priority to group goals. Standing out (achievement) is culturally seen as problematic: "The peg that stands out is pounded down."

Harmonious social relations are more important than personal achievement. Success is seen as a group goal, feeling good about oneself is dependent on harmony with group wishes and expectations (Nisbett, 2003). This is a subgroup of **sociocentric** societies which can be found in Asian and other cultures.

Indigenism: Defining the self in terms of relationships to other people and groups and giving priority to group goals, in terms of place (ecology), (mythic or ceremonial) stories, ancestors, spirit (or spirits or gods or goddesses), and so on. **Indigenist** cultures are the other subgroup of sociocentric cultures.

The following table summarizes these points:

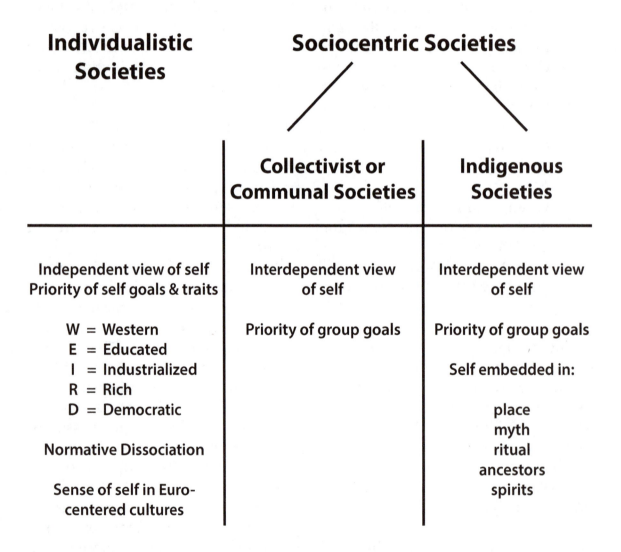

Figure 2.1. Three different perspectives on the self.

Two things are important to keep in mind when looking at the self and culture:

1. Culture and self make each other up; they are interdependent.
2. Within each of the three groupings of societies or cultures there are variations. For example, you may have grown up in an **individualistic** culture, but your family system was more interdependent.

The WEIRD cultures

Henrich, Heine & Norenzayan (2010) have reviewed research on human psychology and behavior regarding its generalizability, given that research evidence is largely based on narrow samples from Eurocentered societies. Research topics have included issues like human perception, fairness, cooperation, spatial reasoning, moral reasoning, and other self–concepts. Their conclusion is that "members of Western, educated, industrialized, rich, and democratic societies, including young children, are among the least representative populations one can find for generalizing about humans" (p. 2). They use the acronym **WEIRD** — *Western, educated, industrialized, rich* and *democratic* — "to refer to the exceptional nature of this sample, and do not intend any negative connotations or moral judgments by the acronym" (p. 44).

Most psychological research has been conducted with members of (post)–modern **individualistic** or Eurocentered cultures, which has biased psychological results in a particular fashion. Importantly, it has created a particular normative image of human beings that cannot easily be generalized across cultures. In addition, based on the available research evidence Henrich, Heine & Norenzayan concluded that "American college students…may be outliers within an outlier population" meaning that "their psychological characteristics are more extreme within individualistic societies" (p. 36). This profound difference in personality process (separateness vs. interdependence) affects everything, from responses to "Who are you?" to basic visual perception and thinking style. "The WEIRDer you are, the more you see a world full of separate objects, rather than relationships" (Haidt, 2011, p. 184). Also, within the West or Eurocentered cultures the U.S. is a more extreme outlier than Europe.

WEIRD people list internal psychological characteristics when talking about themselves (happy, introverted, interested in cars etc.), while East Asians, for example, see themselves in terms of their roles and relationships. WEIRD individuals think more analytically (they detach the focal point from its context), while most other people think holistically by taking context and relationships among parts into account (see also Nisbett, 2003). WEIRD cultures developed systems theories to begin putting things back together what in other cultures was never analytically separated. One could also say that WEIRD cultures are normatively dissociated (split off) from what is a natural part of the self in **sociocentric** and Indigenous societies. The WEIRD norm is that individuals have split themselves off from the priority of group goals, place, myth and ritual, ancestry, and spirits or gods/goddesses.

Cushman (1995) similarly talks about the well–bounded (boundaried), and the masterful self in the U.S. He traces its history and shows that the European settler self rejected the options of developing a self–structure like the Native Americans they encountered and the African Americans they brought as slaves. Since the "white race" saw itself as inherently intellectually and morally superior, it could not choose these avenues. Upon their arrival settlers usually did not want to be who they were culturally before (because they escaped persecution, oppression, poverty, etc.). Yet, what were their alternatives? Native Americans were seen as "wild Indians" and uncivilized and could not serve as cultural model to emulate. And neither could the African slave self that represented a race seen as inferior and of lower intelligence. The two possible alternatives present on the North American continent were not viable and neither was the option of continuing the cultural traditions of the settlers' countries of origin full force. Devoid of many of the traditions and attachments early settlers left behind, with seemingly no viable

attachment options in front, the contemporary self, conceived as well-boundaried and masterful, also became empty. It is, Cushman argues, a self unmoored from tradition and place. It is ready to be filled through consumerism, occupied with a cult of celebrities, and uses psychotherapy to address its **individualistic** concerns and suffering. It is also a self that is easily manipulated.

Sociocentric **societies or non–***WEIRD* **cultures**

Sociocentric refers to individuals who complete an "I am…" sentence more likely by referring to their families, communities, or religious groups. One's relationship to others, the thoughts, feelings, and behavior of others matters significantly and impact one's own actions. Such perceptions became apparent, for example, in cognitive tests where objects (fish) were shown with a background (water plants, etc.). While Americans and Japanese people made the same number of references to the fish, the Japanese participants referred to the relationship between the focal object and the background. Notably, the first sentence of Americans was three times as likely to refer to the focal fish, while Japanese would begin with a general statement about the environment (Nisbett, 2003). This example is taken from a host of cognitive and other research that has found differences between **individualistic** and **sociocentric** cultures. The figure contrasting the Eastern and Western view shows how the self locates itself differently in relation to the group it is affiliated with and groups outside the culture.

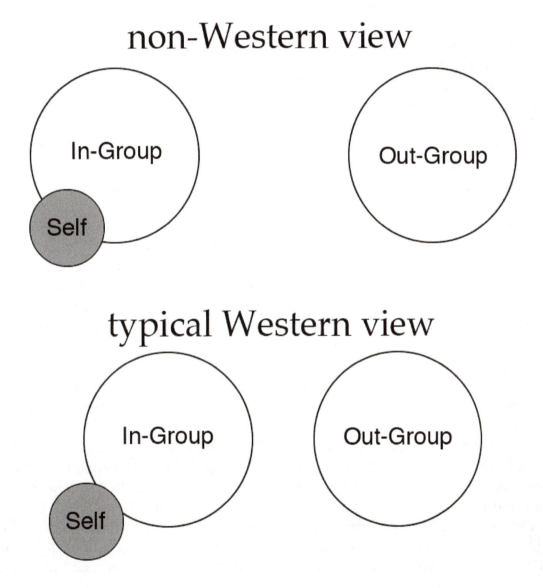

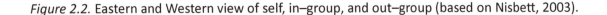

Figure 2.2. Eastern and Western view of self, in–group, and out–group (based on Nisbett, 2003).

Sociocentrism with a twist — Indigenous cultures

There are approximately 250 million Indigenous peoples worldwide — 4% of the global population — living in over 70 countries. In the glossary we provide a more detailed discussion and definitions of who is considered Indigenous. **Indigenism** is likely the least familiar self–perspective. It is also the perspective that is most central to the endeavor of enthnoautobirography. Let us therefore explain this perspective at greater length.

Indigenous traditions are consciously based on locally, ecologically, and seasonally contextualized truths that are narratively anchored — their stories are embedded — in natural communities. It is the practice of a worldview or knowing that is not dualistic with spirits far removed from humans in a transcendent realm; instead they are an active part of ongoing conversations. Stories and ceremonies help individuals find internal and external balance within a conversation that participates in the life of ancestors, animals, plants, stars, humans, rocks, mountains, and other beings. As with all the labels we have introduced, it is important to use them lightly. We understand this general characterization as paradigmatic for Indigenous cultures, but not necessarily as fully achieved (just as all societies often fail to live up to their own ideals). Idealizing Indigenous cultures can easily lead to a romanticization that prevents a realistic look both at ourselves as well as Indigenous cultures.

Many Indigenous authors speak of the ongoing conversation with all beings — animals, plants, humans, stars, ancestors, spirits, etc. In the Sámi language, this has been expressed as *humalan eatnama*: "I converse with the earth." In Aymara, it becomes *nayasa kollo achachilampi uywaysastssta*: "I am letting myself be nurtured by the apu — the spirit of the mountain — as I am nurturing the spirit of the mountain" Peruvians use the Spanish *criar y dejarse criar*, "to nurture and let oneself be nurtured," as equivalent to the Aymara wording.

Such participatory conversation is described using terms in native languages that don't necessarily translate obviously into the language of "spirituality." Native languages are commonly difficult to tranlate into English and other Indo–European languages and have very different structures than the latter languages. When elders or Indigenous authors use words such as "pray," they are typically making adjustments; frequently the native equivalent seems to mean "to talk" or "to converse." The native word then does not have any associations with church or religion, but refers to a common everyday activity that is necessary, obvious, and natural, just like the conversaion in his monumental poem *Beaivi, Áhčažan*:

Beaivi	The sun
Máilmmi áhčči	the world's father
Eanan	The earth
giđa nieida	spring's daughter
almmiravdda gollerásit	the horizon's gold flower
háisuoinnit	the fragrant grass
humahalan eatnama	I converse with the earth
ja gulan ádjagiid	and hear the creeks answer
jietnasilbbain silbajienain	their voices the
vástideame	sounds of silver
humahalan eatnama	I converse with the earth
meaddel áiggiid	beyond time
Beaivi	The sun
máilmmi áhčči	the world's father
Eanan	The earth
eallima eadni	life's mother
almmiravdda iđitguovssu	the horizon's red dawn
nástegáissit	starry peaks
humahalan eatnama	I converse with the earth

The goal of these Indigenous "conversations" — "I converse with the earth" — is not to attain abstract knowledge. The goal rather is balanced living, becoming present in a particular place and at a particular time to the obligations that arise from one's being there (no matter how we may construe our getting there in the first place). Knowing and being in this way is a *participatory* activity (participatory with everything that surrounds us) that could be written as one word: *beingknowing*. It is arguably a kind of inquiry that is also deeply spiritual, as Lapena (1999, p. 18) notes: "[Elders] learn the earth's secret language by quietly observing. It is a secret language called knowledge that releases the spirit from stone and heals by tone of voice and by changing sickness into elements that flow instead of blocking life." The individual does not seem boundaried as is typical in contemporary Western personalities, but rather individual consciousness seems to extend through permeable and fluid boundaries of self into the consciousness of other beings, whether human, animal, plant, rock, or star (and vice versa!). The goal of the nurturing conversation is the fulfillment of obligations, because happiness and balance, and health and fulfillment, are seen as the possible and likely results of such endeavors and presence.

The Mihilakawna Pomo elder Lucy Smith (Peri & Patterson, 1979, n.p.) describes this sense of participation when she recalls her mother's teachings:

> We had many relatives and...we all had to live together; so we'd better learn how to get along with each other. She said it wasn't too hard to do. It was just like taking care of your younger brother or sister. You got to know them, find out what they liked and what made them cry, so you'd know what to do. If you took good care of them you didn't have to work as hard. Sounds like it's not true, but it is. When that baby gets to be a man or woman they're going to help you out. You know, I thought she was talking about us Indians and how we are supposed to get along. I found out later by my older sister that mother wasn't just talking about Indians, but the plants, animals, birds — everything on this earth. They are our relatives and we better know how to act around them or they'll get after us.

In this context, Indigenous spiritual practice can be seen as an engagement that arises from local presence to include other life forms, and, beyond that, life outside one's community.

Traditional Hopis see their responsibility for keeping their villages in balance not just as an obligation to their own tribe, but to the entire world. In their thinking, imbalance and the loss of the **original instructions** to live a simple and ecologically sound life in their southwestern locale means a serious threat to the balance of the entire world (Mails & Evehema, 1995). They also describe the personal commitment to the sources of life through purification, blessings, sacrifices, or offerings and prayerful conversation.

Members of the group PRATEC (Proyecto Andino de Tecnologias Campesinas, the "Andean Project of Peasant Technologies") work with the notion of decolonization through the affirmation of traditional or Indigenous Andean cultural knowledge (Apffel–Marglin, 1994; Apffel–Marglin, with PRATEC, 1998). Their spiritual, scientific, and political work is understood in the framework of such native discourse:

> The conversations held between persons and the other inhabitants of the world are not primarily engaged in for the purpose of "knowing reality." They are engaged in as part of the activity of *criar y dejarse criar*, of nurturing (raising) and letting oneself be nurtured (raised). The verb *criar* is used to speak of raising children, animals, plants, relationships, etc. It is the activity that fosters the growth and development of any potentiality or generativity. It is a fundamentally mutual or reciprocal activity: as one nurtures one is simultaneously nurtured. The action in the world does not leave the actor untransformed; acting in

the world is being in relationship with that world, so the language of conversation is more appropriate than the language of knowledge. There is here no knower and known, no subject and object. Rather there are actors in relationships of mutuality. By acting one transforms not only the world but oneself as well. Therefore it is a fundamentally dynamic world, always moving, always changing, always in flux. There is, as it were, no simple act of knowing as we moderns understand the term for such knowledge–acquiring activity presupposes that there is something to be known, irrespective of who knows it. (Apffel–Marglin, 1994, p. 9)

If Indigenous spiritual practice is so construed, then this suggests that a person might be developing Indigenous awareness, whether or not the person meets established definitions of being Indigenous (genetic ancestry, language, etc.). Similarly, a person of Indigenous ancestry does not inevitably manifest such awareness. In other words, and we will reiterate this important point below,

Indigenous awareness is potentially open to all persons who are regularly engaged in the kind of "nurturing conversation" described above. Indigenous spirituality will be addressed further in Chapter 14: Faith, Spirituality, Skepticism.

Given how early we learn our sense of self, given how a similar sense of self has been modeled over the generations, changing one's self in the profound way we are discussing it here is a tall order. It is easy to see that the recovery of Indigenous mind is a multi–generational project, one where we should humbly acknowledge the small steps we are taking and refrain from any large claims as far as Indigenous awareness is concerned. The following icons are inspired by the Chinese–born and German–raised artist Yang Liu (n.d.). They serve to summarize the discussion of this chapter. The three images contrast the size of the sense of self; the way of life, from **individualistic** to people being connected to individuals being connected in a circle; and, finally, how opinions are seen as linear, circuitous, or as a circuitous interweaving of stories that pertain.

Figure 2.3. The self in Western, Asian, and Indigenous cultures (inspired by Lang Yiu).

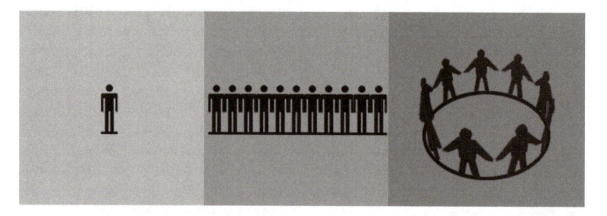

Figure 2.4. Lifeworld in Western, Asian, and Indigenous cultures (inspired by Lang Yiu).

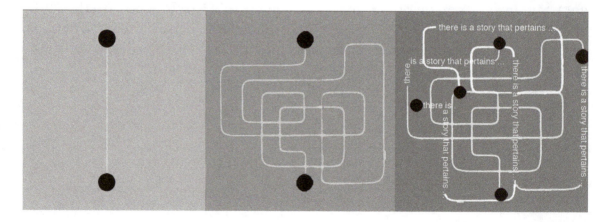

Figure 2.5. Opinions in Western, Asian, and Indigenous cultures (inspired by Lang Yiu).

Activity

Activity 1

Overview of a Contemporary Indigenous Culture

Choose a contemporary Indigenous culture that lives within what is currently the United States (including Hawaii and Alaska), and provide a basic overview of their culture. Make certain to include the following aspects of their culture: where they lived before conquest, and where they live currently; general descriptions of their cultural traditions including language, spirituality, artistry, seasonal activities, and so on; at least two current issues or challenges that they face, such as treaty rights, social or environmental issues.

Given that Smith (2012) and others have noted the complicated and oftentimes problematic (i.e. colonizing) manner that research is conducted about Indigenous peoples, reflect on what issues might be present in this activity? As this inquiry is conducted pay attention to issues, feelings, and the complications that might arise in yourself as you learn about an Indigenous people, including the history of conquest that has brought us to be here in the first place.

This may be completed in a 500–word written reflection, or shared as an oral presentation with others.

Some internet–based resources include:

News from Indian Country, (http://www.indiancountrynews.com/)
National Native News, (http://www.nativenews.net/)
Native American Rights Fund, (http://www.narf.org/)
Indigenous Environmental Network, (http://www.ienearth.org/)

Activity 2

Mapping Your Self

Create a drawing or map of your self in relation to the people and beings around you (family, friends, pets, animals, etc.). For example, there can be multiple dimensions, such as inner relationships, more immediate and outer ones. They might interact, or be more distinct from each other. Allow yourself to be creative (schematic drawing, family tree type drawings, collages with images, etc.).

Share your map with others.

Note: If you are completing these activities on your own, and do not have an organized group to do oral presentations for (such as in a classroom, community organization and so on), it is encouraged that you present the work you are doing to a friend, family member or spouse to experience sharing your process in oral form.

Chapter Summary

Core beliefs about the self are learned very early, and various cultures have different "boundaries" of the self: **independent** &/or **interdependent**. Though the **individualism** of the **modern** western self is an outlier, especially in light of **collectivism** and **Indigenism**, ethnoautobiography helps to understand the self in terms of the group, place, ritual & story.

Concept Check

Name some of the earliest experiences that impact the development of the self.

Name several characteristics of both **independent** and **interdependent** views of self.

Use one sentence to summarize modern **individualistic, interdependent** and **Indigenous** sense of self.

What was the conclusion of Henrich, Heine & Norenzayan (2010) about members of **WEIRD** societies?

What distinguished Japanese research participants from their US counterparts when identifying fish with a background?

An **Indigenous** conversation might include which beings?

NOTES

Chapter 3
Why Not Simply 'Autobiography'?

Riff

I Am a White Man

I am a white man.
I am a white man, it is obvious – isn't it?
White is short for "European."
I am German, so I am white.
White is short for "settler from Europe."
White is short for "socialized into a European frame of mind."
White is the name of forgetting.
Forgetting so much of how we came to be where we are.
I am a white man.
Boxed into a box that likes to forget its name.

I do not walk alone.
Something walks with me.
Something walks with other white men like me.
With me walks a shadow.
Before me I project the shadow of forgetting where I came from.
Behind me trails the shadow of the tears of native peoples.
Below me I march on the shadow of the lands my peoples have raped.
Above me looms the shadow of the spirits which I am blind to.
All around me
Walks the shadow of

domination,
colonization,
witchhunts,
genocides,
holocausts,
sexism,
racism.
I do not walk alone.
We do not walk alone.

How can I heal
When these shadows walk with me?
How can we heal?

How can we walk into healing?
How can I heal
When the shadows obscure what lies beyond them?

Yet, as I walk
I am filled with hope.

I hope to heal
By remembering and seeing
The shadows that walk with me.
So that I may become more complete.
So that I am not made of illusions.
So that I don't die in fantasyland.
So that I may die with the riches of presence and imagination.

I hope to heal
By purifying the shadows I project.
So that I am not boxed in a box without names.
So that I walk with the
Multitude,
Richness,
And plurality
That is me.

Til árs ok til friðar—
So that there may be fertility and the balancing of the great peace.
So that there may be *friður* and *heill* before me—
Balance, wholeness, and health.
May there be *friður* and *heill* behind me...
May there be *friður* and *heill* below me...
May there be *friður* and *heill* above me...
May there be *friður* and *heill* all around me.
So that, maybe, I can go on in beauty, *friður* and *heill*.
And so that, maybe, we all can go on in greater beauty, *friður* and *heill*.
So that, maybe, I can walk with all my relations.
So that, maybe, I get healed.

JWK

Chapter Outline	Core Concepts	Ethnoautobiographical Perspectives	Expected Outcomes
I am a White man	Collective shadow	Acknowledging our collective shadow is healing	Finding the courage to explore collective shadow issues
Reader, beware!	Assumptions as barriers	Setting aside our assumptions opens us to new perspectives	Receptivity to new information and perspectives
Motivations for ethnoauto-biography	Integrated approach to telling our stories	Ethnoautobiographical ingredients (history, myth, place, identity, etc.) inquire into and critique dominant society	Learn how ethno-autobiography transforms dominant society
Origins & ancestors	Ancestors are central in Indigenous thinking	Acknowledging ancestry provides grounding for cultural self reflection	Remembering ancestors
Narrative nature of humans	Humans are storytellers	Emphasize the narrative nature of people and increase awareness of hybridity	Begin to tell your own story
Indigenist & cosmopolitan conversations	Provincialism and cosmopolitanism	As a decolonization practice, ethnoautobio-graphy integrates the dilemmas created by our simultaneous presence in the local and the global	Understand the integration of Indigenist and cosmopolitan perspectives
Space for conversations that nurture	Nurturing conversation	Engaging in nurturing conversations allows us to see ourselves in a more complete light	Acknowledging conversations with humans and other beings around us
Reviving radical otherness	The other is within us	Remembering the other within us makes us more complete	Remembrance of parts we have neglected in ourselves

Chapter Outline	Core Concepts	Ethnoautobiographical Perspectives	Expected Outcomes
Stories of release	Creativity & healing are triggered by our stories	Ethnoautobiography addresses multiculturaism, encourages personal and cultural self–exploration, and honors multiple stories	Finding a more inclusive sense of self
Qualities of Indigenous self–understanding	How the self is rooted in society & nature	Being aware of the networks we are always part of enriches our sense of well–being	Remembering our networked self
What do Indigenous peoples think about this?	Changing our sense of self is critical for species survival	Ethnoautobiography matters to Indigenous peoples	Finding the support of Indigenous peoples for this process

Key Terms

Autoethnography
Cosmopolitan
Deconstruction
Essentialist, or essentialism
(Hi)story, or (hi)stories
Holosexuality
Indigenous self
Masterful self
Objective, or objectivity
Presence, or coming–to–presence
Subject, or subjective
Transgress

Note: All key terms in this textbook are highlighted in bold and can be found in the Glossary at the end of the book.

Resources Alongside This Chapter

Hogan, L. (2001). *The woman who watches over the world.* New York, NY: Norton.

Krupat, A. (Ed.). (1994). *Native American autobiography: An anthology.* Madison: University of Wisconsin Press.

Silko, L. M. (1997, 2006). *Ceremony.* New York, NY: Penguin.

The riff, " I Am a White Man," is juxtaposed with the image at the beginning of the chapter and points to the disconnections and questions that arise for us today. It is a riff that echoes lines that occur in many chants of the Diné (Navajo) people:

> In beauty I walk
> With beauty before me I walk
> With beauty behind me I walk
> With beauty above me I walk
> With beauty around me I walk
> It has become beauty again
> It has become beauty again
> It has become beauty again
> It has become beauty again

> *Hózhóogo naasháa doo*
> *Shitsiji' hózhóogo naasháa doo*
> *Shikéédéé hózhóogo naasháa doo*
> *Shideigi hózhóogo naasháa doo*
> *T'áá altso shinaagóó hózhóogo*
>   *naasháa doo*
> *Hózhó náhásdlíí'*
> *Hózhó náhásdlíí'*
> *Hózhó náhásdlíí'*
> *Hózhó náhásdlíí*

This prayer is an example from the end of Blessingway, a central chantway ceremony for the Diné people. It is a blessing, it is an affirmation, and it invokes balance. In contrast, the riff addresses the loss of such balancing interconnection in the (post)modern European traditions. It invokes the shadow of material that has culturally been difficult to deal with or has been denied. Just as the Blessingway prayer invokes balance and beauty for healing, so this riff invokes shadow material so that balancing and beauty may have a healing impact as we work to find gold in the shadows. A major psychological assumption, especially in Jungian psychology, is that there is always shadow material, and denying the shadow will not make it go away (Jung, 1959). Rather exploring shadow material creates the potential of renewal and unexpected riches.

The image at the beginning of this chapter evokes the worldview of the oldest, Indigenous layers of the European north. Here we find the shaman in the center, sitting in what looks like a Native American tipi (such structures were used from the earliest times in Eurasia), which is connected via a tree upward to the stars (especially the north star), and also downward to the river in which a salmon swims. The shaman's tipi (either a woman or man) sits in the center of the community, with other tipis nearby, and reindeer. The shaman is working ceremonially with the drum, connecting the community ritually with the above and below as s/he is in the middle world, keeping the community in balance or to keep the peace (friður). Or, as the Diné would say, to create beauty or hózhó. This quality of worldview inspires or inspirits this workbook. Such an understanding of interconnection and balance is something that we can learn from for our future. This particular understanding of the world is the archetype we work from.

Stories of the self, or autobiographies, are as much personal as they are visionary, spiritual, and political acts. Ethnoautobiography encourages narrations of our identity that address the following sample questions:

- What qualities of storytelling help us to navigate our way amidst our present personal and global crises?
- Which qualities of autobiography are emancipatory, healing, and supportive of creativity and imagination?

an opening to the possibility of seeing our world in a way that transcends established frames and of developing understandings and meanings that do not fit current categories.

Accordingly, in reading this workbook there may be the temptation to view certain statements within the conventional political spectrum of left to right. When encountering language traditionally associated with a particular political discourse (e.g., left–liberal), we want to caution against the use of these categories and encourage a mindful opening

> **Ethnoautobiography is defined as creative writing (and/or oral presentation) that grounds itself in the ethnic, cultural, historical, ecological, and gender self–exploration of the author.**

- What stories of self implicitly foster racism, sexism, identity politics, or fundamentalism?
- Which stories support social engagement, and cultivating our personal richness that has been under attack in modern times?

Reader, beware!

Let us offer cautionary notes as we are getting more deeply into the experience of ethnoautobiography. We encourage the reader to set aside old lenses (whether political, religious, or socio-cultural). Ethnoautobiography intends

to other possibilities. This includes alternatives that even we can barely glimpse. In fact, we find the polar left – right one–dimensional political spectrum not at all helpful when trying to envision solutions to our current socio–political conundrums. Indeed, this particular approach creates obstacles to discovering innovative, visionary pathways and solutions. Though we cannot help but use language that has particular historical and socio-political associations, we encourage them to be viewed in a new light and context where ideas are put together in a way that seeks solutions beyond established political and cultural paradigms.

A second consideration: We talk a lot about Indigenous civilizations and societies. This is not because they are necessarily ideal per se (in fact, there are numerous instances where they clearly were or are not). Instead, we discuss them because Indigenous worldviews are a dramatic contrast to those of Western and Eurocentered societies and it is this very contrast that contains new perspectives on our current social ills. We cannot go back in history and it is vital to acknowledge that the romance of Natives is nothing but the continuation of a shameful and violent history, as well as a distorted way to see them. However, we can contemplate Indigenous worldviews to see what pointers and answers we might find for our future. Indigenous civilizations have been, and continue to be, dramatically misrepresented in Western eyes. Such a misrepresentation, in our view, not only has led to tremendous suffering among Indigenous peoples, but also furthers Western society's loss of humanity and marks a fundamental disadvantage as we move into the future. It is important to mention that Indigenous societies have provided inspiration for reflective and critical responses to our current socio–political and cultural challenges. We will offer possible directions to develop our own answers using ethnoautobiography.

So, why write ethnoautobiography?

Why not just write an autobiography? We summarize our answer by saying: to encourage critical discourse, critical self reflection, and personal growth. But to be a bit more specific and provocative:

- The overarching context for ethnoautobiographical inquiries is the decolonization of the centers (Europe, U.S.). Colonization (in its overt and covert manifestations) is the political force that so often has emanated from the centers. Ethnoautobiography is the creation of margin upon margin throughout the centers, fissures for the remembrance of tribal origins (alternate cultures, subcultures, "minority" cultures, etc.) and the healing of abuse of minorities and Indigenous cultures. When we tell our ethnoautobiographical stories we acknowledge and share the fissures and diversity we each carry.

- The unlearning or **deconstruction** of Whiteness (as Eurocentered, hegemonic, colonizing, economically globalizing consciousness) is a more specific context that seeks the end of racialism and identity politics, the trauma and fear–based assertion of uniform cultural identities that denies our individual diversity and cultural interconnectedness. The idea of 'Whiteness' leads to the forget-

Motivations for Ethnoautobiography
Decolonization of the centers of power
Affirmation of alternatives outside the centers
Unlearning Whiteness
Affirmation of cultural multiplicity
Remembrance of local knowledge
Affirmation of intimacy with place in a cosmopolitan world
Demise of unrestrained individualism
Affirmation of individuals, and individual difference, in community
Deconstruction of binary gender categories
Affirmation of the spectrum of gender identities
Remembrance of Indigenous visionary ceremonies
Affirmation of spiritual experiences
Enactment of visionary stories and healing endeavors
Affirmation of multiple ways of beingknowing
Unlearning separation and dichotomous approach to the world
Affirmation of participatory engagement with the world

ting of the underlying cultural diversity that we all have. This work **transgresses** White minds and their **essentialist**, and often enough fantastic, notions of pure origin, race, Indians, etc. "White" is, of course, a state of mind that hides diversity and diverse origins. Ethnoautobiography here means healing from supremacy and uncovering the underlying diversity whites have forgotten.

sions between the two may be transformed into playful conversations supportive of individual vision, as well as the multivocality of communal histories: "personal stories are coherent and name individual identities within tribal communities and are not an obvious opposition to communal values" (Vizenor 1994a, p. 57). Such endeavors also support struggles for social justice and

> **At this time we are sharing with all our family relations, we nurture to be nurtured ourselves.**
>
> Machaca & Machaca (1996, personal communication)

- In an ecological context this means the remembrance of local knowledge, and the province (home, family, roots). It means the affirmation of intimacy with place and its histories. Such an **Indigenist** perspective deconstructs the objectification of nature as mere resource and facilitates ecological healing.
- In the context of the social world, ethnoautobiography facilitates the demise of narcissistic individualism (the handmaiden of the destruction of communities). Seeking the downfall of this modern norm aids in resolving antagonisms between individual and community. Now the ten-

equality. When we acknowledge and bear witness to each other's stories, especially stories of suffering, the opportunities to create justice and improve equality can arise. For example, hearing how the most recent depression in the U.S. has impacted families can help us think about how to prevent economic suffering. Hearing how apartheid in South Africa has impacted its citizens in front of a Truth and Reconciliation Commission can lead to healing and become an incentive for legal measures to increase social justice.
- In the context of gender roles, this means the **deconstruction**

of binary fe/male categories. Rigid gender oppositions only serve the supremacy of men. Ethnoautobiography encourages the creation of flexible gender identities, not of a vapid and unimaginative androgyny, but the celebration of a diverse **holo-sexuality**, a vibrant celebration of erotic energies that may take many forms along a multidimensional spectrum.

- Shamans are practitioners in Indigenous traditions who are a combination of medical doctor, priest, and psychotherapist. In the context of shamanism (the oldest stream of endeavors labeled '**transpersonal**' by modern minds) and spirituality, ethnoautobiography means the remembrance of the visionary experiences, healing stories and ceremonies and importantly the communal cultural context from which they arise. This facilitates the examination of visions that are motivated by dollar signs and are inflated to comical, yet dangerous proportions.

- In the context of the modernist effort called **transpersonal** psychology, it means the celebration of participatory events. For example, when we research, inquire, or investigate we also create. These are ways to participate in the creation of reality. Acknowledging the creative element in our inquiries deconstructs the objectifying and dogmatic interpretations of what seems unbelievable to the blinders of the integrated mind (parapsychological phenomena, synchronicities, intuitions, ecstasy, etc.).

Origins and ancestors

As described thus far, ancestry is one of the key ingredients of ethnoautobiography. Leslie Marmon Silko (1979, p. 213) has noted that White or Eurocentered consciousness "violates a fundamental belief held by the tribal people they desire to emulate: they deny their history, their very origins." This chapter addresses this concern and responds with various examples of how ethnoautobiographical stories acknowledge and embrace the complicated and convoluted history of our origins. When we begin to reclaim a participatory sense of self and society we embark on a journey that can be compared to the adventures of previous inner explorers, shamans of old and modern day depth psychologists. The particular journey of this workbook challenges us to survey outer territories and inner worlds, and to engage profoundly in a dialectic of both outer facts and inner experiences. When we look at origins and history, we wonder about the aspects of our experiences that we know well, and yet we aim to focus on those parts of the experiences that are confusing, maybe conflicted, and difficult to verbalize. The process of ethnoautobiography guides us to find answers to these possibly hidden parts of our experience. Origins and ancestors are among the things that are so often difficult to talk about. This is quite in contrast to how people looked at it in earlier times.

> [The] conscious awareness of the singularity of each individual life is the late product of a specific civilization. Throughout most of *human* history, the individual does not oppose himself (sic!) to all others; he does not feel himself to exist outside of others, and still less against others, but very much *with* others in an independent existence that asserts its rhythms everywhere in the community. No one is rightful possessor of his life or his death; lives are so thoroughly entangled that each of them has its center everywhere and its circumference nowhere. (Georges Gusdorf, Autobiography, from Vizenor, 1994b, pp. 156–7)

Ethnoautobiography is a version of autobiography that contrasts with conventional, Eurocentered autobiography. Commonly people write autobiographies either during the final stages of their lives as a way of integrating their experience or earlier in life because they are famous and the autobiography becomes part of their promotional activities. Ethnoautobiography requires that additional information be present, not just simple (or simplistic) biographical sketches of family, career, and major historical events.

As portrayed in the film, *In the Light of Reverence* (McLeod, 2001), the conception of personal, individual identity is intricately woven with nature, ancestors, history, spirit, and community — whether we are aware of it or not. For example, in this documentary we observe an annual ritual race circle around the Black Hills, a central part of the tribal homeland of the Lakota tribe. This is not a race like we might observe at the Olympics, rather, it is an enactment of Lakota identity that is deeply anchored in the Black Hills. Participating in the race is part of what constitutes being Lakota, where individual identity cannot be separated from the cultural identity grounded in the landscape that tribal members circle. Features of this landscape reflect the Lakota view of the stars, thus, fulfilling the adage "as above, so below." The different ceremonial aspects associated with the race invoke these connections, whether in prayer, the structural design of the tipi, or a star constellation. The mythic story of how humans came to see themselves, as they do now in relation to the buffalo and other beings, is part of the Lakota sense of identity.

Responses to "Who am I? And who are you?" concerning the content of these questions have varied across the ages, but also regarding the qualities of self–inquiry. Ancient cultures, such as the Hebrews and Greeks, did not have selves that were firmly boundaried. They had direct lines of communication with their gods and goddesses and to

Notions of ethnoautobiography and **autoethnography** have emerged in recent years as part of interdisciplinary courses addressing issues of race, multiculturalism, etc., as well as in literary criticism (e.g., Shirinian, 2001; Ellis and Bochner, 2000). Autoethnography

> **Ethnoautobiographical inquiry emphasizes the narrative nature of human beings and works to deconstruct essentialist notions of self, other, truth, origin, history, ethnicity, authenticity, colonialism, religion, emotion, and similar concepts.**

the local spirits. In that sense, the self was much more porous and connected to the spiritual, religious or **transpersonal** realms. What is often called the mythic sense of self allowed for direct communion with **presences**, whether it was Yahweh in the Hebrew tradition or the Delphic oracle revealing insights (prophecies) in the Greek traditions.

The modern self we are so familiar with is of rather recent origin and probably only two hundred or so years old. The term 'autobiography' emerged in the English language at the beginning of the 19th century. As an expression of the modern self, autobiography is an equally recent event. It represents the self–conscious telling and creating of who we think we are and how we would like to be seen. Ethnoautobiography provides access to understanding the social constructions of, and ways to revise, the self.

arose out of the self–awareness of the anthropological researcher's experience of the research itself that she was conducting. That awareness then impacted the research, and further increased the self–awareness of the researcher as a research instrument or lens, so to speak. Ethnoautobiography is a specific variant of such self–reflexivity. In a nutshell, it is defined as creative writing (and/or oral presentation) that grounds itself in the ethnic, cultural, historical, ecological, and gender self–exploration of the author. Part of such narratives is the investigation of **hybridity**, the **borderlands** between categories and **transgression** of those boundaries. Additionally, such stories address the multiple **(hi)stories** carried both outside and inside how the dominant society defines and narrates a particular place and time. For instance, while we, the authors, write in contemporary California and Texas, respectively, there are a multitude of stories that are counter to, and larger than, the dominant stories told in these places. As creative and evocative writing and storytelling ethnoautobiography explores conscious self–awareness. Such consciousness is the combination of individual self–representations brought into relationship with **objective** factors (history, politics, religion, ancestry, gender, and so on), which are related to personal identity construction.

The term ethnoautobiography highlights issues of ethnicity. It should be seen, particularly, in the context of the history of self–identity, which shows

matters, here, but three aspects of one human being. (p. 85)

This statement is a good illustration of what ethnoautobiography seeks. Consequently, this means we inquire about the beginning places of our ancestry or ancestries in the sense of specific genealogy; our ethnicity or ethnicities; inquiry about Indigenous roots; history of place; gender and the Indigenous diversity of gender constructions; place and ecology; culture; and origin stories and creation myths. We take the answers we find as tentative answers, woven together into some temporary statement

> As an expression of the modern self, autobiography is a recent event.

that the **modernist** or **White self** emerged using ethnic self–denials. That is, a Eurocentered sense of self attempts to deny cultural, gendered, historical, and ecological aspects of the self. We use an Indigenous sense of **presence** for the interpretation of the **ethno–** part of the word; it is an umbrella for issues of culture, place (ecology), gender, history, and time. Osage Carter Revard (quoted in Nabokov, 2002) stated that

> the "wild" Indian was tied to land, to people, to origins and way of life by every kind of human ordering we can imagine. "History" and "Myth" and "Identity" are not three separate

— only to be woven again — made new in the next telling. The dimensions just listed constitute the necessary and minimal ingredients for ethnoautobiographical explorations, without which **presence** in an Indigenous sense is not possible.

Narrative nature of human beings

Ethnoautobiographical inquiry emphasizes the narrative nature of human beings. Humans are natural storytellers, and have a storytelling brain (Gottschall, 2012). We use stories to create meaning and to deal with uncertainty. We hunger for stories, love stories, and have a natural inclination to create them. Stories **deconstruct essentialist** notions of self, other, truth, origin, history, ethnicity, authenticity, colonialism, religion, emotion (*true* feeling),and similar concepts. Such an interpretative understanding reveals that we are not unfolding from some presumed true essence. Rather, we flexibly emerge as human beings in time and place through imaginative acts of survival grounded in personal observation and experience. We are entangled in multiple stories and carry many voices.

met. This is the beginning of creation; it is where life starts. It is an image of polarities that give rise to something new, entering and acknowledging the space of **hybridity** we emerge with a new sense of our selves.

Acknowledging uniqueness and individuality, together with our connection to stories and conditions larger than an individualistic self acknowledges, creates **presence**, a special quality of being in the world. In fact, ethnoautobiographical

> ## We may elude the politics of polarity and emerge as the others of our selves.
>
> Bhabha (1994, p. 56)

This consciousness can, inevitably, lead to an awareness of **hybridity** (mixture), seeing gaps between stories, and experiences of awkward categories. Neither cultures nor individuals are unitary or simplistic phenomena. They carry diverse stories, definitions, histories, etc. which are embodied in individuals. Just as likely, these are narratives which individuals may **transgress**. Acknowledging **hybridity** opens up what has been called a "Third Space." Exploring a third space, "we may elude the politics of polarity and emerge as the others of our selves" (Bhabha, 1994, p. 56). **Presence** arises out of the fissures between such polarities. In the mythic traditions of the Old Norse *Ginnung gap*, the creative gap of gaps from which everything arise, was where fire and ice

inquiry can be seen as one of the possible definitions for honoring the process of **coming–to–presence**.

One of our key points is that looking at Indigenous traditions is not a way to go back to the past, but a way to go forward. In fact, the Old Norse traditions just mentioned had an image of time in which you could only move forward if you were able to step back through the past to bring it forward with you. This requires the integration of the past for the future. So the movement, the step backward to look at Indigenous roots is in the service of going forward.

This is also a call to open the harmful limitations of **modernity** that are destructive and denying the relevance of our Indigenous past. When we step through the past into the future we come to presence. Community, historical awareness, and egalitarian politics are among the conditions in which we can develop integrated practices that replace **essentialist** notions of authenticity. Authenticity is always fluid, it is an ever

Vizenor notes, "the autobiographical narrative must be ironic; otherwise some narratives would be more natural and essential than others" (1994a, pp. 177–8). The need for irony certainly relates to countering the invented glorious asser-

> Part of ethnoautobiography is the investigation of hybridity, the border-lands between categories and disobedience to those boundaries.

changing process in which we discover our evolving sense of self. Authenticity is never a thing, nothing we ever have, it is never a given; it is a way of being in the world. We have to question: what do community, historical awareness, and other terms mean to us? When we come to **presence**, then the creativity of such **presence** confronts our current challenges and requires the remembrance of **Indigenous** roots.

Creative writing and oral presentations are important tools for ethnoautobiographical investigations. By telling our story we reveal ourselves as 'in–process'. This removes any **essentialist** understanding of self. The assumption that there is an essential, unchanging sense of self with one true root denies the process we are always in as individuals. Essentialist notions of self are usually romantic or nostalgic in nature and part of nationalistic or chauvinistic ideologies asserting a form of racial purity. What are ways to overcome essentialist notions of self?

tions of the modernist self. Additionally, narratives that **deconstruct** White–ness and remember Indigenous roots find much **anti–essentialism** in their persistent critique and honesty regarding ethnoautobiographical stories. Amidst pain and tears, laugter at White grandiosities will help to burst personal and cultural narcissistic bubbles.

Ethnoautobiography is not autobiography. By virtue of its ingredients (history, myth, place, identity, etc.) it inevitably inquires into the definitions and discussions of the dominant society of a particular place and time and questions them (the German *hinterfragen*, to question or inquire behind the appearances, provides a good image). It does not merely comply with the boundaries offered, but critiques them creatively. Again, ethnoautobiography explores self–awareness — the **subjective** — and, importantly, relates it to external — the **objective** — factors. Thus, it is also a moral and politico–historical narrative, invigorated by the narrative of the teller.

Indigenist and *cosmopolitan* conversations

When we use the term 'Indigenist' or 'Indigenous tradition', we could associate the 'local' and 'provincial', meaning something with a narrow focus on a particular place. Then its opposite might be 'cosmopolitanism', or a position that is open to the international world (see Appiah, 2006; Breckenridge, Pollock, Bhabha & Chakrabarty, 2002; Derrida, 2001; Krupat, 2002; Rabinow, 1986). Where does ethnoautobiography locate itself between provincialism and cosmopolitanism? Does it emphasize a narrow focus that is rather parochial in nature?

In Eurocentered thinking, **cosmopolitanism** and provincialism are generally seen as opposites. The practices of ethnoautobiography suggest a reframing of both of these terms where the immersion in the local (provincialism, Indigenism) and the commitment to connections within and across cultures (cosmopolitanism) are equally important. This is similar to the importance of interplay between subjective and objective.

Cosmopolitanism comes out of a philosophical tradition reaching back to the Stoics and Kant. In this Eurocentered understanding some of the terms associated with cosmopolitanism are "universal", "theoretical", "abstract", and "conceptual". They imply a masculinized sense of mastery, distance from experience, indifference to the particular, and a focus on absolutes. This leads to an individualistic sense of self that now becomes a unit of world culture and international politics. Thus underlying this notion of cosmopolitanism is the assumption of individualistically bounded selves focused on individualistic rights. This cosmopolitanism sees a center with culture diffused from the center. We can think of London as the center of the British Empire or Paris as the center of France or New York City as the center of the arts. The centers are **cosmopolitan**, and the surrounding areas are provincial in this understanding.

The opposite of cosmopolitanism, **provincialism**, generally is associated with "insularity," "narrow–mindedness," and "a lack of sophistication." Life and the way of thinking outside the center, the sophisticated capital city or metropolis, is seen as unsophisticated, and narrow–minded. You can imagine opposites like New York City and Fargo, North Dakota or Los Angeles and Eureka, California. Here the individual is not an abstraction, and the specifics of personhood (home, family, roots, etc.) matter.

The notion of cosmopolitanism emerged from a liberal paradigm of individualism and emphasizes the larger, more abstract view to the detriment of the intimate and particular. The universal supersedes the specific. This model is affiliated with Western notions of democracy and the free market economy.

When we emphasize *both/and* throughout this book, what does that mean for cosmopolitanism and Indigenism or provincialism? Such *both/and* is difficult to imagine when we understand these terms as the opposites just described. Yet, we are challenged to think outside the box and develop new forms of understanding cosmopolitanism and provincialism. What could a diversity of universals look like?

We emphasize that cosmopolitanism is a question about relationship to the world that has multiple answers. There isn't just one cosmopolitanism, there are many. There is diversity in cosmopolitanism. This manifests today in multiple forms as we find refugees throughout the world, people who live in a diaspora, migrants, and exiles. They all carry the spirit of **cosmopolitanism**. Since we emphasize that humans are hybrid, mixed bloods, or crossbloods, we are, and never were, pure. Origins are always mixed right from the start. Ethno-autobiography not only questions notions of purity, but it also affirms the riches that come from acknowledging the multiplicity in our origins.

As we assert cosmopolitanism as a question, we also acknowledge it as process. It is an unfolding acknowledgment of exchanges, migrations, historical memories and wounds, of trade and artistic imagination. When we think of the *both/and*, we can conceive of our domestic personal sphere as a part of cosmopolitanism. This is a cosmopolitanism of minorities and carries with it a critique of modernity. In this way we recognize the diversity of universals and their particularity. Cosmopolitanism is now no longer abstract, but situated with particular traditions and groups.

Cosmopolitanism in this sense is not something new. We can think of Plains Indian council meetings where diversity within a tradition met to find common solutions while honoring the knowledge of each group. We can think of the circulation of Sanskrit poetry in Asia, or the purported gatherings of tribes in Monte Alban outside of Oaxaca, Mexico. We can think of the pochteca, the merchants of the Aztec empire that traveled and traded on routes reaching into the historical sites of Chaco Canyon, New Mexico. There are numerous other historical examples where people have acted beyond the local.

When we engage with others in this way we may end up living at home while abroad or living abroad while at home. We may inhabit multiple places at once and become different beings at once. Taking seriously the "province", the place where we live, the specific ecology we are a part of, leads to an intimate understanding of our community, locale, and history. Then we may see the larger, cosmopolitan picture.

Our increasing global awareness needs to find balance in our rootedness. There needs to be a capacity to integrate the dilemmas created by our simultaneous presence in the local and the global. It is in this way that we may be able to travel with roots and address issues of sovereignty imaginatively, as, for example, Vizenor (1998, p. 190) suggests by noting in the Native American context that, "clearly, the notions of native sovereignty must embrace more than mere reservation territory." Gerald Vizenor, a prolific Native American author so often has a visionary way of subverting assumptions present in Eurocentered cultural descriptions. Sovereignty is generally understood as authority of a particular territory, the power to rule it, and to make laws. Vizenor suggests that reservation territory is too limited a notion of sovereignty for Native Americans.

Vizenor states that in stories of emergence and migration, i.e., stories of origins, the sovereignty associated with movement is mythic, concrete, and full of vision. Such motion is not solely in the realm of territory or land, as in colonialism and nationalism. Native **transmotion** is the natural union in stories that connects humans to an environment and to the spiritual and political meaning of other animals and beings. "Monotheism is dominance over nature" Vizenor (1998, p. 183) writes, "transmotion is natural reason, and native creation with other creatures." Vizenor sees monotheism as part of a split from nature, taking humans out of nature, and thus ultimately leading to environmental crises.

This notion of sovereignty is different from **Eurocentered** political thinking that shuns anything resembling transmotion. Asserting sovereignty beyond notions of territorial rule as *non*-Indigenous peoples leads us back to the consideration of the tribal origins of the White mind, part of the decolonization encouraged by ethnoautobiography.

As a **decolonization** practice, ethnoautobiography begins this conversation with cosmopolitanism and provincialism. On the one hand, local knowledge, Indigenous worldviews, place and so on are sources of knowledge and value that provide specificity, or **groundwork** (Clark & Powell, 2008); and on the other, a **cosmopolitan** critique that respects provincial or Indigenous knowledge is a res-ponse to Eurocentrism that offers a broad vision. Thus we creatively inquire about narratives outside the boundaries and structures of "the West" or "Europe."

Space for conversations that nurture

Ethnoautobiography seeks to create spaces for the Indigenous that are no longer presented in a stereotypical colonial parade, with any certainty of fixed identities. In ethnoautobiographical storytelling twisted notions of individualism, nature, gender, and sovereignty melt into a process of co–creation. Humor helps the plural roots of Whiteness emerge from the shadows. Facing such varied Indigenous roots can be healing and reassuring, while the search for true and essential origins is an unnecessary and dangerous distraction.

Out of decolonizing efforts comes no certainty of knowledge and self, but the assurance of conversations that nurture. We have mentioned the Andean notion of presence, *criar y dejarse criar*, "to nurture and be nurtured;" it mirrors the Quechua *kauan pachari kawsach-kauchik, kawsaynuichikunawau, uywaypaqmi wywanakuckkanchik* – "at this time we are sharing with all our family relations, we nurture to be nurtured ourselves" (Machaca & Machaca, 1996, personal communication; see also Machaca & Machaca, 1994). The Projecto Andino de Tecnologias Campesinas, PRATEC for short, is dedicated to decolonization and cultural affirmation. They embrace notions that nurture the diversity or heterogeneity of life in the *ayllu*, the community consisting of much more than humans.

> What happens between the Andean communities of humans, deities and nature is reciprocal dialogue, a relationship which does not assume any distancing and objectification between those dialoguing, but rather an attitude of tenderness and understanding towards the life of the other. Such dialogue does not lead one to a knowledge about the other, but rather to empathize and attune oneself with its mode of being, and in company with that other, to generate and regenerate life. It is a dialogue — that leads [not to knowledge but] to wisdom. (Rengifo, 1993, p. 168, translation by Apffel–Marglin; also Apffel–Marglin, 1998)

Nurturing conversation may occur among humans, and may also occur with a hill where a landslide has occurred, or a mountain in front of us, or a condor. There is a communicative circle of giving and taking where everyone is nurtured, whether through reciprocity in a human community or reciprocity with llamas, guinea pigs, quinoa or corn.

This is ancient business for tomorrow. Betty Bastien (2003, 2004) is a Native person from Canada who has worked extensively with the reaffirmation of her Indigenous roots. One of the tribal Elders tells her: "In order to regain our identity and maintain our way of life we need to have good relations. We don't leave out prayer in anything that we do" (2004, p. 85). She also gives descriptions of her understanding of Siksikaitsitapi (Blackfoot) cultural practices where the ceremonial transfer of socially significant medicine bundles serves to maintain the web of interconnection of human and non–human beings. Everybody has a responsibility to participate in ceremony: "As long as I live I will continue to do my ceremonial work. We share love, kindness, and generosity. We help each other. We are helping each other. My friend here is going to open his Medicine Pipe bundle. I will always help my friend in his ceremonial work, too. The gifts you gave me, I gave them to him" (p. 88). These participatory visions and communal obligations maintain alliances among humans and with the natural presences of spirit(s). Indeed, such visionary presence in place and time affords a precision of imagination that is healing. For people of White mind – when working to attain this level of Indigenous connection – such precision has a decolonizing effect. Such precision interrupts fantasy and narcissism that may twist what could be healing toward individualistic needs.

Transpersonal psychology explores dimensions of the self that are beyond *(trans–)* our usual everyday experience. The discipline has encountered difficulties understanding and theorizing unusual or anomalous experiences, such as trances or precognitive dreams. Frequently they are seen as transcendental and beyond the personal, hence *trans*personal. In recent years Jorge Ferrer (2002) has developed a

> nature to interact with a spiritual power in the co–creation of spiritual worlds. (p. 117, italics in original)

Rather than focusing exclusively on the inner experience, this approach sees the encounter with a spirit during trance, for example, as an event that can arise in different places. Such a spiritual trance world is co–created as human nature interacts with the world of the unseen (the spiritual, divine, numinous, etc.). Ethnoautobiography emerges from a

> ## Ethnoautobiography is ancient business for tomorrow.

framework that is akin to Indigenous ways of knowing. He suggests that spiritual knowing should be conceived as "creative participation of not only our minds, but also our hearts, bodies, souls, and most vital essence" (p. 115). His participatory vision of human spirituality emerges from a thorough critique of the constructions of what is "trans–" in modern minds. Ferrer's participatory vision

> conceives **transpersonal** phenomena as (1) *events*, in contrast to **intrasubjective** experiences; (2) *multilocal*, in that they can arise in different loci, such as an individual, a relationship, a community, a collective identity, or a place; and (3) *participatory*, in that they can invite the generative power and dynamism of all dimensions of human

thorough critique of the constructions of the self, of what is personal to modern minds, and conceives of the self as participatory event. Either approach gives rise to visions of self and the **transpersonal** as participatory events, one inevitably implying the other.

Reviving radical otherness

Normative dissociation — the splitting and separating of self from origins, place, time, history, etc. — is the central process and shield that **modernity** created. To put it differently: it is the splitting from Indigenous origins in the Eurocentered traditions that is one of the hallmarks of **modernism**. This disconnect is ready to be filled with the meaningless distractions **postmodernity** endlessly creates.

This is the colonization of what once was a given for participatory selves. Ethnoautobiography as practice of **radical presence** is designed to release us into realms where the traces of our Indigenous presences can be recovered. Such presence is not transcendent, that is, beyond the ordinary and difficult to access; it is immanent, accessible, and ever present.

Released from the bondage of modernist constructions of the self is the revenge of the other, as Baudrillard (1993) would have it. He evokes a powerful image that brings to mind the breakdown of the Berlin Wall. Nobody expected it, yet

That revenge may be seen in the way in which the Whites have been mysteriously made aware of the disarray of their own culture, the way in which they have been overwhelmed by an ancestral torpor and are now succumbing little by little to the grip of 'dreamtime.' This reversal is a worldwide phenomenon. It is now becoming clear that everything we once thought dead and buried, everything we thought left behind for ever by the ineluctable march of universal progress, is not dead at all, but on the contrary likely to return – not as some archaic or nostalgic

> Ethnoautobiography is a visionary and imaginative process that grounds itself in time (smaller and larger planetary and celestial cycles), place (ecology, history of place), history (stories and myths), ancestry, and stories of origin and creation.

the East Bloc communist states collapsed from the inside with citizens marching toward the wall, and as they climbed it they were subverting a social structure that seemed as unshakable as the progress of modernity. In his visionary quote he sees the assumptions of our modern world undermined by the remembrance and reappearance of our Indigenous roots, the radical otherness in ourselves and in our societies that we have denied and forgotten. Baudrillard sees this as the revenge of the shadow material we have created:

vestige, but with a vehemence and a virulence that are modern in every sense – and to reach the very heart of our ultra–sophisticated but ultra–vulnerable systems, which it will easily convulse from within without mounting a frontal attack. Such is the destiny of radical otherness – a destiny that no homily of reconciliation and no apologia for difference is going to alter. (p. 138)

Reviving radical otherness in our selves through ethnoautobiographical inquiry and thereby liberating participatory events from **modernity** that serve social justice is a humbling endeavor that requires compassion and patience. The literal and imaginative destinations of our decolonization is as much in the release of the spirit of radical otherness within ourselves, as is confrontations with colonial Whiteness, sexism, ecocide as they become part of our healing **presence**. It is also creative renewal and regeneration for the future. By acknowledging our roots, and telling these stories, we find a place to stand beyond Whiteness.

Stories of release

It is easy to see that contemporary identities are challenged as economic globalization, the Internet and other forces impact how we see ourselves and others, as communities less often provide reassuring ground. This often

disorientation caused by the lack of local attachments (the disruptions in community, for example), the indiscriminate inundation with global information (genocides, pirates, droughts), or experiences of strange–seeming cultures flooding what is familiar. Identities, more often than not, are no longer secure and anxiety is one of the consequences. Ethnoautobiography takes these ominous voids seriously as they seem to grow in power, directing our lives in unconscious ways.

How we construct or understand our identity culturally also matters for our religious and spiritual understandings of the world. What happens when we bring the divine or God or Gods and Goddesses or spirits closer into ourselves (as they were in ancient Hebrew times)? What if they are no longer "out there" but within closer reach? What does it mean to consider spiritual

> Such practice of ethnoautobiography is emancipatory not in the sense of progress, but emancipatory from the paradigm of progress.

leaves our sense of identity threatened. The apparent certainties provided by various forms of chauvinism or fundamentalism, whether in politics or religion, seem to provide a refuge from contemporary anxieties, especially unconscious ones. It is these types of dogmatism that are among the motivations for bloody wars. Consider the

events not as individualistic, but participatory, creative in nature as human possibilities are explored in multiple ways? Who is the self that is participating in these events?

We also ask which qualities of autobiography are emancipatory and healing, promoting creativity and imagination? Indigenous peoples provide a number of inspirational models, as do writings by other people of color. To this day Indigenous peoples embody social systems based on a participatory spiritual understanding of reality. Far from vanished and dead, they may provide us with inspirations about decolonizing stories of self that need to be told. These stories release us from the colonizing forces of **modernism**, its addiction to progress, and may help restore balancing. The participatory visions of Indigenous peoples have shown in **White minds** seems both possible and imminent. These stories attest to human resilience and the healing powers of an ancient way of being in the world that can be affirmed and renewed for the future.

In order to develop a sense of self akin to that exhibited by Indigenous peoples, it seems necessary that we start where we are. For one, that is facing our modern malaise shown clearly in the London (2011) or Paris (2005) riots where hopelessness, despera-

> When speaking about Wintu culture, we cannot speak of the self and society, but rather of the self in society.
>
> Lee (1959, p. 132)

an almost unbelievable capacity to accommodate and dialogue with a wide spectrum of spiritual and religious traditions. Understanding how autobiographical stories are told in Indigenous contexts can thus be enlightening, especially since native stories seem to address major contemporary challenges: connection to place, relationship with community, etc. They provide avenues to retell our selves that may influence our personal identities in a significant way.

Today, in the midst of and with the help of Indigenous leaders, cross–cultural exchange opportunities, Internet technology, and many other factors, the re–emergence of participatory visions

tion, and fear culminated in violence. A participatory sense of self can only emerge successfully if we avoid nostalgic romanticism (the heroism of the stoic Plains Indian or the Eden of the Bible) or nationalistic and religious fundamentalisms. Learning from what Indigenous peoples exemplify we, as participants in and inheritors of colonialism, may similarly engage in decolonizing enterprises that Indigenous peoples have developed as part of their resistance and survivance.

In terms of **cosmopolitanism** and provincialism, the **cosmopolitan** societies from which colonial activities originated, can now decolonize as provincialism or Indigenism appear inside the centers. This is the return of radical otherness within our sophisticated (post) modern system that catalyzes a transformation of the centers. Decolonizing the modern well–boundaried self and developing creative stories may help dissolve the identity politics that fuel wars and violence. Ethnoautobiography is designed to decolonize and promises to tell stories in community that extends place, history, and spirits into the self. Thus we can celebrate our visionary **sovereignty** through the creation of our psycho–spiritual selves – a move that leaves the colonial, well–boundaried self of **modernity** behind.

As introduced above, the autobiographical understanding of Indigenous peoples is, it seems, automatically and inevitably ethnoautobiographical. Such

(1969), and *House Made of Dawn* (1966); or Gerald Vizenor's *Interior Landscapes* (1990), *Dead Voices* (1992), and *Hiroshima Bugi* (2003).

Qualities of *Indigenous self–understanding*

Spending time with Indigenous peoples has increased our awareness of the social construction and storied nature of our selves, identities, individualities, or personhoods beyond the notions developed by Eurocentered theorists. For example: Jürgen was talking to an old Hopi man about his understanding of our current crisis. His answer discussed the original instructions the Hopi had received in ancient times, the responsibilities of different clans, the Hopi mesas they were on, the springs that provided water,

> **Telling stories of the self, or autobiographies, are as much personal as they are visionary, spiritual, and political acts.**

stories exemplify a sense of self embedded in community in the broadest sense of the term. When looking at novels and autobiographies this becomes immediately apparent. Examples are Arnold Krupat's collections: *Native American Autobiography* (1994), *Here First* (2000, with Swann), and *I Tell You Now* (1987, with Swann); or Leslie Marmon Silko's *Ceremony* (1977) and *Storyteller* (1981); or N. Scott Momaday's *The Names* (1976), *The Way to Rainy Mountain*

the sacred items buried in the plaza of his village, the arrival of Columbus, and how the white brother has lost his way by not following original instructions. This was said in the present tense and in a way where all these different aspects were a part of himself, a part of his own struggle to find balance in life. Columbus, the way he spoke, had not just arrived 500 years ago, but had just arrived or was still arriving. A violation of sacred objects buried in the plaza was not just an unfortunate desecration, but a cut into his self.

Experiences like this have led us to contrast the White modern constructions of self (a racialized and colonized existence) with qualities that define Indigenous self–understanding. Ethnoautobiography emphasizes that our self is always in process and never a

clan, band, etc. – of their respective societies. (p. 4)

Part of their self–definition, beyond clan, etc. were also relationships with (sacred) places and ceremonies. These are part of their cultures that they specifically participated in. Personal greatness or fame was always achieved on

> In order to develop a sense of self akin to that exhibited by Indigenous peoples, it seems necessary that we start where we are.

thing or essence. We are always changing, unfolding, and refolding. When we pay attention to how the matrix that we are a part of constructs us and impacts how we present ourselves, then the process of our self becoming reveals itself.

Arnold Krupat (1994), scholar of Native American autobiographies, has observed that

> Native American conceptions of the self tend toward integrative rather than oppositional relations with others. Whereas the modern West has tended to define personal identity as involving the successful mediation of an opposition between the individual and society, Native Americans have instead tended to define themselves as persons by successfully integrating themselves into the relevant social groupings – kin,

behalf of the people. Celebrating solitary heroes or heroines who cultivated originality and difference was incomprehensible in this paradigm. The emphasis of Native autobiographical stories is thus not merely on inward reflection and individualism, but just as much on the embedded–ness in the whole – community, the stories and histories community carries, places. Krupat's notions have not gone uncontested (see Vizenor & Lee, 1999). However, even where we find a greater emphasis on individual visions and other experiences, the communal background remains ever present.

Dorothy Lee used linguistic analyses to explore notions of self in Wintu culture in northern California.

> When speaking about Wintu culture, we cannot speak of the self and society, but rather of the self in society.

...A study of the grammatical expression of identity, relationship and otherness, shows that the Wintu conceive of the self not as strictly delimited or defined, but as a concentration, at most, which gradually fades and gives place to the other. Most of what is other for us, is for the Wintu completely or partially or upon occasion, identified with the self. (1959, pp. 132–134)

Though raised far from Wintun notions of self, we see our writing as attempts to recapture an entry into this quality of process by paying attention to dreams and visions as well as critical socio–political reflections in the telling of stories. By doing so our self may expand into what is around us, what we so often think of as "other". Our self thus becomes aware of its immersion in society and nature.

Decolonizing the **masterful** self simultaneously reconnects personal identity with an existence that is more integrated, and communal. In short, a self that is not modern.

What do Indigenous peoples think about this?

Of course, Indigenous peoples are just as diverse as any other group. However, there are numerous statements by Elders, Indigenous intellectuals, and writers that speak to the importance of ethnoautobiographical projects.

Indeed, a number of Indigenous authors and Elders have encouraged non–Indigenous people to reconnect with their own Indigeneity or to "recover their own Indigenous roots or Indigenous mind", another way of talking about ethnoautobiography. We are using the terms Indigenous roots, and Indigenous consciousness not out of any presumption that any such recovery

> Ethnoautobiography is designed to decolonize and promises to tell stories in community that extends place, history, and spirits into the self.

Ultimately, ethnoautobiography is spiritual and communal research into how we form and maintain our individual identities. Such inquiry into senses of self seeks to understand how we function in particular social roles, situations, and places, and what the psychological, ecological, moral, historical process of our individualities is.

can be achieved within one lifetime. On the contrary, it is work for generations. Also, we cannot have closure alone in our personal process of decolonization and re–connection with Indigenous spirituality. We do not believe that individual closure is possible without the healing of the communal contexts. This is not something only achieved for our selves.

WHY NOT SIMPLY 'AUTOBIOGRAPHY'?

Apela Colorado has worked extensively with retraditionalization among Indigenous peoples and the recovery of Indigenous mind with non–Indigenous people. She has stated (1994, p. 47):

way these were applied to living in this world — not the terms imposed upon it by the order which set out to destroy it. You must learn to put your knowledge of this heritage to

> **Here we are once more at the seams with pronouns and imagination in an autumn thunderstorm.**
>
> **Vizenor (1987, p. 2)**

The goal of the recovery of Indigenous mind [is] to reunite people with their tribal minds. Each of the races of humankind was given a sacred circle or original instruction to live by. If our species is to survive, Euro–Americans must be supported in their effort to regain the Earth-based knowledge of their ancestors. Native Americans will help.

use as a lens through which you can clarify your present circumstance ... You must begin with the decolonization of your own minds, with a restoration of your understanding of who you are, where you come from, what it is that has been done to you to take you to the place in which you now find yourselves. (pp. 386–7)

These sentences express a sentiment that can be found among many native peoples. It emphasizes a moral obligation all humans have, the gift of original instruction of how to live in ecological balance, and the challenge of survival in our contemporary crisis.

Churchill (1996) spoke similarly when addressing an audience of Germans:

> You must set yourselves to reclaiming your own Indigenous past. You must come to know it in its own terms — the terms of its internal values and understandings, and the

Within the framework of his own **Indigenist** approach he urges the expression of "German Indigenism" (p. 389). Mohawk (1997, personal communication) speaks to the same issue: "I do not want people to adopt Indian rituals, because I want them to own their own rituals. I want them to come to ownership of experiences that are real for them. Then I'll come and celebrate with them." Our struggles with these issues are described in some of the recommended readings (Kremer 2000a; Jackson–Paton, 2008).

According to the native and Indigenous peoples (shamans, medicine people and intellectuals) we have spoken to, the crucial point here is that Indigenous roots are always recoverable. Ancestral roots can be accessed. Indeed, Indigenous leaders see such a task as an historic necessity in our times. This is where their hope for the resolution of the current crises, particularly the ecological crisis, rests. For example, Bob Hazous, Chiricahua Apache, has stated: "Don't come to Indian people and look for feathers and sweats and medicine men and stuff like that. Go

of these original instructions and the conversations with all beings in a particular place at a particular time. This is where ethnoautobiography leads. While consciousness is a psychological term that has arisen from the individualism facilitated by the Eurocentered paradigm, it assumes quite a different meaning in an Indigenous context. Instead of being merely an individual psychological phenomenon, consciousness refers to a fluid and embedded awareness of and connection with all our relations

> The goal of the recovery of Indigenous mind [is] to reunite people with their tribal minds. Each of the races of humankind was given a sacred circle or original instruction to live by. If our species is to survive, Euro–Americans must be supported in their effort to regain the Earth–based knowledge of their ancestors. Native Americans will help.
>
> Colorado (1994, p. 47)

back to your own history and find out who you are so that you can look at yourselves and see how beautiful you are" (Rae & Taplin, 1994). Implicit here is an assumption about "original instruction — words about purpose, words rooted in our creation, words that allow the human being an identity beyond the illusion of civilization," as Gabriel Horn (Narragansett /Wampanoag) puts it (1996, p. 49). We examine this further in Chapter 10 on mythic stories.

Reconstructing Indigenous consciousness is about the remembrance

— humans, ancestors, animals, plants, earth, stars, sun, and all others. All of this exists in the storied, imaginative, communal reflections of lived participation, meaning our self is not merely contained within a well–boundaried husk, but is an ongoing process that is engaged in creative participation with the elements around us.

The temptation to romanticize or idealize Indigenous peoples is an indication of the lack of these elements that modern people feel. This temptation can lead to an ethnoautobiographical journey as we heal the experience of something that is lacking in us. There is no presumption that Indigenous roots help us remember some ideal paradise from which romantic minds can concoct yet another utopia. This would be entirely misguided. What matters is the difference between modernist thought and Indigenous paradigms. Here, it seems, the modern mind can learn something urgently needed for the future. Ignoring the **presence** of Indigenous European roots and the history of distortions empowers romantic and nostalgic projections onto Native American and other tribal peoples. For example, the "ecological Indian" and similar notions come the perverse dynamic of idealization and an unconscious yearning to be Indian or some other Native on the one hand, and racism and Indian hating on the other (Deloria, 1998; M. K. Nelson, 2006). This will be addressed in Chapter 8 on Nature below.

That we were all tribal at some point in history is a critical point to remember. Equally critical to be aware of is a lack of integration of tribal pasts and the resulting racist and genocidal horrors. Each tribe or people or nation has to deal with its history, including the history of whatever violence has or is occurring (whether slavery, clitorectomy, or other atrocities). What remains stunning is the difference in scale and quality of the colonial violence (against women, nature, and Native peoples) that the modern Eurocentered

mind has perpetrated. We fail to see something comparable in the violence among peoples engaged in what we have described as the struggle for conversational **presence** and balancing in a particular place and time.

The work of ethnoautobiography is a tall order for non–Indigenous people as Indigenous peoples continue to struggle for survival and recognition. Indigenous is a term with important political meanings. Any person of Eurocentered mind needs to be aware of the challenging political context for Indigenous peoples. The personal and social struggle for decolonization inevitably includes the resistance to genocide, racism, sexism, and ecocide. Engaging with Indigenous or earth–based spiritualities requires a confrontation with these painful issues.

We may, indeed, feel guilt and shame as we look at our histories and as shadow material emerges. However, that is only a part of the process, not the goal. Many of the events and actions we may feel guilt or shame about are not anything we did ourselves. However, we need to recognize the benefits we gain from systems of oppression and act creatively to dismantle these systems. This means taking responsibility for a continuing history as we move forward. Taking responsibility for how the destruction of the Native American cultures or the Middle Passage continue to play out opens the doors to imagine things differently. However, if we get stuck with the experience of guilt and shame, there will be no resulting renewal.

Is that all? Taking responsibility? This central move of witnessing, acknowledging, and supporting healing leads to a freeing of our spirit and our imagination. It enables an affirmation of the possibility of liberation in community, of multicultural celebrations that arise from the depths of our ancestral connections, of creative imagination for social change and the healing of history. Ethnoautobiography is a creative endeavor that will likely encourage the use of our imagination in a process that is fun and freeing. It will also help find actions that suit and express our personal gifts.

Activity

Activity 1

Create an Ancestral Altar or Collage

Create a collage (or other visual representation) with pictures, images of people, places and items from where your ancestry is or might be from. These can be copies of family images, or inferred, imagined ones. They can be over several generations, showing change in people and/or location, or they can be focused on a particularly significant "positive" or "negative" time period or event.

Share a brief oral description of your piece with others.

Additional resources:

Oakland Museum: dia de los muertos (http://museumca.org/share-your-odestothe-passed)

San Francisco's Annual Day of the Dead celebration: (http://www.dayofthedeadsf.org/). Search for a local Day of the Dead celebration in your area.

Activity 2

Visualizing Settlement

This activity is designed as a guided visualization, and yet there are numerous ways to practice this on your own. You may read through it, underline particularly challenging or moving phrases and meditate, or reflect on them. You may read it out load and see what emerges as you hear your own voice reading the script. You may record yourself reading the script and then allow yourself to be guided by your own voice. You may ask a friend or family member to assist you by reading it out loud to you. There are many different ways to practice this, the goal is to begin to examine what may be taken for granted, unknown, or invisible about where you live and how you came to live there.

This may be completed in a 500–word written reflection, or shared as an oral presentation with others.

Note: If you are completing these activities on your own, and do not have an organized group to do oral presentations for (such as in a classroom, community organization and so on), it is encouraged that you present the work you are doing to a friend, family member or spouse to experience sharing your process in oral form.

✳✳✳

Please close your eyes
If you are not comfortable, or do not feel
safe doing so
You may keep your eyes partially open
Only do what is comfortable

[a period of brief silence can be taken
between each paragraph depending on
the circumstances]

Now please
Take a deep breath
Know that you are sharing that breath
with others in the room
You may or may not know them personally
But you are sharing breath
Please take another breath
And as you exhale

Please bring into your awareness
A place that is from your family memories
For this exercise please choose a place
Located in what is now considered the
United States
It can be somewhere you lived
Somewhere you grew up
Where you went to school

But it can also be a place
You have heard about in stories
Even somewhat mythic

That you've heard people talk about in
your family
But all you need right now is to visualize
That place you and/or your family lived
Recently or generations ago
If you are having trouble concentrating
If your mind is wandering elsewhere
Return to your breath
It anchors you in your body
It anchors you in the room

Perhaps you now have a place in your
mind's eye
Now focus your attention on what family
life
Was or might have been like
There could be memories that you have
You might have some information to go on
From family stories, or research
Or information that could be inferred
Suggested by what you imagine
Life was like
All that matters is you get some image
of life
The people, the time period
Where there children?
Was there hardship?
Had they moved recently from some-
where else?
Were they planning to move elsewhere
in the future?

Take a few breaths as you bring those images into your full awareness

Now wherever or whenever your consciousness has gone
I would now like you to focus your attention
To the people who are Native to that place
The people who were Indigenous there when White people settled
Do you know who they are?
Did they sign treaties allowing White settlement?

Are there reservations nearby?
Does a local school have a Native mascot?
Are there current Native land claims in process?

Are any of the place names Native in origin?
Were there massacres or other atrocities that occurred nearby?
Do you know?

Did anyone every talk about the Native people?
What stories were told?
Or were the Native people made invisible?

Regardless of your answers to these questions
What feelings are you aware of?
Whether you know something
Or know nothing
How does that feel?
About you as a person?
About the country in which we live?

How does that make you feel
About the place you were imagining?
What feelings arise between the stories in your awareness?

Take a few breaths
Bring those feelings into your full awareness

Take a deep breath as we prepare to come back together to the room

Take another deep breath knowing that you share that breath
With others in thr room
I will now count back from
5 – 4 – 3 – 2 – 1

Welcome back!

Chapter Summary

Ethnoautobiography is an integrated approach to telling our stories, since humans are storytellers and ancestors are central in **Indigenous** thinking. Understanding that assumptions are barriers helps have nurturing conversations. Healing comes from our stories, whereby we can acknowledge **provincialism**, **cosmopolitanism** and how the self is rooted in society and nature. While the other is within us, changing our sense of self is critical for species survival.

Concept Check

Since **Indigenous peoples** are far from vanished or dead, what inspiration might their stories provide?

What are some outcomes of ethnoautobiographical **decolonization**?

What comes out of decolonizing efforts?

The U.S. **White** self emerged from what?

What is the splitting of self from origins, and history, called and what is a consequence?

NOTES

Chapter 4
Ethnoautobiography Defined

Riff

The Old Ones Would Say

The Old Ones would say:
Above
the stars, the galaxies, the planets, the sun –
they guide you through the wonder of time cycles
and story upon history
to where you stand now – look up!

The Old Ones would say:
Below
Earth, with all our
animal, plant, rock, and human relations,
she yields nurturing medicine – look around! Listen!

The Old Ones would say:
At birth
you began to bring forth the gifts of your medicine,
your uniqueness, your fate and story, your give–away,
woven between Above and Below, weaving.

The Old Ones would say:
These are the things
that tell you who you are
and where you come from
and why you are here –
stories upon stories,
gifts from the ancestors.

The Old Ones would say:
These are the gifts you hold
to understand Indigenous roots
and what they may mean today

The Old Ones would say:
you have been provided for:
nurturance is around you.

The Old Ones would say:
We are here to help you
find your story of balancing.

The Old Ones would say:
As you come to presence
of the Above and the Below
we are here to help you discover who you are
as you weave your life's story.

JWK

Chapter Outline	Core Concepts	Ethnoautobiographical Perspectives	Expected Outcomes
The Old Ones would say	Indigenous worldview	An Indigenous worldview is accessible to people of all colors & cultural backgrounds	Feel encouraged to discover the diversity & Indigenous roots that are obscured by Whiteness
Map: Ethno-autobiography makes explicit that identity is shaped by many factors beyond ethnicity	Understand the multi-dimensionality and necessary ingredients of successful ethnoauto-biography	The complexity of our self provides us with rich inner resources	Identify the elements of ethnoauto-biography
Storytelling (Ch. 15)	Humans are storytellers	Storytelling can be healing	Appreciate the different styles of ethnoauto-biographical writing exemplified by published authors
Community (Ch. 6)	Communities need to serves their members	Community is central to our sense of well–being & health	Critical thinking about various aspects of community
Place (Ch. 7)	Place is part of identity	Consciously connecting with place provides us with sources of inspiration & memory	Acknowledge place as part of our sense of self
Nature (Ch. 8)	Humans are part of nature, not outside of it	Awareness of our interconnectedness helps us find balance	Awareness that we are a part of nature
History (Ch. 9)	History has psychological consequences	History is part of our self identity	Bring history into self
Mythic stories (Ch. 10)	Mythic stories help us to make meaning in our lives	Mythic stories provide a source of inspiration & connect us with the realm of visions & dreams	Acknowledgment that mythic stories contain important truths

Chapter Outline	Core Concepts	Ethnoautobiographical Perspectives	Expected Outcomes
Ancestry (Ch. 11)	Ancestry is central to an Indigenous understanding of self	Knowing where we come from helps us to be rooted in our self	Begin investigating one's ancestry
Gender (Ch. 12)	Gender is more than male vs. female	The multidimensionality of gender reveals new levels of interconnectedness	Look behind the gender label we use for ourselves
Dreams (Ch. 13)	Dreams are an important realm where our self acts for two hours or more every night	Dreams provide a nightly experience of our tremendous creativity & the depth of our self	Remember dreams & live with dreams
Spirituality, religion & atheism (Ch. 14)	Finding answers to ultimate questions about meaning is unavoidable as we seek to understand ourselves	Connecting with possible answers deepens our experience & understanding, whatever our stance	Understand that spiritual aspects of Indigenous cultures are immanent and ever present (rather than transcendent)
Indigenous presence	The Sámi worldview is an exemplar of Indigenous presence & worldview	Within this worldview the Sámi people lived successfully for centuries in the challenging arctic environment	Understand an example of Indigenous presence
Hybridity	All humans are hybrids	Acknowledging our hybridity prevents supremacist or racist thinking	Find ways to acknowledge our own hybridity
Example of EA	EA has different voices	Finding our own voice gives us strength & direction	Begin constructing an ethnoautobiography
Feeling lucky	In an Indigenous context, there is no random event	All of our stories form relationships	See connection to multiple events in our lives

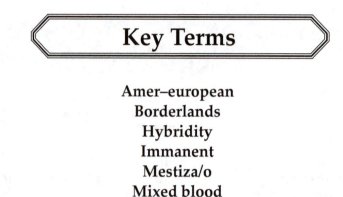

Key Terms

Amer–european
Borderlands
Hybridity
Immanent
Mestiza/o
Mixed blood

Note: All key terms in this textbook are highlighted in bold and can be found in the Glossary at the end of the book.

Resources Alongside This Chapter

Krupat, A., & Swann, B. (2000). *Here first: Autobiographical essay by Native American writers*. New York, NY: The Modern Library.

Swann, B., & Krupat, A. (Eds.). (1987). *I tell you now – Autobiographical essay by Native American writers*. Lincoln: University of Nebraska Press.

The Old Ones Would Say, the riff that opens this chapter, invokes the contents of this workbook in a nutshell. It provides an ancient definition of what the self is, yet with tremendous relevance for our future as we address our contemporary dilemmas. In this chapter, we first talk about ethnoautobiography in a contemporary vein, and then provide an older example from an Indigenous culture that is a source of our inspiration.

The previous chapter provided an overview of the context for ethnoautobiography. As a broad summary we can say that it is designed to meet three interrelated goals: first, to help examine perhaps familiar social and personal experiences in a new light; second, to help articulate those aspects of these experiences that may be confusing, difficult to articulate, or conflicted; and, finally, to offer a *process* that allows us to find our own answers and resolutions to obvious and hidden contemporary confusions and challenges. Expanding our senses of self is a source of hope for the resolution of our current crises and challenges.

Ethnoautobiography, or EA for short, is a particular way of telling our story to foster a greater awareness of our selves and what is around us. There are specific ingredients that make an autobiography and an *ethno*autobiography. This chapter provides an overview of these elements. They are discussed in greater detail, together with practical exercises and suggested readings, and activities, in the chapters that follow. Even with this detail, however, it is important to be aware that each of the chapter topics are highly complex and can only be briefly introduced. All we can hope to do is to point to central issues and give some introductory directions. Remember that one of the intents of this workbook is to increase the ability to pay attention and encourage our capacities for well–reasoned analysis. This means both critical reflection and critical *self*–reflection. The goal is to open up our perspectives so that we look at ourselves anew and *re*–imagine our complex social and natural environments.

We seek to reclaim the origins of the word *ethnic* (which derives from the Greek *ethnos*, meaning tribe, people, or nation). Ethnic came to have a pejorative implication, meaning heathen or pagan, when used in reference to cultures outside the Christian or Jewish faith. We use *ethnic* and *Indigenous* interchangeably in reference to tribal or Indigenous practices that value more expansive and inclusive earth–based worldviews. Thus, ethnoautobiography explicitly acknowledges that a person's identity is profoundly shaped by many additional factors beyond ethnicity, including but not limited to: place, nature, community, ancestry, gender, **hybridity**, history, dreams, storytelling, creativity, and so on. This is the Indigenous perspective invoked in the riff *The Old Ones Would Say*. It also shows that White people are not stuck with a white mind set, but that there are ways to uncover the rich diversity underneath 'White', a creative diversity that seems critical for our future. Ethno-autobiography also points to the existence of White mind in many different people due to the consequences of colonialism. The practice of ethnoautobiography has religious and spiritual implications that will be addressed below. The rock carving opening this chapter — depicting a person with ceremonial staffs in the middle of a herd of elk — gives a sense of the an Indigenous sense of the person, immersed through ritual connections in its natural surroundings. The image from Nämforsen, Sweden, is four to five thousand years old.

Similarly, Figure 4.1 is a graphic representation of the different elements of ethnoautobiography. This figure places the storytelling self in the center of nine factors that importantly impact our sense of our selves, whether we are aware of them or not. We might say that the figure represents an *ethnic* or Indigenous view of the self. We introduce each of these ten elements briefly below. They are all considered in greater depth in subsequent chapters. These nine aspects effect and combine with the storytelling of who we are. Questioning and investigating each of these sources of identity facilitates a process of personal self–reflection that allows us to both affirm and shift our values, commitments and experience of the world. This workbook suggests what such an expanded view of the self might mean for the future, for the lives we are living today and the lives of future generations.

Figure 4.1. Elements of ethnoautobiography.

Storytelling (Ch. 15)

We discuss the storytelling element first, since it is the center — the self, the pivot — of the ethnoautobiographical endeavor. We return to it at the end of the workbook as we integrate the various dimensions of ethnoautobiography. At that time we will pull things together into a new story of our own.

One of the central facts of the human animal is that we are storytellers (Gottschall, 2012). Our minds are storytelling minds. Some like to say: "The truth about stories is that that's all we are" (King, 2003, p. 2). Ethnoautobiography builds on this important capacity and desire. We can imagine early humans telling stories around the fire or singing them while completing chores or performing them ritualistically. Modern humans persist in storytelling, despite the fact that novels have been pronounced dead repeatedly. We tell stories on T.V., in numerous shows, when we try to get to know strangers, and when we remember important events in our lives or our daily experiences. Storytelling is thus at the center of the ethnoautobiographical endeavor. We emphasize a particular way of paying attention to the stories we are and the stories we carry.

Chickasaw writer Linda Hogan tells her story in *The Woman Who Watches Over the World* (2001) through a prism that reflects and refracts different memory pieces. "Memory is also a field of healing that has the capacity to restore the world, not only for the one person who recol-lects, but for cultures as well. When a person says 'I remember,' all things are possible" (p. 15). Telling stories of who we are and what we have experienced can be healing and open up new avenues in self and culture.

Importantly, many ethnoautobiographical works directly connect narrative process — oral telling or written word — with personal, familial and cultural identity formation. The French writer Cixous (1997, pp. 203–4) notes this when saying "What I am recounting here (including what is forgotten and omitted) is what for me is indissociable from writing. There is a continuity between my childhoods, my children, and the world of writing – or of the narrative." Her ancestry and how she grew up are inseparable from her storytelling. Ethnoautobiography embraces the self as a story.

There is no one correct way to develop an ethnoautobiography. Throughout this workbook we will continue to provide a diversity of examples. While the form may vary widely, each story examines an individual's connections with ancestry, place, history, etc. The strength of this narrative form lies partly in the fact that it is a creative and imaginative project. These stories begin with autobiography, but do not end there. As Vizenor (1987) states,

> Survival is imagination, a verbal noun, a transitive word in mixed-blood autobiographies; genealogies,

the measured lines in time, place, and dioramas, are never the same in personal memories. Remembrance is a natural current that breaks with the spring tides; the curious imagine a sensual undine on the wash. (pp. 2-3)

While Vizenor specifically refers to tribal or Indigenous survival, we can extend his statement: survival requires active imagination to imbue genealogies and places with the power of personal memories. Such imagination might include a water nymph (an undine) and create its own force once it breaks loose.

Ethnoautobiography (EA) is a story greater than the sum of its parts. For example, ethnoautobiographical writing and storytelling provide openings for stories about place and the ways that nature affects people deeply. It not only allows, but actually encourages, stories that for too long have been at the margins of European–style narratives. In this sense EA provides openings for the telling of stories that might foster personal and cultural healing. Even more so, as Barbara Christian (1993) writes in the context of discussing Toni Morrison's novel *Beloved*, the writing and telling itself will be fixing, that is, it will also help heal the world. Ethnoautobiographical storytelling is healing work. As we tell and retell a story we work with and integrate experiences, whether inspiring or traumatic. Each telling will be somewhat different, each telling is a part of working with an experiences and making it part of or defining our self.

Vizenor (1994a) consistently evokes **natural reason**, a way of thinking that is connected with the world around us in and through stories; storytelling is not separate from the natural world or ecology we live in:

> The coherence of natural reason is created in personal stories, and in elusive unions of shamans with birds, animals, and ancestors. These natural unions are heard in the arch-shadows that outlast translations. The shamans hear their memories in birds, animals, and shadows in our stories. (p. 98)

Thus, natural reason's dependability rests with stories and in mysterious meetings between shamans, animals, and ancestors, and with the immersion in places where the wind rushes through the trees and memories sit. These comprise an expanded and more inclusive sense of self. Such stories of natural alliances permeate the margins and linger beyond the shadows of the spoken word, beyond the initial fleeting numinous experiences of unions with the natural world. Shamans and other storytellers are reminded of their stories by animals or shadows or spirits or ancestors that are reflected in the storytelling of others. The self expands to be permeated by and to permeate the world around us, self and world are in an osmotic process where inside and outside bleed into each other.

As we consider stories that we tell, we might ask: Is there something more to add to my story that I've always longed to tell? Are there shadows of memories that have been neglected in my story? How do I tell my story? What feelings arise when I am asked to tell it? What stories did I grow up hearing, whether about family or history or place? What are the stories I have heard about where I am from and where my parents and grandparents are from?

Ethnoautobiography supports the telling and re/creation of personal and communal stories. In so doing, such stories provide a grounded and dependable worldview, balancing the Eurocentered poles of mind and nature, for example. Further, ethnoautobiography welcomes the inhabitants of the world (human, shaman, bird, animal, ancestor, plant, etc.) long relegated to the margins and shadows, as well as the relationships fostered between them. These mutual relationships form an interconnected web of community that is deep and broad and will long outlast Eurocentered attempts at comprehension.

We might develop a story that explores our love for a particular place, like a rock outcropping by the ocean or a tree in our backyard. We might begin a story by talking about a treasured object. Or we might talk about a family dinner.

Community (Ch. 6)

Humans are communal animals. In a multicultural sense, community refers to the human and **more–than–human** groups that people live amongst. This includes immediate extended family, but also the diverse interconnected web of relationships that are the foundations of a person's sense of self. Our capacity to thrive in communities has resulted not merely in survival, but in achievements that are extraordinary to this day. We can think of Inuit cultures in the arctic. We can think of the incredible star knowledge that humans have manifested in such places as Stonehenge or Newgrange or that the Dogon of Mali celebrate in extended ceremonies.

The hope in ethnoautobiography revolves strongly around nurturing community, whether in a temporary learning community in an academic setting or a more long–term living situation. As mentioned earlier, in nurturing conversations (*criar y dejarse criar*) each part nurtures others and is nurtured by others simultaneously. Ethnoautobiographical writing broadens and enlivens the experience of community; and yes, community includes relationships with the natural world. The experience of community also begins to shift our stories from singular, linear, and modular narrations to visionary stories that are as broad as they are deep.

When we look at communities we can ask questions such as: How well does the individual serve the community and how well does the community serve the individual? What are the communities I am part of? What is the sense of obligation and responsibility in these communities? Is the quality of respect, or equality, present for each of its members? How does a community serve me and how does it serve others around me? Who is included, explicitly and implicitly, in our communities? Does the natural world figure in our sense of community? There are various dimensions to understand communities, including those special moments, called *communitas*, when there is a common experience of collective joy.

Allen (1998) also illustrates the extensive connections — what she calls a confluence — that she considers as her community:

> We live on the road that the dead walk down. We ride it out of town and back. By its meanders we discover what is there, what is not. By its power we are drawn into a confluence of minds, of beings, of perceptions, of styles. (p. 12)

You might walk around your campus and acknowledge who and what is all there — the buildings, maybe a pond, ducks and geese, the trees, students and faculty meandering about or rushing between buildings, the sky overhead. You might even imagine who lived in the place of the campus before it was created. An Indigenous sense of community includes all of this, and more.

Place (Ch. 7)

The environment where individuals and their families or kin live, or have lived, shapes and influences community and personal identity. Someone may have lived in roughly the same place all of their life or may have moved several times and experienced a succession of very different places. Ethnoautobiography suggests that place affects a person, whether they acknowledge it or not, whether city or countryside. Thus, Allen's (1998, pp. 3–9) sections, "Stories are roads, stories are fences" and "The highway is forever", characterize the depth of place in the development of communal and individual personality.

> The land, the family, the road–three themes that haunt my mind and form my muse, these and the music... The sounds I grew up with, the sounds of the voices, the instruments, the rhythms, the sounds of the land and the creatures. These are my source, and these are my home.

Allen mentions sound, reminding us that our experience of place is not merely visual — sights, sound, smells, tactile experiences, temperature, they all combine to create our experience of place. Our sense of smell, our oldest sense, is particularly powerful in evoking memories of place.

Anzaldua (1987) echoes the strength of place even in light of her needing to leave her family home and its constraints upon her. She writes "I was the first in six generations to leave the Valley, the only one in my family to ever leave home. But I didn't leave all the parts of me: I kept the ground of my own being.

On it I walked away, taking with me the land, the Valley, Texas" (p. 16)

Inquires about place include questions about who inhabited where you live or lived. Where were we, our parents, and our grandparents, born? What was the place like at that time? What is the history of settlement there? What major human migrations affected the place? Describe changes to the place that have happened over the course of ten, twenty–five or one hundred years. What is the origin of place names? Who are the other inhabitants (human and **more–than–human**) of the places we inhabit? Is there any awareness of the more–than–human world in our stories of place? Do we have extra special places that we visit, remember, or honor in some way in our lives?

These and other such questions mean to decolonize our sense of place. That is, we hope to break down barriers about where we live in order to have a fuller sense of our selves. An important aspect is understanding and remembering the history of place (who has lived here?). Additionally we also question ecological practices that help reduce our carbon footprint and help our nature relations flourish (from recycling to starting our own garden to walking in our neighborhood more).

Ethnoautobiography then is an attempt to account for the multiple ways that place impacts and nurtures story, even in its purported absence. While the elements present in ethnoautobiographical writing are not hierarchical, this is mentioned early to encourage the decolonization (that is,

a humble critic of self and society) of the places we live and to remember where we come from and where we have been. Further, stories of place provide a gateway into appreciating more complex ecological relationships with nature.

Nature (Ch. 8)

Expanding further on a fuller sense of place, attitudes about nature provide characteristics, stories, and numerous influences upon a person's sense of themselves. How much time did we or do we spend in nature? Do we have easy access to nature, both in terms of material, as well as cultural, resources? Do we feel comfortable in nature? Is nature "out" there, or is it more integrated in our lives? Is a particular season a favorite, and if so, why? Do specific animals have special meaning in our lives? Do we hunt them, and/or do they appear in our dreams?

Vizenor (1987) expresses his relationships with nature, or this aspect of **natural reason**, in his "narrative on the slow death of a common red squirrel." In this short autobiographical essay, or imaginative history, the lessons learned from the squirrel inform all aspects of Vizenor's sense of self as writer, **mixed blood**, and critic. He describes the process of shooting a squirrel and the image of the squirrel's dying haunts him.

> The squirrels in his autobiographies are mythic redemptions; he remembers their death and absolves an instance of his own separation in the

world.... He learned that hunters and squirrels were never opposites; the opposite of both is separation. Both the hunter and the hunted are tested by their separation from the same landscapes. (Vizenor, 1987, p. 5)

Thus, nature becomes the teacher about all relationships, amongst humans and between humans and the more–than–human world. Vizenor's imaginative 'autocritical' autobiography teaches him, and us as readers, that hunters and squirrels are never opposites, by virtue of their relationships with each other. For the opposite of relationship is separation; both the hunter and the hunted are in relationship with the same landscape, the question is the quality of their relationship.

For 99% of human history humans where hunter–gatherers and lived as part of nature with a level of intimacy that may be hard to imagine for us moderns. Here "the weaving of nature and culture is like the exchange between living cells and their surroundings: the vital breathing in and out, the flux of water and nutrients, the comminglings of outer world and inner flesh" (R. Nelson, 1993, p. 205). The Indigenous sense of nature is very different from our own; for example among the Alaskan Koyukon peoples "the physical world is considered a part of the 'nonliving' community — earth, mountains, rivers, lakes, ice, snow, storms, lightning, sun, moon, stars — all have spirit and consciousness. The soil

underfoot is aware of those who bend to touch it or dig into it" (p. 217).

As is common among Indigenous narratives, the film *In the Light of Reverence* (McLeod, 2001) makes the relationship between personal identities and nature explicit. We see how personal identity, spiritual understandings, and mythic story are woven into the landscape and emerge from the landscape, from a particular sacred place. However, as the three segments of the film illustrate Indigenous identities are fundamentally challenged by White people who also claim a relationship with nature: whether rock climbers in the case of Mato Tipila, miners in the case of the Hopi, and so-called New Age celebrants at Mt. Shasta.

What makes these examples instructive is that Indigenous communities include various aspects of themselves in their stories, such as colonization, cultural conflict, etc., not simply relationships with nature. In contrast, White stories of nature in the film (and more generally in most environmental narratives) exclude all other relationships creating a separation the likes of which Vizenor felt tested by. Vizenor's experience was tested by the relationship the squirrel has with the same landscape. Similarly, then, we might ask how are the White relationships at Mato Tipila or Mt. Shasta tested by other human and more–than–human relationships?

As with Vizenor above, Indigenous stories frequently refer to inter–species communication, as well as creatures that take on personal, communal, and cultural importance, such as totems, or power animals. Indeed, *In the Light of Reverence* offers examples of such powerful relationships only with larger "entities," sacred places.

What is the significance of these oppositional mindsets that we see so vividly displayed in *In the Light of Reverence* that seem so irreconcilable? What is at the source of this opposition, and how did it come about? All peoples — European, Asian, Native American, etc. — had a worldview at one point in history that was similar to, say, the Koyukon people. The rise of modern agriculture and societies emerging from the **Enlightenment Period** has led to an increasing separation of humans from nature. The rise of modernity also impacts the relationship between Indigenous peoples and nature. Okanagan native Jeannette Armstrong, in discussing the prophecies and teachings of her tradition in an interview, states that "we were told that we are cutting ourselves off from the ability to live well by distancing ourselves from the natural world. … We are cutting off the abilities that we previously had that gave us the best chance to be in a healthy relationship with ourselves as people and with the rest of the world" (Gomes, 2000, p. 7). Yet, this is exactly what has happened as part of the rise of Euro–American cultures.

But has our relationship with nature been permanently severed? Many scholars make the claim that "Euro-Americans also carry inside them a deep affinity for life" (R. Nelson, 1993, p. 223), what is sometimes called the "biophilia hypoth-esis" (see Wilson, 1984; Kellert & Wilson, 1993). Biophilia suggests that all people carry inside themselves the seeds to see our selves as wholly a part of nature. Further, we do not need to control nature, but can engage with nature in generative conversations and collaborations, and that we are all a part of the same moral order. Indeed being in nature, nature requires our moral consideration as much as our fellow human beings. Ethnoautobiography works to connect with this sense of biophilia, the love for life that we carry where we can acknowledge a redwood tree, rock or red–tail hawk as a part of the place and community where we live.

The opportunity offered by ethnoautobiography is to include a complex sense of community that is explicitly inclusive of nature. Thus, we respond expansively and imaginatively to the habits of the Eurocentered mind that is focused on linear time (i.e. progress, evolution, etc.), to the near complete exclusion of nature and place. EA also encourages and expects the full tapestry of human experiences to be relayed in story. Such stories are inclusive, flexible and have grown of ongoing inter–relationships with and among the natural world. These more inclusive stories come to resemble **(hi)stories** of our selves.

History (Ch. 9)

The historian Marc Bloch wrote about the importance of history: "When all is said and done, a single word, "understanding", is the beacon light of our [historical] studies ... For in the last analysis it is human consciousness which is the subject matter of history ... Historical facts are, in essence, psychological facts" (quoted from Anderson, 2012, p. 8). Ethnoautobiography is interested in the psychology of historical facts and the history of psychological facts. History thus is a part of who we are, integral to our sense of self.

More than a linear narrative of events, history in an ethnoautobiographical sense, includes varied social and cultural histories, as well. Such an historical sense of events also manifests as critical, activist, and decolonization projects such as the author introductions seen in Chapter 1, "Who am I?" hooks (1997) explicitly names the politics inherent in this historical work: "acknowledging race changes how we can talk about gender. ... It's a class thing too" (p. 221).

History always involves specific people, as each person is impacted by the historical circumstance in which s/he lives. This is true for us now, as well as when tracing our ancestral lineages. What were the historical circumstances of our families? How did those situations lead them to certain decisions (to migrate or leave their culture behind, for example)? Where there major events, such as wars, political or religious upheavals that motivated people to migrate? How were names and cultural identities modified during migrations?

Anzaldua (1987) in her articulation of the **borderlands** also manifests an overtly political, and in turn, decolonizing agenda.

What I want is an accounting with all three cultures—white, Mexican, Indian. I want the freedom to carve and chisel my own face, to staunch the bleeding with ashes, to fashion my own gods out of my entrails. And if going home is denied me then I will have to stand and claim my space, making a new culture — *una cultura mestiza* — with my own lumber, my own bricks and mortar and my own feminist architecture. (p. 22)

History created the specific borderland that Anzaldua carried, history has created a new culture inside of her, a new home.

Allen (1998) speaks to the politics, and the complexity, made explicit in ethnoautobiography. History is present in the streets of Cubero; the dead are present.

If they came to colonize, those non–Indians in my family, they didn't succeed. The dead still walk Cubero, as they walk this entire land. Capitalism, imperialism, racial hatred, and racial strife notwithstanding. Perhaps Mr. Bibo, Mr. Gottlieb, Mr. Francis né Hassen did not come here to steal Indian land. Perhaps they came to keep the dead alive. (p. 10)

The possibility put forth by ethnoautobiography allows for renewed historical narratives enriched with diverse stories and storytellers. What historical events you have witnessed? How did they impact you? Which events shaped your parents? As has been the case, time and again, ethnoautobiographical stories break apart the fixed boundaries of academic disciplines. In this sense then, history is inclusive rather than exclusive, visionary rather than limited. The visionary story is our entry into myth.

Mythic stories (Ch. 10)

Humans, as storytellers, tell all kinds of different stories, of which mythic stories are the oldest. The concept of "myth" was developed in the 19th century in the European academic traditions. Stories that people had told for centuries were now written down (and often severely edited to suit the taste of the times) and subjected to analysis. We prefer to use the term mythic *stories* (rather than myths) to emphasize their origins in storytelling and the oral traditions. Folk tales and fairy tales often contain reflections of older mythic stories, for example.

In an interesting way myths are related to dreams; you might say that they are collective dreams. Many of them clearly have originated from dreamlike or visionary experiences and they have persisted across time, because people found them meaningful. Dreams connect us to aspects of ourselves we are not necessarily aware of in waking life. Myths have the capacity to help us understand the deeper meaning of a par-

ticular cultural tradition. The blending of everyday reality and dreamlike or visionary realms gives them a special quality (there is more on dreams below).

Mythic stories of creation and anthropogenesis (how humans of a particular tradition came to be) are of particular interest here, since they contain so–called '**original instructions**.' Original instructions can be described as central information about the ways in which a particular tradition sees the world and what it tells them about the balanced ways to be in the world. Mythic stories of healing are also important and tell us a lot about how a culture looks at illness and health. Native peoples generally consider star stories the most sacred and secret stories; they may contain vital information about the origins and cosmic connections of a tradition.

Thus, some questions to consider are: is there a creation story in our ancestries? What does it portray about relationships between humans and the **more–than–human** world? Does the creation story offer instruction about the origin of humans in the world? What is the **original instruction** regarding health or balance in an individual? Are the stories accessible or are they obscure, and convoluted? What does the obscurity mean toward your self–understanding? Are there other symbolic representations of mythic stories amongst your ancestry?

Rock carvings, for example, are also related to mythic stories. At times they record a particular myth in images (e.g., we find the god Thor blessing a couple during a bonding ceremony in Scandinavia). Indeed, we use these archetypal images throughout this book to connect with and evoke the realm of mythic stories. The intrigue of these often simple but powerful images may open the doors to cultural and ancestral memories we were not aware of.

Ancestry (Ch. 11)

Ethnoautobiographical approaches to ancestry include both literal genealogical history, as well as the imaginative and mythic relationships with ancestors and ancestral places. Thus, there are at least two approaches to ancestral work in EA. First, in doing genealogical research we answer more straightforward questions: who are my parents, grandparents, great–grandparents, and so on? Where were they born, and where did they die? What were their occupations, and religious affiliations? Were there any written records left behind? Are there stories of family members heard in childhood? And so on.

At the same time, imaginative or mythic relationships are also vitally important to EA. This is especially the case for people who are descendants of persecuted or oppressed peoples, such as some early European settlers, enslaved Africans, relocated Native Americans, exiled Palestinians and other survivors of forced migrations. Another example would be descendants of survivors of the Nazi holocaust, Bosnian or Rwandan genocides and other instances when literal family connection is interrupted (with horrific consequences, to say the least!). On a more individual level, such imaginative ancestral relationships are also vitally important for people who have been themselves or are descended from people who have been adopted. In situations such as these, broader inquiries are necessary: Can someone overcome the loss and disconnection that was forced upon a people in order to find membership and relationship? Are there clues about place of origin, ethnic identity, language, and so on, that might provide access to some ancestral relationship? Is it possible to feel connection and relationship across great distances in time and space? What diversity of ancestral spirits are available to connect with?

Cixous (1997) expresses the interconnected web that is the foundation of her sense of self. She includes an expansive notion of **genealogy** along with her sense of immediate family relationships. She says

I see a sort of genealogy of graves. When I was little, it seemed to me that the grave of my father came out of that grave of the North. My father's grave is also a lost grave. It is in Algeria. No one ever goes there any more or will ever go.

When I speak today in terms of genealogy, it is no longer only Europe that I see, but, in an astral way, the totality of the universe. (p. 189)

These literal and imaginative affinities significantly influence community and personal identity, once again whether acknowledged or not. Leslie rootprints, she describes what can be considered the beginning point of an ethnoautobiographical inquiry: "all my imaginary affinities are Nordic."

> In this workbook activities will ask for genealogies, collages of photos or images, and a story about a family object. This is early notice to get in touch with family members who may have done some of this work or who have a family object to use. Perhaps it is time to begin genealogical research in your family and put lineages together. It will be good if you can trace your ancestry at least back to your great–grandparents. In any event, this is the time to begin thinking about this work, since it does take some preparation.

Marmon Silko, as illustrated in our quote in Chapter 1, has been an outspoken critic of the denial of ancestral roots by Anglo–Americans. In her view they have "failed to create a satisfactory identity for themselves" (1979, p. 213). Ethnoautobiography addresses this central cultural issue: personal identity is inextricably connected to history and culture, in short, ancestral origin. Investigating our ancestries leads to the discovery of healing identities, and allows us to become more whole.

While ancestral honoring may be associated with Indigenous communities, ethnoautobiographical writings provide examples from other communities as well. Autobiographies and memoirs are life stories that may or may not, depending on the life and work of the author, address any of the various dimensions of ethnoautobiography. When the French feminist thinker Hélène Cixous (1997) writes about

Similarly, hooks (1997) acknowledges the deep influence and support of her ancestors in her personal work, as well as her expression of self.

> I feel that the spirits of all of my ancestors, the women in my family, want me to do this, to speak out. I accept this because I see it as a divine calling even though it does not express the innermost me. Mack and I talk endlessly about the struggle I am having, trying to forge my own identity. (p. 223)

Ethnoautobiography seeks to ground stories in the ancestral processes that shape human lives. This includes imaginative and literal family ties, as well as critical and creative personal narratives. While ancestry is a necessary ingredient in ethnoautobiography, this is not to suggest that it is the sole or sufficient explanation of who we are. Our intent is to facilitate dialogues and identify ancestral connections, even where unexpected.

Gender (Ch. 12)

Gender identity in all forms and variations plays a vital aspect to ethnoautobiography for several reasons. In modern, Eurocentered societies gender is generally constructed around the binary of male/female, rather than a continuum that allows for multiple expressions of who we are as gendered beings. As Vizenor (1994a, p.97) reminds us, "We must need new pronouns that would misconstrue gender binaries." Gender reflects the fullness of who a person is, and as Anzaldua (1987) and hooks (1997) exemplify, challenging dominant norms of gender often leads to more diverse personal identities. Finally, violence, trauma and their resulting vulnerabilities are often connected to gendered experiences of power and domination such as those expressed by Jensen (2000) and Vizenor (1987).

Storytellers are, naturally and inevitably, always gendered. This includes all of us, and all of our stories. Along with other aspects of self, how we are gendered is culturally determined, in some instances as a part of a binary male/female scheme of Eurocentered societies, or of a more complex scheme that include third and further genders. The manner in which a story is understood, and even told, is enmeshed with their gender. Anzaldua (1987, p. 19) connects her sense of cultural

identity with her simultaneous experience in gender **borderlands** "But I, like other queer people, am two in one body, both male and female. I am the embodiment of the *hieros gamos*: the coming together of opposite qualities within."

Indigenous cultures offer innumerable examples of alternate gender constructions. For example, looking at the Inuit view of gender (d'Anglure, 1992), we find gender enmeshed with the understanding of the seasons, spirituality, land and sea, the cycle of game animals, and more. Gender is a part of the map offered in this workbook, not separate from who we are in place, nature, community or spirit. Instead of laying gender down as a line from female to male, we enter a complex matrix of gender and **holosexuality**.

Ethnoautobiography emphasizes gender in order to decolonize the Eurocentered polar construction of gender, which tends to be relegated to the repressed and denied personal and cultural shadows. These narratives seek to encourage and welcome the varieties of human experience, long judged and filtered through gendered lenses. Investigations involving gender identity might include questions such as: Is gender approached as rigid 'boxes' that determine appropriate behavior? Have you ever been attracted to someone of the same gender? How are emotions and feelings expressed in your family of origin? What attitudes about the body have been inherited from society and/or your family? Does the body have presence, in other words, is there awareness of the body as a dancer, or athlete? How is sensuality and sexuality expressed among your peers? Do you have dreams that are of a sexual or gendered nature?

yond our imagination. Either way these are created by and through our mind. Given that we dream about 20% of the time we sleep, dreams take up a significant portion of our lives. There is a rich source of

> Given the importance of dreams, both in terms of time spent dreaming during our lives and their significance for our sense of self, we recommend beginning to keep track of your dreams. In Chapter 13 there is an activity related to dreams for which keeping a dream diary will be helpful. There will be an opportunity to analyze one of your dreams in greater depth. A dream journal helps to record the nocturnal elements of integrating your ethnoautobiographical process.

Dreams (Ch. 13)

Carl Gustav Jung was a depth psychologist who emphasized the role of dreams in the process of individuation, i.e., our sense of wholeness and integration or what he calls the "Self" archetype (see his 1965 memoir). Before the beginnings of modern psychology, Indigenous peoples in ancient Europe and elsewhere paid close attention to dreams. Shamans and medicine people would interpret both their own dreams as well as dreams brought to them. People often tried to discern what they might tell about the future, and regarded dreams as messages from the spirits or gods. An old Germanic saying, *träume sind gäume*, states that dreams are observations (Grimm, 1976, p. 1145).

Every night our sense of self manifests in our dreams, whether we recap the previous day in a dream or fly through a fantastic world that seems be-

creativity, not just of information, that we naturally produce every day. Each one of us manifests an incredible creativity every night, an incredible reservoir for self understanding and inspiration.

Dreams open us up to a larger sense of self. They are a particular integrative state of consciousness that humans have paid attention to since the beginnings of humanity. They weave us into what is inside and around us — nature, family, community, the divine, etc. — and they are part of our sense of self. Integrative states of consciousness help us connect with parts of ourselves that we are not routinely aware of.

We may encounter one of our parents and understand what s/he means to us in a new light; we may fly, as a bird or in an airplane or in our human body; we may walk around naked and feel entirely comfortable or experience great discomfort; the sexual imagination of our dreams may disturb, amuse, or enlighten us; we may do something in a dream that we have always wanted to do or that we miss doing. The riches our dreams provide are endless and stunningly creative.

Questions to reflect upon regarding dreams include: Are there recurring dreams in your experience? Have you ever been able to control your dream (often called lucid dreaming)? Did you have so-called nightmares in childhood? Do you tend to view your dreams in a literal, matter-of-fact manner, or are you open to more symbolic interpretations of your dreams? How often do you remember your dreams? Can you describe them in detail, both in terms of activities and feelings? Do you notice variations in the frequency of dreams (or remembering them) in different periods of your life?

Dream Recall Techniques

by Karen Jaenke

How to remember dreams? Some of us remember dreams almost every morning, and some of us might never seem to. Whatever our current rate of recall, we all can practice dream remembering. Here are some basic tips:

Preparations:

1. Get a journal especially to record your dreams. Keep a pen and dream journal next to the bed, so that you can write notes quickly without having to get up. (A small flashlight beside the bed can be handy so as not to disturb a partner.) It is best to write down dreams immediately upon awaking from them, when dream access and recall is usually strongest.

2. Before going to sleep, it can help to read excerpts from your dream journal. Record hypnagogic imagery (images you have just before falling asleep).

3. Set firm intentions for dream recall. Repeat inwardly your intention before going to bed (e.g., "Tonight I will dream and remember a dream") and anytime you wake up during the night. Visualize yourself dreaming, waking up after the dream ends, and writing it down.

4. Try to keep a regular sleep routine. Go to bed and arise at approximately the same times.

5. Get a good night's sleep, sleep as long as you can naturally. If possible, plan on awakening leisurely and naturally, without an alarm clock.

Upon awakening:

6. Upon waking up, keep your eyes closed and move the body as little as possible. If you already moved, it often helps to return to the position you just awakened from.

7. Focus you mind's eye on the experience you were having just before awakening. Rehearse the images in your mind and take mental note of your feelings.

8. Catch an image and "rewind" the dream backwards or forwards from there.

9. Write down your dream as soon as possible. Write what you remember even if it is only a fragment or feeling. Honoring the fragments you receive will assist in recalling longer series of images. Using drawing and sketches. Give your dream a title.

Additional tips:

10. If you have trouble writing down your dreams, use a voice–activated tape recorder.

11. If you can't remember a dream, as a drastic measure, you can set an alarm clock (using a non–intrusive alarm rather than the radio) for an earlier awakening when you might be in REM sleep. You will recall dreams or dream fragments about 80% of the time if awakened during this stage.

12. Avoid alcohol before going to bed, as it reduces the amount of REM sleep.

13. Go to a bookstore or library and read about the dreams and dream theories. The more your conscious mind is involved in the process, the more the unconscious will cooperate. Avoid dream interpretation books.

14. Join a dream group, attend dream workshops, or meet with others to share dreams. The unconscious mind rewards us once it knows we care about its contents and have a safe container within which to share dreams.

15. Slowly over several weeks, you may be able to write down one or more dreams a night. The average person has 3 — 5 dreams a night. The first few may be vague, consisting of images or residue from the previous day. Later dreams get longer and more detailed and move more deeply into the unconscious, becoming more "movie–like." The last two dreams are usually the ones we remember most.

Spirituality, religion, and atheism (Ch. 14)

We all seek answers to what can be called spiritual questions about the meaning of life. Some find such answers in atheism and a belief in the power of science and technology. Some feel comfortable with a doctrinal belief (such as Judaism, Buddhism, Hinduism, Islam, or the various Christian tradi- tions) where sacred texts provide the substance for religious practices. Others feel more comfortable stressing the importance of spiritual experiences over any particular dogma. While these may seem to be three positions that are mutually exclusive, this is not necessarily the case. Individuals have found their own combinations of these three basic approaches to grappling with the meaning of our existence. We all need to find the answers that work for each of us individually.

We encourage an experiential approach to inquiries about our spirituality that can be enriching for anybody, whether we subscribe to a particular faith or dogma or whether we have more questions than answers. It is important to honor what is important in our spiritual belief system while paying close attention to where we have unknowns and would like to go deeper. This can lead to a deeper engagement with life from whatever vantage point we approach it.

This workbook encourages reflection on spiritual or religious questions openly and without prejudice. While encouraging a broad approach based on an inclusive Indigenous model, there is no specific stance that you should feel pressured to adopt. In our observations, Indigenous peoples tend to be inclusive rather than exclusionary, dogmatic, and divisive. For example, we have encountered Native American medicine people who regularly welcome Jesus into their sweat lodge ceremony. We have seen Native people pray with different religious traditions while also maintaining their own spiritual ways. (While this also reflects the history of colonialism and missionization, it also indicates an accommodating and inclusive spiritual worldview.)

A significant difference between Indigenous or earth–based spiritualities and the so–called major religions is that the former see spirits and gods/goddesses as **immanent**, as present in their lives and communities and place. The major religions and Western understandings of religion emphasize the divine as a transcendent god wholly independent of the material world we humans live in.

We recommend that this workbook is an opportunity to reflect upon spiritual and religious beliefs. It is a chance to double check what feels right. Spiritual inquiries might include: Do you see yourself as a spiritual person? Have you found meaning and comfort in a particular denomination? Are you convinced that science and technology provide all the answers? Do you experience contradiction or paradox between your personal spiritual experience and residing in a particular religious tradition?

This brief overview of the elements of ethnoautobiography roughly espouses an Indigenous view of being in the world. The following readings and descriptions in the workbook will provide some keystones for reflection and review. Each of the subsequent chapters addresses these nine aspects of ethnoautobiography, and are structured like these overview chapters, including riffs, key terms, concept questions, and activities for further reflection. These self–reflections taken together are informed by the broad stance of Indigenous traditions, what we call Indigenous presence.

Indigenous presence

The model of ethnoautobiography used in this workbook is based on an Indigenous sense of self that we find in multiple forms in the rich diversity of native cultures. Yet, their sense of self seems to have at least the nine elements we just discussed in common: the importance of storytelling, community, place, nature, history and mythic stories, ancestry, gender, and dreams or visions. The movie segment *Mato Tipila* from *In the Light of Reverence* gives an idea of the Lakota sense of self. Listen carefully how people talk about the importance of the mountain and the meaning of the race they undertake each year. This place, these events are all closely interwoven with the Lakota sense of who they are as a people.

Let us look at another example: the Sámi culture in the arctic north, (an area where we both have traveled and learned much from friends and colleagues). The Sámi people live in an area they call Sápmi, which covers northern Norway, Sweden, Finland, and parts of the Russian Kola Peninsula. In earlier times Sápmi extended further south in these countries. The people speak several languages that are not always mutually intelligible. They are expert reindeer herders and fishing people along the coast and rivers where the salmon run. In the northerly parts of this arctic area the sun shines twenty–four hours a day during the summer and in the winter darkness prevails for several months.

Despite a long history of taxation, missionization, and colonization, the Sámi culture has persisted and in recent decades has become quite visible in the Nordic countries. The traditional skills of reindeer leather bags and sewing with pewter thread, of carved birch vessels and exquisite knives have produced extraordinary pieces for tourists and museums; at the same time, theatre, yoiking (the traditional form of Sámi singing), sculpture, and painting have developed contemporary expressions that honor history and tradition. The growing season is short in the arctic and in the southern latitudes of Sápmi we find the taiga (boreal forest) and further north the tundra. Reindeer, moose, ptarmigan, wolf, bear, loon, salmon, seal, and many other animals are part of this world. Sápmi is a modern country that is profoundly connected with its Indigenous roots. Traveling there provides experiences of both modern Europe and a vibrant Indigenous culture. Below is an image representing the Sámi worldview as reconstructed by Mulk & Bayliss–Smith (2006).

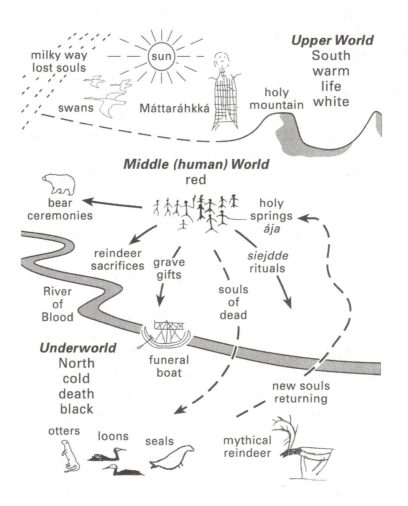

Figure 4.2. Reconstructed Sami worldview (by permission, Mulk & Bayliss–Smith, 2006).

The Sámi world has three aspects: the Upper World (the world of the sun, the main female spirit or goddess *Máttaráhkká* and her daughters, the milky way, swans, holy mountains, and lost souls); the Middle or Human World (where people live and conduct their rituals at sacred places and attend to the transition to the realm of the dead); and the Underworld (where the souls of the dead go and whence they return). Each of these worlds has particular associations:

- The Upper World is associated with the south, the headwaters of rivers, mountains, and the heavens. Its symbolic color is white.
- The Middle or Human World is the connector or intermediary between the two worlds. Fir trees

connect with the heaven; gifts are made for the dead and their safe transition to the Underworld. Its symbolic color is red.

- The Underworld, separated by the River of Blood, is the place of death and cold. It is the realm of otters, loons, and seals, but also the place of the mythical reindeer. Boats travel here from the Middle World bringing the souls of the dead. Its symbolic color is black.

Máttaráhkká is the central figure in the Upper World, she is the Old Woman of the South, the mistress of life, she is a protector of birth and motherhood. Migratory water fowl (swans, ducks, and geese) can serve as messengers to this realm; they bring the new year in spring and symbolize human and animal souls. Holy mountains are a place where the Upper World can be accessed.

While the headwaters of rivers lead us to connect with the Upper World, the mouth of the World River flows into the icy seas of the far north where we access the land of the dead and evil. The Island of the Dead may be under the water or under the earth. The loons that dwell here are associated with shamans and are also seen as bad spirits.

In the middle world life proceeds by insuring the transition of the dead to the Underworld, making offerings at sacred places (*siejdde*) and springs (*ája*), offering sacrifices to honor reindeer, and bear ceremonies.

How does this relate to ethnoautobiography? Traditionally the Sámi person, living in the Middle World, is telling the story of who s/he is in the weave of the community, aware of how gender is constructed differently (women are powerful and own reindeer herds), with intense awareness of the seasons (the Sámi people count eight seasons in their arctic home), an intimate understanding of the terrain (where to fish, where reindeer can graze, where to find moose and ptarmigan, etc.), the history of invasions (from taxation to missionization), the stories of the mythical reindeer Mjandasj, and the memories and stories of the people who have gone before. The images that come from dreams and the inspiration for a yoik (traditional Sámi singing) are all part of the weave that eventually results in a personal story.

With all of these elements alive and acknowledged, the Sámi person has, what we call, **Indigenous presence**. This is a possible decolonizing outcome of ethnoautobiography. As has been stated, however, we are aware (as is the Sámi or Lakota person), that there is rarely, if ever, any possibility of purity or absolute cultural homogeneity. On the contrary, Indigenous presence openly acknowledges and embraces **hybridity** and the **borderlands** as a mark of both the reality of the world we live in (with countless migrations, for example), as well as a measure of potentiality for our common future.

Hybridity

Hybridity — mixing, impurity, the **mixed blood**, both/and, the crossblood, the migrant — is something we have and will continue to touch upon throughout this workbook. The search for purity, whether an imagined pristine ethnic origin or the purity of race is usually dangerous and has led to innumerable destructive fantasies, sometimes including genocides. The search for an ideal purity and supremacist thinking often are in each other's company. Cultures and ethnicities have always changed as history has moved along. Exploring the hybrid aspect of who we are is thus both inevitable and mandatory. We will revisit this theme again and again.

Jürgen, being born and raised in Germany, often encounters this response when he asks students to research their ancestries: "Well, that's easy for you to say. You are German, that's very straightforward. I'm an American mutt, it's all mixed up." Many individuals who are settlers in the U.S. are obvious hybrids, whether their ancestors arrived here long ago or whether it was only their parents that chose to live here. But once you scratch the surface of Jürgen's identity (German), things quickly get complicated, as you have seen in his self–introduction in Chapter 1. One of his lineages leads from Hamburg up in Northern Germany down to the River Rhine Valley and on through the Alsace–Lorraine into France; at the time his ancestors lived there the Alsace was rather remote and many Jewish people migrated through

there to change their identities to evade the pervasive anti–Semitism; Kremer (a name for which there are quite a few variant spellings ranging from Kramer to Craemer) is often a Jewish name. His other, maternal, lineage moves along the Baltic Sea toward Gdansk (Poland) and into an area where the border shifted several times between Lithuania and Poland and where there were many shtetls or Jewish towns, and some of the names he found are frequently Jewish. In addition, Jürgen settled in the U.S. and has lived here about half of his life. Thus, there is nothing simple about him being German — hidden below that label is a complex ancestral history.

R offers another variation of the hybridity that lies beneath the surface of homogenized White identity. With an ancestry predominantly from England (also with lineages from Ireland, Scotland and France), many Quaker English ancestors, while Christian, suffered extreme persecution at the hands, prisons and executioners of the Church of England. More recently, R has openly questioned White racial privileges and gender identities often leading to complex, confused and, at best, ridiculed positions in society. Thus, there is nothing straightforward about R being raised in the U.S. as a descendant of Quakers. Further, any outward appearance as a White person belies a much more complex, hybrid, identity.

As all of these factors, and many others attest, ethnoautobiography is generally described as an alternative narrative form, often reflecting elements of storytelling. Vizenor (1987, p. 1), for example, eloquently — and provocatively — incorporates Indigenous storytelling traditions to suggest "The mixedblood is a new metaphor... a transitive contradancer between communal tribal cultures and those material and urban pretensions that counter conservative traditions."

A more complex, creative and imaginative self–identification is frequently reflected in ethnoautobiographical narratives. These identities are referred to as mixedblood (Vizenor), a confluence (Allen), or **mestiza** (Anzaldua). Such diversity within self challenges Eurocentered standards of a pure, or essential, cultural identity. Vizenor (1987) introduces himself by noting "Gerald Vizenor believes that autobiographies are imaginative histories; a remembrance past the barriers; wild pastimes over the pronouns. ... mixedbloods loosen the seams in the shrouds of identities" (p. 1).

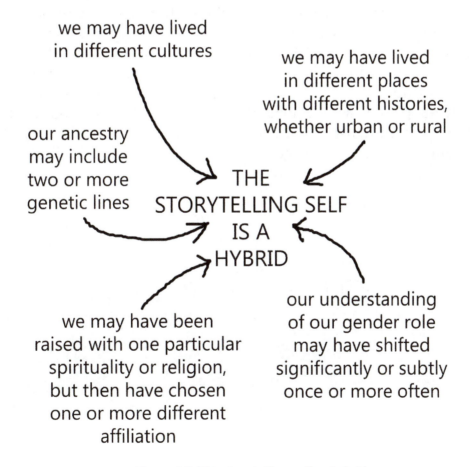

Figure 4.3. The storytelling self as hybrid.

Hybridity means many different things: the figure illustrating only a few of the innumerable hybrid possibilities. For one, openness to hybrid identities allows for seeing diversity where the White mind has attempted to portray homogeneity (or sameness). The existence of Scottish–Germans would be but one example, Korean–Japanese another, **amer–europeans** yet another. Similarly, migration creates hybrid senses of self and community by movement through space and time. Hybridity also creates room for the distinction between biological and cultural ancestries (we may be genetically one or more particular ancestries, yet we may have grown up in an entirely different tradition).

Allen (1998, p. 2) likewise embodies supposedly contradictory identities when noting "Most of the cowboys I knew were Indians." She continues, reflecting both/and identities in keeping with the diverse senses of self within ethnoautobiography: "My life is the pause. The space between. The not this, not that, not the other. The place that the others go around. Or around about. It's more a Möbius strip than a line" (p. 9).

Thus, ethnoautobiography is the ideal residence for hybrid stories of self, because narratives are no longer bound by the constraints of category, purity, or certainty. All that matters is the author's naming of the parts that make their story true using the coordinates we discuss here. When we look below the surface, we are all multi–vocal beings — there are many voices and many aspects to us and they are not necessarily consistent or logical. And that is worth celebrating.

Activity 1

Accepting Origins

Choose at least two dimensions of ethnoautobiography (place, nature, community, ancestry, gender, hybridity, history, dreams and storytelling, explored with imagination and creativity) and expand on your initial autobiography from the Self Introduction activity in Chapter 1. This can be done orally and/or in writing. Also consider why did you chose these additional factors. Are certain elements more accessible to you than others? Why do you feel that might be?

Activity 2

Elements of Your Ethnoautobiography

Using figure 4.1 as a starting point, construct a simple diagram of the specific elements that contribute to your ethnoautobiography. Refer to previous activities such as your Self Introduction in Chapter 1, your Map of Self in Chapter 2, and Activity 1 in this chapter, Accepting Origins. Is it possible to have at least one of your own specific element for each of the dimensions of ethnoautobiography?

Share your diagram as an oral presentation with others.

Note: If you are completing these activities on your own, and do not have an organized group to do oral presentations for (such as in a classroom, community organization and so on), it is encouraged that you present the work you are doing to a friend, family member or spouse to experience sharing your process in oral form.

Chapter Summary

Ethnoautobiography is defined as **storytelling** involving the dimensions of community, place, nature, history, mythic stories, ancestry, gender, dreams, and **spirituality** (including atheism). It is designed to create a participatory or Indigenous sense of **presence**. The acknowledgment of **hybridity** is an important aspect of ethnoautobiography.

Concept Check

In addition to ethnicity, what additional factors of a person's identity does ethnoautobiography explicitly acknowledge?

What do you learn from the conflict at sacred sites from the video *In the Light of Reverence* about identity and self?

Gerald Vizenor (1987) believes that autobiographies are what?

Riff

Feeling Lucky; or, Embodying Radical Presence
Dallas, Texas, 26 June 2012

I have always read more into coincidence
Than perhaps most people do
Thus many years ago when I came upon
The Sámi word *boazulihkku*
(you could try saying *boaatsoolichkoo*)
Roughly translated as "reindeer luck"
It made perfect sense to me
Reindeer luck is an attempt to describe—for an outsider—
The everyday occurrence of things
Once immersed in the world of the reindeer
There is no happenstance, no random event,
If one lives fully in the world
Of the tundra, the hills, the herd…
They all are participants in that way of life
As are history, spirit, dreams, ecology, ancestry, everything
All are present

For me this was an introduction to
Radical or Indigenous presence
The process and product of
The decolonization work before us
Where we might find healing
From habits born of wounds
As we embody knowing of self and Other
In relationship with the human and
More–than–human world
In other words: feeling lucky —
Boazulihkku

Bonnie Bainbridge Cohen connects
embodiment and presence
Perhaps even describing this idea of luck
Boazulihkku
Embodiment, she says, *is automatic presence,*
Clarity and knowing,

Without having to search for it or pay attention.
Zen master Thich Nhat Hanh could as well
Be talking about *boazulihkku*
With his sentiment of interbeing:
If you are a poet,
You will see clearly that there is a cloud
Floating in this sheet of paper.
Looking even more deeply,
We can see we are in it too.
Everything co—exists with this sheet of paper.

The heart of reindeer luck
As the heart of ecology and
As the heart of decolonization
Are rooted in the same soil of
Connection and relationship
David Abram asks
What if the curious curve of thought
Is engendered by the difficult eros and tension
Between our flesh and the flesh of the earth?

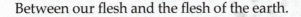 

Between our flesh and the flesh of the earth.

The same participation is the foundation of both
Knowing self and knowing other
So the old habits that maintain division
Fall away

To create renewal and healing
Anzaldua calls this place the borderlands
I want the freedom to carve and chisel
My own face, she says,
To staunch the bleeding with ashes,
To fashion my own gods out of my entrails.

Gerald Vizenor, the woodland trickster in academe, notes that
Survival is imagination, a verbal noun,
A transitive word in mixedblood autobiographies.

Remembrance is a natural current
That breaks with the spring tides.
Survival implies facing hard realities
Of personal and cultural histories

Linda Hogan reminds us that
Touching bottom enough
To have a foot push me back to the surface,
As if swimming,
Was what saved me.

Perhaps the telling of our stories is
That bottom to push off from
Telling stories initiates practices
Of interconnection, of interbeing that
Nurture presence
Link survivance and sense of place
Foster healing and embodiment
Shailja Patel tells of her relationship with words
I walk a lot of my writing, the way you walk a dog –
It completes itself in motion

Now in motion, these words
Form relationships with reader, speaker, listener
And our stories connect us
With each other and history
With the more–than–human world and our dreams
Once those relationships are renewed
The connections flowing out into the world
The stories, our awareness, consciousness
Expand and envelop all that surrounds us

Contact improviser Steve Paxton observes that
Consciousness can be felt to change
According to what it experiences
This expanded picture
Becomes the new ground for moving

John Berger moves on this ground:
I have never had the impression
That my experience is entirely my own and it often seems
That it preceded me

This reminds me
Of a recent article on neuroscience
It asserts that
Consciousness
Might be more about
Relationship
Than most of us hold in our awareness
The rainbow, offers Manzotti, *is a good metaphor*
Awareness of the rainbow
Is consciousness spread between
Sun, rain, and a person's sight

So, when I see a rainbow
I am thinking this is rainbow luck
My being spreading out
Participating with sunlight and raindrops
Into a rainbow experience

Finding *boazulihkku*
Finding rainbow luck
Finding reindeer luck
Is the creative work of
Radical presence
Interbeing
Relationship
Spread between surrounding, memory, and self

The goal before all of us now
In these times
Is to do the work necessary
So that we can feel that lucky
Boazulihkku

RJP

NOTES

Chapter 5
We Are Moral Beings

Riff

Nazis in the Closet

I grew up in the ruins
of the Second World War
In a city devastated by
Allied bombing
Hamburg, Germany
In front of our house
Bombs were fished
Out of the river
Every few weeks
I walked to school
Amidst skeletons
Of houses

Our family meals
Had presences that
Could not be spoken
Nobody knew
How to talk about the
Tremendousness
Of the disappearance
Of millions
Of neighbors
Jews
Gays and lesbians
Roma, Sinti
And others
I felt the unspoken
In my gut
I held it
In my body
I inhaled it
Unknowingly

One day we kids
Climbed into the attic
Of a neighbor's house
And discovered
A chest filled with
Symbols and paraphernalia
Of Hitler's maniacal genocidal
Rantings and actions
A chest of illegal possessions
We were unsettled
By the shameful memorabilia
Of the Shoah
The unimaginable heaps
Of murdered neighbors
In Bergen–Belsen and elsewhere
Not knowing these images yet

Nonetheless
The German collective shadow
Had materialized in front of us

Fear and fascination with the darkness
In front of us joined
The unspeakable
That already exerted its
Tremendous power
From behind the walls of denial
Reeling in more denial

In high school, the Gymnasium,
We explored
The history of
The Third Reich
I asked what the teacher did
During this time
When he already was
In his adult years
We did not know what happened
In the prison down the road
How could I have known?
I wondered
How can you not notice
Your neighbors disappearing?
How can you not ask
Where they went?

Asking these questions
At school and elsewhere
Led to writing pamphlets
And school newspapers
And staging happenings
Struggling to speak the unspoken
Struggling to make it visible
And visceral

One day
I showed slides
Of Bergen–Belsen
The way the British army
Discovered the nightmare
Of Hitler's deeds manifest in
53,000 half–starved and ill prisoners
And 13,000 unburied corpses
Human atrocity at a scale
Unimaginable
Even today
As you walk around Bergen–Belsen
The earthen mounds of hundreds and thousands
Of bodies create the presence
Of people incomprehensibly defined
As vermin
By Hitler's willing executioners

The slides I showed
To disturbing electronic music
Booming bubbling screeching
Did not make me new friends
Six people showed up for the event

My determination
To tread where most
Fear to tread
Became stronger

JWK

Chapter Outline	Core Concepts	Ethnoautobiographical Perspectives	Expected Outcomes
Nazis in the closet	Power of the shadow of history	Historical events impact our moral sense of self	Appreciate the power of denying issues
Brain, self & morals	Spontaneous moral behavior is largely regulated by habitual and unconscious parts of ourselves. Moral discourse usually occurs after rationalization	Moral behavior does not change easily	Grasp the deep level at which moral behavior is anchored
Moral psychology	The sense of self and morals vary significantly across cultures	We need to be aware of different moral assumptions between cultures	Sensitivity to cultural difference, including assumptions we can't even imagine
Dimensions of morality	Humans seem to have a limited number of "moral taste buds"	Different dimensions of morality help us understand polarities, such as those between Republican & Democratic parties	Understanding that there is more than one morality
Hall of mirrors	Left hemisphere should be servant of right hemisphere; predominance of left hemisphere has led us into hall of mirrors	Inviting right hemispheric processes is critical for exploring values and morals	Understand the foundational importance of integrative, intuitive processes
Radical hope	Hope can arise even when we can't see beyond the horizon	Without radical & active hope there can only be despair	Develop sources of hope
Integrative states of consciousness	Humans have always sought integrative states of consciousness; they synchronize the two hemispheres	Experiences beyond the rational are central for understanding who we are	Value the loosening of the boundaries of the individualistic self

Chapter Outline	Core Concepts	Ethnoautobiographical Perspectives	Expected Outcomes
Personal & cultural shadow	All individuals & all cultures have denied our shadow aspects	What we don't or can't talk about impacts our daily life significantly	Acknowledging the healing & creative force that stems from acknowledging shadow material
Transformative learning (TL)	Unconscious parts of moral behavior can be accessed and changed, but rational discourse alone is probably least effective	Dramatic changes in the world require radical changes in self & our capacity to make such changes	Connect with unconscious and non–rational processes when trying to make deeper changes in self
From the desert into the city	Individuals have complex moral identities	Complex moral identities shape complex people	Allow moral values to seep into unsuspecting places

Key Terms

Active hope
Dimensions of morality
Integrative states of consciousness
Left– and right–brain hemisphere
Personal and cultural shadow
Radical hope
Reptilian, palaeo–mammalian, and neo–mammalian brains
Systems 1 and 2
Transformative learning

Note: All key terms in this textbook are highlighted in bold and can be found in the Glossary at the end of the book.

Resources Alongside this Chapter

Haidt, J. (2008). *The moral roots of liberals and conservatives*. Retrieved from http://www.ted.com/talks/jonathan_haidt_on_the_moral_mind.html

Hanson, R. (with Mendius, R). (2009). *Buddha's brain: The practical neuroscience of happiness, love & wisdom*. Oakland, CA: New Harbinger.

McGilchrist, I. (2011). *The divided brain*. Retrieved from http://www.ted.com/talks/iain_mcgilchrist_the_divided_brain.html

Suttie, J. (2013, November 7). *How to close the gap between us and them: A Q&A with Moral Tribes author Joshua Greene about emotion, reason, and conflict*. Retrieved from http://greatergood.berkeley.edu/article/item/how_to_close_the_gap_between_us_and_them

The brain, the self, and morals

As questions about our sense of self and morals are continually raised, we also ask about where they reside inside of ourselves. Is our self–identity housed in the brain? Is our moral sense of our selves located in the mind? Where might they be located in our body? A single psychological event (such as a moral decision) can be looked at from several vantage points: *cognitive* (the reasoning behind the decision), *emotional* (the feelings that accompanied and impacted the decision), *behavioral* (past and present behavioral consequences based on the decision), and *physiological* (what is going on in our body and nervous system, including our brain while making the decision). When we make a moral decision all of these dimensions are involved simultaneously, some more consciously, others less so (or even entirely unconsciously), and some kicking in notably faster than others.

In recent years brain research has allowed us to follow neurological processes in much greater detail than ever before. This knowledge is very helpful, *not* because it offers ultimate explanations — it does not. Rather, understanding the neuropsychology of moral decision–making offers useful insights that help increase our awareness of our moral behavior, the process of moral decisions, and how to change moral perceptions. These important insights, however, are not the final answers, and neurophysiology is only one of several aspects that impacts moral decision–making. This is similar to what we now know about genetics: the science of epigenetics that has shown how our genetic makeup is impacted and how a genetic predisposition may or may not be triggered. Indeed, our genetic code does not actually provide ultimate explanations about our behavior, and who we are.

An overview brain map of sorts will provide some orientation. The basic rule here is that evolutionarily older parts of the brain are more difficult to impact by conscious decisions and rationality than younger parts of the brain. Also, each aspect of the brain is, in a sense, a domain with its own specific rules. What works with younger parts of the brain may not work with older parts, because they function differently. This is important to remember when we consider changing ourselves, or integrating insights that we have about our sense of self. Our basic sense of self develops very early and its roots are in the evolutionarily older parts of the brain.

The map of the triune brain, developed by MacLean (1973), provides useful basic distinctions between evolutionarily older and younger parts of the brain:

- *Reptilian brain* – The oldest part of our brain that performs basic functions which continue when we sleep or even faint: breathing, blood pressure, heartbeat, etc. It regulates our basic survival functions.

- *Palaeo–mammalian brain* — This is the area of the brain where our habits and our sense of self reside. It is critical for emotional responses and processing, both in waking and dreaming life. Another name for this part of our brain would be the "emotional brain". Importantly, the language of the emotional brain is not necessarily rational (think of how irrational your dreams seem at times), rather it is the poetic language of images. The emotional brain is difficult to access through cognitive reflection, while the arts, dreams, movement and dance, trances, rituals, and so on access the palaeo–mammalian brain.

- *Neo–mammalian brain* – The part of the brain that most people think of when they hear the word "brain", this is our executive center, where rational thought (cogitation) and self–reflection reside. This is often referred to as the frontal cortex.

Another important aspect of our basic brain map is that it is divided into **left and right hemispheres.** Early discoveries of split brain research led to conclusions that are now safely regarded as dated and incorrect. However, this basic division of the brain *does* have major implications that we discuss shortly. Kahneman (2011) discusses useful distinctions of two systems in the brain that relate to MacLean's model. *System 1* is the quick and dirty response to reality, the draft of our reality that emerges from association and metaphor. It recognizes faces and understands speech instantly. Without involving conscious awareness it makes judgments and takes action. It has instant access to our memory bank that guides its judgments. These judgments are biased toward memories that are emotionally intense (fear, pain, hatred) and are therefore often mistaken. Frequently, aspects of what **System 1** does are called intuition, since we don't have a sense of voluntary control while it just does its job. By contrast, *System 2* is where we make rational choices and explicate our beliefs. It is the slow critical examination of the evidence at hand, including the evaluation of actions System 1 has taken. **System 2** allows us to plan and create art and culture. System 2 consists of effortful mental activities and give us the sense of choice, agency, and concentration. Presumably System 2 evolved more recently than System 1.

System 2 helps us stand back and reflect on what is happening immediately in front of us. We can analyze, strategize, outwit somebody, read other people's intentions, or even deceive someone. Importantly, stepping back from what is right in front of us also allows us to be empathic and understand somebody else's world. Creating such distance from immediate events is a critical aspect of making us human and is profoundly creative of all that is human.

If this is case, why not give up the error prone **System 1** and build our lives on **System 2**? System 2, in fact, takes much mental effort, time, and calories. System 1 takes care of many routine tasks without much effort. From an evolutionary perspective, it is advantageous to be fast and wrong instead of slow and right. (For example, think about a situation where you might see a puff viper. System 1 makes you jump backwards, whether it actually is a puff viper or not. That is a better outcome than making sure it is one and getting bitten). Of course, System 2 is not error free either, as psychological research has shown (e.g., when we base judgments on the most quickly available memory rather than the most appropriate memory; this is the so-called availability bias).

Just as we would like to believe that the **neo–mammalian brain** is boss, we also would like **System 2** to be boss. However, there is a notable difference in processing speed: the **palaeo–mammalian brain** and System 1 respond very quickly, while the neo–mammalian brain and System 2 need to slow things down for analysis. We have immediate "gut reactions" and cannot necessarily translate them into well–reasoned responses. System 2 is a slower processor and it is easier to accept the swift and automatic responses of **System 1**, even though

they may be unreliable. System 1 is convenient, fast, expresses our habits and helps us with immediate judgments (you may have an instant feeling of like or dislike for a person, for example).

Probably the most important conclusion from recent neuroscience research is that automatic, habitual, and unconscious responses play a highly significant part in our behavior, in our emotional process, and our sense of self. Our judgments depend significantly on very fast intuitive flashes. Haidt (2012) applies this knowledge to our moral behavior by talking about the rider and the elephant: The rider can be seen as System 2 and the neo–mammalian brain, while the much larger elephant would be System 1 and the reptilian and palaeo–mammalian brains. Haidt (p. 141–142) asserts that "the elephant (automatic processes) is where most of the action is in moral psychology." Nonetheless, "intuitions can be shaped by reasoning, especially when reasons are embedded in a friendly conversation or an emotionally compelling novel, movie, or news story." The role of reason pales somewhat by comparison to the role of automatic responses. It is therefore important to keep the power of the elephant in mind and to understand that the reasonableness of the rider is limited by the size and power of the elephant.

The implications of all this for moral behavior and reflections on "who am I?" are threefold:

1. We need to slow down in order to reflect deeply and critically.
2. We need to find ways to access those parts of ourselves (and our brain) that are not easily accessed via rational cogitation.
3. Never underestimate the power of the elephant.

As you might imagine, the readings and activities in this workbook are designed to support such a process of slowing down and accessing "the elephant".

Moral psychology

It might not then come as a surprise that moral systems of people in Western, educated, individualistic, rich, and democratic (**WEIRD**) societies, are "individualistic, rule–based, and universalist" (Haidt, 2011), emphasizing harm and fairness. By contrast, the sociocentric cultures mentioned above, and non–WEIRD cultures in general, place the needs of social groups or institutions before the needs of individuals. This means that moral behavior, rather than being codified in a set of rules, is collected more anecdotally and a case–by–case analysis is more important (casuistics). A concern with harm and fairness is insufficient to understand moral challenges as additional dimensions come into play. We will discuss these dimensions below.

The towering figure at the beginnings of research in moral psychology was Lawrence Kohlberg (1981). He developed a rational system of moral stages, modeled on Jean Piaget's stages of cognitive development that was groundbreaking and compelling in its time. It also reflected a left–liberal view of human beings that at that time was well supported by acceptable empirical evidence. Kohlberg assumed that our moral decisions are fundamentally the result of reasoning and he extensively researched the variety of reasons at the foundation of moral behavior. Carol Gilligan (1982) was among the first to point out that from a feminist perspective this is hardly how humans in general, and women, in particular, function most of the time. Yet, neither Kohlberg nor Gilligan address cross–cultural differences in any significant way, though there has been an increase in research exploring cultural issues.

Here are some moral dilemmas to ponder (from Haidt, 2012):

1. While walking, a man saw a dog sleeping on the road. He walked up to it and kicked it.
2. A father said to his son, "If you do well on the exam, I will buy you a pen." The son did well on the exam, but the father did not give him anything.
3. A man had a married son and a married daughter. After his death his son claimed most of the property. His daughter got little.

4. In a family, a twenty–five–
year–old son addresses his
father by his first name.

Is it okay to kick the dog? To not give the son the pen, as promised? Is the daughter entitled to an equal share of the inheritance? Do you call your father by his first name? Responses to these moral dilemmas vary across cultures. People in India and the U.S., for example, offer quite different responses to these situations: the first two examples are generally judged immoral by both Indians and Americans; in the third example, Americans said the son acted wrongly, while Indians thought it was acceptable; and the reverse was true for the final example. This suggests that our moral gut responses can vary dramatically across cultures and that we cannot expect that our moral elephant respond in the same way as the deep–seated sense of morals of a person from another culture. Thus, the majority of our moral responses seem "natural" and it is because of our quick and habitual responses that we do not experience moral dilemmas much of the time. Our answers feel like givens that we rarely question.

When watching *In the Light of Reverence*, the emotional charge behind opposing moral positions is quite apparent. They seem only natural to each group and a deep sense of violation results when a moral system is violated or in danger of being violated. The actions of the climbers at Mato Tipila violate not just the Lakota sense of what is right and wrong, they invade and threaten their personal and cultural sense of themselves. The same is true in a different way for the settlers who have arrived more recently on Lakota lands. Understanding the depth of moral responses, their rootedness in the core sense of self, can help move toward mutual understanding and creative conflict resolution. Accordingly, it is even more difficult to discuss traumatic history when the emotions and the violation of personhood are not acknowledged and are not made part of the discussion.

Dimensions of morality

Jonathan Haidt (2011, pp. 128ff.) posits that we have six major moral modules, that is, processors for particular types of input. Different cultures develop these six modules differentially; different modules are more or less important in different cultures. Whether the number of moral dimensions is actually complete or not, they are useful in looking at the different dimensions of ethnoautobiography.

- *Care/harm dimension*: This module is a response to the adaptive challenge of protecting and caring for children. It was originally triggered when we saw suffering, distress, or neediness in children. Contemporary triggers are baby seals and cute cartoon characters. Compassion is the related emotion and caring and kindness are the related virtues.

- *Fairness/cheating dimension:* The adaptive challenge is to reap benefits from two–way partnerships. It was originally triggered by cheating, cooperation, and deception. Examples of contemporary triggers are marital (in)fidelity and broken vending machines. Anger, gratitude, and guilt are characteristic emotions of this module. Relevant virtues are fairness, proportionality, justice, and trustworthiness.

- *Loyalty/betrayal dimension:* The adaptive challenge is to form cohesive coalitions. This module was originally triggered by threats or challenges to a group. Current trigger examples are sports teams and nations. Emotions connected with this module are pride in the group and rage at traitors. Loyalty, patriotism, and self–sacrifice are relevant virtues.

- *Authority/subversion dimension:* This module deals with the adaptive challenge of forging beneficial relationships within hierarchies and was originally triggered by signs of dominance and submission. Examples of contemporary triggers are bosses and respected professionals. Respect and fear are associated emotions. Obedience and deference are associated virtues.

- *Sanctity/degradation dimension:* This module evolved in response to the adaptive challenge to avoid contaminants. It was originally triggered by waste products and diseased people. Examples of triggers are taboos such as communism, racism, or marriage equality. The characteristic emotion associated with this module is disgust. Temperance, chastity, piety, cleanliness are associated virtues.

- *Liberty/oppression dimension:* This module deals with the adaptive challenge of the domination of individuals. Its original triggers were dealing with bullies and tyrants. An example of contemporary triggers are people who abuse the social safety net. Anger is an associated emotion (dislike of oppression). Equality is an associated virtue.

Haidt's descriptive model is based on extensive research and has an empirical strength that is considerable. His research included other cultures (although Indigenous cultures were not included in notable ways.) As is true for all descriptive models, the descriptions can only reflect current reality, the status quo. Yet, descriptive models may give good ideas about potential or current evolutionary challenges or what additional dimensions there could be that our current lens might not see. For example, it is obvious that we are much more cosmopolitan as a result of globalization, which makes moral decisions even more complex. What is our responsibility about deforestation of the Amazon? What about our responsibility when we receive information about genocide in another country? Do we have responsibility when a tribal culture is threatened by extinction because of missionization or mining? If we see ourselves as part of nature, what moral obligations do we have?

We can ask additional questions. How much globalization can we take? Do we have the moral equipment to resolve our current global challenges? Is the only major option for us to relegate these issues to **shadow** material by way of denial? Based on his research, Robert Kegan (1998) has argued that we may be in over our heads. The majority of citizens may not have the cognitive capacities to sufficiently understand the complexities of global warming, a global economy, or the spread of new viruses. What are the implications if our **System 2** is not sufficiently trained or educated not only to understand these critical issues, but also to grapple with their moral implications?

In situations when our human system gets overwhelmed (whether by the level of cognitive complexity or emotional challenges that it has to cope with), we tend to fall back on evolutionarily earlier or moral primitive ways of processing. This is where the elephant steps into action and **System 1** acts in full force. How can we enhance both our moral reasoning *and* our moral elephant? We see **transformative learning**, an approach involving both cognitive and emotional processes, as a way to address these challenges and will discuss it below.

The limitations of descriptive models notwithstanding, Haidt fruitfully applies his findings, for example, to the division between Republicans and Democrats in the U.S. with potentially significant implications for political strategies. Liberals have a primary focus on the care/harm, liberty/oppression, and fairness/cheating dimensions. Libertarians focus primarily on the liberty/oppression and fairness/cheating dimensions, while social conservatives have a more evenly distributed focus on all six moral dimensions (Haidt, 2011).

It is important to keep in mind that different political parties, different religions and spiritualities, and different (sub)cultures find different resolutions in each of these dimensions. Not only does each culture need to find moral answers in each of these dimensions (usually valuing one or more dimensions over the remaining), we as individuals need to find moral responses in each of them.

Hall of mirrors

The basic brain map presented above has shown us how our brain can be divided into older and younger parts. One of the major implications of this division in the brain is that moral decisions and values related to our sense of self can be impacted by the reasoning power of our frontal cortex (the "rider"), but the rapid responses of our habits anchored in the older parts of our brains (the "elephant") are where much of our sense of self and morals resides. Add to this basic map another important aspect: the brain's division into two hemispheres. Understanding this division is critical for reflecting on our sense of self as well as our contemporary challenges.

McGilchrist (2009, 2011) reviewed existing brain research and came to some very important conclusions about why we have two hemispheres. They serve very different functions: the *right hemisphere* provides sustained, open, broad alertness or vigilance for what might be, and is concerned with patterns and making connections; the *left hemisphere*, in contrast, has a narrow, sharply focused attention to detail.

Research shows that the **right hemisphere** helps identify what is different from what we expect. It perceives things in context, understands metaphor, body language, implicit meanings, and facial expressions. The right hemisphere is concerned with individuals (not categories) and the embodied world, the living as opposed the mechanical. It looks at embodied beings as part of the lived world. It also deals with things that can never be fully grasped, such as spirituality.

By contrast, the **left hemisphere** concerns itself with what we already know and provides a simplified map of reality. Its goal is precision and it works to pin things down and breaks them into parts in the process. The result is clarity and the capacity to manipulate things that can be known and isolated, things that are static. The knowledge of the left hemisphere is decontextualized and it uses denotative language; what it knows is explicit and general in nature, but ultimately lifeless. The body gets broken down into its constituent parts. The system the left hemisphere creates is closed and it has the advantage of attempting perfection.

The two hemispheres, therefore, offer two versions of the world that we combine all the time in various ways and give different weight to each depending on circumstance. For a broad understanding of a situation we rely more on knowledge from the **right hemisphere**, for specific technical tasks we rely more on the left. We have two hemispheres for a reason and we need them both.

Historically, humans started out with both hemispheres in a balance of mutual benefit. However, in more recent centuries the view of the **left hemisphere** began to dominate, and currently we primarily look at the world through that perspective. Our world is taking on the semblance of the left hemisphere: the technical is becoming all important, the virtual is emphasized over the real, bureaucracies keep expanding, there is no clear sense of a whole, and the big picture is fragmented. The "what" is much more important than the "how" as the left hemisphere usurps the functions of the right. We have riches of information, but do we have the wisdom to understand and integrate it?

The power of the left hemisphere is impressive. It creates a view of reality that is entirely self–consistent, because it is made from itself. Everything that does not fit gets discarded. While the left hemisphere is very vocal on its own behalf, the **right hemisphere** cannot construct arguments. As a result we seem to be trapped in a hall of mirrors: the stronger the view of the left hemisphere, the more it prevents us from seeing ways out of our dilemmas. "We just get reflected back into more of what we know about what we know about what we know" (McGilchrist, 2011).

McGilchrist reminds us of Einstein's statement that the intuitive mind is a sacred gift and the rational mind its faithful servant, critically adding: "We honor the servant but have forgotten the gift." This metaphor informs McGilchrist's (2011) title, *The Master and His Emissary*. The emissary, the **left hemisphere**, as his argument goes, has usurped the role of the master, which is the **right hemisphere**, the holder of the big picture, the integrator. He asserts the importance of reason and good language while alerting us to the dangers of a one–dimensional rationality.

The implications of our hemispheric division for the purposes of ethno-autobiography — and to understand and address our contemporary crises — seems to be that we need to rebalance the use of our brains. Personal and social transformation can only result from a balanced use of left and right–brain processes. Our self and our morals will not change by force of reason alone. Rather, we need to engage the right hemisphere in the process. Our current crises (whether economic or ecological or personal) will not be resolved solely by a technical and rational analysis, we need to integrate our scientific knowledge with the big picture that our right–brain provides. We need to honor the servant of rationality while remembering the sacred gift of intuition. When looking at the morals we believe in we need to use reason to see if, indeed, they are reasonable and we need to use our **right hemisphere** to work with the personal roots of our values. Responding to a crisis requires that we use our best integrative functions to put it all together into a meaningful whole.

Dörner (1989) conducted research where participants had to improve on a complex system in a specific ecological or social environment. Those who used their intuitive capacities to work with complexity generally did better than those who did not. The force of rationality alone inevitably seemed to crash the system that participants intended to improve. Thus, understanding the scientific evidence for global warming is one thing, what to do about it quite another.

Radical hope

Arguably we are confronted with social, cultural, and environmental challenges that could signal the collapse of the world we know. As the former head of the US National Oceanic and Atmospheric Administration asserts: "Only Newton's laws of motion may enjoy a wider scientific consensus than a human–enhanced greenhouse effect" (reported in Jones, 2013, p. 3). The dramatic and accelerating technological, social, and cultural changes we are witnessing are giving rise, it seems, to an increase in fear among people who see and feel, but do not necessarily understand or trust current developments. The rise of fear and the rise of a variety of fundamentalisms seem to be correlated (and such fundamentalism may be spiritual, religious, ecological, scientific, or of another stripe). Socio-cultural disorientation and threats to basic survival give rise to an unconscious sense of despair as assurances about the future are more and more difficult to come by. This level of fear may be masked by an optimistic belief in science and technology or a fundamentalist religious belief system or an immersion in the immediate future while disregarding larger trends. The world as we have known it could actually cease to exist and we scarcely have a vision of what might take its place. The possibility of cultural devastation on a planetary level may be looming just below the horizon.

Cultural devastation, of course, has occurred many times in human history, including the genocide of numerous Native American cultures. Lear (2006) analyzed the destruction of the Crow Nation, as one specific example. Plenty Coups, the last great chief of the crow, stated that "when the buffalo went away the hearts of my people fell to the ground and they could not lift them up again. After that nothing happened." The world the Crow had known had ended. What can you hope for in such a dire situation? Plenty Coups had a dream in which there were buffalo–like animals with spots, "strange animals from another world" (p. 70). Then a tremendous storm knocks down all trees except for one, the lodge of the Chickadee, which is "least in strength but strongest of mind among his kind".

Plenty Coups is unable to understand the meaning of his dream, but the Elders of the tribe listen to the dream and interpret it. One of them states: "The tribes who have fought the white man have all been beaten, wiped out. By listening as the Chickadee listens we may escape this and keep our lands." The consequence is that the Crow Nation acknowledged that buffalo hunting had come to an end and that they would need to ally with the white man against their traditional enemies.

Lear (2006) discusses this situation in terms of "radical hope":

> What makes this hope radical is that it is directed toward a future goodness that transcends the current ability to understand what it is. Radical hope anticipates a good for which those who have hope as yet lack the appropriate concepts with which to understand it. (p. 103)

We contend that our current situation is not unlike the situation of the Crow Nation as we consider our planetary crises. How can we acknowledge our feelings (fear, despair, pessimism, etc.) and look toward a future goodness that may arise out of our malaise? Radical hope is what may carry us beyond ideological divisions and historical traumas. Ethnoautobiography is founded on radical hope.

It is significant that the Crow Nation's approach to their cultural devastation emerges from Plenty Coup's dream, an aspect not emphasized by Lear. Theirs was not a strategic decision merely based on rational analysis, but on insights arising from the dream state and the qualities of the **right hemisphere** as well as the older parts of the brain. Of course, Indigenous peoples take dreams very seriously and have always seen them as meaningful.

Interestingly something very similar occurred when Christianity was about to arrive in Iceland around 1000 CE. After divisive discussions in the Allthingi, the Icelandic parliament, Thorgeir Thorkelsson, a trusted and reasonable man, was appointed to resolve the conflict. He spent a night under a fur blanket, a traditional way of talking to ancestral spirits, and based on this meditative quest resolved that Iceland should convert to Christianity. Thorgeir himself was a pagan priest and he threw his spirit figures into a tremendous waterfall now known as the waterfall of the gods (Goðafoss). This resolution prevented civic strife by welcoming Christianity but also allowing the continuation of its heathen traditions in private. Both Christianity and pagan traditions have co–existed in Iceland ever since. Just as in the Crow example we find the use of an **integrative state of consciousness** (a one night vision quest or meditation with the ancestors) that leads to resolution. The two examples are in many respects parallel, although the Icelanders probably had a better sense of what was below the horizon.

Similarly, Macy and Johnstone (2012) contrast passive and **active hope**:

> Active Hope is a practice....The guiding impetus is intention: we *choose* what we aim to bring about, act for or express. Rather than weighing our chances and proceeding only when we feel hopeful, we focus

on our intention and let it be our guide" (p. 3).

Based on their visionary insight the Crow actively engaged hope, despite the fact that they could not even begin to guess what was beyond the horizon. Ethnoautobiography actively builds hope by engaging each individual in a transformative process that utilizes left–and right–brain, rational analysis and intuitive, visionary processes.

Integrative states of consciousness

All humans have the capacity to experience altered and visionary states, and we all do so every night when we dream. Dreaming is among the states of consciousness where different parts of our brain become more synchronized or integrated, especially as we bring our dreams into our everyday awareness. We may also experience integrative states of consciousness or have experiences of the sacred when we are out in nature, when we are in a temple, church, or cathedral, or when we are in a cave, sacred circle or labyrinth. We have evolved to be religious and experience the numinous that is larger than we are. Seeing sacredness is part of being human. For millennia humans have sought experiences of the divine through rituals.

In more recent centuries Western traditions have changed and attempt to exclude regular experiences beyond our small selves. The strong boundaries of the individualistic self make such random and unpredictable experiences, other than our nightly dreams, no longer a part of the social fabric. Experiences of life as sacred and that our small selves are a part of a larger whole is no longer common, but considered marginal.

Experiences of sacredness and **integrative states of consciousness** give us access to the deeper parts of our sense of self not accessible via rationality. Such experiences validate right–brain processes and synchronize our two hemispheres. They give us access to our emotional brain and help us deal with experiences that may be difficult to acknowledge (such as **shadow** material). Insight, inspiration, and guidance may explicitly be gained by having such integrative awareness which may also trigger intuitions and visionary experiences. They are also critically important for cultural renewal. At one time, almost all cultures had socially endorsed trance rituals, whether the Plains Indian sun dance, trance dances during carnival, or equinoctial and solstitial celebrations.

Personal and cultural shadow

With all of this background, what we call the self and our immediate responses to political and moral issues are, to a significant extent, unconscious (they tend to be habitual and immediate). An important aspect of the unconscious is what Carl Gustav Jung called "the shadow". He saw it as "the 'negative' side of the personality, the sum of all those unpleasant qualities we like to hide, together with the insufficiently developed functions and the content of the personal unconscious" (Jung 1917/1966, 66n). Von Franz (1968, p. 174) believed that the individual **shadow** "represents unknown or little–known attributes and qualities of the ego." Yet the shadow also carries energies and insights necessary for the wholeness of what Jung called the "Self". Hence, Jung counseled learning about one's shadow and entering into what he called "long and difficult negotiations" with the shadow. Through such "shadow work," one becomes enlightened and reduces the shadow's destructive potential, not so much, as it were, by waging war against the darkness, or abandoning the darkness for an abode of light, but by bringing the darkness to the light, the light to the darkness.

Jung was also concerned with the collective manifestation of shadow material. To speak of the collective shadow is to refer to what historically has often been labeled "evil." Jung identified the "principle of evil" as involving "naked injustice, tyranny, lies, slavery, and coercion of conscience" (Jung, 1963, p. 328) and believed that the contemporary world has very little understanding of, or ability to respond to, such evil. Jung suggested that the primary response to evil by the individual must be the quest for self–knowledge, for wholeness, which presumes the assimilation of shadow material. The individual "must know relent-

lessly how much good s/he can do, and what crimes s/he is capable of" (Jung, 1963, p. 330).

Collective and individual shadows intertwine in each individual. Exploring individual shadow material may lead to collective shadow material and vice versa. Collective shadow material is held in individuals as well as in socio–cultural structures.

A common saying among Jungian psychologists is that there is gold in the shadows. This means that looking at personal and cultural material that we have a difficult time with, or that make us feel uneasy, or we would rather deny will in actuality lead us to finding gold. Ethnoautobiography delves into thorny issues, such as "whiteness" or "privilege" or "colonialism" not to make ourselves feel bad or to flagellate ourselves with guilt. On the contrary, it is to find the gold of renewal and future vision as we confront history and take responsibility for the issues that continue to mar our personal and social wellbeing. We may indeed experience guilt along the way, but the purpose of exploring **shadow** material is not to create shame. On the contrary, it is to move beyond these feelings to form a more satisfying sense of self. Psychology teaches us that there are no shortcuts to accomplish this, and that avoiding shadow issues will only make them loom larger (like the shadow of Nosferatu in the alleys in Murnau's Dracula movie). Guilt and shame in and of themselves are worth nothing, it is their exploration that can lead us toward healing, integration, and new territory in our communities.

Ethnoautobiography can be understood as a "collective learning process" encouraging self–reflection in a learning community, intentional community, or a natural community. Approaching our **shadow** material opens the road to a different self–understanding, different behavior, and the possibility of a different perception of our social and natural world.

Transformative learning

The rational mind alone is hardly sufficient to effect personal growth and transformative learning. An increase in reflexivity and insight results from both rational and non–rational processes. The elephant is insufficiently explored by rational means. Exploring **shadow** material, dreams, and the arts is just as important as a well–reasoned argument. We have to become adept in being the rider and being the elephant. Transformative learning, the overall framework for the process of this workbook, utilizes the many tools available that facilitate such **dialectic** process.

This type of learning is a process of looking at our assumptions about our selves and the world and facilitating changes that we desire. The goal of transformative learning is to develop the capacity to take self-reflective looks at our selves and to increase our capac-

ity for choice because of an increase in awareness and the integration of non–rational aspects of ourselves.

Reading this book may have caused reactions to certain words sometimes. For example: supremacy, decolonization or spirituality may be confusing or overly challenging. The transformative learning approach encourages us to observe our reactions and to monitor our feelings and thoughts as they occur. Observing ourselves without judgment (being non–judgmental or having compassionate ruthlessness is a critical ingredient!) will gradually strengthen both the capacity to have insight into our own process and the capacity to make choices that feel morally stronger.

Transformative learning is not only rational process; it involves our heart (feelings, emotions), actions (behavior), and other dimensions. Mezirow (1991) focuses on our capacity to reflect upon our assumptions as we encounter what he calls "disorienting dilemmas". For example, in order to reduce the number of crack babies, a wealthy donor offers a monetary reward that is significant for men and women using crack. In return they have to undergo long term or permanent birth control. Is this a moral thing to do? Sandel (2012) explores this moral dilemma, which, at first, may appear to have a straightforward answer: Fewer babies born with crack addiction is a good thing, isn't it? But then further questions are likely to arise: Do crack addicts actually have the free will to make such a decision because of their addiction? Is it moral to potentially deepen their addiction and accelerate their death? Does this mean crack addicts are damaged baby–making machines? This is a disorienting dilemma where a number of your values and assumptions about the world may clash. Mezirow sees this as a generative moment that can lead to changes in worldview.

> Transformative learning is the transformation of meaning schemes (specific beliefs about self or world) and meaning perspectives (comprehensive worldviews) through reflection on underlying premises, leading to meaning perspectives that are more inclusive, differentiated, permeable, and integrated (1991, pp. 6 – 7)

Other aspects have been added to Mezirow's particular understanding, mostly emphasizing the importance of dimensions that are not immediately cognitively rational. The importance of artistic (self)–exploration, somatic practices (yoga, tai chi, dance, sports), emotional (self)–exploration (e.g., feeling responses to particular phrases or images), dreams, experimentally trying out alternate behavior, and other non–linear processes has become clearer. For example, Jungian theory (Jung, 1964), talks about

the importance of the "compensatory function" of dreams, which is their capacity to bring messages from the unconscious to the conscious. This can result in significant changes when a dream is worked with.

An expanded definition of **transformative learning** is

> the expansions of consciousness *in any human system* through transforming basic worldview and specific capacities of the self; transformative learning is facilitated through consciously directed processes such as appreciatively accessing and receiving the symbolic contents of the unconscious and critically analyzing underlying premises. (Elias, 1997, p. 5, italics in original)

This workbook touches upon various dimensions of the learning process and may trigger disorienting dilemmas. It is our hope that every reader — for different reasons and on different occasions — will encounter opportunities for transformative learning. Such an opportunity may occur during various practices, or activities, such as telling the story of an important family object. Or, it may arise when critically analyzing a suggested reading. Or, even when spending some time in nature.

We have described ethnoautobiography as a process involving ten dimensions, i.e. storytelling, ancestry, community, place, etc. Exploring each of these dimensions holds the potential of **transformative learning**, and yet we can make this picture even more detailed and rich, as we see how each of these dimensions has four qualities. If we juxtapose one over another, it illuminates additional aspects of transformative learning. Following Wilber (1995), we can divide our perceptions into those of inner experiences and those that are perceptions of the outer world (interior vs. exterior). And we can look at a single object and multiple objects (individual vs. collective). This gives us four fundamental quadrants:

1. I: Interior — individual (intentional, subjective).
2. WE: Interior — collective (cultural, intersubjective).
3. IT: Exterior — individual (behavioral, objective).
4. ITS: Exterior — collective (social, interobjective).

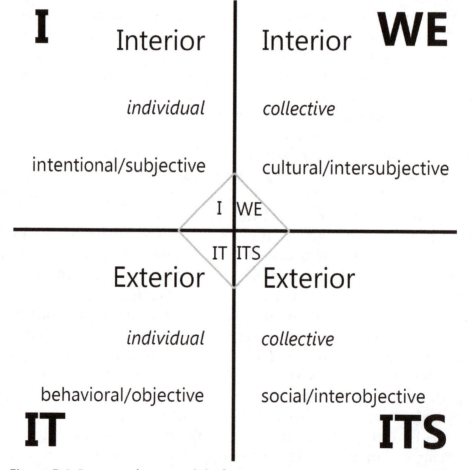

Figure 5.1. Four quadrant model of perceptions (based on Wilber, 1995).

In considering these four different perspectives, and we look at a person or an object or ourselves from all four perspectives, then almost inevitably fresh insights occur and we begin to enter the realm of **transformative learning**. We broaden our horizon by using multiple perspectives and thus likely become more aware of how we perceive another person or object or ourselves. This means we have an opportunity to become aware of our assumptions or meaning perspectives (Mezirow, 1991).

Two brief examples: Jürgen has a cat named Atigo. He has certain thoughts and feelings about Atigo, which are primarily positive (individual interior experience, I). His perceptions are generally shared with his wife and daughter (collective interior experience, WE). They see the cat as loving, playful, a lover of water, and at times behaving like a sea otter when lying on his back.

Jürgen sees the physical creature of the cat with its musculature, sharp claws, and tiger markings (individual exterior, IT). He is part of the family together with four rabbits (collective exterior, ITS).

We also have complex feelings about objects, such as our computers (individual interior experience, I). We have an ongoing human–machine relationship with our computers that may range from excitement to outrage (collective interior experience, WE). Of course, we see them as physical, technological objects (individual exterior, IT). We also may have a number of networked computers at home or at our workplace (collective exterior, ITS).

On pages 158 and 159 are some catchwords that describe how this quadrant map applies to ethnoautobiography. In each cell you will find additional examples in italics.

	I	WE	IT	ITS
Community	My experience of community *I love my church* *I love my dojo*	The values I share with the communities of which I am a part *We believe in the compassion of Christ* *Preserving local wildlife is of foremost importance to us*	The behavior I observe of an individual in community *I see him behaving like a good Samaritan*	The social structure of the community *Our organization is a nonprofit* *Our organization makes decisions by consensus*
Place	My experience of place *I feel a fondness for my grandmother's house* *I feel the divine when entering Chartres Cathedral*	The shared experience of a place *A family picnic, or lunch in a cafeteria* *The shared story about the meaning of National Parks*	The physical characteristics of a specific place *The Lincoln Memorial* *The Nile River*	The ecology of a specific place (city, park, wilderness, etc.) *The Russian River watershed*
Nature	My experience of nature *Watching ocean waves* *Sitting in a redwood forest makes me feel serene*	The shared experience of nature *Backpacking or horseback riding with a group* *A family picnic*	Characteristics of a specific organism *the Douglas fir tree in your backyard* *your pet rabbit nuzzles under your arm*	The complex ecology of the environment *Redwood forest* *Alpine tundra*
History	My personal experience of a historical event (as it happens or as I read/hear about it) *Terrorist attacks make me fear for my own security* *The end of apartheid in South Africa has given me hope*	The shared experience of a historical event *The 2008 crash of the housing market* *Hurricane Sandy in 2012*	Specific details and observations related to a historic event *The location of a US Civil War battle* *Observable changes in the Dow Jones Industrial Average*	Broader human movements and consequences of historical events *Economic mechanisms behind historical events* *Government ideologies, e.g., fascism, manifest destiny, liberalism*
Mythic stories	The myths I can tell; the experience of the myths I read *I find myths entirely puzzling* *Myths put me in touch with my childhood imagination*	The mythic stories that are part of my culture *Oisin, the Irish bard* *Brünhilde in Django Unchained*	The form & function of myths *Greek tragedies* *Raven tales are trickster stories*	Rituals & ceremonies embodying myths *The Dine Blessingway* *Halloween*

	I	WE	IT	ITS
Ancestry	My lineage *I look forward to learning more about my ancestry* *Since I'm adopted I have many emotions about family history*	Shared ancestral stories in my family *My ancestors owned enslaved Africans* *My grandparents are survivors of the Shoah*	Specific information about an ancestor *My grandmother was a Socialist* *Our grandfather was born in 1882 in Indiana*	My family tree *I can trace my family to the Isle of Man*
Gender	My own definition of my gender *I feel comfortable with how others see me as wo/man* *I feel fluid in my gender identity, every day it is a bit different*	The gender assumptions I share with my social group *Men are from Mars; Women are from Venus (Gray, 1992)* *Marriage can only be between a man and a woman*	My actions as a gendered being *I never allow others to see me cry* *I want to be a mother*	Socio–political factors that impact my gender definition *Courts allowing same gender marriages* *One in four women survive rape*
Dreams	The dream I remember *The dreams I remember are deeply puzzling* *Now and then I have had dreams that have blown me away*	The cultural meaning attributed to dreams *Dreams are private & only matter to the individual* *Dreams provide access to other realms*	Descriptions or details of the dream or dreamer *Neurological processing while dreaming* *The significance of Rapid Eye Movement (REM)*	Relationship between consciousness & dreams *The interaction of my dreaming brain with the rest of the body* *Do androids dream of electric sheep? (Dick, 1996)*
Spirituality	My beliefs related to spirituality or atheism *I believe a protective spirit always walks with me* *I grew up going to church, but now science is my answer*	The beliefs shared with my social group *We believe in a higher power* *They believe in reincarnation*	Personal ritual behavior in church &/or elsewhere *Trances in Sufi dancing* *"Witnessing" in Christian churches*	Socio–political factors that impact (non) spirituality *The economic structure of a church organization* *Prayer in schools*
Storytelling	My life story *R & Jürgen writing the EA examples at the beginning of the workbook*	The sharing of family stories *R's grandmother always said: 'everything in moderation, including moderation'* *Jenny's dad drove a car from Chicago to Texas when he was 14*	Impact of the structure & wording of stories *Brain processing while telling a story* *Clarifying a memory when hearing a story*	Social meaning and impact of a story *Different points of view pertaining to a story* *Telling or writing or publishing your story*

This table illustrates in greater detail something mentioned earlier: Ethnoautobiographical explorations moving between the subjective (both I and WE) and the objective (IT and ITS) is generative and transformative. It challenges us to look at our assumptions (meaning perspectives and schemes) about the world and how they mesh with external realities (IT and ITS) and how our internal realities (our perceptions, habits, felt responses, etc.) respond in turn.

When we engage in this process **transformative learning** is the inevitable result that engages both the rider (our reasoning, our frontal cortex) and the elephant (our emotional, intuitive processing). We can use our rationality (self–reflection) to trigger transformative learning or we can use artistic means (expressive arts, dreams, storytelling, etc.) to evoke explorations that connect our experiences with our reflexivity.

The information provided in the workbook and the various activities are designed to trigger transformative learning from both ends: from the end of our cognitive reflexivity (readings, web searches, etc.) and from the experiential end of stories, collages, visits to places, etc.

The process of ethnoautobiography

With these first six chapters we have laid the foundation for the work of ethnoautobiography. Given the multidimensionality of this process the work can seem confusing or even overwhelming. Each of the aspects or branches of ethnoautobiography provides a fair amount of information. The work of integrating this information and tracking one's personal responses can lead us down circuitous roads. Perhaps a good metaphor is that the EA process is like a ride down a winding river. We can't see past the next bend. Every now and then a stream joins the river and we may disembark to explore what the stream has to offer. We may take a swim and explore the bottom of the riverbed. At times the river seems to wind back on itself. Sometimes the vistas are open and wide and we gaze across a plain, other times we may be carried through the depth of a forest where we feel totally immersed in t he deep green of the trees. Ethnoautobiography is like this, and just like a river ride has an ending, ethnoautobiography moves toward closure, temporary as it may be. When we start the journey we can't completely see it. We have to trust that the twists and turns of the river will lead us somewhere, and that our story will carry us somewhere, somewhere we cannot see at the beginning. **Transformative learning** leads us into explorations, reflections, and encounters with ourselves and others where we can't quite see the destination, yet our body, our memories, and our intentions will bring it all together.

Activity 1

Transformative Learning Experience

Identify one learning experience you would describe as significant and transformative. Describe it, discuss what happened and how it was transformative. Use as much detail as possible, without getting bogged down in precision. What were the different aspects of the experience? What type of educational setting did it take place in (school, workshop, seminar, etc.)? What helped the learning process? What was the subject matter that the experience took place in (art, music, literature, psychology, ecology)? Can you identify and reflect on which parts of you were involved in the experience?

This may be completed in a 500–word written reflection, or shared as an oral presentation with others.

Activity 2

Moral Dilemma

Using one of the three examples of cultural conflict at sacred sites (Bear Lodge, Mt. Shasta, Hopi) from the movie, *In the Light of Reverence,* discuss (preferably with others in a small group) possible resolutions to the dilemma. Discuss pros and cons, move beyond either/or, toward both/and. Strive for consensus. Be supportive of each other's positions, feelings and ideas. Be creative, inspired and practice living outside the box.

Describe how you would attempt to resolve the moral challenge in front of you. Do your best to take all sides into consideration. See if you can come up with a resolution for yourself that both feels right and is intellectually defensible.

During this process also pay attention to your emotional and rational processes in light of the information provided in this chapter (and workbook). What are your gut reactions and what were your reflections? Keep notes to strengthen your skills of self–observation. What is your experience of being self–reflective? Can you identify both what you learned about the specific moral dilemma you choose, as well as, how you responded to the assignment.

What did you learn about how you make moral decisions? What was new? What aspects of yourself, and the ways in which you respond to such dilemmas, would you want to attend to in this workbook? Identify which moral dimensions described by Jonathan Haidt (2008, 2011) were present in your statements and in your discussion.

Note: If you are completing these activities on your own, and do not have an organized group to do oral presentations for (such as in a classroom, community organization and so on), it is encouraged that you present the work you are doing to a friend, family member or spouse to experience sharing your process in oral form.

Chapter Summary

Moral behavior often occurs by unconscious attitudes and/or habit, and moral discourse usually occurs after a rationalization. Morals, like the sense of self, vary significantly across cultures. Hope can arise even when we can't see beyond the horizon, even though taking into account that all individuals and cultures have denied our shadow aspects. The unconscious parts of moral behavior can be accessed and changed, though rational discourse is probably the least effective way of doing so.

Concept Check

Where does the process of moral judgment begin in our selves?

How might we describe the majority of our moral responses?

How many dimensions of morality are there, and briefly describe each one?

Radical hope might carry us where?

Ethnoautobiography delves into thorny issues, in part, to find what?

Transformative learning goes beyond rational processes to involve what other dimensions?

Riff

From the Desert Into the City

The base we lived in for those four months was nothing more than about one hundred cement slabs and large areas of flat desert land, all outlined by metal pickets and thick layers of concertina wire to form a square mile perimeter. The base itself was just off of the Iraq border and about thirty miles from Kuwait City. Once every couple of weeks we would drive from the desert base into Kuwait City to pick up supplies, use their showering facilities, computers, etc., at the main seaport base that all US forces used for importing and exporting goods into Kuwait. Sometimes we would be forced to wear civilian clothes and take Kuwaiti public transit shuttles so as to hide the fact that we were US soldiers traveling in this Arab state. Other times we drove in a convoy of our military vehicles with live ammunition next to our vehicle's weapon system. I was a "gunner" on the lieutenant's truck and the weapon attached to our vehicle was a .50 caliber machine gun.

I remember moving through the vast desert paths, and finally coming to a paved road. Shortly after driving on that road for a while we approached a freeway system that took us into the main area of Kuwait City. I was uncomfortable and nervous, as I was standing out of the turret in the last vehicle of our convoy. In basic military convoy transpor-

tation formations, the last vehicle orients their weapon system to the rear of the convoy to serve as eyes behind the group. This meant that I alone was standing up in our turret, hands holding the ".50 cal" and facing all of the traffic behind me. I vividly remember the looks on several faces of those that drove behind us or passed us by. Expressions of disgust and uncertainty were on the faces of people as they looked at this white American male grasping a huge weapon pointed in their direction as they drove home from work or were out shopping. I remember asking myself what I would think or feel if I encountered some strange man in military dress driving down the freeway back in Phoenix, Arizona. I wanted to disappear.

> In our time, direct colonialism has largely ended; imperialism, as we shall see, lingers where it has always been, in a kind of general cultural sphere as well as in specific political, ideological, economic, and social practices. Neither imperialism nor colonialism is a simple act of accumulation and acquisition. Both are supported and perhaps even impelled by impressive ideological formations that include notions that certain territories and people require and beseech domination. (Said, 1993 p. 9)
>
> CB

NOTES

Chapter 6
Community and *Communitas*

Riff

Looking for Cynthia Ann Parker

Dog–sitting at a friend's house
On one level seems to be a ridiculous
Opening to telling a story
About searching for the ghosts of
Cynthia Ann Parker
Practically a mythological figure in both
The White settlement of Texas
As well as resistance to it
And yet, at the same time, where I am
Makes all the sense in the world

I have the habit of needing to know more
About the places in which I live
And so it was when I first came to Texas

Within a month of our move I was reading
Empire of the Summer Moon
In fact, reading it out loud to Jenny
As we drove back from California
We were shaken by the remarkable story of
Quanah Parker
The last free leader of the Comanche people
Both as a warrior and diplomat
And also the tragic, heartbreaking story of his White mother
Cynthia Ann

As we drove south on I–35 in Oklahoma
A little internet research located
The final resting place of
Quanah and Cynthia Ann

And though it was nearly 2 a.m.
When we pulled up to the gates of Fort Sill

We still had to see their graves
To honor their lives
To acknowledge all that they signify
And the longer we've lived here in Texas
The more I've needed to know
What they mean

So we also went south a hundred miles
To the reconstructed site of Parker Fort
Where Cynthia Ann was taken at age 9 or so
By the Comanche, in 1836
This location is treated by some as another Alamo
A monument to decontextualized settlement
Forgetting or ignoring the arrogance and
Ignorance of White actions

We needed to visit Palo Duro Canyon as well
The location of the last battle
Between the US and the Comanche
Where Colonel Mackenzie ordered the slaughter of
Over a thousand horses
To ensure the Comanche would not
Recapture them

We hope some day
There will be a monument
To the Comanche and the horses
At Palo Duro Canyon
We did see bats at sundown and
A rattlesnake crossed our path

Most telling of all, though
Was our visit to the so–called
Battle of Pease River
On a tributary to the Red River
Near the Texas Panhandle
Some have called it a massacre

This was where Cynthia Ann
Was kidnapped, again
This time by White settlers

Though she was now Naudah
Had married a Comanche chief and
Had three part–Comanche children

Taken back to the White world
She attempted to escape numerous times
A stranger in a strange world, twice over now

So on a blisteringly hot summer day
We drove down old country roads
To find the stone monument
Hysterical markers, Jenny calls them

On the map it looked like there might be more
Perhaps a historic site of some kind
There was an open gate
And a road
So we went in

But immediately it didn't look very inviting
There were cars, trailers
It did not feel like a public place at all
Yet, as we hastily left
A White woman walks towards us
Attempting to get our attention
We stop and get out

No, there was nothing more than the historical marker
This is private land, it turns out
Her family has lived here for generations
They have a family reunion here every year
Have for the last 75 years or so
She says there's another marker down the road
Honoring her great–grandmother
The first White child born in the county

She definitely knows of the significance of the place
Says that the historical marker was practically in
Her family's front yard
And that she thinks there's a stake
Where Cynthia Ann's husband died
During the attack by the Calvary
She doesn't know where
And will have to ask her mom to show her
The place that Quanah Parker's father
Peta Nocona, supposedly died

And that brings it all back together
To being at my friend's house
Dog sitting
As I leave, they show me a picture
Of a young woman holding a calf
It's my friend's mother
On their family farm
That has been in the family for generations
Since her great–grandparents
In Nocona, Texas

RJP

Chapter Outline	Core Concepts	Ethnoautobiographical Perspectives	Expected Outcomes
Looking for Cynthia Ann Parker	Communities have histories & shadows	Histories of place continue to impact communities	Begin looking for the history of communities
Moral dimensions of groups	We can assess the well–being of a community by using the six moral dimensions	Most social issues are complex, and looking at these from multiple perspectives enriches our understanding	Develop critical analyses of the communities to which we belong
(In)equality	Inequality has signifi-cant consequences in the lives of all citizens	Longevity, health, education, happiness, etc., are impacted by levels of inequality	Appreciate the consequences of inequalities
Racial contract	The social contract is a racial contract	The racial social contract impacts the life of millions of citizens to this day	Challenge estab-lished moral & political agree-ments; include taboo topics in conversations
Privilege	If you carry privilege you may not see it, if you do not carry privilege you probably know very well who is privileged	Privilege, and lack thereof, impacts our sense of self & entitlement	Make the unseen seen
Legitimation & legitimation crisis	Social institutions claim legitimacy which may become questionable when it does not achieve its own goals	In the US the legitimacy of numerous social institutions is coming into question because citizens do not feel they serve them sufficiently	Assess the level of legitimacy of existing political & social institutions
Culture of fear	Fear is an important factor in political manipulation	Non–specific fear has become a potent factor in contemporary life	Appreciate the power of fear
Communitas	Experiences of communitas are important for the well–being of a community	Modern humans are deprived of ecstatic experiences & communitas	Look for the positive potential in communities
The soul & people of the Arabic desert	The divine dwells everywhere, and in all things	Dissolving rigid boundaries of self allows for sensing of the sacred	Notice the sacred in all things

Key Terms

Communitas
Fear
(In)equality
Legitimation and legitimation crisis
Privilege
Racial contract

Note: All key terms in this textbook are highlighted in bold and can be found in the Glossary at the end of the book.

Resources Alongside This Chapter

Bongiovi, N. Y., Whitaker, F., (Producers), & Coogler, R. (2013). *Fruitvale Station* [Motion picture]. United States: Significant Productions.

Gaiman, N., & McKean, D. (2008). *The graveyard book*. New York, NY: HarperCollins Publishers.

Ignatiev, N. (1995). *How the Irish became White*. New York, NY: Routledge.

Lee, H. (1960). *To kill a mockingbird*. Philadelphia, PA: Lippincott.

White Privilege Conference (n.d.) http://www.whiteprivilegeconference.com/

Wise, T. (n.d.). *The Pathology of Privilege*. Retrieved from http://vimeo.com/25637392

The riff that opens this chapter about community was chosen for several reasons. The story itself about Cynthia Ann Parker is foundational in North Texas. There are countless places, streets, and institutions named for the Parker family. As the riff illustrates, the story of Cynthia Ann is so tied up with various aspects of settlement that her story is in some ways like the air north Texans breathe. Ironically, or perhaps not, few people are aware of it. It is as though a part of the community is completely invisible. Of course, this historical invisibility translates into a variety of legacies that will be addressed in this chapter, such as the **racial contract**. One of the gifts of ethnoautobiography is a broader sense of self that emerges from expanding our historical awareness and making events visible that previously have been largely invisible. Indeed, decolonization practices foster significant relationships between self and community.

Similarly, the image for this chapter evokes a sense of community that goes beyond the human to include the animal world. In Andean traditions community (*ayllu*) is understood to include the natural world where humans live and their practice of nurturing conversation includes the conversations with non–human beings, including the mountains, streams, etc. At the most fundamental level we need to ask: Where do we draw the boundaries, or circumference, of our community? Are all humans included or are some excluded? Why are some deemed unworthy of membership in a given community (whether implicitly or explicitly)? Are non–humans, or objects regarded as inanimate, included?

In trying to analyze the state of a society or community we can look at a few questions: Does it walk its talk? Can publicly espoused politics, values, and/or philosophies be found in reality? Does a government or an organization serve one group more than another, and to what extent is privilege present? Another way to look at these issues is from the perspective of ideology critique, whereby we examine whether the public pronouncements by political leaders covers up problems, making them taboo and controlling the public discourse. Further, we might inquire about whether conflicts exist in a social body that are difficult to talk about.

Of course, these are not simply abstract questions. They can be felt very personally, such as whether someone feels privileged or disenfranchised in their community or society. Or, if certain social issues are difficult to discuss in different communities. Perhaps there is something that feels unfair in my society, or an organization to which I belong. Do I even trust my political leaders, and why or why not? Finally, are there social issues I see on a daily basis deserving the attention of politicians and community leaders?

We will touch upon these and related questions by considering:

- **Privilege** and how privilege tends to be difficult to see by the privileged (while those disenfranchised tend to see it very clearly).
- The ideal social contract vs. the **racial contract**.
- Research on the social consequences of **(in)equality**.
- **Legitimation**, what happens when a government can no longer legitimize itself sufficiently? This occurs when citizens feel the governmental structure is failing them and no longer experience it as legitimate.
- The moral dimensions we introduced in Chapter 5 and how they can be used to understand the complexity of contemporary societies.
- The role of **fear** (and a culture of fear) in maintaining highly ideological positions and the status quo in societies.
- Special times and circumstances when a community congeals into **communitas**, a particularly intense experience of the sense of community.

These highlights give some central dimensions that help in our self–exploration and reflection of how we see our selves as members of a community and society. We are embedded in various social networks and experience each of them differently. There is family, college, town/city, clubs, churches and innumerable other possible groups to consider. In all of these social (and ecological, for that matter) groupings we find ourselves a part of layers and dimensions of relationship, many of which are unnoticed. An initial consideration is to view the communities we are a part of through moral dimensions mentioned earlier in Chapter 5, "We are Moral Beings."

Moral dimensions of social groups

Vine Deloria, in his interview for *In the Light of Reverence* (McLeod, 2001), notes the differences between societies of rights and entitlements (such as Western societies) and societies of responsibilities (many Indigenous societies). We could inquire into the moral, ethical, and legal foundations of societies through investigations about balancing rights and responsibilities. Further, there may be responsibilities that come with rights, rather than impinging on them. We use the moral dimensions presented in Chapter 5 to look at social groups and societies:

- In the *care/harm dimension,* we ask whether society manages to protect its citizens, especially its children. We also consider social mores and whether people treat each other with caring and kindness; we consider the quality of social functioning. Does the level of inequality in our society create more harm than we can morally accept?

- In the *fairness/cheating dimension*, we consider whether a society is fair and whether bribery is part of its functioning (white collar crime, for example). Questions about whether justice is administered equally to all citizens are central to this dimension. An equally strong challenge is to ask about the ability for people to trust that government institutions act fairly. For example, during the 2008 US housing market crash we could investigate whether the support banks received was fair in comparison to individual citizens. Additionally, we could address whether access to education is unfairly distributed among citizens.

- In the *loyalty/betrayal dimension*, questions about how loyalty is created among a group of people are central to feelings of membership. We want to understand what role symbols play — whether at a national or regional level (such as a flag or anthem), or in an organization (such as the Boy Scouts) — in fostering feelings of loyalty or betrayal. Additionally, such inquiries detail whether everybody is asked to sacrifice on behalf of their nation, organization, or group in the same way.

- In the *authority/subversion dimension*, we investigate how respect for authority is generated, or whether it has been undermined and subverted. Do central institutions, like Congress and the Supreme Court, command respect and deference, or have they been undermined? We inquire about whether authority is backed by deeds that represent what they stand for. Issues about marriage equality and electoral campaign contributions in the US, for example, both have critically focused on how authority is respected. Once again, questions about the 2008 housing market crisis relate to impacts about the authority of the banking system in the US.

- In the *sanctity/degradation dimension*, we need to as about what issues are taboo in society and organizations. Questions about what taboos might be appropriate aid in understanding if taboos cover shadow issues and deny history. We could investigate the role of the Vietnam Memorial, for example, and learn lessons about appropriate symbols and monuments. Or, we could ask more fundamentally: Should there be taboos, and how do we distinguish between "good" (useful, healing) and "bad" (oppressive, unnecessary) taboos? We also consider how we might be able to generate a public discourse on taboos.

- Finally, in the *liberty/oppression dimension*, we consider if the level of liberty is sufficient or if liberties are eroding. Most importantly, we investigate if there are citizens in our society that are oppressed. Central to this dimension are questions about whether members of society have well functioning social networks, if they are supportive enough, or if these networks are abused. Ultimately, is the level of inequality in our society acceptable?

Haidt's descriptions are useful when we look critically at the efficacy of communities and societies. However, his model may not be complete. We can certainly imagine other moral dimensions that have been seen in other societies (such as courage among the Crow Indian Nation). The ability to have open discourse about the questions along the six moral dimensions speaks to the amount of integrity and cohesion a society or community has.

For example, when watching *In the Light of Reverence* (McLoed, et al, 2002) it is a useful exercise to ask your self about the moral responses to issues presented in the film. Do particular moral dimensions get activated more than others? We might consider the liberty of the rock climbers to scale Mato Tipila, or even Mount Rushmore. It is important that we consider what issues create the strongest reactions, both in terms of the actions of the rock climbers, as well the taboo of the Lakota people against climbing Mato Tipila. Finally, it is important to consider how our reasoning might, or might not be consistent with our gut reactions. Observing one's internal process around moral questions and dilemmas can illuminate aspects of ourselves that we hold dear, but we may have little awareness of. It may also show us areas where we don't know or are open to learning about and revising our assumptions.

Discussing a social body, a society, or organization and questioning how successfully they function in these six dimensions leads to questions about inequality and legitimacy. Thus, we can ask how legitimate a government is that fails to protect its citizens from harm, or fosters high levels of inequality? Questions of this nature help us identify various crisis points — such as inequality, **privilege** and the **racial contract** — within a society, community or organization.

(In)equality

An important focus of **(in)equality** relates to defining income and wealth distribution. The Gini index is a widely accepted index of (in)equality, where 0 means perfect equality and 100 means maximal inequality. Global inequality is generally estimated between 61 and 68. South Africa has roughly the highest in level of inequality (70 or so). Whereas countries of the European north (Denmark, Sweden, etc.), generally have lower income inequality than other countries. The Gini index of the US has been steadily rising in recent years. Within the US there are also notable differences in income inequalities between states (with Arkansas and Utah at the low end of inequality and New York and California at the high end, to give a few examples). The Gini index, while not without limitations, provides a useful measure of income inequality.

While we may think of inequality solely as a moral or ethical issue, inequality has very real consequences in the lives of a country's citizens. For example, research shows that inequality and **fear** are correlated, meaning the higher the income inequality, the higher the level of mistrust among citizens (Wilkinson & Pickett, 2009). Research now shows that income inequality is also correlated to the wellbeing of children, the level of health and social problems (see graph below), obesity, size of prison population, and the amount of recycling, in addition to a number of other factors. In this sense, inequality is an issue that puts moral considerations (such as how much inequality is acceptable) into the context of that particular moral stance. Paying attention to the research on inequality leads to profound questions about the type of society we want to live in. After all, different levels of inequality impact the lives of citizens in significant ways, shortening or lengthening their life

span or supporting (or failing to support) social mobility.

The following two graphs based on the book, *Spirit Level* (Wilkinson & Pickett, 2009), illustrate interrelationships between inequality and various factors. The general rule seems to be that higher levels of income inequality are associated with higher levels of health and social problems. Not surprisingly then, life expectancy is longer in more equal and rich countries. When looking at education we find patters that go with these general trends: In US states with greater income inequality math and literacy scores of eighth–graders tend to be lower and high school drop out rates higher. In countries with lower income inequality math and literacy scores of 15–year–olds tend to be higher (Wilkinson & Pickett, 2009). Certainly, in societies with legacies of racial inequality and White supremacy these issues require focus on the **racial contract**.

Racial contract

One place to understand the concept of community and **(in)equality** is in the realm of the social contract. According to *The Racial Contract* by Charles Mills (1997), we have had 2000 years of Western political thought. In the humanities, philosophy has remained a "white" discipline uninfluenced by multiculturalism, ethnic studies, women's studies, feminist studies, third world studies. The social contract, as developed during the Age of Contract theory from 1650–1800, overlaps with the growth of European

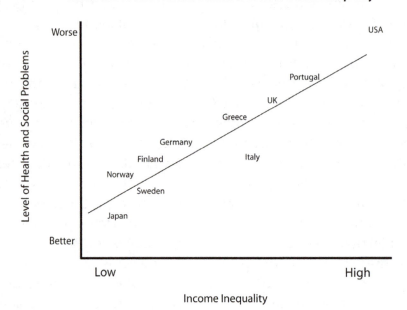

Figure 6.1. Health/social problems in relation to income inequality (based on Wilkinson & Pickett, 2009).

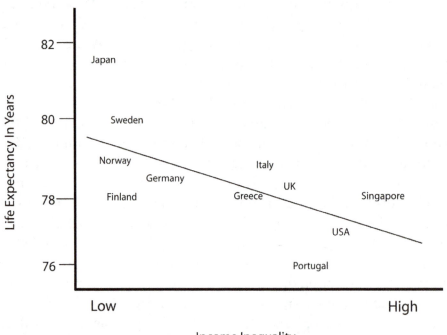

Figure 6.2. Life expectancy in relation to income inequality (based on Wilkinson & Pickett, 2009).

capitalism giving the social contract its racial subtext.

Mills (1997) uses the classic understanding of the social contract (Hobbes, Locke, Rousseau, and Kant) to generate judgments about a society and to explain everything from a person's moral psychology to the way the government functions and society is structured. The fundamental idea is that human beings started out in a "state of nature" and then decided to establish civil societies and a government, implying that government is founded on "the popular consent of individuals taken as equals" (p. 3). Further, "The ideal contract explains how a just society would by formed, ruled by a moral government, and regulated by a defensible moral code" (p. 5).

The European social contracts definition what it means to be "human" derives from the political, moral, and epistemological dimensions of the contract. The political dimensions of Eurocentered social contracts explain the origins of government and our obligations to the state, and describe human nature as an evolution from "natural" to "political man" or from "savage" to "civilized." These dimensions form a basis for the development of polity, state, and judicial systems that pre–suppose that citizens regulate their behavior through a moral code. This moral code is expressed in both theological and secular code.

What Rousseau calls a deceitful social contract, Mills (1997) terms a *nonideal/ naturalized contract* and explains "how an unjust, *exploitative* society, ruled by an *oppressive* government and regulated by an *immoral* code, comes into existence" (p. 5). Mills poses the challenges to demystify and condemn such nonideal/naturalized contracts, i.e., to uncover their ideological nature and lack of **legitimation**. He states that "White supremacy is the unnamed political system that has made the modern world what it is today" (p. 1). He argues that global white supremacy "is *itself* a political system, a particular power structure of formal or informal rule, socioeconomic privilege, and norms for the differential distribution of material wealth and opportunities, benefits and burdens, rights and duties" (p. 3).

The worldview dimension of the **racial contract** prescribes norms of thought and behavior as agreed to by participants (signatories). Therefore, our concepts — theories by which we learn, remember, explain, generalize, categorize, problem solve — are derived from the racial contract. For example, terms like "invention of the Americas, Orient, Africa", or "colonization, enslavement, conquest" are all located in historical events creating the modern world by European colonialism, also including voyages of "discovery." These norms of thought are located in pacts, papal bulls, treaties, legal documents, academic discourses, and legal structures. Our vocabulary of "discovery," "exploration," "heart of darkness," "new world," refers to the ways in which the "other/them" came to be known, and is founded in the **racial contract**.

The moral dimension of the racial contract establishes who is a person and who is a subperson. In order to justify colonial conquests, non–white people were considered as incapable of forming a political, legal, moral society compared to white Europeans that could. By using racial conceptions, especially through the lens of religion, subpersons were considered monstrous and in need of taming and redemption by Christianity.

Europe became dominant through colonialism. In colonized countries, inhabitants were considered defective ("subperson"), in need of intervention and redemptions by "persons." The racial contract assumed that Whites ought to be better off than non–Whites not simply because of the racial contract but because Whites are naturally better than non–Whites morally, cognitively, and physically. According to this thinking, Whites are invented by the racial contract in the modern period. Further, during Europe's hegemony of the Age of Conquest, White supremacy was established by *de jure* (formal, judicial) means. In sum, the racial contract is an exploitative economic and political contract that is enforced through violence and ideological conditioning. We might consider all of the colonized places within the U.S. and in other parts of the world.

Thus, contrary to the common thinking that racism and White supremacy is a

deviation, Mills (1997) contends that it is in fact a naturalized account of the actual historical record. He accuses European ethical theorists of complicity in the racial contract by failing to acknowledge the centrality of racist thinking in the development of the modern world.

Today, white supremacy is a "de facto" reality — a matter of economic, social, political and cultural privilege — composed of the actual moral and political consciousness of White people. According to Mills (1997), Whites act in racist ways while thinking of themselves as acting morally. He outlines the phases of cognition that make this possible: 1) developing concepts that legitimize the racial order; 2) Whites assess how well they are doing by how non–Whites are doing; and, 3) Whites cultivate patterns of affect and empathy for non–white suffering. Evasion and self–deception become the norm because to agree that the "other" is human will turn their world upside down. How else can colonialism and conquest be justified if the "other" is a person just like one's self? The norm Mills describes becomes part of habitual and largely unconscious parts of personal and social patterns.

As the racial contract established the reality of the inferiority of non–Whites there were numerous effects and consequences. Today it is rare to ask questions about the racial status quo. Among Whites, it is rare to ask questions about the racial status quo (as is true among any privileged group: men, the wealthy, heterosexuals, the able–bodied, and so on).The racial social contract erases certain societies and these are now subsumed under the categories "third world" or "developing countries." In the US, we pretend that Whites and nonwhites are equal. Mills (1997) calls this our epistemological ignorance and dysfunction. Epistemological dysfunction results in the failure to grasp the whole system. Its psychological equivalent is denial with the creation of shadow material.

The racial social contract has always been recognized by non–Whites as the real determinant of most White moral and political practice and thus, as the moral and political agreement to be challenged. Even as the social construction of race is acknowledged today, its political foundation remains and thus the **racial contract** continues its whitening process.

Through ethnoautobiographical inquiry about the communities that we belong to, we can repudiate the racial social contract. By withdrawing our consent from the racial contract, we are able to view the realities of **privilege** as well as the great social costs, to *all* individuals and societies. Further, in these questions about communities we begin to interrupt the habit of denying personal and collective shadow material. By making visible how the social contract is racialized and acknowledging the epistemological, political, and moral dysfunction in the modern world,

only then can we begin to re–imagine another world, a different world.

Privilege

Mills' (1997) analysis of the racial contract identifies important sources in White supremacy or White **privilege**. Those who hold privilege are commonly not at all, or only dimly, aware of their privilege, as they can take it for granted. Privilege is the air they breathe; it is a given. In the US, White and male privileges are generally invisible to people identified as white and male. "I think whites are carefully taught not to recognize white privilege as males are taught not to recognize male privilege" (McIntosh, 1990, p. 97). However, privilege is obvious to people in unprivileged or subordinate positions (Morrison, 1992; Smith, 2012)

It is important to become aware of unearned advantages in order to address issues of oppression, and to face shadow or denied aspects of self and/or society. Making the unseen seen is the first order of business. "Describing White privilege makes one newly accountable" (McIntosh, 1990, p. 97). As we have indicated previously, this is a task that can be challenging because of habits that are encoded in the deeper parts of our brain, not to mention family, community and society.

Tim Wise (n.d.) is an example of White **privilege** self–awareness. Wise begins to take responsibility for who he is, and how this might impact others. This responsibility includes the obvious in his role as invited speaker, and how such an invitation is already a function of privilege. Thus, we can add issues of privilege (and lack thereof) to the factors that we are usually unconscious of and yet impact our sense of self, morality, and values a great deal. Seeing and acknowledging privilege in our selves and others enlarges the space for what can be talked about and the choices for intentional behavior.

Through these foundational issues of inequality, the **racial contract** and **privilege** we can see ways in which our sense of self and our membership in various communities is more complex than previously considered. Furthermore, we may develop perspectives that critique society and its various organizations. Sometimes this leads to questions about the legitimacy of certain institutions and even governments.

Legitimation and legitimation crisis

We have touched upon a number of factors or dimensions that allow us to look at societies critically. In one case we may say that a country has a governing structure that is legal, or has legal authority, and it demonstrates that it fulfills its ends (the reason for its existence) successfully. In another case we may discover that a governing structure may have legal authority, but fails to show that it can actually reach the ends for which it purportedly was instituted. For example, does a government provide sufficient education with adequate access for its citizens? Do all citizens have a fair chance at economic success? A critical analysis along the lines mentioned above may lead us to discover that a government has lost its legitimacy, or that its legitimacy is questionable, or even that it may be in a crisis of **legitimation**. When looking at the civil war in Syria that began in 2011, or the 2011 Egyptian revolution centered in Tahrir Square, or the 2013 Taksim Square demonstrations in Istanbul, Turkey, we see peaceful and violent responses that question the legitimacy of the government in power.

In the US, as result of the great recession 2007 – 2009, movements like Occupy Wall Street question the legitimacy of the current governing structure. The resulting discussion about 1% of the population having greater access to wealth and political power raises issues of legitimacy by pointing to an increase in social inequality throughout the country. People often proclaim that Washington is deadlocked and that many citizens do not expect Congress to act effectively. Voter participation in the U.S. is significantly lower than in many other countries, particularly European countries. Lack of voter participation and ongoing demonstrations indicate a loss of confidence, a sense of inefficiency as far as the working of government is concerned. They also indicate economic crisis. Citizens seem to be less motivated to participate in politics. We find that central ideologies of the US are now in question: social mobility and the American Dream. Jürgen Habermas (1975) has written extensively on **legitimation crises** in Western countries. His framework would lead us to believe that the U.S. has entered a crisis in which many citizens do not feel that the governing structure succeeds in reaching its goals and question the legitimacy of the powers assumed in Washington. We have observed both an economic crisis and an ongoing crisis of motivation among citizens. Popular support for the current governing structure has notably decreased. These issues have crystallized in recent years around rights to privacy (and the legitimate extent of surveillance), the banking industry, the use of drone technology, and other issues. Identifying a **legitimation crisis** is an important question where we analyze economic, sociological, psychological, and other data.

When trying to understand controversial social issues, it is important to attempt to separate moral concerns from research evidence. In public discussions these issues commonly get entangled in ways that make it difficult to separate ideological commitments from empirical support for

such commitments. Of course, these issues are not always easy to separate; however, it is critical that we do our best to understand research evidence before coming to conclusions about their meaning. For example, when we talk about social mobility, a first step would be to look at what research shows: what is the rate of upward and downward social mobility? Should a government intervene to increase social mobility? If you think a government should support a high level of social opportunity and mobility, what would be appropriate ways to do so?

Thus, **legitimation** issues have two sides: on the one hand, governments that act with apparent lack of legitimacy; and, on the other, citizens who accuse the governments of being illegitimate.

Interestingly enough **fear** resides on both sides of these **legitimation** issues: governments fear losing power and prestige; citizens fear less economic or social stability.

The role of fear

Within the practices of ethnoautobiography, issues of community place particular emphasis on the healing and undoing of a culture of **fear** that seemingly pervades Eurocentered societies, and especially the United States. Glassner (2009) opens *The Culture of Fear* with the question: "Why are there so many fears in the air, and so many of them unfounded?" (p. xix).

Ethnoautobiography offers many approaches to understanding both why there are so many fears, and additionally why many of them are unfounded. In the context of this chapter about community, one potential reason is the breakdown of the connections and relationships that are part of community. Much of present–day fear seems to be caused by unknowns resulting from the rapidity of technological developments and the breakdown of many hopes and assumptions about the future. Assurances about our place in society seem to be more and more tentative (from jobs disappearing, such as type-setters, to the challenges of retirement plans). Žižek (2013) comments on the 2013 protests in Brazil, Turkey, and elsewhere: "What the majority of those who have participated in the protests are aware of is a fluid feeling of unease and discontent that sustains and unites various specific demands" (p.11). The unease, fear, and discontent is felt not only by protesters, it is the tip of an iceberg that indicates more widespread feelings.

The manipulation of **fear** has a long history in politics because our fear responses are powerful and easily over-ride rationality and careful thinking. If a politician manages to speak to our amygdala, the part of the brain that is central in the process of fear genera-tion, then she or he has a tremendous power over us. Once the amygdala (the palaeo–mammalian brain) has been activated rational thought is easily overrun by irrational responses (think Hitler, think 9/11 — history is littered with examples of irrational behavior in times of real or imagined threat). Interestingly, research has shown that the greater the income inequality in a society, the more distrust among its citizens: inequal-ity and fear are interrelated.

In the riff at the beginning of this chapter, there are two ways that the culture of **fear** is undone. First, on a more immediate level, by learning the story of the places we live in our experience of commu-nity grows. This includes learn-ing about a deeper history, ecologi-cal relationships, culture, politics and so on. That is especially brought to bear in the riff when it turned out that the friends featured in the story have family that live in Nocona, named for Cynthia Ann's husband. Such a rel-atively simple story suddenly builds relationships which are an antidote to fear. Second, however, in the process some of the older "historical" fear is put to rest. Once we begin to know another per-son's story, all the history that shapes them might begin to seep into our story, too. Thus, much of the history of settlement of Texas — which is rife with brutality, conquest, hard-ship, and misunderstanding — is made somehow more plain and accessible when R learned this story about a friend's family. It didn't heal all of the historical harm to the communities involved, but it did make the complexity more human.

Numerous authors have connected the contemporary culture of **fear** with the history of conquest and it's legacy, both in the United States and in US foreign policy (Chomsky, 1988; Davis, 1998). Silko (1991) is one who makes such a connection: "The spirits whisper in the brains of loners, the crazed young white men with automatic rifles who slaughter crowds in shopping malls or school yards as casually as hunters shoot buffalo" (p. 723). By acknowledging the conquest of Texas, for example, and beginning to accept all the terror, anguish, and fear that is a part of it (McMurtry, 2005), we might begin to build more community and lay fear to rest.

Fear may be a central factor that can get in the way of exploring the depths of ethnoautobiography. Some of our questions and reflections may lead us into taboo territory and fear may outweigh the power of our rational insight. And fear may block access to our awareness about certain beliefs and memories we hold. When we run into a barrier or stumbling block (or fear the reaction of someone we are talking to), it is always good to take a moment of pause and acknowledge the power of fear. Awareness of its power, and understanding where it arises from, may allow us to follow our line of questioning toward insights that we find personally more satisfactory.

Communitas

In the previous chapter (Chapter 5) we discussed the hall of mirrors of left–brain dominance, the particular reality of one–dimensional rationality we seem to be stuck in. In the past, cultures had institutionalized ways to open the way to inspiration and for individuals to experience themselves as part of something larger. Our dominant contemporary individualism has made it difficult to attain experiences where we are part of a larger whole (experiences that significantly involve the emotional parts of our brain). Of course, given that humans seem to have evolved to be spiritual beings, the search for such experiences of sacredness and communal bonding has never abated. We can observe this today in various religious and spiritual movements as well as communal events, such as Grateful Dead concerts, election rallies, and even holiday picnics. We seem to have the need to experience ourselves beyond the confines of our individual self, yet in individualistic societies we don't have any traditionally established ways to enter this realm anymore. More often than not we get there by happenstance.

Victor Turner (1969) asserted the importance of the experience of **communitas**. His widow Edith describes it as "a group's pleasure in sharing common experiences with one's fellows. This may come into existence anywhere. [It is] found in festivals, in music, in work situations, in times of stress, in disaster, in revolution, and in nature" (E. Turner, 2012, p. 2). And even war and natural catastrophes can trigger experiences of **communitas**, with profound solidarity, and self–transcendence. People may bond in clamorous processions where intensely masked individuals chase out the winter (as in the European Alps), or in joyous dances around the Maypole celebrating the arrival of spring (as we see to this day in Northern Europe and some pockets of the US), or communal fertility rites that include hilarious mock copulations and births (as in the ritual of the Kukeri in Bulgaria), or in the ecstatic dances of the Sufi traditions. Edith Turner describes her work as "the anthropology of collective joy", the subtitle of her book. Communitas serves to cement social bonds and its ritual experience is the beginning point of religion. It helps us experience love and bonding beyond the confines of our intimate relationships in a larger community. It often also allows us to explore cultural shadow material through ritual enactment in order to release our capacities for ecstasy and connection.

Ehrenreich (2007) traced the "history of collective joy" from its archaic roots, humanity's ancient ecstatic practices, to ecstatic Christianity, carnival and the prohibitions to "dance in the streets". She discusses the repression of experiences of communitas in ancient Rome, the repression during the time of reformation in Europe, the destruction of Indigenous ecstatic rituals during the

periods of imperialism, and its perversion in political spectacles whether during the French Revolution or in Nazi Germany and Mussolini's fascist Italy. The rebellion of the Sixties, the emergence of rock 'n roll with its roots in African ecstatic traditions, and the use of psychedelics are expressions of the persistent desire for ecstatic and social bonding experiences. Communitas entails an alteration in awareness, where participants enter a mild or stronger form of an integrated state of consciousness. Of course, such experiences, in the European view, were appropriate for "savages" but not civilized humans. At best it was legitimate for the lower classes. Ehrenreich (2007, p. 9) notes that "the essence of the Western mind, and particularly Western male, upper–class mind, was its ability to resist the contagious rhythm of the drums, to wall itself up in a fortress of ego and rationality against the seductive wildness of the world".

The capacity for ecstasy and communitas, as research has shown, exists in all of us. Almost all cultures around the world had communal trance ritual at one point or another in their history (Bourguigon, 1973). It is a natural capacity that can be used for good or ill. We have seen it abused in fascist rituals inciting the population to total war or to extract cult conformity from group members. These dangers are particularly present when a society has lost its "cultural container", the traditional rituals, stories, and guidance for interpretation. When we are in an ecstatic state we can become vulnerable to malevolent influences. Politicians of authoritarian regimes often seek this vulnerability and malleability to implement their goals over well–reasoned objections by citizens. Cult leaders thrive on the creation of impressionable states of consciousness to have obedient followers. The general lack of culturally endorsed rituals results in a spiritual hunger among modern individuals that makes them particularly vulnerable to abuse. Clearly, of utmost importance, is whether the behavior among participants and leadership is ethical. Yet, **communitas** can also be an arena where the trickster appears and established boundaries are challenged. For example, carnival and other ceremonies are a time when established mores are suspended for the duration of the ceremony.

Our need for religious, ecstatic experiences will not go away; it seems to be what we have evolved to and it seemingly continues to have an important evolutionary function — for our survival, for our well–being, for our happiness. Indeed, experiences of communitas and **integrative states of consciousness** through ritual seem to be our natural way out of the hall of mirrors we have created for ourselves. Our right hemisphere and the older parts of our brain are of critical importance, from all we can tell, for resolving our contemporary dilemmas. Left brain or one–dimensional rationality alone is insufficient. We need to activate all our internal resources and bring them into our own awareness and into the public arena. Personal and collective rituals, as history attests and anthropology has shown us again and again, provide an opportunity to do this.

Activity

Community Mapping

Draw a map of any of the communities that you belong to. For example, you might begin with where you live (either in a home, or apartment), your workplace, a school or community organization you attend, and perhaps where family or good friends live.

As a second layer, you could add places you visit regularly, whether they are shops, involve entertainment, or are outside. Also, consider the routes that you take to get from one place to the next. Do you drive, walk, or take public transit? Are there communities that you pass through as you move to and fro?

Have the communities you are a member of remained constant, or have they changed over time? Are some communities you belong to temporary, such as schools, or community groups? Is there continuity in some communities, in that have you maintained connections and relationships over time? Is **privilege** and/or **fear** present in any of the communities in which you belong? How does it manifest?

Write a minimum 500–word narrative description about these communities and how you participate with them.

Chapter Summary

Communities have histories and shadows and can be assessed morally. Community shadows include **(in)equality**, the **racial contract**, **privilege** and **fear**. Claims of legitimacy may become questionable when communities or societies do not achieve their own goals. Experiences of **communitas** are important for the well being of a community and remind us that the divine dwells everywhere.

Concept Check

Why is **(in)equality** such an important social issue?

What makes the social contract a **racial contract**?

What is a crisis of **legitimation**?

Why is **fear** such a potent tool in political manipulation?

What is the constructive potential in **communitas**?

Riff

The Soul and People of the Arabic Desert

We would be participating in some extensive training practice of land navigation, or refamiliarizing ourselves with our land–surveillance equipment, when out of nowhere we would be right in the middle of a migrating herd of camels or sheep. I would get out of our vehicles and walk down the line of animals and find a single man peacefully walking behind them. I would work to try and communicate with him hoping that he may recognize even the most basic English I could think of. But the only sense of communication we had with one another was the universal sign of gesturing for drinking water: moving a half–cupped hand up to my mouth. With this motion he smiled and nodded his head "yes!" I ran back to my vehicle and pulled off a few bottles of water to give him. He graciously accepted and thanked me in his own way, as he continued moving through the desert. I walked with him for a while and although we did not speak I felt a unique presence emitting from him. I have not encountered anything like it since those days in the desert, but I suppose the best word to describe it would be the "presence of the divine."

For a short moment walking with this god–like man I was conscious of my own perception of (my)self and the lens that I viewed the world from. I won't say that I fully realized the extent of my diluted perspective of the world that this man reflected in me, but again, subconsciously I was aware of something very profound even though I could not voice it. I stopped walking and smiled at this marvelous being and returned to my vehicle as he continued walking off on some path that was invisible to my eyes.

There were only a few incidents of running into these divine nomads, even though I longed to interact with them on a daily basis. The next time I was fortunate enough to cross paths with a similar being was when we drove in proximity to his home. Again I stopped as he was out walking with his sheep and smiled and waved at our two vehicles out on patrol. I calmly went out to greet him with as many bottles of water and food as I could carry. He gratefully accepted the water but declined the food. His refusal of food came as a huge shock to me. I glanced over at the tiny, shanty structure that he had no doubt assembled out of spare pieces of cloth, wood, metal, and whatever else he found nearby, and thought that surely he must be in need of food. I looked away from his home and back at him. Looking into his eyes, and he into mine, I had an unearthly feeling that he was communicating with me from a place beyond words.

The presence of divinity poured out of his being and called to me like a gateway to another world. Immediately I had the realization that this man possessed a deep, unknowable joy that I had never encountered, let alone even entertained. I had a type of vision or moment of understanding that this sentient being did not have the same outlook on life as I did. In fact, although we walked on the Earth at the same time, we existed in two very different worlds. In this moment of illumination I glimpsed a devotion to a spiritually devoted path that was so close to God, and so alien to anything I had ever experienced, that I had trouble holding all that he was showing me. For this moment I experienced the divine, and my life was forever altered.

***

In *Autoethnography As Method*, Heewon Chong discusses border–crossing which helps Blackhawk understand his experience with the nomadic herders. She suggests that "another possible autobiographical timeline is one that zooms in on border–crossing experiences that occur when you become friends with others of difference or opposition or when you place your self in unfamiliar places or situation" (p. 73). She continues to elaborate on these cultural experiences by stating that they can essentially be instances of "enlightenment."

CB

Notes

Chapter 7
Where am I?
Ethnoautobiography as Gateway to Place

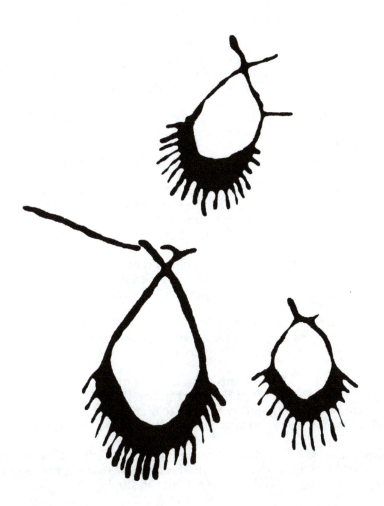

Riff

Coaquannok, The Place of the Long Trees

Dallas, Texas, July 2010

The fireflies last night sent me through time and space
To the one childhood summer I spent with my father's parents
Who lived outside of Philadelphia
Where I had been born about nine summers prior

Born there, yet never really living there
I have still always felt deeply connected to what
The Native Lenni Lenape call, Coaquannok
"The place of the long trees"

Strangely, just before walking in the dusk twilight
Amid the tiny flashes
I had told a story from the last time I visited my birthplace
After my paternal grandmother had died in 1997

Giving myself several days prior to grandmother's memorial
I hoped to locate long forgotten family trails
Because numerous ancestors had lived there
Many Quakers among them

I had just arrived, still laden with my backpack
When I happened by the Arch Street Meetinghouse
It's the heart of the Quakerism in North America

I marveled at the expansive, yet serene, meeting room
The docent, Sandy, noted the twenty foot long benches were cut
From single planks of wood

I told her the reasons for my trip
Precipitated by my grandmother's death
Sandy inquired, and when she realized she had known her
She was no longer an anonymous docent, but old family friend

Sandy led me to an adjacent room with an exhibit of Quaker quilts
She pointed out two in particular that she had learned about
In preparing them for display

One was all white, with intricate stitching, and an equally
Intricate story woven into the fabric
When Sandy had gently washed it
Small black specks had emerged
Fearing she had ruined it

She had actually brought history to the surface
The quilt was made in a Quaker family
Who had refused ginned cotton
Because of its ties to the slavery economy
Using hand–ginned cotton had left seeds, and
A story, behind

Another quilt came from Christiana, Pennsylvania
Where the violence of slavery
Spilled into the White community in 1851
A participant in the so–called Christiana Riot
Had been given this quilt as a gift

This brief visit to the Arch Street Meetinghouse
Had already reminded me that I was connected here
Many of my ancestors had sat on similar benches
Those benches, remnants of the long trees
On those benches many testimonies were heard
About how to live properly in this world
Amongst Native and African, and each other

In my family, the story goes, that the first Chandler, Jane,
Landed at Philadelphia in 1687
My grandmother's maiden — and my father's middle — name is Chandler
While not all Quaker, Chandlers have been a part of settlement
From nearly the beginning

Jane Chandler landed with eight children
After her husband, George, died at sea
Old family papers tell of Jane living in a cave
Along the Delaware River
"The pity was felt towards herself…
Even by the Indians, who brought them gifts"

People from Philadelphia
Can't justify avoiding conversations about the
Interactions among Whites and Africans or
Between Native and settler
Legacies of high expectations and bitter deceit
Are woven into the fabric of my family, too
Contradictions, and all

After I left the Arch Street Meetinghouse
I encountered a statue with a plaque
"This sculpture commemorates Tamanend…
Who resided in the Delaware Valley when
Philadelphia or Coaquannok was established"

The statue includes an eagle with a wampum belt in its mouth
The plaque continues
"This belt recognizes the friendship treaty…
Between William Penn (Mikwon)… and
Other leaders of the Lenni Lenape Nation
It reads: 'to live in peace
As long as the waters are in the rivers and creeks and
As long as the stars and moon endure'"
Perhaps the "lie of the land" endures longer than the treaty

Sources suggest that Penn showed respect for the Lenni Lenape
He learned and spoke Algonkian
Penn was given Lenape and Iroquois names
He advised that disputes involving Natives have
Juries that included Natives

An idealized settlement story such as this one
Would have to be repeated?
For example, Benjamin West's famous painting
Praising Penn's Treaty, and the
Scholars who critique the painting
But not settlement, of course

The lie of the land took root
With the so–called Walking Purchase
When a fair agreement was interpreted
To the settler's benefit and they
Ran away with the remaining Lenape land
In eastern Pennsylvania

***

I was born and raised Quaker
My parents met at Earlham, a Quaker college in Indiana
My mother's family had long since migrated from the Delaware Valley
First to North Carolina, then Indiana in the 1850s
Most of them Quakers

Much of my family entered North America
Through the Delaware Valley
I grew up with family stories of working for justice
I was raised with open–mindedness
In religion and politics, with deep roots

Quaker settlers brought with them many things
Including experiences of persecution
Over 14,000 Quakers were imprisoned for their beliefs
Many lost their lives
Penn's "holy experiment" emerged from this
"world turned upside down"

Primarily a rural movement from northwest England
The Religious Society of Friends
Took root during the English Civil War of the 1640s
George Fox and his Quakers were among many
Radical movements countering Crown and Church

In 1649 George Fox experienced a conversion on Pendle Hill
He gathered people to preach and
Thus began Quakerism, a Christian movement
Encouraging direct personal experience with god
Quakers criticized establishment priests,
Allowed women ministers
They refused to pay tithes, often leading to imprisonment
Religion and politics blended in the Peace Testimony
As pacifism was adopted in 1680

Settling in North America, they embraced Protestant ethics
But believed strongly in plurality, liberty and equality
These ideas made an impression on
Philadelphia, the country, and my own life

As is often the case, interpretations varied
Freedom motivated the critics of human enslavement
Similarly, democracy and privilege meant change
Came at a slow, often contradictory pace

***

On my way to the Philadelphia suburb of Germantown
I felt that contradiction in my whole being
As I made a pilgrimage to the tomb of
Pennsylvania Anti–Slavery Society founder and Suffragist
Lucretia Coffin Mott supposedly at Fair Hills Burying Ground

The burying ground was in a run–down
Neglected Philadelphia neighborhood
I never found her final resting place
But I saw my inherited Whiteness
Looking for a White mother of abolition
All I could see was the legacy of slavery

Yet, German Quakers did produce the first formal
Anti–slavery position in the Western world
In Germantown, in 1688
By 1776 slave holding was banned among Friends

One story tells of Abner Woolman
Brother of Abolitionist John Woolman
Abner's wife inherited two enslaved people, and
Wanted to know how much to compensate them
For the wealth they had created for the family's estate
But there are also stories of Quaker merchants
Fully entwined with the slavery economy
Similarly, Abolitionist Levi Coffin was so frustrated
By the intransigence and reluctance among Quakers
That he formed his own Anti–Slavery Quaker meeting in Indiana

Philadelphia, itself, also embodies these contradictions
The city became a thriving center of Abolition and freedom,
But has an ugly racist history, too
It is a place of possibility, fraught with complication

***

Coaquannok, the place of the long trees,
An intersection of where my ancestors sat
In spiritual reflection, and political upheaval
Those benches mark the Lenape
Presence in the land, and
The presence of the place in my ancestors' lives

Penn's vision for Philadelphia was a well planned
Great green city by the Delaware
Quakers have many naturalists among them
And are well known gardeners
Like my Grandfather Paton and émigré ancestor Thomas Meehan

Three–greats grandfather Meehan
Brought his botanical sense with him from England
After working at Kew Gardens
He emigrated to Philadelphia in 1848
His nursery, and related gardening skills, would become famous
There is a Meehan Street now in Germantown
In his honor

Perhaps these settler ancestors felt relationship around them
Grandfather Meehan wrote about it in botany
Penn wanted to institutionalize fairness with the Lenape
Lucretia Coffin Mott sought to establish justice for enslaved Africans

Following them, I am learning to see with a Native eye
Beginning to notice and speak about relationships
Noticing interconnection, where place, spirit, ancestry come together

This is a beginning, a process of learning about the complexities in me
The connections have always been there
The stories have been telling me who I am, and
Where I come from
Philadelphia, Coaquannok
The place of the long trees
RJP

The following sources were used in this riff: Carter (1996), Merrell (1999), Hill (1991), Soderlund (1985), Coffin (1991), Nichols (2006), Oberle (1997), Capps (1976).

Chapter Outline	Core Concepts	Ethnoautobiographical Perspectives	Expected Outcomes
Coaquannok	There are many stories of place	The better we know a place, the better we know ourselves	Learn practices to reconnect with complex stories of a place
How do we meet the ground?	There is much more to know about the places we live	Place includes history, geography, environmentalism, and more	See the connection between decolonization and stories about place
Remembrance asks questions about place to provide information about presence in place	Shallow presence lacks deep roots in place	Knowledge about places questions and enriches our relationships	Describe the nature of relationship with place
Remembrance of self, other and self–with–other	Remembrance provides access to knowing about people and place	Knowing where one is and who one is are inseparable	Illustrate how remembrance connects people to place
Restor(y)ing weaves new healing stories	Stories can heal and restore relationships between people and place	Restoring a place and telling a story both are healing	Tell ways that restor(y)ing reconnects people and place
Genealogical imagination revives relationships	Genealogy includes place	Relationships with place are highly creative and imaginative	Understand what role imagination has in ethnoautobiography
Where does the self find groundwork?	Ethnoautobiography decolonizes and reconnects human narratives with place	Groundwork has the fundamental goal of building radical presence with the land and deepening our lives	Become familiar with approaches for building groundwork
Millennial twins	Telling the story of self is telling the story of place and its history	Telling ethnoautobiographical stories of place can help heal historical traumas	Experience one particular way of EA storytelling with place

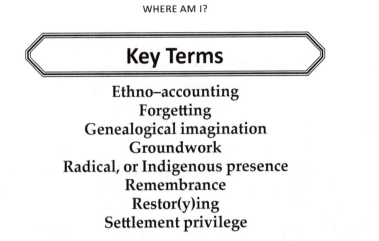

Key Terms

Ethno–accounting
Forgetting
Genealogical imagination
Groundwork
Radical, or Indigenous presence
Remembrance
Restor(y)ing
Settlement privilege

Note: All key terms in this textbook are highlighted in bold and can be found in the Glossary at the end of the book.

Resources Alongside This Chapter

Basso, K. H. (1996). *Wisdom sits in places: Landscape and language among the Western Apache*. Albuquerque: University of New Mexico Press.

Brody, H. (1998). *Maps and dreams: Indians and the British Columbia frontier*. Prospect Heights, IL: Waveland Press.

Deloria, V., Jr. (1991). Reflection and revelation: Knowing land, places, and ourselves. In J. A. Swan (Ed.), *The power of place: Sacred ground in natural and human environments* (pp. 28–40). Wheaton, IL: Quest Books.

Greenwood, D. A. (2009). Place, survivance, and white remembrance: A decolonizing challenge to rural education in mobile modernity. *Journal of Research in Rural Education*, 24(10). Retrieved from http://jrre.vmhost.psu.edu/wp-content/uploads/2014/02/24-10.pdf

Kremer, J. W. (2000a). *Millennial twins: An essay into time and place*. Retrieved from http://online.santarosa.edu/homepage/jkremer/millennialtwins.pdf

Sacred Land Film Project (SLFP). (n.d.). Retrieved from http://www.sacredland.org/

Sarris, G. (n.d.). *The last woman from Petaluma*. Retrieved from http://www.sonoma-countygazette.com/editions/wcg200802_021.pdf

Williams, T. T. (1992). *Refuge: An unnatural history of family and place*. New York, NY: Vintage Books.

The above Riff, "Coaquannok," tells an aspect of R's birthplace. R briefly describes learning more about this place, while also learning about an expanded sense of self. There are two significant lessons from this narrative directly applicable to practicing ethno-autobiography. First, there is always more to know about what came before in the places we live, especially given Eurocentered and settler practices of disconnection and **forgetting**. Second, in the act of opening to know more about a place, you learn more about yourself, your relationships with the place, and all of the people who live and have lived there.

There are many stories told about the places we live, and there are many names for them: history, geography, or environmentalism. For example, Cunningham's (2010) book, *A State of Change — Forgotten Landscapes of California*, provides a clear sense of how the ecology in the state has changed over the centuries, whether the marshes, the grasslands, or the presence converge around forests in the southwestern U.S. including the intersecting issues of heroin trafficking, firewood cutting, forest management and White environmentalism.

Ethnoautobiography does not supersede or even replace these topics rather it seeks to re–integrate fields of inquiry that usually are kept separate. Indeed, ethnoautobiography seeks to fully connect these varied topics with each other and with the places we inhabit. Further, in the process of making connections and integrating experiences and information about a place, the place itself takes on a greater presence in the narratives told.

How do we meet the ground?

Ethnoautobiography about place might be summed up by the question: "Where is the ground, and how do you meet it?" In asking the seemingly straightforward question about where the ground is, we encourage the intention to develop a fuller **ethno–accounting** of *where* we live. Once we begin to be more

> Old, red Manhattan lies, like an Indian arrowhead under a steam factory, below New York.
>
> Stevenson, quoted in Proulx, (2010, p. 163)

of bear, salmon, and condor. Or Kosek's (2006) *Understories: The Political Life of Forests in Northern New Mexico*, shows how race, class and cultural identity fully in relationship with the places we inhabit, as we know more about who and what was there before, as we honor and respect changes that have occurred, then the second part of the question comes to full meaning: *how* do we meet the ground? Is our presence shallow and incomplete? Do we behave as if we have deep roots in place? What is missing from ourselves, our own stories, and the narratives told by and about where we live, and how does that manifest in our lives?

A shallow presence with the land might be exemplified by rampant resource extraction without regard for the future of the people or the place. But

of ethnoautobiography. Using the term **ethno–accounting** does for place, what ethnoautobiography does for personal identity and the stories we tell about our selves and our communities. The prefix *"ethno–"* brings genealogy, history, gender, seasons, spirits, and so on, to narratives about place. Most importantly, it decolonizes and reconnects human narratives with place. Here are a couple of practices by way of example: *Remembrance* and *Genealogical imagination*.

> **Knowledge of places is closely linked to knowledge of the self, to grasping one's position in the larger scheme of things, including one's own community, and to securing a confident sense of who one is as a person.**
>
> Pewewardy, in Clark & Powell (2008, p. 2)

at the same time, we contend that an environmentalism that relegates to the shadows the conquest that brought this land to **amer–european** settlers is shallow as well. Behaving with the cultural arrogance and **settler forgetfulness** to argue that amer–europeans can somehow have deep roots, or be native to a place, without also having to face the underworlds of conquest, whiteness, colonization, and enslavement is similarly incomplete.

Thus, practices that bring forth a two-way relationship with place as evoked in the above quote by Cornel Pewewardy, "knowledge of the self", are a central goal

Remembrance

As briefly mentioned in the conversation pieces in Chapter 0, ethnoautobiography encourages **remembrance**: "self–remembrance," "remembrance of the other," and "remembering self–with–other." Self-remembrance in this context might include the migration stories of how people came to live in particular places, including the other narratives that are intertwined. Thus, in the case of R, as a descendant of White Quaker settlers, what are some of the stories carried along even though having barely lived in Philadelphia? Additionally, what narratives are present when reaching back to ancestral connections there? For Jürgen, how did his migration to the United States impact upon how he is connected to the place that is northern California?

Remembering the other is exemplified by the riff about Coaquannok, especially if there is little personal knowledge of the details of conquest and colonization. This riff, and ethnoautobiographical narrative generally, seeks to integrate stories often relegated to the margins or forgotten. Thus, R's story about Philadelphia is bound up in the history of stereotypically good dealings between English colonists and the Lenape, as well as the equally complex relationships among Quakers and Africans, whether enslaved or free.

Another example of such interwoven histories of place, but from a native northern California perspective, is the Greg Sarris (n.d.) story "The Last Woman from Petaluma":

> Her Indian name, or at least one of her Indian names, the only one any of us know, was Tsupu. She was my great-great-grandfather's mother, or my great-great great grandmother, and, again as far as any of us know, the last native of Petaluma, not the city we know today, but the ancient Coast Miwok village of the same name. Certainly, she was the last to pass down any memory of the place. She was quite young, perhaps fourteen, when she left, beginning what would become a chaotic, wholly incredible journey to find and keep a home in and about Sonoma County. Though the village was abandoned once and for all after the 1838 smallpox epidemic claimed its remaining citizens and though American farmers demolished its large midden, using the centuries-old refuse of decomposed shells for fertilizer, eradicating any trace of the village, Tsupu never forgot it. The last time she visited she was completely blind, yet nodding with her chin to an empty hillside, she said "there," as if she could see Petaluma plain as day, tule huts and fire smoke. (p. 1)

The process and product of this ethnoautobiographical practice is to acknowledge the breadth and depth of stories that are woven into the places we live. Included in these stories must be the family and cultural shadow material associated with forced migration, family upheaval and colonization. Remembering self–with–other might be described as an outcome of these inquiries themselves. In other words, ethnoautobiography fosters relationships with self, other and between the two.

However, such personal inquiry and **groundwork** is not a linear process at all. In fact, the process of **restor(y)ing** a place is ongoing, fluid and flexible. Developing the groundwork upon which to stand requires patience and openness. The stories might begin in an historically significant place that has some family meaning. There could be a family member or ancestor whose experience in some place touches something alive for you, as in R's experience of opening up to Philadelphia. It took the death of a grandparent to return there. There are field trips, library visits, conversations with people, and so on. The entrances are many, and they all lead to a fuller, interconnected experience of place.

Appropriately, an example of ethnoautobiographical writing about place is Annie Proulx's (2011) *Bird Cloud: A Memoir of Place*. Proulx weaves together the place itself, the routes and roots that brought her to it, as well as some of the checkered past that she acknowledges in her quote of Robert Louis Stevenson above. Norman Denzin (2008) makes similar entrées in *Searching for Yellowstone*. He does so in a variety of voices, "part memoir, part ethnography, part performance text" (p. 16) providing precisely the kind of imagined and creative energy to the otherwise sometimes dull and/or harsh material that ethnoautobiographical inquiry challenges.

Seamus Heaney's poem, *North* (1998, p. 11), is an imaginative exploration of a specific place. He explores mythic and historical meanings as he is walking by a particular bay in Ireland, reaching across the sea to the past "pathetic" colonies on Greenland, to Iceland, and remembering the old parliament of the Icelanders, the Althingi:

the hatreds and behind backs
of the althing, lies and women,
exhaustions nominated peace,
memory incubating the spilled blood.

His sense of place is entwined with memories of swords, the Old Norse god Thor, re–imaginings of the past, yet the beginning of the poem states that he "found only the secular powers of the Atlantic thundering".

Genealogical imagination

Ethnoautobiographical reflections on place require visionary approaches, employing genealogical imagination. Not only does the creative act of imagining a relationship with a place and the people who inhabited it break down the Eurocentered habits of disconnection and rationalism, building connection with places also importantly decolonizes **settlement privilege**. If settlement relies on **forgetting** about relationships, genealogical imaginings revive and forge them anew.

At the turn of the millennium, Jürgen (Kremer, 2000b) wrote and essay in which he explored the relationships between his place of retreat, the ecology of the hilly chaparral outside of Red Bluff, California, he spent time in, its history, and what it all means to him. In this piece he makes the local pine trees part of the conversations by inserting their images as "chapters". Their pine nuts were an important source of nutrition for the local

Nomlaki Indians. The Nomlaki and the place both suffered great violence at the hands of European settlement. The closing riff of this chapter contains an excerpt from Jürgen's essay.

Integrity comes down to being true to words and true to its place and time. Severing the connection between language and place signifies a lack of integrity. **Forgetting** or denying or destroying the language of a place is not just murder of people, but it is just as much violence to the plants and animals. Ethnoautobiographical stories about place seek to restore integrity and interrupt the cycles of **forgetting** and violence.

Building and nurturing relationship lies at the heart of ethnoautobiographical inquiry. Such relationship includes the joyful, imaginative, and creative connections with real and imagined people, in the form of biography and autobiography. It also includes the underworld stories, as well. Denzin (2008) writes:

> But remember, the American West was stolen from Native Americans. The reservations are a direct result of the Indian wars of resistance to the nineteenth– and twentieth–century colonial efforts to seize native lands and resources. At this level the story of the West is not a story of native self–determination, sovereignty, and Indigenousness. It is a story of theft, genocide, violence, and tyranny. What kind of postmodern self anchors itself in this cultural space? (p. 207)

We contend it is an autobiographical self. For the purposes of this introduction to **ethno–accountings** of place, Denzin's earlier question could be rephrased: *Where* does some kind of **postmodern** self anchor itself in this cultural space? It is for this reason that in building ethnoautobiography we also simultaneously grow and nurture relationships with place. The place we live, the prior and present inhabitants, the conflicts and renewal that occurred (and still occur), all contribute to the identities that we carry with us each day. Gaining fuller insight into such **groundwork** is an important step toward **radical presence**. Then not only are we clearer about how a **postmodern** self might anchor itself, but also what groundwork we have upon which to stand (Clark & Powell, 2008).

Activity

A Place in Time

Visit a place in nature. Choose a place that feels comfortable, even familiar, to you. You may go to a place close to an urban area (such as a city park, along a creek, or other natural place within a city) or something more remote; it doesn't matter. Spend at least 30 minutes being in the place. Find a place where you can comfortably rest, quiet yourself, and sit.

If it feels safer to have somebody nearby, bring a friend or partner. In this case, once you have selected your spot make an agreement not to talk to each other for at least 30 minutes and to not intrude upon each other's space.

As you sit, develop a sense of the place. See who is all there: trees? flowers? birds? butterflies? water? humans? What are the smells? What are the sounds? What is the light like? What time of day is it? What season is it, and what is the weather like? What does the ground feel and look like under where you are sitting? Do your best to immerse yourself completely in all that you observe, sense and feel.

Once you have a sense of immersion or sinking into the place, imagine yourself backward through time at this place. What was this place like 10 years ago? 20? 50? 100 years ago? 500 years ago? See if you can transport yourself back through time. Precision is not important as much as whether you can successfully get senses of how change may have happened at this place. Is there something that has changed that is more obvious to you, than others?

Write a minimum 500–word reflection about the experience being sure to include three elements:

1. a "natural history" type description of the place, incorporating as many senses (touch, hearing, smell, sight, and even taste) as you can recall;
2. the reflection of the place through time; and,
3. a self–reflection of how it felt to complete the activity. How much effort did it require to do the two parts of the activity? How did it feel? Was it simple, or really difficult

to open up to the place, and to imagine how it may have changed over time? Is this something that you might attempt other places, and repeat as a way to further your experience of a place?

Take 4 pictures (one in each direction from where you were sitting), and attach them to your reflection.

Chapter Summary

There is much more to know about the places we live, suggesting many varied stories of place. Shallow presence lacks deep roots in place, while **remembrance** provides access to knowing about people and place. Stories can decolonize, heal, restore and reconnect relationships between people and place. Telling stories of self includes telling the story of place and its history.

Concept Check

What would or could be included in an ethno–accounting of place?

What are possible results of **restor(y)ing**?

In what ways does **ethno–accounting** decolonize people and place?

How would ethnoautobiography about place be summarized?

Riff

Millennial Twins

I am not of the land where I am writing this, yet I live on it and I am becoming part of it. This is where I have settled. My ancestors are of the European lands; there they and I grew up, yet nothing but storysherds have been passed on to me from those centuries of being in particular places. Taking care of my storysherds may make it possible to reimagine the stories from which they broke away. In order to do so in a sacred way means caring for the sherds first and foremost; taking the risk of picking up the sherds. In renewing a vessel I not only need to visualize its pattern as whole and complete, but I need to give particular attention to the points of breakage, the patterns of the broken lines. This is my obligation as storyteller. Maybe then, later, I can make one story new. And, to be sure, it won't be the story my ancestors handed down to me. But it will.

*****

Driving toward my place of writing retreat I parallel the Sacramento River northward. To the right and left of the interstate are rice paddies; the air is filled with insects and numerous low flying airplanes dispense toxic insecticides. I sneeze frequently as my body reacts to the noxious pollutants entering the car. Before the history of the agricultural abuse of this former vernal lake was possible, something else had to occur. It was the prize winning story making its way across what is now called California.

> The banks of the Sacramento river, in its whole course through the valley, were studded with Indian villages, the houses of which in the spring, during the day time were red with the salmon the aborigines were curing…. On our return, late in the summer of 1833, we found the valleys depopulated. From the head of the Sacramento to the great bend and Slough of the San Joaquin, we did not see more than six or eight live Indians, while large numbers of their skulls and dead bodies were to be seen under almost every shade tree, near the water, where the uninhabited village had been converted into graveyards. (E. G. Lewis 1880, 49, quoted from Goldschmidt 1978, p. 342)

Where I go has aboriginal names that are not recorded on any of the AAA maps I have in my car. Sunsunu, Noykewel, Nomlaka, Waltoykewel, Waykewel, Memwaylaka. Tehemet and Paskenti seem to be the only Nomlaki names that have survived in the forms of the county name Tehama and the town name Paskenta. Where I go is aboriginal Nomlaki territory. Here is how the prize winning story played itself out among them:

> The malaria epidemic of 1833 was the first serious blow Western civilization struck against the Nomlaki. ... There is no evidence of direct contact between Whites and Indians until mid–century ... By 1851 settlers began to request that the Indians be segregated from the White population on a reservation. ... In 1854 ... Thomas J. Henley, established the Nome Lackee Reservation on a tract of 25,000 acres in the foothills of western Tehama County between Elder and Thomes creeks. .. By 1856, with the threat of Indian retaliation dissipated, the settlers became covetous of the "magnificent farm of 25,000 acres" and brought pressure for its abandonment. The Nomlakis and other Sacramento valley Indians were literally herded over the mountain to Round Valley in 1863, the Nome Lackee Reservation having already been taken over by Whites. ... After several years a number of Nomlakis returned to settle in the foothills of their old territory. ...By this time [1930s] there were but three rancherias left ... , with probably no more than a score of households identifying themselves as Nomlaki. (Goldschmidt 1978, p. 342)

I recap to grasp what I have just read:

1833 Unknown number of Nomlakis killed by malaria epidemic brought in by White settlers.

1850 First direct contact between Nomlaki Indians and Whites.

1851 Segregation of Nomlaki Indians from Whites.

1854 Nome Lackee Reservation established.

1856 Pressures for the termination of Nome Lackee Reservation.

1863 Nomlaki Indians and others herded to Round Valley.

1870s Return of some Nomlaki Indians to their old territory.
1930s Three rancherias with half a dozen Nomlaki house
        holds each.
1970s Only scattered descendants are said to survive.

One of the Nomlaki Indians has described the trail of tears to
Round Valley, the Nome Cult Reserve, in these words:

> They drove them like stock. Indians had to carry their own food.
> Some of the old people began to give out when they got to the hills.
> They shot the old people who couldn't make the trip. They would
> shoot children who were getting tired. (Margolin 1993, p. 165)

Before any direct contact the 2,000 plus Nomlaki Indians are
severely decimated by disease brought in by White settlers.
Within fifteen years of direct contact their Indigenous culture is
effectively destroyed. Eighty years after direct contact and one
hundred years after indirect lethal contact only a few households

identify themselves as Nomlaki in their traditional territory. This all began to happen a mere century and a half ago. It continues to be the prize winning story.

Down from where I sit and write I watch the seasonal creek waxing and waning. Every morning the rill flows, ripples, and glitters in the sun. By afternoon I see nothing but a little wet sand and pebbles in the stream bed across which the tracks of my car tires deepen as I come and go. Butterflies still gather for the remaining moisture.

*****

Maybe it is impossible to think of the past millennium without interference of the recency effect. But maybe what has happened during this century is a crystallization of what has built over the previous 900 years, and not merely a perceptual distortion. Summarizing the current century Habermas (1998, p. 73) has pointed to the

> horrifying traits of an age that 'invented' the gas chamber and total war, governmentally administrated genocide and extermination camps, brain washing, the system of government surveillance and panoptic observation of entire populations. This century 'produced' more victims, and resulted in more soldiers killed, more citizens murdered, civilians killed, and minorities expelled, more people tortured, maltreated, starved, and frozen, more political prisoners and refugees than was even imaginable until now. (Transl. J.W.K.)

I notice how I find it increasingly difficult to think about the purported advances Eurocentrism has offered the world. As long as I look at history or the sciences within this story, advances and advantages are visible, despite all the horrors. When I leave the framework of the Eurocentric story even the seemingly most obvious ways in which it has improved on people's lives end up with a question mark. I notice how many advances have come about in order to address ills wrought by the prize winning story itself; to discern what advantages remain when I don't take the story for granted is challenging. The story was not inevitable. Its continuation is not inevitable.

Human rights, such an obvious and persuasive example resulting from European intellectual traditions. Yet: to what extent were
they drafted in order to address human catastrophes precipitated and perpetrated by the Eurocentric traditions themselves?

Historically they were developed in response to atrocities perpetrated as a consequence of actions stemming from Eurocentric
thinking. Not as result of enlightened thinking or of debates about
cultural ethics. Yet, one could not think about the rights of Indigenous
peoples or genocide as legal concepts without the idea of human
rights. And surely they also address imbalances, evil, and excess
created by other cultures than those ensconced in the European
intellectual milieu.

Or the European enlightenment tradition, and so many scientific discoveries. Surely I don't want to toss all of it out as I
confront the horrors Eurocentrism has wrought; but just as surely
the purported and celebrated advantages seem increasingly relative and questionable.

Is it possible to think about their value from a viewpoint outside of or before the prize winning story? How could I do that? Where and how is a healing standpoint possible that allows me to keep its totalizing tendencies at bay?

*****

Raven flies by many times this morning. I am reading stories by a bear. Over the last few days I have begun reading and re–reading all of N. Scott Momaday's works. House Made of Dawn. The Ancient Child. So often, as in the following quote, he beautifully speaks something I feel, like in this case about the place where I am sitting and writing. Reading the quote I react to his male language. I assume that he uses the male gender because he speaks primarily of himself.

> Once in his life a man ought to concentrate his mind upon the re-
> membered earth, I believe. He ought to give himself up to a particular
> landscape in his experience, to look at it from as many angles as
> he can, to wonder about it, to dwell upon it. He ought to imagine
> that he touches it with his hands at every season and listens to the
> sounds that are made upon it. He ought to imagine the creatures
> there and all the faintest motions of the wind. He ought to recollect
> the glare of noon and all the colors of the dawn and dusk. (Mom-
> aday, 1969, p. 83)

Momaday's Kiowa name is Tsoai–ta–lee, Rock Tree Boy (1999). This is in reference to Devil's Tower in South Dakota, a place sacred to the Kiowas, made famous in the movie *Close Encounters of the Third Kind*. According to the Kiowa tale it is a tree stump, scarred by bear claws, tsoai–ta. Momaday is a bear. Much of his writing centers upon bear medicine, including the aspects which are diffi-cult and unmanageable. After reading I drive the thirty–odd miles to town, on my way to the San Francisco Bay Area. After driving for a short while I surprise a bear as I turn around a bend on the dirt road. The bear seems young with beautiful brown fur. It turns and races toward the next bend and plunges down the steep hill. I get out of the car and hear it crashing through the brush. I find the tracks of its galloping and leave offerings in them. A red–tail hawk circles above.

Returning from the San Francisco Bay Area I drive again on the interstate through rice paddies, orchards, and olive groves. Interspersed are several wildlife refuges. I daydream of Native American names on the signposts. In some bi– or multilingual countries I have found bilingual signs, at least in areas where the minorities are the majority. I remember the Gaelic and English signs in Eire; and the Sámegiella and Norwegian signs in Finnmarku in the European Arctic North. I imagine not just seeing the town name Winters on the green sign, but also Liwai. Not just Yolo, but also Churup. Grimes together with Palo. Colusa together with Til–til. Paskenta and Paskenti. Bilingual signs have probably been a contentious issue in most places where they exist. They seem impossible in California or elsewhere in the U.S. where the memory of residential schools is largely suppressed, and where bilingualism is quickly experienced as a threat to the "white" ideal of what makes an American. So I imagine for the sake of remembrance, for the sake of a different story, for the sake of completion and balance.

*****

I return into the hills of Waltoykewel. Easing the car down the hill and across the seasonal creek I notice that my dome tent doesn't quite look the same. In fact, it is rather flat. On the way up I had noticed a tall Towani pine that had fallen across the road, and an entire roof that had been blown off a house. I wonder whether there had been high winds during my absence.

I walk around the pancake tent and notice scratch marks. Even some of the cement bags that I had used to secure the tent had been torn open. Nearby I now notice bags of steer manure ripped open. I walk toward the building and notice clearly visible bear tracks. Parts of the provisional plastic covering have been torn from its sides, with claws marks and muddy swipes identifying the inspector clearly. I take the tent apart to find two flattened mice. The surviving deer mouse scoots downhill.

At night I sit outside and listen to the wind. It is because of the pine trees that I can follow the movements of the wind spirit. At times nothing stirs where I am, yet I hear the wind rushing through a pine tree 20 yards away, rustling its needles.

Now I hear the wind way far in the distance on top of the next hill; I follow its course as it descends downhill through the individual pines, touching trees spaced wide apart, stirring a pine over here into a whisper, then one to the right. The wind's breath moves, fingering the needle bunches, brushing them, prompting them to talk, then moves upward toward me, whispering, now moving more toward the left, then toward the right, snaking uphill. Wind brushes my face, and throws my hair into disarray. Wind teaches me about the lay of the land, its movements. Wind spirit.

*****

A member of the neighboring Wintu tribe has given beautiful words to the process of learning through intimate relationship with place. The elders "learn the earth's secrets by quietly observing. It is a secret language called knowledge that releases the spirit from stone and heals by tone of voice and by changing sickness into elements that flow instead of blocking life" (LaPena, 1999, p.18). This is what it means to follow our original instructions in a particular place and time.

> Sacred names, dreams, and visions are images that connect the bearer to the earth; shamans and other tribal healers and visionaries speak the various languages of plants and animals and feel the special dream power to travel backward from familiar times and places. (Vizenor, 1981, xvii)

This is what seers, seeresses, healers, shamans, medicine people, and Indian doctors did and do. We are at risk in the presence of words. We are in the presence of awesome power. Getting it right is healing, getting it wrong creates imbalance and excess. To be sure, there isn't a singular way of getting it right. There are many ways of balance. Getting it right means being and acting from time, place, and history, roots. All relations. Being present.

Words are sacred. Always. Spirit breath. They have power. Always. They create even when we forget their power. Forgetting it often means creating imbalance, since forgetting the sacred breath and wind in words is imbalance.

JWK

Notes

Chapter 8

Connecting Nature, Self and History

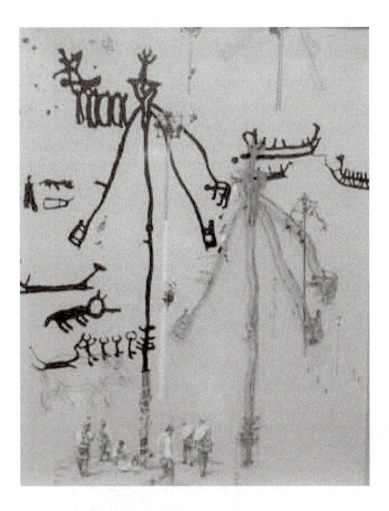

Riff

Timbisha Transformations
Fall 1996

I will never forget talking with Richard, Timbisha Shoshone tribal administrator and member of the Timbisha Land Restoration Committee. He asks me pointedly, "why is reclaiming our homeland in Death Valley such a threat to White environmentalists?" I begin to understand the connection between being an environmental activist and my recent work defending Indigenous conservation. For the first time I glimpse the link between the two and the responsibility I have. It was after this conversation that I first used the phrase "environmentalism as a settler narrative".

If Death Valley is not wilderness as I have learned, how do Whites get away from it all? What is it that we need to get away from anyway? Is it just city life, or is it the wounds of our history? Yet, if we are trying to refresh ourselves by going to someone else's — stolen — homeland that should force us to look ourselves in the mirror.

These contradictions necessitate that I begin to think about how environmentalism is more complex than a simple longing for connection to place. I feel that longing even more deeply as everything is being reclaimed from me. I am stripped of my stolen riches, seeing my poverty of spirit.

I have to go a long way in time and space to rekindle that sense of connection with place. Is it possible to do that here in North America? Is it possible to (re)inhabit the land here, as many deep ecologists suggest? Interactions with place are so complicated now. Why can't I just go camping and not have to worry about all this stuff? Doesn't this muddy the water of progressive environmental agendas? Doesn't this deflect attention away from the urgent tasks of preservation, diluting conservation's power?

This conversation with Richard marks my turning point. Until now most of my work has been learning from Indigenous peoples about their practice of conservation. Richard finally puts the mirror in front of my face to note explicitly that there is a profound connection between the kind of environmentalism that I have been involved with (i.e., deep ecology) and the current crisis facing Indigenous peoples. Indeed it seems to me, as Richard framed it, the crisis faced by the Timbisha was actually worsened by environmentalists, not the other way around. How can I reconcile this within myself? What did this mean for who I was and who I wanted to be? Wasn't environmentalism supposed to be about making the world a better place, and reconnecting alienated people with nature?

RJP

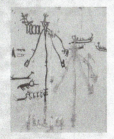

Chapter Outline	Core Concepts	Ethnoautobiographical Perspectives	Expected Outcomes
Timbisha Transformations	People have various relationships with nature	Decolonization of nature and the stories we tell are an outcome of ethnoautobiography	Pay attention to more complex stories about human–nature relationships
Wilderness	Wilderness is often the standard for understandings of nature	We develop more complex relationships with nature by seeing the relationship between history & nature	Provide complex stories of human–nature relationship
Colonial environmentalism	Much environmentalism has unseen roots in colonialism	Decolonizing environmentalism provides openings for more stories	Understand various examples of colonial environmental
Romantic nature	Colonial environmentalism gave rise to romantic approaches	Opening to more complex stories of nature allows for self and cultural awareness	See legacies of colonial and romantic environmental practices
Econobility	Stereotypical measures of good/bad relationships with nature	Self and cultural understandings of econobility aid in transformation	Detail ways econobility impacts environmentalism
Biophilia	Innate human relationship with nature	Biophilia supports close connections with nature	Re–examine relationships with nature
(Re)placing	Restor(y)ing relationships reconnect us with nature	Ethnoautobiography requires histories that reconnect humans with nature	Describe ways relationships with nature are transformed & are transformative

Key Terms

Biophilia
Colonial environmentalism
Econobility
More–than–human
(Re)placing
Wilderness

Note: All key terms in this textbook are highlighted in bold and can be found in the Glossary at the end of the book.

Resources Alongside This Chapter

Abram, D. (2010). *Becoming animal: An earthly cosmology*. New York, NY: Vintage Books.

Albanese, C. (1990). *Nature religion in America: From the Algonkian Indian to the New Age*. Chicago, IL: University of Chicago Press.

Callicott, J. B., & Nelson, M. P. (1998). *The great new wilderness debate*. Athens: University of Georgia Press.

Hames, R. (2007). The ecologically noble savage debate. *Annual Review of Anthropology* 36, 177–190. doi: 10.1146/annurev.anthro.35.081705.123321

Kellert, S. R., & Wilson, E. O. (1993). *The biophilia hypothesis*. Washington, DC: Island Press.

Kitchell, M. (Producer & Director). (2013). *A fierce green fire: The battle for a living planet* [Documentary]. United States: Bullfrog Films.

Mann, C. (2005, September 1). America's pristine myth. *The Christian Science Monitor*, p. 09.

Nelson, M. K. (2006, Fall). Ravens, storms, and the ecological Indian at the National Museum of the American Indian. *Wicazo Sa Review*, 21(2), 41–60. Retrieved from http://www.earthdiver.org/pdf/nelson_WSR.pdf

Takahata, I. (Producer), & Miyazaki, H. (Director). (1985). *Nausicaä of the valley of the wind* [Motion picture]. United States: Walt Disney Home Entertainment.

Waller, D. (1996). Friendly fire: When environmentalists dehumanize American Indians. *American Indian Culture and Research Journal*, 20(2), 107–126.

The previous chapter offered stories and practices to illustrate the importance of sense of place in ethnoautobiography. In many ways, deepening relationships with place also expands into broader connections with the natural world. When faced with all of the implications of the survivance of the Timbisha — as described in this chapter's riff, Timbisha Transformations — R's relationships with nature and people changed dramatically. Indeed, the changes went far beyond the particular locale where

enough in the process of decolonizing our selves. Acknowledging presence in the totality of nature is a monumental undertaking, most especially for those raised in Eurocentered consciousness that relegates nature to the shadows, that denies the amount of connection that might exist between humans and the **more–than–human** world.

In a similar way that the prefix "ethno–" brings fuller, connected and embodied stories to personal autobiography, so do **ethno–accounts** about

> **What in this place needs to be remembered, restored, conserved, transformed, or created? There are many possible answers to these questions, and...such questions can only be pursued in collaboration with the diverse others who inhabit shared spaces.**
>
> Greenwood (2009, p. 5)

the Timbisha reside, far beyond the particularities of that place, to encompass inherited colonial and romantic attitudes about nature. More importantly, this **decolonization** process opened into more authentic connections with the natural world, once the separation fostered by Eurocentered environmentalism began to fall away.

Discussions of place allow us to broaden our scope and grant us an opportunity to increase our awareness of all that surrounds and envelopes us. Sense of place is a helpful starting point because learning the complexity in individual locations is challenging

place begin to more thoroughly decolonize our relationships with nature. This provides entrance into a first consideration for ethnoautobiographical narratives about nature: we suggest that there is no primordial, pristine pure nature removed from human contact whether through story or physical presence. Thus, there can be no question that we are in relationship with the natural world; the only question is the quality of that relationship.

Wilderness

When the term nature is mentioned, most people immediately think of pristine **wilderness** and related imagery. For the purposes of this chapter, a fundamental question to consider is the nature of people's relationships with nature. Can people be in wilderness? If people used to live in a place, can it later be called wilderness? What really is wilderness? How might different cultures view wilderness, or nature?

By acknowledging greater depths of human–nature relationships we have already initiated **decolonization** because there are such strong tendencies within environmentalism that consider **wilderness** as wholly pristine, that is devoid of any human contact. Such approaches are a central and foundational value in various strands of environmentalism. Roderick Nash (1982, p. xi), for example, makes that clear with the statement that "wilderness was the basic ingredient of American civilization", equating the very identity of the U.S. as being dependent on wilderness. However, that there could be different cultural experiences of nature — what Nash is uniformly describing as wilderness — is never explicitly addressed. He goes on to state categorically that such a pure appreciation by environmentalists of nature–as–wilderness is revolutionary.

An irony that is frequently missed, or avoided, is that this basic ingredient does two simultaneously powerful things: first, it places a dichotomy between humans and nature, implying that pure nature is out there, away from human contact or contamination; and second, by suggesting that **wilderness** even existed, environmentalists are claiming land taken by conquest from Indigenous peoples. In other words, when R visited so–called Death Valley, it was as a guest of the Timbisha. The visit was not motivated by any awareness that the place was wilderness. In contrast, most visitors to this and other National Parks regard the place as wilderness, meaning devoid of human presence. If no one knows that these places are actually claimed, inhabited, or homelands by Indigenous peoples, then Indigenous peoples are rendered invisible, at best.

The purpose of an ethnoautobiographical approach to nature is to establish all of the connections and stories, to **restor(y)** our experiences of nature, so that we may have a bigger picture available to us. Thus, a critique of environmentalism that gives a more honest **ethno–accounting** actually makes space for alternative and non–traditional experiences, such as those expressed in the chapter on place and this chapter's riff. Without some awareness of the colonial impact on Indigenous peoples in the U.S. it was very challenging for R to make any sense of what the Timbisha were really saying. Connecting the return of some of their land with environmentalism proved very unsettling. Indeed, many environmentalists were, and still are, threatened by the notion of Indigenous peoples having any claim to National Parks. Ethnoautobiographical stories about nature see beauty and richness in fuller and more complex narratives about nature.

Cronon (1995) assists in developing such greater understanding of our ecological context when making clear the connection between colonial expansion in the U.S. and **wilderness**:

> Thus in the story of a vanishing frontier lay the seeds of wilderness preservation in the United States, for as wild land had been so crucial in the making of the nation, then surely one must save its last remnants as monuments to the American past—and as an insurance policy to protect its future. It is no accident that the movement to set aside national parks and wilderness areas began to gain real momentum at precisely the time that laments about the passing frontier reached their peak. To protect wilderness was in a very real sense to protect the nation's most sacred myth of origin. (pp. 76–77)

The first myth of origin in the U.S. (which have their roots in Eurocentered religion and science) are that humans are separate from nature, and that our presence spoils it. This is codified in the Wilderness Act of 1964 which stated that wilderness "is hereby recognized as an area where the earth and community of life are untrammeled by man, where man himself is a visitor who does not remain." Such a view is purist, over–simplified and very exclusive to the White experience of settlement.

This leads to a second related myth of origin: that **wilderness** is even available because it is devoid of people or the people living there don't matter. Present in the controversies about wilderness is often the assumption that North America was empty of people at the time of European conquest and settlement. Jennings' (1976) challenges such assumptions: "Incapable of conquering true wilderness, the Europeans were highly competent in the skill of conquering other people and that is what they did" (p. 13). In calling land pristine wilderness, environmentalists erase human presence from that land, and when that presence happens to be Indigenous peoples this furthers conquest and settlement.

Indigenous delegates to the Fifth World Parks Congress understand this connection, just as Richard did in the riff: "First we were dispossessed in the name of kings and emperors, later in the name of state development, and now in the name of conservation" (cited in Dowie, 2009, p. xv).

Such direct connections to **colonial environmentalism**, or ecocolonialism, are vital to point out, because it is critical to view nature within the scope of history and the varied cultural experiences that people have with nature. That is, ethnoautobiographical approaches to history, which are the stories told about the natural world, are not simple, or simplistic, natural history. As with place, there are a variety of labels attached to these narratives, and natural history is certainly one of them. As has been shown elsewhere, ethnoautobiography can take many forms, and varied stories of nature are among them.

Colonial environmentalism

The environmental colonialism just described links Eurocentered approaches to the self, other and the relationships between them. Indeed, during the 1980's when mainstream, White environmental groups were being challenged by low–income, communities of color with allegations of environmental racism, it was a Native activist, Winona LaDuke, who brought such Whiteness and racism

ing some differences. Colonial environmental perceptions were predominantly grounded in resource acquisition and use, solidly within a Eurocentered frame. "It is now clear that modern environmentalism, rather than being exclusively a product of European or North American predicaments and philosophies, emerged as a direct response to the destructive social and ecological conditions of colonial rule" (Grove, 1995, p. 486).

While varied Indigenous land use was a reality throughout the Americas, colonists were mostly unable to *even* see this was the case. The experience of nature, as with the Indigenous inhabitants, was one of rapacious consumption, without thought to the long–term consequences of such actions. While the colonial norm was one of violent dominance over the natural world and Indigenous peoples, there were

> There can be no question that we are in relationship with the natural world; the only question is the quality of that relationship.

back to its colonial roots: "the environmental movement...exceeds the charge of contributing to environmental racism and is charged more appropriately with environmental colonialism" (1994, p. 148).

There are two faces of **colonial environmentalism** that are part of the same worldview, even while retain-

nearly always some voices of dissent (Albanese, 1990; Drinnon, 1990). While acknowledging the many complicated outcomes of environmentalism, the expression of care and connection with nature was importantly expressed in the likes of Henry Thoreau, John Muir, Mary Austin, and others. While these environmental and social critics, among others, questioned the dominant relationships between White settlers and nature, they also maintained certain colonial outlooks with nature and Indigenous people.

Romantic nature

Thus, colonial disregard for nature at the beginnings of environmental movements gave way to romantic environmentalism, which forms the foundation of what most people currently associate with environmentalism. Romantic views run a spectrum from support for some measured use of natural resources (roughly termed conservation) to the often, at least theoretical, opposition to resource use of

retain colonial perceptions. Winona LaDuke's comment about environmental colonialism makes this connection. Similarly, this is some of what R addresses in the riff when calling environmentalism a settler narrative. The crux of settler environmentalism is how Indigenous peoples are removed from a landscape, whether literally or in environmental awareness. Only then does it become **wilderness** for Eurocentered environmentalist to protect. This is in keeping with what Cronon describes as protecting "the nation's most sacred myth of origin".

Underlying these themes of colonial environmentalism are implicit attitudes about how Indigenous peoples interact with nature. There are roughly two

> What if thought is not born within the human skull, but is a creativity proper to the body as a whole, arising spontaneously from the slippage between an organism and the folding terrain that it wanders?
>
> Abram (2010, p. 4)

any kind (roughly termed preservation). Romantic views of nature often include the restorative power of **wilderness** for human health as popularized by Thoreau's statement: "In wildness is the preservation of the world."

What is important to understand is that while the more overt colonial period had romantic views of nature within it, so do romantic attitudes about nature

positions: first, is the North–America–as–barren–wilderness assumption, as addressed above. The implication of this for Indigenous peoples is that even if they were here, their numbers probably were few, and they certainly did not have any significant impact on the environment. We could call this the "open–for–the–taking" position based on Jaimes (1992): "Another core tenet of

Eurocentric doctrine is that the invading European population did not really displace anyone in North America because the land was largely an uninhabited vacuum, vacant and open for the taking" (p. 16).

Solnit (1994) critiques such a settler version of the Yosemite story in her *Savage Dreams: Inside the Hidden Wars of the West*:

> [environmentalists want] to imagine this continent as uninhabited and untouched, as a nature made apart from man, and he mourns for the end of its independence (in much the way that earlier writers lamented the vanishing tribes). The implication is either very hostile — that native peoples don't constitute a human presence — or very idolizing — that they lived in such utter harmony they had no effect on their surroundings at all, but either way they don't count. (p, 295)

The second position might be described as the ecological Indian assumption (Harkin & Lewis, 2007; Krech, 1999; Redford, 1990), which suggests that Indigenous peoples are actually destructive to nature and lack any scientific ability to learn from their ecological mistakes. While both of these assumptions are hotly debated and controversial, what matters most for ethnoautobiographical writings about nature is that they both avoid personal and cultural self–reflection. At the center of these critiques are identities bound up in **econobility**, or the notion that people have essential, pure relationships with nature, whether for good or ill. In other words, according to this assumption being econoble means carrying out idealized environmental protection of **wilderness** or nature, in general. While being innoble means that the Eurocentered separation between nature and human is not a part of a culture. Thus, the opposite of being econoble means that the Eurocentered worldview separating nature and humans is not valued.

Econobility

A cornerstone of romantic views of nature are econobility and its companion "playing Indian" (P. Deloria, 1998). Econobility creates criteria whereby stereotypical, primarily Eurocentered environmental agendas are deemed appropriate, such as wilderness preservation, National Parks, animal species protection. Everything else is not environmentalism at all, such as urban gardening, or treaty rights. As explained above, one often invisible outcome of econobility is that Indigenous peoples do not have any rightful place in wilderness, thus justifying their removal. Econobility sets up White environmentalists as being the true arbiters of what ecology is, and acts as the enforcer of who measures up.

In an environmental context, **Playing Indian** is the ironic act of environmentalists claiming to be somehow Native to a place, making them the rightful caretakers, instead of the Indigenous peoples who have a long history with specific places, that are now called wilderness by environmentalists. Econobility ensures that Indigenous peoples have no right to the land, as the assumption is that they will not adequately protect nature or even destroy it. This makes way for White environmentalists to be the rightful guardians and protectors of the land, thus creating themselves in the ideal image of a stereotypical Indian. Nadasdy (2005) identifies the dangers and confusion this assumption holds.

> Part of the reason the debate over ecological nobility has been unable to transcend its imperialist roots…is that scholars have focused on only half of the problem. While they have painstakingly examined the cultural assumptions underlying Euro–American notions of "Indigenousness," they have paid relatively scant attention to the equally problematic assumptions about "environmentalism" that underlie the image of ecological nobility. (p. 293)

An ethnoautobiographical approach to nature emerges to pay greater attention to all the assumptions that underlie environmentalism, nature, and **wilderness**.

It is through the practices of ethnoautobiography that we can begin to bring these stories together once again, and see how thy weave together to make us whole. Kremer (2000) in "Millennial Twins" addresses this directly,

> We need to remember ourselves as natural history, we need to remember ourselves as land, as stars, we need to remember our stories, we need to remember ourselves as plants and as rocks. Such memory can heal us from participation in an arbitrary count foisted upon ourselves and others. It may heal us all the way to the roots of our origins. And then we may see, then we may hear, and all our relations may assist us. Our grievous sounds may turn to song, and song may help see and heal. It just may help us pay attention. (Section 47, p. 41)

That is the irony of critiques of colonial and romantic environmental stories and the beauty of ethnoautobiographical approaches to nature and place. Rather than elevate one narrative about nature to be the only true one, we seek to include as many stories as possible with the goal of bringing humans and nature closer together and to create healing conversations in community. For at the heart of all this is the deep longing that humans have with the **more–than–human** world.

Biophilia

Consistent with the decolonizing work put forth in this book, finding the histories of nature within our own stories provides expanding awareness of the relationships that have always been there, relationships many people are disconnected from. As Kellert (1993, p. 20) relates, "The biophilia hypothesis proclaims a human dependence on nature that extends far beyond the simple issues of material and physical sustenance to encompass as well the human craving for aesthetic, intellectual, cognitive, and even spiritual meaning and satisfaction." Ethnoautobiography is motivated by a similar belief.

Nature provides a grand scale of our sense — and for our senses — of who we are in the scheme of things. Jürgen (Kremer, 2000) notes these connections when he writes that "Words originate from a matrix of place and time, from landscape, myth, and history" (Section 5). Abram (1996, 2010) describes this same relationship in both, *The Spell of the Sensuous,* and *Becoming Animal.* In keeping with our suggestion that all people are and have been in relationship with nature, Abram (2010) writes:

> What if thought is not born within the human skull, but is a creativity proper to the body as a whole, arising spontaneously from the slippage between an organism and the folding terrain that it wanders?

> What if the curious curve of thought is engendered by the difficult eros and tension between our flesh and the flesh of the earth? (p. 4)

This linkage is alive and well in ethnoautobiography as the process of decolonizing the self creates ripple effects into the manner in which we view nature and can be in relationship with it. We call this **(re)placing**, putting our selves back in nature and, in turn, transforming ourselves.

(Re)placing

We have a chapter on nature in addition to place in this book to make abundantly clear that a purpose of ethnoautobiography is to nurture many conversations with and across long separate disciplines and philosophies. In this process nature and history meet in order to provide a broader context for the events and beings that contribute to our stories of self, community and culture. Thus, overviews such as Ponting's (1991), *A Green History of the World,* and Schama's (1995), *Landscape and Memory,* provide valuable context for understanding the rise of Eurocentered environmental philosophies and practices. The healing, through remembrance of many ecological stories, is what we call **(re)placing**. It is the act of consciously weaving ourselves back into nature, seeing the ways that we participate with nature in all of its manifestations, down through time to the present moment. More critically engaged are Merchant's (1980), *The Death of Nature*, and Cronon's (1983), *Changes in the Land*. Ethnoautobiography encourages conversations across boundaries populated by these, and many other works. These stories follow the arc of long cycles of time, as well as the shorter historical periods of cultures and individuals. But all of these stories of nature must be present.

Activity 1

Ecological Research

Choose an ecological issue that is important and has meaning for you. Describe, with as much complexity as possible, how you conceive of it. This includes popular or familiar positions about the issue, the history of it, different parties to it, controversies associated with it, and so on. For example, animal rights campaigns against using fur. Important aspects to address would be the history of using fur in clothing cross–culturally, how different societies and economies view this, and the ways this may have changed historically. Be creative in the way that you present the issue, using images, multimedia, and multiple sources of information. Further, you should also address if there are issues raised in this chapter related to the issue, such a as **colonial environmentalism**, **biophilia**, and so on.

This may be completed in a 500–word written reflection, or shared as an oral presentation with others.

Activity 2

Local Nature

Identify an ecological issue near where you live. This issue should be visible in the landscape and community. You will need to be able to take pictures of it. What are some questions you have about the issue? For example, how is trash, recycling and composting handled in your community? Is solar and other alternative energies present and supported? Is there a predominant cultural, class, and gender makeup of a particular organization that focuses on ecological issues?

Document what you see, then look at the various factors or dimensions that are part of the this specific ecological issue. Feel free to draw on the literature or to interview people to understand the issue as best as you can in all its complexity.

How does the history of place effect this issue? Walk around the location, investigate, take photos, create art — do what helps you to document, understand, and ask questions.

This may be completed in a 500–word written reflection, or shared as an oral presentation with others.

Note: If you are completing these activities on your own, and do not have an organized group to do oral presentations for (such as in a classroom, community organization and so on), it is encouraged that you present the work you are doing to a friend, family member or spouse to experience sharing your process in oral form.

Chapter Summary

Ethnoautobiographical approaches to nature pay attention to assumptions that have been inherited from colonial and romantic views. By connecting nature, history and culture we can restor(y) relationships between people and nature. Such decolonization requires stories about self and nature to be seen, heard and healed.

Concept Check

Why do more complex stories of human–nature relationships foster decolonization?

What are two characteristics of romantic and/or colonial views of nature?

Name two characteristics of how **econobility** impacts environmentalism.

What are the possible effects of **Playing Indian** in an environmental context?

Describe **biophilia** and offer one example of its presence in your life or society.

What are some elements of **(re)placing**?

NOTES

Chapter 9
History — Memory and Imagination

Riff

To Sand Creek
August 2010

While Jenny and I were nearby, it really was out of the way. There aren't many who would just happen by the Sand Creek Massacre National Historic Site. The eight–mile dirt road would ensure that. And though the road was long, we were silent. Perhaps the length of the road and the silence were related. More than once I thought about saying that it was too far to go! It is difficult to name the many emotions that swirl through you at a time and place such as this: sorrow, guilt, and shame. Then there was the weather: it was over 100 degrees. But when the ranger suggested we drive closer, we declined. It seemed appropriate to walk. And walk we did, again in near silence. As we walked, I thought of other such places, and wondered about witnessing the horror of the Nazi death camp Auschwitz, someday.

As we approached the marble memorial, the weight of the agony and suffering was too much to bear and I wept. It may have been for the actual event all those years ago, and also the accumulation through the generations. For many years I have known of this place, read about it in books. Now I was here: not in time, but in place. The place still held the wounds, the sorrows. When I looked at the many offerings left at the memorial, I noticed a flag. Looking more closely, I was amazed to see that it was from Poland, the location of Auschwitz. I guess I'm not the only one who feels a connection between these places.

When we returned to the visitor center, we spoke with the ranger some more. We began to talk about the potential for healing the place holds. She told us about an annual run Native youth make to heal the place. Then she said that descendants of soldiers have visited and some say, "Sorry." We talked about trauma being passed through generations of victims, and perpetrators.

RJP

Healing

Though the Sand Creek Massacre has long passed, memories live on. Many Cheyenne and Arapaho return here to pray and pay tribute to ancestors who both perished and survived that dreadful day.

Ever resilient, the Cheyenne and Arapaho nations of today number in the thousands. Many reside in communities in western Oklahoma and on reservations lands near Ethete, Wyoming and Lame Deer, Montana.

Sand Creek Massacre National Historic Site reminds us not only of the atrocities that occurred here, but those that continue to be inflicted on cultures throughout the world. It is a place to rest torments of the past, but moreover, to inspire us to keep them from happening again.

Chapter Outline	Core Concepts	Ethnoautobiography Matters	Expected Outcomes
To Sand Creek	Healing historical places	Sand Creek is insufficiently represented in textbooks with unresolved issues for descendants	Understand why Sand Creek continues to be an issue for society
At the intersection of the personal and the historical	Family stories & photos carry history	History has a psychological impact & shapes our sense of self	Ability to discern in family stories & photos how the personal & historical specifically intersect
The history I did not read	Official histories neglect important aspects of historical events	Textbooks generally give an incomplete view of history to students	Awareness of issues that may not be part of official history
Radical history is multivocal	Accurate historical accounts require multiple voices	Validating suppressed voices supports genuine multiculturalism	Inclusion of historical voices previously unheard
Empathic and well–imagined memories	Multivocal histories require accuracy, empathy, & imagination	Neglected history continues to have social & individual impact	Visualize multivocal histories & understand the complexity of history

Key Terms

Multivocality

Note: All key terms in this textbook are highlighted in bold and can be found in the Glossary at the end of the book.

Resources Alongside This Chapter

Consedine, R., & Consedine, J. (2005). *Healing our history: The challenge of the Treaty of Waitangi* (2nd ed.). Auckland, New Zealand: Penguin.

Kelman, A. (2013). *A misplaced massacre: Struggling over the memory of Sand Creek.* Cambridge, MA: Harvard University Press.

Patel, S. (2010). *Migritude.* New York, NY: Kaya Press.

Regan, P. (2010). *Unsettling the settler within: Indian residential schools, truth telling, and reconciliation in Canada.* Vancouver, Canada: University of British Columbia Press.

Reid, F. (Producer), Hoffman, D., & Reid, F. (Directors). (2000). *Long night's journey into day* [Documentary]. United States: Reid–Hoffman Productions.

Tutu, D. (1999). *No future without forgiveness.* New York, NY: Doubleday.

Zinn, H. (n.d.). *What is radical history?* Retrieved from http://www.historyisaweapon.com/defcon1/zinnwhatisradicalhistory.html

At the intersection of the personal and the historical

In the opening riff, "To Sand Creek," we glimpse how unresolved history can have a lasting effect on people and society. These implications exist for families, as well. Can we visualize what our parents or grandparents lived through remember the atmosphere of your childhood. The dress or coat grandparents are wearing may indicate the social mores of the time. A military uniform may remind of a war. Annette Kuhn (2002), in her book *Family Secrets*, uses photos to explore both family and cultural history. She comments:

> In the oral tradition, the mythic origins of tribal people are creative expressions, original eruptions in time, not a mere recitation or a recorded narrative in grammatical time.
>
> Vizenor (1984, p. 7)

as children? Perhaps answers to such questions can be found by collecting stories from our relatives.

Following these inquiries further, we consider the history of the place(s) where we grew up. In so doing, we consider both what the history books describe, and what stories may be alluded to, but can't be found in the textbooks. How has the population of your community changed over time? Searching for answers to all these questions will not only enrich our understanding of how we came to be who we are, but it will also enrich our historical understanding. What might have seemed remote and dry may find life in the stories of relatives or the remembrances of people recorded on film.

Photos can be helpful in remembering our own story and help family members remember stories. They may help you

Memory work can create new understandings of both past and present, while yet refusing a nostalgia that embalms the past in a perfect, irretrievable moment. ... It demonstrates that political action need not be undertaken at the cost of the inner life, nor that attention to matters of the psyche necessarily entails a retreat from the world of collective action. (p. 10)

Kuhn here acknowledges and emphasizes the importance of our personal psychology for our actions in the world.

One example is a photo of herself as a little girl: "To mark the Coronation of the Queen, my mother made me a special frock; and on Coronation Day I was photographed wearing it" (Kuhn, 2002, p. 70). She then looks beyond her personal experience (a memory of sickness, because she had bronchial pneumonia at the time) to the larger cultural meanings:

> This photograph of a little girl in her Coronation Day outfit belongs to none of the usual categories of the formal family photograph. Rather, it calls to mind other sorts of formal photograph — the soldier in uniform, for instance, or the school portrait ... Even if destined to have no currency beyond family album or mantelpiece, a ceremonial image may none the less voice a profound desire not merely to be witness to, but actively participate in, rituals through which a recognition of some collective destiny, a social sense of belonging, is sustained. (p. 73)

The pose we see in a photo can be indicative of the times, the way people are grouped (formally arranged like in a Velasquez painting or people standing more casually next to each other). The photo from "the old country" may tell us something about nostalgia or persecution or conflict. The car in a photo may help us see how well our ancestors fared in past historical times.

Jürgen grew up with family photos of beautiful Florida sunsets amidst images of his father as a prisoner of war in Florida. These photos held the memory of war survival, the escape from Nazi dictatorship through the capture by the US military in Africa, the tropical beauty inspiring fond memo-ries of comradeship. Hardship, intimacy, and hope were evoked when they were talked about. The history of prisoners of war during World War II is commonly not known among Americans, yet it inspired not only his father, but also Jürgen.

The history I did not read

Every country has an official or primary version of history. This version ends up in school textbooks and gets recounted in public celebrations. However, this dominant voice usually neglects experiences that do not quite fit this official version. History, once we scratch the surface of its public version, becomes multivocal and we see that it is actually composed of many voices, identities, and stories that are woven together. History, like society itself is not homogeneous, despite presentations as such ("We Americans", "We Germans", etc.). Sarris (1996) writes about this from a personal perspective:

> Who I am as a writer, as a person, is someone continuing the conflict, the coming together, of histories, cultures. My education and training as an academic and writer only add voices, inner disputants, to a world of multiple voices. ...What I hope to have done is provide a way for us to start talking interculturally and interpersonally about what is in fact intercultural and interpersonal. (pp. 37–8)

Shailja Patel (2010) addresses multi-vocal history powerfully in her piece, "History Lesson", (pp. 15–19). She describes her struggle with the information from textbooks at school and information she wasn't taught at school. She contrasts throughout what she learned and didn't learn. Reading the entire poem is revelatory. Here are a few excerpts:

Less than twenty years before I was born, there was a gulag in my country. I know nothing of it until 2006.

This is the history I learned in school (Standard Three to Standard Five, Hospital Hill Primary School, Nairobi).

The first man and first woman were Gikuyu and Mumbi. They gave birth to the nine clans of the Kikuyu. The Mugwe was the leader who parted the waters, long before Moses, and led his people to freedom. Koitalel arao Samoei predicted the coming of the white man and the railway (a long snake, spitting fire). He led the Nandi people against the first British invaders. Waiyaki wa Hinga, paramount chief, went unarmed to a supposedly friendly meeting with British Officer Purkiss. He was killed!

We scribbled Purkiss Pig–Face into the margins of our textbook. We burned with the righteous outrage of nine–year–olds. (…)

The British incarcerated, tortured, and murdered approximately 25,000 Kenyans. Men, women, and children. More than a million Kenyans were detained for over eight years in concentration camps — barbed wire villages where forced labour, starvation, and death were routine

This is the history we read in school. (…)

Patel then explores other aspects of Kenyan history not learned at school. In the middle of the poem she quotes President Kenyatta saying "Let us agree that we shall never refer to the past", a stance taken by many politicians in respect to a problematic or traumatic past. Patel then reveals the past existence of concentration camps in Kenya.

This is the history we didn't read...

The white officers had no shame. They would rape women in full view of everyone. Swing women by the hair. Put women in sacks, douse in paraffin, set alight.

They burned us with cigarette butts. Forced us to walk on hot coals. (…)

In April 1956, Britain's Sunday Post ran an interview with Katherine Warren–Gash, the officer in charge of Kamiti women's camp. She said:

Confession and "rehabilitation" of women in the camp is proving better than a course of beauty treatment! The women arrive sullen, sour, unpleasant, downright ugly. But after confession and rehabilitation, many of them become really pretty.

The title of this chapter — "History—Memory and Imagination "— points to the fact that history is constructed, as Patel's poem powerfully illustrates. The history we learn in school curricula or in any history book is a particular story that is being told and it can be quite a way off from what could be called inclusive or objective. The California school curriculum, for example, requires teaching about the history of the Spanish missions. Commonly such teaching does not include discussion of their impact on the local Native American tribes. The Natives were condemned to forced labor and became serfs or slaves. The death toll among the tribes was disastrous. This is one of the shadows of public California history. Jack Norton (in Bastien et al., 1999, p. 14) notes:

California, for example, passed what was euphemistically called "The Act for the Governance and Protection of California Indians" in 1850, but most historians call it the Indian Slave Law (Heizer 1974). By that law Indian people could be sold into slavery for varying periods, usually from 20 to 25 years. Then in 1860, the California legislature made it easier for slave hunters, and by 1860, 4,000 Indian children had been sold into slavery. Indians were also denied protection by the law. They could not bring any charges against a white person until the 1890s. In addition, thousands of Indian people were killed outright. Professional killing squads formed by citizen groups were funded by the state for the sole purpose of murdering Indian people. In fact, two of California's governors, Peter Burnett and John McDougal, called for a war of extermination against the California Indians (Carranco and Beard 1963).

We find similar denials of Indigenous voices in Scandinavian countries. The history of the exploration of the Nordic countries commonly does not discuss much about the impact on the Sámi, the Indigenous people of the Arctic European North (ranging from prohibitions to speak the Sámi language and missionization, to torture with electro shock therapy, etc). Nearly every country has aspects of a denied history, whether it is the Armenian genocide in Turkey or the right–wing involvement of Zen Buddhists in Japan.

When we try to make the memories we carry more complete we are challenged to include voices that frequently are excluded from the dominant narrative, i.e., from the history books that are used in government institutions.

When we add voice and make history multivocal we begin to overcome the divides between us and them and to empathically imagine and understand the worlds of others. Instead of a singular authoritative textbook voice we now develop and begin to listen to a multiplicity of voices.

The Truth and Reconciliation Commission in South Africa was a society–wide attempt to bring in neglected voices, to explore cultural shadow material, and to heal a historical trauma. "The TRC was a key part of the negotiated compromise that permitted the transition from racial dictatorship to democracy by providing amnesty for perpetrators of apartheid–related human rights violations so long as they publicly acknowledged their deeds and named names" (Statman, 1999, p. 40). It was not necessary for people "to feel contrite or even to regret his or her crimes, so long as the truth of the matter would emerge". The profound witnessing that occurred did have a healing effect, yet the residual structural and ideological residues of apartheid need continued attention and exploration. The Commission can be seen as a model of how very difficult historical issues can be addressed and pave the way toward reconciliation.

Radical history is multivocal

Striving for "radical presence", i.e., making ourselves present to the current moment and to what went before, to the present and past, includes radical history (Zinn, n.d.). The term radical, or going to the root, implies a search for a more complete view of history. While seeking completeness suggests something may be incomplete, it also can produce a critique of what dominant historical narratives present. This suggests an inclusion of voices insufficiently — or not at all — heard, producing a history of many voices.

Becoming radically present makes us aware of the pieces we have disconnected or dissociated from, whether in history or other areas of our lives. Thus, developing critical histories requires understanding how the victims of history are impacted. Radical histories investigate the biases and interests that are represented by governments and that lead to the perpetration of social ills (instead of seeing them as neutral and benevolent).

In order to write successful ethnoautobiographies we need to develop empathic historical imagination. This way we can work our way through feelings of guilt and shame and begin to heal history by understanding traumatic events, witnessing them, and taking responsibility. This opens the possibility of a different sense of our selves and a different quality of action in the world.

Empathic and well–imagined memories

Ethnoautobiographical writing restores the creative nature of understanding our lives. Autobiographies and memoirs are life stories that may or may not, depending on the life and work of the author, address the various dimensions of ethnoautobiography. When the French feminist thinker Hélène Cixous (1997) writes about "rootprints", she describes what can be considered the beginning point of an ethnoautobiographical inquiry:

> What constitutes the originary earth, the native country of my writing is a vast expanse of time and lands where my long, my double childhood unfolds. I have a childhood with two memories. My own childhood was accompanied and illustrated by the childhood of my mother. The German childhood of my mother came to recount and resuscitate itself in my childhood like an immense North in my South. With Omi, my grandmother, the North went back even further. Consequently, although I am profoundly Mediterranean of body, of appearance, of jouissances [pleasures], all my imaginary affinities are Nordic. (p. 181)

The "Albums and legends" chapter of her book, from which the above quote is taken, touches upon numerous themes that could be points of departure for ethnoautobiographical writing. In this autobiographical statement she anchors the creation of her feminist critical presence to the "originary earth," or native countries of her hybridity.

Paul John Eakin (1985) has pointed out:

> Adventurous twentieth–century autobiographers … no longer believe that autobiography can offer a faithful and unmediated reconstruction of a historically verifiable past; instead, it expresses the play of the autobiographical act itself, in which the materials of the past are shaped by memory and imagination to serve the needs of present consciousness. Autobiography in our time is increasingly understood as both an art of memory and an art of imagination; indeed, memory and imagination become so intimately complementary in the autobiographical act that it is usually impossible to distinguish between them in practice. (pp. 5–6)

Autobiography in our time is increasingly understood as both an art of memory and an art of imagination.

Eakin (1985, p. 6)

Ethnoautobiography is in this sense a particular act of the imagination that strives to overcome modern restrictions. In so doing, it re–imagines a tribal or native sense of self–actualization and **sovereignty** as it investigates critically and self–critically "the needs of present consciousness." It engages with historical events critically and imaginatively. In the process it may generate playful openings that interrupt the seemingly self–destructive forces of modernist limitations in a global world where imagination rarely seems to have roots. It validates and stresses the importance of each individual member of a social body or community. Ethnoautobiography shows the psychological importance of historical events and how history is part of each one of us.

In her poem Eastern War Time, Adrienne Rich (1991) illustrates that such historical imagination, if acknowledging complexity and hybridity, is likely a far cry from a romantic return to roots. In this poem, she powerfully acknowledges difficult and shameful parts of history and makes them a part of herself and, as we read the poem, they become a part of our selves: we become the woman bargaining for a chicken; we are waiting for a gas mask.

Memory says: Want to do right? Don't count on me.
I'm a canal in Europe where bodies are floating
I'm a mass grave I'm the life that returns
I'm a table set with room for the Stranger
I'm a field with corners left for the landless
I'm accused of child–death of drinking blood
I'm a man–child praising God he's a man
I'm a woman bargaining for a chicken
I'm a woman who sells for a boat ticket
I'm a family dispersed between night and fog
I'm an immigrant tailor who says A coat
is not a piece of cloth only I sway
in the learning of the master–mystics
I have dreamed of Zion I've dreamed of world revolution
I have dreamed that my children could live at last like others
I have walked the children of others through ranks of hatred
I'm a corpse dredged from a canal in Berlin
a river in Mississippi I'm a woman standing
with other women dressed in black
on the streets of Haifa, Tel Aviv, Jerusalem
there is spit on my sleeve there are phone calls in the night
I am a woman standing in line for gasmasks

I stand on a road in Ramallah with naked face listening
I am standing here in your poem unsatisfied
lifting my smoky mirror (p. 44)

Here the awareness of history, myth and identity are, indeed, not three separate matters, but are three aspects of one human being. They are the **remembrance** of storytelling that displaces nostalgia for essentialist origins. Ethnoautobiographical inquiries into roots and origins assume such multiplicity, **multivocality**, or plurality in our beginning points. Their critical celebration in imaginative stories creates the potential for native presence.

The crossblood Anishinaabe author Gerald Vizenor (1984) asserts this anti–essentialist approach from a native perspective:

> The woodland creation stories are told from visual memories and ecstatic strategies, not from scriptures. In the oral tradition, the mythic origins of tribal people are creative expressions, original eruptions in time, not a mere recitation or a recorded narrative in grammatical time. The teller of stories is an artist, a person of wit and imagination, who relumes [illuminates] the diverse memories of the visual past into the experiences and metaphors of the present. The past is familiar enough in the circles of the seasons, woodland places, lake and rivers, to focus a listener on an environmental metaphor and an intersection where the earth started in mythic time, where a trickster or a little woodland person stopped to imagine the earth. The tribal creation takes place at the time of the telling in the oral tradition; the variations in mythic stories are the imaginative desires of tribal artists. (p.7)

Adrienne Rich writes, "I sway in the learnings of the master–mystics ... I have dreamed of Zion ... I have dreamed of world revolution." Keeshkemun, an orator of the Anishinaabe crane totem, proclaims to the English colonizer at the beginning of a resistance speech: "I am a bird who rises from the earth, and flies far up, into the skies, out of human sight; but though not visible to the eye, my voice is heard from afar, and resounds over the earth." His speech was "strategic, diplomatic, and literary, evidence of native transmotion and survivance" (Vizenor 1998, p. 120) — a deliberate act of defiance and native self–affirmation. Thus, the presence of trickster figures, *naanabozho* in Vizenor's writing or Loki in the Old Norse stories, is an inevitable and mandatory ingredient in ethnoautobiographical creations.

Remembering excluded voices from the authority of government approved history textbooks evokes the trickster. In this process, we are transformed and cannot continue to be who we once were. When we are

present to the multiplicity of historical voices and have the courage to
witness them there is no telling what
may occur. Importantly, this opens us
to our creative potential for different
and responsible action in the world.

Activity

Making Pilgrimages

Conduct research about a place in the United States where it would be appropriate
to make a pilgrimage as a consequence of White settlement, violence, genocide,
slavery, etc. Additionally, this may be a place near where you live, in which you can
travel to. If this is possible, it is highly encouraged, especially if you are able to do so
with a group of people, whether other students, friends, family members and so on.

The place must have general cultural significance (such as local Native American
history, immigration points, local African, Asian, Latino American history, sites of
genocide, internment or concentration camps, etc.). In your discussion, whether in
written or oral form, be sure to include the following: the location, the reason for
choice, a brief history of the place, any current activities that take place at the site, and
organizations or groups that are involved in those activities at the site.

This may be completed in a 500–word written reflection, or shared as an oral presentation with others.

Note: If you are completing these activities on your own, and do not have an organized
group to do oral presentations for (such as in a classroom, community organization
and so on), it is encouraged that you present the work you are doing to a friend, family
member or spouse to experience sharing your process in oral form.

A select list of resources with Online information:

African Burial Ground, New York City (http://www.nps.gov/afbg/index.htm)

Angel Island Immigration Station, SF Bay Area (http://www.aiisf.org/)

Indian Country Diaries: California Missions and Genocide (http://www.pbs.org/indiancountry/history/calif.html)

Indian Island Candlelight Vigil, Wiyot Tribe, northern California (http://www.wiyot.com/cultural-activities)

Manzanar Relocation Center, California (http://www.nps.gov/manz/index.htm)

Sand Creek Massacre National Historic Site, Colorado (http://www.nps.gov/sand/index.htm)

Toni Morrison Society, A Bench by the Road Project (South Carolina, Ohio, Mississippi) (http://www.tonimorrisonsociety.org/bench.html)

Tulsa Race Riot, Oklahoma (http://digital.library.okstate.edu/encyclopedia/entries/t/tu013.html)

Washita Battlefield National Historic Site, Oklahoma (http://www.nps.gov/waba/index.htm)

There are many other places that are not "official" historic sites, but are very important and have lots of information available. For example, the Wounded Knee Massacre site in South Dakota, the Quanah and Cynthia Ann Parker tomb in Oklahoma, and so on. Be creative.

Chapter Summary

Official histories neglect important aspects of historical events including what is often contained in family stories and photos. Understanding the **multivocality** and complexity of histories forms more accurate historical accounts. Requiring multiple voices brings accuracy, empathy and imagination to history.

Concept Check

What might bring seemingly dry and remote history to life?

When we add voice and make history **multivocal** what do we begin to overcome?

What are some outcomes of multivocal history?

What does imagination encourage ethnoautobiography to overcome?

The **remembrance** of storytelling displaces what?

How does Cixous describe her **hybridity**?

NOTES

Chapter 10
Mythic Stories

Riff

Mythic Tricksters at Play

I. An important trickster story, this one

At the time of beginnings Raven was bored, so he decided to find out what was inside the mysterious house over the hill. Eagle advised against it, but there was no stopping Raven. He had observed a young woman coming and going from the house, appearing on various sides, yet he had never been able to find an entrance. He knew she would need to fetch water sooner or later. So Raven turned himself into a pine needle and floated down the river just as the young woman immersed her vessel into the water. She swallowed the pine needle as she drank and became pregnant with Raven. As it turned out, Raven was quite an unusual baby given to insistent complaining. He became expert at getting the woman's father to release the gifts he had been given to take care of. So whenever Ravenchild's complaining would reach a paroxysm he would open one of the boxes to first release the stars and the northern lights, then the moon, and, finally, the sun. With the sun up in the sky the world turned green and changed into the world we know. (Retold Northwest Coast story; see Bringhurst, 1999 for Haida translations and discussion.)

II. Another important trickster story, this one too

Loki [the trickster of the Old Norse] was interested in things
because he was interested in them, and in the way they were
in the world, and worked in the world. He was neither kind
nor gentle, not anyway when he inhabited the world of myth.
In the world of folk tales he was a fire demon, mostly benign,
providing warmth for hearths and ovens. In the world of Asgard
[the home of the Old Norse gods] he was smiling and reckless,
a forest fire devouring what stood in its path. …

He studied, most of all, fire and water. Fire was his element but
he also changed himself into a great salmon and treaded his way
swiftly through the crash of the waterfall, across the eddies of
the deep pool, over its lip into the rushing river, which parted
round a great stone, and joined again, twisting and bubbling. …

Loki wanted to learn from it — not exactly to master fire or
water, but to map them. But beyond the curiosity there was
delight. Chaos pleased him. He liked things to get more and
more furious, more wild, more ungraspable, he was at home
in turbulence. He would provoke turbulence to please himself
and tried to understand it in order to make more of it. He was
reckless and cunning, both. … (Byatt, 2011, pp. 113 – 115)

III. This one just in, yet another important trickster story

One day the trickster Loki goes to the theater. Theater is one
of his current loves. A play by the Spanish playwright Arrabal
is featured. As Loki enters the foyer, much to his surprise, Fer-
nando Arrabal grabs his arm and swiftly leads him back stage
and then on to the stage. The playwright challenges Loki to a
game of pinball to prove the existence of the spirit of shamanism. It takes one million points for the proof. With the ironic
gesture of a magician pulling a rabbit out of the hat, Arrabal
hands Loki an iPad. It is projected on a large screen at the back
of the stage. The words WILD WEST, JAIL, INDIAN VILLAGE,
KILL DIRTY HARRY, SHERIFF show in large letters. Loki is, of
course, not one to turn down a challenge and an opportunity to
create mischief. "Once I reach one million points, that's proof of
the existence of the spirit of shamanism?" Arrabal affirms: "Yes,
that's how the game is played, that's what is at stake." Loki gets
impatient. The existence of the spirit of shamanism was all in
his hands. He was bound and determined to end the reign of
modernity and get the trickster fully into the game. He would
shatter the hall of mirrors modernity had built. He was going
to demonstrate his powers. He would provide definitive proof
of the spirit of shamanism, something modernity had failed to

accomplish. No better way than a game of chance! The manuals of mythology and shamanism would have to be re–written to honor his name. Loki plays with great skill and excitement as the ball rolls through the Wild West pinball setting. The ball stays in the game, bounces through the Indian Village, Dirty Harry gets killed, the ball rolls through the bank twice, 950,000 points, 960,000, 962,000 … The stagehands gather around him to get a close–up look. Loki pushes the buttons on the iPad screen with unnecessary force, shakes the tablet wildly, his thumbs in constant action, 980,000 and the ball is still up. It accelerates on the train tracks traversing the Wild West, hits the closed bank, almost enters the Indian Village, 982,000, 984,000. The ball obeys Loki's intense interventions, it submits to his trickster force. He only needs one million points. How could he lose now? 996,000, 998,000, 999,000. Loki goes crazy inside. The spirit of shamanism had chosen him to prove his existence. What a trick. 999,200, 999,600, 999,800, 999,900. At that moment the iPad goes dark and the LCD projector shows a blue screen with "no signal." Arrabal breaks into a big belly laugh. Finally he shouts: "Vive la différance!" to honor Jacques Derrida's deconstructive and trick-sterish philosophy, puts on a top hat, and bows to the audience.

JWK

Chapter Outline	Core Concepts	Ethnoautobiographical Perspectives	Expected Outcomes
Tricksters at play	Myths can be renewed	Myths help to explore cultural meanings	Develop an appreciation for the potential of mythic storytelling
What is a myth?	Myths tell the stories of gods & spirits in ways that are culturally meaningful	Understanding myths means understanding deep cultural patterns	Appreciate the contemporary significance of mythic stories
Myths and dreams	Myths & dreams are related: Dreams are individual, myths are communal	Dreams can play an important role in the renewal of mythic stories	Understand the dream–like quality of mythic stories
Mythic stories in the oral tradition	Myths were originally trans-mitted through storytelling or the oral tradition	The loss of oral traditions means an atrophy of particular aspects of our brain processes	Finding ways to renew myths by re–telling them & making them your own
The invention of mythology	Mythology primarily refers to the written versions of mythic stories & their study	The common academic understanding of mythic stories limits the appreciation of their psycho–cultural power	Overcome the limitations posed by the focus on written versions of mythic stories
Historical layers	Mythic stories have changed through time	When we begin to re–tell myths we are adding to their history & enliven them	Look beyond the surface of a mythic story & identify its historical depths
Different types of myths	Mythic stories have different qualities, purposes, & origins	Humans have created a diversity of mythic stories & this diversity reflects the richness & complexity of cultures	Differentiate between different types of myths

Chapter Outline	Core Concepts	Ethnoautobiographical Perspectives	Expected Outcomes
Creation myths	Creation myths usually hold central cultural information	Remembering creation myths can help us remember important cultural patterns	Appreciate the psycho–cultural depth creation myths hold for a particular tradition
The truth of myths	The truth of mythic stories is communal & may contain scientific knowledge	Myths are not false, they contain truths that are different from scientific truths	Find a variety of truths in mythic stories
National myths	National myths reflect a nations self understanding & ideals	National myths can be misguided or exclude parts of a nation	Identify which social contradictions are masked by American national myths
Myths today	Myths continue to inspire art	Mythic stories consciously & unconsciously continue to exert power in individuals & social bodies	Discern myths in contemporary art (film, theater, literature, visual art)

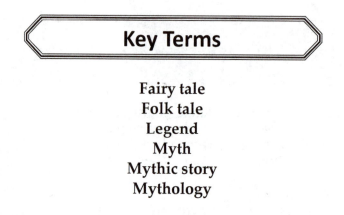

Key Terms

Fairy tale
Folk tale
Legend
Myth
Mythic story
Mythology

Note: All key terms in this textbook are highlighted in bold and can be found in the Glossary at the end of the book.

Resources Alongside This Chapter

Byatt, A. S. (2011). *Ragnarök*. New York, NY: Canongate.

Cuarón, A., Del Toro, G., Navarro, B., Torresblanco, F. (Producers), & Del Toro, G. (Director). (2007). *Pan's labyrinth* [Motion picture]. United States: New Line Home Entertainment.

Jones, G. R., Miller, R. P., Newman, P., Renzi, M., Sloss, J. (Producers), & Sayles, J. (Director). (2000). *The secret of Roan Inish*. [DVD]. United States: Sony Pictures Home Entertainment.

Prechtel, M. (2001). *The disobedience of the daughter of the sun*. Berkeley, CA: North Atlantic Books.

Silko, L. M. (1977). *Ceremony*. New York, NY: Penguin.

Go to any library or (online) bookstore and look for any collection of creation stories from different cultures. Numerous such collections are available.

The riff above gives three stories, two ancient mythic stories that have been told over and over again across the centuries, and one a quasi–**myth**, made up of modern elements. The **trickster** is important in many mythologies. It is the character that shakes things up (in Native American stories Coyote throws the stars into the sky in a jumble and disturbs the way they were organized before) or breaks things loose (Raven liberates the sun so that life as we know it can begin in Northwest Coast Indian stories). The third story above provocatively challenges any certainties around spiritual realities and encourages questions, inquiries, and questing. The trickster, usually male, is a pervasive mythological figure who changes stability into instability; he deconstructs what has been carefully constructed; he challenges traditions so that they can be renewed and strengthened.

The rock carving image appears to show trees of life and a spirit boat (a vessel in which we can travel between realities). The tree of life makes a frequent appearance in mythic stories and was, and continues to be, honored as the center of communities. It is also the place where we shift between realities when move up and down the tree, from the middle world to the upper world or down into the underworld, which is not the same as hell. In the tradition of the Old Norse the tree is attached to the north star. The rock carving is a mythic image of the ancient **Indo–European** people of the European north.

What is a myth?

Myths are stories that involve supernatural characters (gods, goddesses, spirits, etc.). They are narratives considered sacred or central to a particular culture and originally transmitted in oral traditions. Mythology refers either to a collection of myth or the study of myths. In our text we generally prefer the term "mythic stories" to indicate the oral nature of their original transmission from generation to generation. They provide existential, philosophical, and spiritual guidance in narrative form capturing a particular understanding, as well as, a self–understanding of what it means to live successfully as a society or community in a particular place.

For the purposes of this workbook we are particularly interested in myths that emerged from a particular cultural practice, which is not to claim that all myths necessarily came about in this way. We can describe myths as emergent from the lived experience of a people in a particular place and time, either through individual dreaming or visioning or during communal rituals or ceremonies. Such mythic stories provide the original instructions for a culture which changes as stories are transmitted and rituals continue. Mythic stories in this sense are never fixed, they are always evolving from a central core. Mythic stories deal with the socio–cultural truths of a people, and provide guidance and instruction that emerged out of the visionary presence of a community in a particular ecology and historical moment. The visionary cultural presence emerges between the astronomical and archetypal spiritual readings of the cosmos and the skills and cultural practices developed through survival in the place. While their primary focus is on answers to existential questions, they also may contain Indigenous scientific knowledge reflecting careful observations of sky and earth (astronomy, meteorology, ecology, etc.).

In evolutionary schemes myths or the mythic times are generally considered a thing of the past that has been superseded by later developments leading into modernity and postmodernity. An alternate view is held by cultural philosophers like Jean Gebser who wrote about *The Ever-Present Origin* (1986). While he talks about archaic, magic, mythical, mental, and integral structures, he thinks it is misguided to put these structures of consciousness into an evolutionary line and to look for development and progress (where something needs to be left behind); rather, he regarded them as an unfolding of different qualities of consciousness. Our view is consistent with this approach, which affirms the continuing importance of mythic consciousness and mythic stories. It does not deny or reject the importance of science, and seeks a quality of **postmodern** integration that brings different qualities of consciousness together in creative and visionary play. One of our contemporary challenges may be how to hold these different qualities of consciousness together in our awareness and how to integrate them into our cultural practices.

Myths and dreams

Myths and dreams have an intimate relationship. It is not only that myths oftentimes contain dreams and visions, but we could say that in some sense myths are records of our collective dreaming. Within Indigenous worldviews they connect us with the **immanent** world of spirits, often called the 'dreamtime', and help us remember our connections to ancestors and other sources of in-spiritedness (by contrast, in Eurocentered thinking these aspects are considered **transcendent**). In this sense myths are the stories that have survived in communities as record of profound encounters with spiritual realms and that help us to keep the portal to them open.

From a Eurocentered perspective, myths connect us to what Jung (1959) calls the collective unconscious filled with archetypes, collectively inherited patterns or recurring symbols, such as the archetype of the hero, the mother, the trickster, and what Indigenous people would call the spirit world or dreamtime. We each have several personal dreams every night that provide opportunities to connect with deeper levels within and beyond ourselves; some of the dreams and visions we have, especially if they come to us during rituals or ceremony, connect us with our collective dreaming. Such dreams, if they enter the conscious life of a community, inspire, reflect, and shape the deep structure of a society; they may provide guidance or instruction, motivate community members to certain actions, help members bond, and teach about challenges and how to cope with them. Myths hold cultural meaning that are accessed through what Jung called "big dreams" (1965), ceremonial visioning and dreaming. This description of **myth** represents an important type of myth, however, it is important to keep in mind that myths come in great variety.

Mythic stories in the oral tradition

While we now almost exclusively *read* mythic stories, for centuries and millennia they were passed down in *oral* traditions — told and retold and changing in the process of transmission. The invention of writing, and especially the alphabet, starting about 5,000 years ago, constitutes a major turning point in both cultural practices and the use of the human brain (Abram 1996, 2010). It is part of a large shift from hunting and gathering, nomadism, and horticulture to increasingly large-scale agriculture. With it comes a shift away from the importance of female spirits or goddesses within a complex male and female spiritual universe (gods and goddesses connected with vegetation and hunting). We see the emergence of patriarchy and priests who are in charge of the spiritual and religious affairs of people. It is a shift away from an engagement in a nurturing conversation in which female nurturing spirits play a significant role, to a controlling approach to the environment in which humans are increasingly separated from their sources of sustenance.

Leslie Marmon Silko (1996) gives an excellent description of an oral tradition in action:

> Communal storytelling was a self-correcting process in which listeners were encouraged to speak up if they noted an important fact or detail omitted. ... Implicit in the Pueblo oral tradition was the awareness that loyalties, grudges, and kinship must always influence the narrator's choices as she emphasizes to listeners that this is the way she has always heard the story told. The ancient Pueblo people sought a communal truth, not an absolute truth. For them this truth lived somewhere within the web of differing versions, disputes over minor points, and outright contradictions tangling with old feuds and village rivalries. (p. 32)

Modern societies are in search of absolute truth, while Pueblo and other oral traditions are looking for communal truths. Of course, epistemological critiques of modern scientific assumptions have shown that the claim to absolute truth is ideological and that modernity similarly is in the business of communal truths, even if the rules of the game are differently defined (Harding, 1997).

The use of alphabets emphasizes linearity, sequential thinking, and abstraction. Now the integrative function of the right brain (with its power of holistic visioning and evaluation) gets usurped by left–brain functions that create a world in which the arts, dreams, and other uses of imaginal faculties are increasingly devalued, while the linear use of scientific rationalism gets elevated. Myths were part of the integrative functioning of the different parts of our brain, the synchronization between hemispheres and younger and older parts of the brain. They often seem so alien to contemporary readers because of the predominant use of left–brain functions, where myths do not make rational sense. Myths only can make sense when we integrate our rational left–brain functions with right–brain processes. In this sense mythic stories provide a potential for the remembering and unfolding of an integral consciousness for the future.

The invention of mythology

With the shift in cultural practices, and thus in the use of our brain potential, stories shifted from inspirited oral tellings to written records that can be read and analyzed. In some sense myths and **mythology** did not exist before writing. They came into existence once scientific endeavors had moved a good distance from alive oral traditions. Historically, myths and mythologies were invented during the 19th century when scholars became concerned with the collection and analysis of stories that had previously been handed down in oral traditions. The Brothers Grimm are probably the most famous example that also shows the many problems that arise when oral stories become fixed in writing. Not only do stories no longer change organically as they are told and retold, they become fixed in an authoritative version, and also get changed so that they sell to readers. It has been shown that the Brothers Grimm worked to cater to their contemporary audience.

The exemplar of the invention of **mythology** is the *Kalevala*, the Finnish national epic (Pentekäinen, 1989). Elias Lönnrot traveled around Karelia, a geographical area divided between Eastern Finland and Russia. Karelians have their own language, closely related to, but distinct, from Finnish. Rising nationalistic awareness and romanticism led to the desire for a poem inspired by *The Iliad*, *Beowulf*, or *The Nibelungenlied*. (The latter, for example, continues to be tied to German national self understanding and has been continuously taught in schools with new editions and commentaries appearing regularly). As Lönnrot traveled around Karelia, he collected so–called runo songs (women were probably the majority of the singers). He compiled these individual songs into a cohesive epic, the *Kalevala*, which was published in its current version in 1849. At that time nationalists were the progressives, while they are today considered politically right wing. Mythology served to inspire nationalistic sentiments as nation states emerged and forged their identities.

The interest in recording **legends**, **folk tales**, and myths and their studies is thus enmeshed both with an emergent national consciousness in Europe as well as the emergence of an academic discipline in the humanities, a discipline primarily interested in cataloging the themes found in these stories and their cross–cultural comparison. While written versions of mythic stories changed their quality in a significant way, they also helped preserve them as the oral traditions began to vanish under the pressures of publications for reading and with modern developments such as the pervasively passive radio and television. More recent multimedia developments, however, allow for the revivification of mythic stories in new forms of audiovisual tellings.

Historical layers

The myths that we have available to us now have always changed as they were told and retold. Silko's quote above illustrates this vividly when she reminds us that "truth lived somewhere within the web of differing versions" of a **mythic story**. We cannot assume that the story we read or hear now was the same a few hundred or thousand years ago. Instead it is useful to think of each of these stories containing historical layers and that we can train ourselves to distinguish younger and older layers.

An example is the prose and poetic *Edda* of the Old Norse. All of these texts were written down after Christianity had arrived and we can discern that influence; for example, here the major male god Odin is more of a Christ–like figure. Once we peel back the younger layers we can identify Indigenous or shamanic layers that are very much akin to contemporary Indigenous cultures. Here Odin is a shaman or healer and the two ravens and the wolves are his totems or animal familiars (*fylgia* in Old Norse terminology) and he engages in questing ceremonies in order to glean spiritual understanding. Odin's rituals as described in the *Eddic* texts are shamanic in nature. It is always important to keep the historical layering of mythic stories in mind so that we can identify distortions stemming from such influences as patriarchal thinking or the major religions.

Different types of myths

Myths come in different varieties and shapes. While we focus on particular myths originating out of a visionary ritual presence in a particular place, not all myths will conform to this model. Myths may describe a hero's or heroine's journey, they may be stories of initiation (such as the Dinè *Kinaldaa* or Apache *na'ii'ees*), they may describe a healing and provide guidance for conducting healings (such as the Dinè chantways), they may teach about virtues, ethics, and morals, or talk about creation, stars, and the origin of a people. We can also distinguish cultural, institutional, familial, and ethnic or nationalistic myths. Other terms for mapping these old stories are myths (generally considered the oldest), **legends** (often understood as historical narratives or explanatory stories of particular features in the landscape that are never entirely refuted nor entirely believed), **folk tales** (often highly structured), and **fairy tales**; usage of these terms overlaps and their definitions vary in the literature.

The origins of these different types of myths will differ and one **mythic story** may fall into several categories. We emphasize here the lived connection to mythic stories and the visionary work with cultural myths through dream and ritual for the sake of discovering their relevance today. Only such depth work will help us understand their meaning for tomorrow. If we are to understand their collective import and potential, we need to go from intellectual analysis to a creative engagement with mythic stories, an engagement that uses all parts of our selves and our brains, both individually and communally. This may lead to renewals that are quite different from nostalgic or romanticizing remembrances of mythic stories.

Ancestral creation stories are a natural starting point for such depth work with mythic stories, since, within an Indigenous paradigm, they provide central guidance for cultures.

Creation myths

Within an Indigenous worldview, ceremonies are an instrumental part in the process of balancing ourselves for individual and social well–being. Different traditions express their understanding of this process differently. Commonly the creation, origin, or emergence stories contain the central or **original instructions** about how to be in balance on earth. Jürgen retells the Old Norse understanding of creation and anthropogenesis at the end of the chapter. The story gives an Old Northern European understanding of the process of balancing or nurturing conversation.

The information contained in this story is at times called "original instructions." **Beingknowing**, in an Indigenous sense of **presence**, flows from a deepening understanding of such stories. All traditions contain such central stories, usually creation stories, which provide a foundational understanding of origins, appropriate behavior, healing, and ceremonies. Working with such stories in ceremony allows a comprehension beyond the cognitive acquisition of a narrative.

The truth of myths

In common parlance we hear people say "That's a myth!", meaning something is false or untrue. Some myths contain elements that can be supported by science, such as the Dogon's knowledge of the white dwarf companion star of Sirius. Though the star cannot be seen with the naked eye they knew of this star before the advent of telescopes. A Native American tribe in Southern Oregon has a narrative that describes the origins of Crater Lake which contains parts that are true in a literal sense of geological history. Yet many aspects of myths are not true in the straightforward positivistic scientific sense. Does that mean all myths are basically false and should be relegated to the realms of fantasy? This would be like saying that all our dreams are nonsense. While they may appear nonsensical on the surface, interpretation commonly leads to the successful garnering of meaning and insight. Similarly, myths may appear nonsensical on the surface, yet careful interpretations using different aspects of knowledge — psychology, history, astronomy, biology, and more — will lead us to insights and understandings that help us see the depths of these stories. The truth myths carry is about existential, socio–cultural, and Indigenous science (to varying degrees, depending on the specific story). The sense that an interpretation is right is similar to the 'aha!' of dream interpretation when insights 'click'.

National myths

We have mentioned the *Kalevala* and *The Ring of the Nibelung* as national myths that continue to be important in a nation's search for self–understanding. These are appropriations and renewals of old stories for particular socio–political purposes. We find notably different qualities in national myths. For example, the U.S. has its own national myths that revolve around manifest destiny, the American dream, and American exceptionalism. This is the view that

> the New World is the last and best chance offered by God to a fallen humanity that has only to look to His exceptional new church for redemption. Thus, America and Americans are special, exceptional, because they are charged with saving the world from itself and, at the same time, America and Americans must sustain a high level of spiritual, political and moral commitment to this exceptional destiny" (Madsen, 1998, p. 2)

Or, regarding the American Dream "first defined by James Truslow Adams as 'that dream of a land in which life should be better and richer and fuller for everyone, with opportunity for each according to ability or achievement'" (Campbell & Kean, 2012, p. 11). Myths function as stories that promote the values and interests of the dominant groups in society and that make the social world easier to cope with as contradictions and complexities are simplified and made more palatable. Nationalistic myths are depoliticized speech that remove certain issues from discussion because they are presented as natural and given. Once we start to question the myths of American exceptionalism and the American dream by asking 'whose dream?' and 'at what cost?' and 'who benefits?' we open up to critical discourse. We can also ask how the origin of these national myths are similar or dissimilar to origins, ceremonial practices, and functioning within Indigenous paradigms.

Myths today

Myths are powerful because they arise from and evoke ancient psycho–cultural patterns and realities. To this day they inspire works of art of all kinds. Anselm Kiefer has created numerous monumental paintings evoking mythic characters and stories. Movies that follow mythic patterns or illustrate mythic stories can be particularly powerful. Terry Gilliam's movie *The Fisher King*, based on the myth of the Fisher King (Hill, Obst & Gilliam, 1991), powerfully illustrates the healing of its main characters through mythic connections. Tolkien's *The Hobbit* (1937) and *The Lord of the Rings* (1954) were inspired by Old Norse and other mythologies. At times artists consciously build on known myths (such as A. S. Byatt's, 2011, retelling of Norse myths in *Ragnarók*; or Margret Atwood's, 2005, exploration of the *Odyssey* from a woman's perspective in her *Penelopiad*). At other times, such as in *The Girl With the Dragon Tattoo*, the artist may perhaps unconsciously connect with or evoke a mythic pattern (Larsson, 2008).

Wagner's *Ring des Nibelungen* (1848–1874) is an extensive *Gesamtkunstwerk* (comprehensive work of art) that continues to capture audiences in operas all over the world. His musical, dramatic, and visual evocation of an old Germanic story, the *Völsungasaga*, never ceases to have a powerful effect through the archetypal spiritual presences and conflicts it portrays. We can see reverberations of this ancient story in Stieg Larsson's *Girl With the Dragon Tattoo* where the superhero Lisbeth Salander is a Brynhilde like figure (Brynhilde also figures in Quentin Tarantino's, 2012, *Django unchained*). Part of the power of Larsson's work stems from these mythic echos, as is true for the work of writer Neil Gaiman (2005, 2011). Similarly, playwright Mary Zimmerman frequently retells mythic stories such as *The Secret in the Wings* (2014), and *Metamorphoses* (2002). Stephen Sondheim also combined numerous folk tales in *Into the Woods* (1993).

Leslie Marmon Silko uses a number of mythic stories that are connected to rituals in her book *Ceremony* (1977). Here she expertly illustrates a contemporary integration of mythic story as part of the healing of the protagonist both from post traumatic stress syndrome and cultural wounds. Silko shows how the old stories can be not only relevant for today, but how they continue to have healing power and how their meaning can be renewed.

Martin Prechtel's, *The Disobedience of the Daughter of the Sun (2001)*, illustrates various levels on which mythic stories can be interpreted, from the psychological to the cultural. Prechtel is not only a wonderful storyteller, he is also expert at showing the richness and multiple facets of myths. His interpretation is an exemplar of honoring a story through its interpretation rather than distancing the reader into a process of rational analysis only.

***

This is the right time and a good place to ask — Venus, the shaman star, the star of the being so important for any healing, is visible and just now high up in the sky. Freyja, "the lady", is the name of this being. And where we are standing here at this tree — it is the center of this community, it is the place which connects us with everything that matters. There is so much to be said about the time, the star, and this place at the tree. Some of it I will tell today, but other things will have to wait for a later night. So, let me start at the beginning, the place of origins, because there is no healing without going to that place. One of the völvas, the ancient seeresses, before me has said: 'In the beginning of time there was nothing: Neither sand nor sea, nor cooling surf; there was no earth, nor upper heaven, no blade of grass - only the Great Void.' This void was fertile, it was filled with magical power, the auður, the life giving power whence everything arises. This is the place of creation, and without placing ourselves at the source of all there will be no healing. If we seek balance when imbalance threatens us, then we need to start over from the place of balance between the ice of the north and the fire of the south. These are the poles of Ginnungagap, the fertile void out of which our world and we ourselves arose. Where heat and cold meet, the deadly hoarfrost from the rivers of the north is melted by the heat of Muspell. All this would mean nothing, if the richness of auður wasn't örlög, destiny or fate. Without the primal law, without timekeepers, without moonwatchers, without sunwatchers - the world would be nothing, it would be without destinies, örloglaus.

And then it all starts when the three giant maidens come along. But these women have all kinds of names, and show up in different guises, at times there are even three times three. Sometimes even twelve. Or they number the thirteen months of the moon calendar. When some see them they call them dísir, protective spirits, others call them nornir, norns, but they also show themselves as valkyrjur, valkyries. Whichever way the maidens are seen, where they are is the power to impart örlög, to awaken a being to move in time. They are the measurers of time and their weaving material are moon beams and sun beams. They alone are not subject to it. Whether they awaken giants, or older Vanir spirits, or younger Æsir spirits, or humans — they are all subject to the cycles of örlög, the cycles of fate, created from the fertile richness of Ginnungagap.

There is time then, measurement, fate. Out of it emerges a primal force, a giant by the name of Ymir, a two gendered being, many generations before the twin couples Freyja and Freyr, Njördhr and Nerþus, and Thor dressing as Freya. Ymir was formed out of the drops at the confluence of the forces streaming out of Niflheimr and Muspellsheims, the homes of mist and fire. He was nurtured by that primal richness in the form of Auðhumla, the nourishing cow of auðr, who is fate as urðr and örlög. She is the hornless mother of all creation, the matrix which makes life possible. Be patient now, why she is hornless I shall tell you later. At this moment in creation we have nothing but the nourishing matrix of auðr, the örlög, fate, in it administered by the nornir, and the giants as primal forces.

Not only does Auðhumla nurture Ymir, she also licks Búri, Born, Creator, Father, out of the salty stones over three days. His son Burr — we have forgotten whether he mated with a giant or created out of himself like Ymir — creates with Bestla, the daughter of the giant Bölthorn, the first divine spirits or gods. Some say their names were Óðinn, Vili, and Vé, some say Óðinn, Hænir, and Lóður were the first divine spirits. One of them became more and more important, and in recent times many people think first of him when they think of our traditions: The auðr of the primal richness sounds very close in name to Auðun, and we have Óðinn who also shows himself in the form of Óðr, who Freyja cries for — but I am rushing ahead... yes, yes, as time passed the maleness of creation was the only thing people would see, now a well known story, but many would say a rather sad story. The first three divine spirits were subject to the örlög, just like everything else, except for the female measurers of time, the nornir.

It was the destiny of the first three divine spirits to create earth, and later human beings, from the primal force which Auðhumla had nurtured in Ymir. They killed — or sacrificed — the two gendered giant and thus formed the earth — the mountains from the bones, the sky from the skull, the seas and lakes from the blood, the trees and vegetation from the hair, middle earth, Miðgarðr, from the brows, the clouds from the brain, the soil from the flesh, and the rocks and scree from the toes and teeth. What remained was food for the maggots, who turned into yet another magical force after feeding on the primal giant: they transformed into dwarfs. One of their duties was to uphold the sky in the four directions, another to dream. Some say that the fire and flames continued to spew out of Muspellsheimr, and these became the stars and planets which the divine spirits ordered to allow humans to measure time.

One day the first three divine spirits wandered the shores and found two tree trunks on the beach. Óðinn or Óðr gave them breath, Atem, Odem, önd; Hænir gave them óðr, soul or understanding and feeling; and Lóður gave them lá and litu, the bodily fluids which gave them color. These first humans, Askr and Embla, ash and elm, were without örlög or örlöglaus, but in the process of becoming human they received fate, örlög, so, somewhere there the nornir must have intervened. Our ancestors don't have much to say about that. It may have been much too obvious to them to even mention it. But some people think it was the nornir who gave them the qualities necessary for human life, and not the sons of Burr.

And, you see, there is an interesting thing here: The first divine spirits killed Ymir to create earth and with it the trees. And out of two of the trees they created the first humans. But there was one more special tree that was created in this process: its roots reach deep down, so far that they even reach Ginnungagap, the gap of gap, and its trunk and branches reach way up into the sky, so far that it touches the pole star at the top. In fact, it covers our world. This is the Tree of Life, and the Tree of the World, it holds auður and Urðarbrunnur, the well of memory, and the nornir; it is the process of life for us here, and you can even say that is the humans. While our ancestors have handed down many stories about the life of this tree, somewhere along the way the story of its creation got lost. Or maybe it didn't, since the Tree of Life is also us humans. Much more needs to be said about this tree.

The tree comes with many names and under different guises. There is Yggdrasill, there is Irminsul, there is Mjötuðr, there is the mysterious Sampo, and there are many other names for it. At times it is an ash, at times a larch, and it has been and continues to make its appearance as different trees in different places. As you will travel and learn about the different names and the different kinds of trees who have become the holder of life, you will learn about the knowledge and gifts of the people in different regions. This tree is the center of the world, when you look up it reaches into the stars, and connects us with the milky way and the different regions where ancestral spirits go to and come from. The roots of the tree reach into the depths of memory, and the örlög which brought us here. There is one important and crucial name for the tree I have not mentioned yet: Heimdallr. The nornir created Heimdallr early on, the nine of them. Although his function has changed over the millennia, I see that he was one of the early divine spirits. He is not only the guardian of Bilröst, the rainbow bridge between worlds, but also one of the measurers; while the nornir are the movement as they keep count scoring the moon cycles in particular, the tree Heimdallr is the rod who helps them do so (and if you are no prude, and your sexual imagination gets sparked, then I shall not be a woman who inhibits the way you feel). Heimdallr holds the horn of the moon honoring this cycle. He was born from the seas, and he easily changes into a seal. He helps making the örlög real for us humans.

The tree is our life, is us. So I could talk about it all night, and I am glad that the night is young, even though Freyja's star has set by now. Let me say this much: The tree is birth and death, becoming and decaying, generation and regeneration. At its root are the nornir, three of them are well known to us by their name: Urðr, the one who holds the memory from which Verðandi creates what is coming to be present; and then there is Skuld, she knows what is owed to the ages, what their meaning is. They keep track of the lunar cycles of time, they score the records as humans have taken the clue from them and scored the movements of the moon for many thousands of years. Then there are the other nornir who connect with different divine spirits, the Æsir and the Vanir, others connect with the giants, the elves, and the dwarves — we don't remember all their names. What each of these women creates has been seen in the form of white clay, aurr, and with this feminine fluid they spatter the tree of life, they cover it with the riches they lift from Urðarbrunnur. And yes, if you are not afraid to lie at the Ginnungagap of woman, whether you are man or woman, then you see this richness formed out of the moisture created from her heat. But their work has also been seen as the weave they create from the threads the sun woman has spun for them.

Thus the tree of life is nourished by the women who live at her roots and ladle the fluids from Urðarbrunnur and other sources. As the tree receives she gives nourishment to others: At her roots snakes gnaw away, and deer eat her leaves. She gives protection to the eagles and hawks in her top. Squirrels run up and down as messengers between the different parts of the world. Because the nornir never cease to spatter the tree with aurr the tree stays green year round. She stretches into all nine worlds, into all nine aspects of being, she connects us with them, and she is all these, she is the above, the below, and the middle.

There is one other things you need to know now: When you look at all this you see how much knowledge the tree has, how much knowledge Heimdallr has as the measurer, as Vindlér, the borer, the turner, the spiraling one, the ram. The tree is living knowledge, including the deepest knowledge of the cycles which is created with aurr from örlög. Of course, this drum here, which I use in ceremony is partly made from a special tree, a tree which also is the world tree, and in the center you see the drawing of the tree. This way the drum is Sampo, the mill, and Yggdrasill, the horse which can take us into other worlds; and it is all the others; this way the drum is knowledge, one way to knowledge. But there is another, actually: there are many others, but an important one is the sacrifice on the tree. We are trees, and to honor our origins and in order to journey across the spirit bridge we can sacrifice our self to spirit on the tree by fasting. (Bjarnadóttir & Kremer, 1998/1999, 141–145, italics in original, abridged, revised to include explanation of Old Norse terminology)

Activity

Recreating a Creation Myth

Locate, investigate, and re–tell a creation myth from one of your cultural (ancestral) backgrounds (in case you really can't find one: choose a story of initiation or healing). Read the story several times, especially before going to sleep (to encourage dreams connected with the story). Attempt to get to know the story well enough that you can tell the basic outline to someone else. Perhaps create some art evoking, or connected, to the story. Or read the story out loud and see how it shows up for you. Write it with new characters, in a new setting, as a dialogue, etc. Stay true to the story while working with it creatively.

As you retell the story make it creatively your own, i.e., present to you today. Your paper or presentation needs to be based on a published myth that must be referenced. This assignment is a paradox: be true to the story and make it your own. You are welcome to include images.

This may be completed in a 500–word paper, or shared as an oral presentation with others.

Note: If you are completing these activities on your own, and do not have an organized group to do oral presentations for (such as in a classroom, community organization and so on), it is encouraged that you present the work you are doing to a friend, family member or spouse to experience sharing your process in oral form.

Chapter Summary

Myths are culturally meaningful stories of gods & spirits, originally trans-mitted through the oral tradition. Mythology is the study of written mythic stories. Myths and dreams are related: dreams are individual, myths are communal. **Mythic stories** have changed through time, and have different qualities, purposes and origins. Creation myths often hold central cultural information, the truth of which is communal perhaps containing scientific truths. National myths reflect a nation's self–understanding and ideals. Myths continue to inspire all types of art.

Concept Check

What is a myth, a mythic story, and mythology?

Describe how mythic stories and dreams are related.

Name some different qualities, purposes and origins of **mythic stories**.

What do **original instructions** provide?

What are some of the national myths of the United States?

Name at least three contemporary books and/or films that draw on mythic stories.

NOTES

Chapter 11
Who are My Ancestors?
Genealogy, Indigenousness and
Ethnoautobiography

Riff

Ancestral Imaginings

R: Learning to honor my ancestors was both really challenging, and something of a next step. I was the family historian, and quite suddenly the genealogy came to life, participating more fully in my everyday life. Thus, my one grandparent who I was close to, Linda Chandler, became an honored ancestor after passing.

Linda Chandler: It was so sweet how that happened, R. You were kind of the misfit in the family that I had been to some degree, as well. I always wanted to look out for you, even though we didn't see each other much. I was really touched and also surprised that you wrote your application essay for teacher education as a conversation with me.

R: But that's how influential you were in my life, even though in some ways I didn't know you that well, or wasn't around you that often. I still regularly quote your "everything in moderation, including moderation" dictum. And I've more than once told your story of affirming, rather than swearing on a Bible during McCarthyism.

Linda: And that is the richness in these relationships once we are open to them. Of course, ancestor worship, as such, would be frowned upon by my generation, and probably still is. But there's more to it than that. It's about remembering how you came to be who you are, about the influences that might be more obvious or not.

R: Yes, it is about learning as much as possible, and sometimes using my imagination in order to fill in gaps. It is intriguing too what can happen, even with "new" ancestors, such as my father–in–law, Bob Reid. He's only been my ancestor–in–law for about a month.

Bob Reid: What a special honor to be in the new ancestor category, and as an in–law, too. It was special on my end, as well, because even though I only knew you as my daughter's spouse for a few years, and at the end of my life, you always seemed interested in hearing stories, knowing more, and really honoring your wife's side of the family.

R: Well, that's what I mean about filling in gaps. For instance, with your childhood in the Panhandle of Texas, as I learned more, it turned out that there were immense settlement wars with the Comanche in that region. Of course, it was before your time, but that provides background to who your ancestors were, what their lives were like, and in turn who you were.

Bob Reid: Once again, you really seemed to be interested, to care, to even respect the stories that are woven into families. That was a wonderful thing to witness. I only wish I had been around longer to tell you more of them.

R: You were a fantastic storyteller! But those stories remain alive in many different places. I recall all of the pictures we looked at and seeing so much of you in them. It's similar with my great–grandmother Edna Frazer. I have a few stories from my mother, but they're deeply informed by a few wonderful pictures.

Edna Frazer: I love those pictures so much. And that they're from the near the beginning and end of my life seems so poetic. The entire middle of my life is missing from the photographic record. The pictures of me as a young girl, with my parents, is one of my absolute favorites, which is why your mother made sure to give it to you. And then my other favorite picture is the one with your great–grandfather Ray Hudelson. We were still so in love.

R: It is really obvious how happy the two of you were. I love that picture also because there is so little about the Hudelsons in the family history. And here is this seemingly warm, caring face leaning next to you. So again, there don't have to be diaries and lots of material to make a connection. Of course, it's easier when that is the case, as in my great–great–great grandfather Meehan.

Thomas Meehan: But again R, even though I have lots of documents left behind about me, not everyone of my descendants knows or cares. So your reaching out to me and continued acknowledgment is deeply meaningful.

R: As your presence is for me. There is so much the power in these ancestral connections; there are all sorts of resonances.

RJP

Chapter Outline	Core Concepts	Ethnoautobiographical Perspectives	Expected Outcomes
Ancestral imaginings	Relationships can be built with any ancestor	Ancestral connections provide clarity of personal and cultural identity issues	Create imaginative genealogical connections
Family trees	Genealogy is fundamental in ethnoautobiographical inquiries	Knowing where we come from helps us affirm who we are	Complete a family tree three or more generations back
Genealogical imagination	Exact genealogical imagination brings the family tree to life	Genealogical imagination helps to recover those parts of family stories that have been forgotten or dismissed	Finding our own creative voice as we understand our genealogy
Indigenous roots	All peoples have Indigenous roots	Remembering our Indigenous roots can guide us in the solution of contemporary dilemmas	Researching information on the world of our Indigenous ancestors

Key Terms

Genealogical imagination
Genealogy
Hybridity
Recovery of Indigenous mind

Note: All key terms in this textbook are highlighted in bold and can be found in the Glossary at the end of the book.

Resources Alongside This Chapter

Coming to the Table [CTTT]. (n.d.). Retrieved from http://www.comingtothetable.org/

Coogan, R., Seaward, T., Tana, G. (Producers), & Frears, S., (Director). (2013). *Philomena* [Motion picture]. England: BBC Films.

DeWolf, T. N. (2008). *Inheriting the trade: A northern family confronts its legacy as the largest slave–trading dynasty in U.S. history*. Boston, MA: Beacon Press.

Freeman, V. (2000). *Distant relations: How my ancestors colonized North America*. Toronto, Canada: McClelland & Stewart.

Kremer, J. W. (2011). *Totem body and the recovery of Indigenous mind*. Retrieved from http://www.earth-awareness.com/Resources/online%20catalgue.pdf

Santos, J. P. (1999). *Places left unfinished at the time of creation*. New York, NY: Penguin.

Taylor, T. (2013). *The forage house: Poems*. Pasadena, CA: Red Hen Press.

Many people have become acquainted with **genealogy** through popular TV shows researching the ancestry of celebrities, such as "Who do you think you are?" and "Finding your roots". Ancestral research is a foundational component of ethnoautobiography, the *ethno–* of it. Yet, we have to approach our explorations of ancestry in a deeper way than TV shows by exploring the cultural transmission we are a part of. There are three elements to an ethnoautobiographical approach to ances-

we can begin to explore the worlds of our ancestors empathically and imaginatively. Then we can make use of our **genealogical imagination** in order to build relationships and create stories among and between the people, places, and beings in the family. We can evoke the worlds of the past through the specifics of our family histories.

Third, and importantly, the constant touchstone in all ethnoautobiographical work is to hold dear the knowledge that all people were Indigenous, at some

> We Indian people who had inhabited the land of the fountain of youth had not been meant to survive and yet we did, some of us, carrying the souls of our ancestors, and now they speak through us. It was this that saved my life, that finally contained me. Or better said, I contained it.
>
> Hogan (2001, p. 4)

try that distinguishes it from popular concerns focused on family trees and famous people in one's lineage.

First, researching our family tree is the necessary and inevitable beginning. It is a foundation for ethnoautobiographical work in general, and subsequent steps lead deeper into working with the meanings of our **genealogy**. While it is a mandatory ingredient, it hardly explains everything about us as the various chapters in this book demonstrate.

Second, once we have the necessary information about our ancestry

time and in some place. In this context, **genealogy** is an inevitable part of the decolonization process. Learning about our Indigenous roots is the beginning point from which we can retell our stories with healing imagination.

Family trees

The first step for the work of this chapter is to research as much of our family tree as we can. We may be lucky and have a family historian to consult or we may have to do the work ourselves. Asking living relatives, especially the oldest, is a good beginning point. There may be members of our family who have important information, though we may have not been in touch with them. We can look through photo albums and ask about the people in the pictures. We may find documents that help reconstruct our family tree; in Christian traditions, the family bible may contain important pieces we are looking for. We can also ask our parents and others about treasured possessions that have been handed down in the family — what is the story of these artifacts? Who was the first owner? For the purposes of this workbook it will be good if you are able to research your ancestry at least back to your great–grandparents and perhaps farther, though that may take some time.

We may end up with something that looks like this:

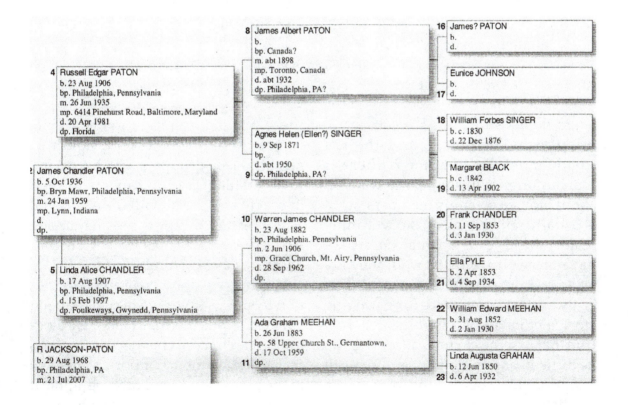

Figure 11.1. R's paternal family tree.

Or like this:

Abraham Meir KLEIN	1844 Smolenitz (Slovakia) — 1924 Tyrnau
Rosa (Rivka) EHRENSTEIN	1846 (about) Skalitze — 1925 Tyrnau

Children:
1. Charlotte
2. Riesa
3. Sidi (…)

1. Charlotte KLEIN   1871 – 1923, Tyrnau
   Jacob EHRLICH   1869, Pressburg — Tyrnau
   a) Hilda Ehrlich
      — Freund
         5 children: 4 died in concentration camp. (…)
2. Riesa KLEIN   1894 — 1975, Tyrnau, Watz, Strasbourg
   Samuel BUCHINGER   1877 — 1936, Watz, Hungary
   7 children, all born in Watz (…)

Figure 11.2. Excerpt from Cixous' family tree: Klein from Tyrnau (Slovakia) family tree (Cixous & Calle–Gruber, 1997, p. 190ff).

As demonstrated in R's self–introduction in Chapter 1, and the riff Coaquannok, in Chapter 7, there is real importance in having information about biological family members, what is usually called family history. Family history includes the actual family we have grown up with, as well; they are also a part of who we have become. This is always a starting place for gathering stories ethnoautobiographically. It is true that in some circumstances this can be difficult and troubling: in the case of adoption, for example. Even more so, for those of African descent whose path back in time is filled with the pain and horror of enslavement and the Middle Passage. Yet, even through this hardship there are many active genealogists in the African American community. Indeed, groups such as Coming to the Table (CTTT, n.d) were formed in part to also assist with the emotional aspects of family history research among African Americans, as well as descendants of slave owning Whites.

At times we don't have any information to start with or we may have been adopted. While this may make genealogical research more challenging, it nonetheless can come to important results. In the process of ethnoautobiographical research a number of people who were adopted did find their biological parents and even siblings who had grown up separately. As has been said before, *we always have to start with where we are*: with any documents or photos we have in our possession, and what they might tell us. We might contact adoption agencies. We can also pay attention to our intuition and our dreams. We could look at what have we surrounded ourselves with in our lives, and see if there is anything that might provide clues. The most important step is to ask questions and listen for all the possible responses and feelings: Who are my parents? Who are my ancestors? Where do I come from? Within an Indigenous paradigm you would ask these questions at a special place (by the ocean or at a tree or a place dear to you) and make an offering of some kind (offer something that is meaningful to you, so that you give it away).

Regardless of personal background, ethnoautobiography encourages relationship building and a good place to do this is with our actual and our biological ancestors. In the riff Coaquannok, R's ancestors provide access to all kinds of stories about Philadelphia, how history is entwined with family, and a rippling out in relationship. Ethnoautobiography does not end with a family tree; in fact, that is only a beginning.

Genealogical imagination

We have discussed the important role of imagination in the exploration of history (Chapter 9). It can help us remember and reconstruct context with larger stories. In much the same way, a genealogical imagination applies a fuller story to our individual and family stories. While we might never know for certain how particular ancestors lived their lives, for example, we may visualize, imagine and creatively put ourselves into those situations to connect with a more complex story of self, community, and place. The visualizing settlement activity at the end of Chapter 3 is an example of such imaginative work.

Engaging our genealogical imagination can happen in many different ways. We can watch documentaries, read historical novels, watch movies set in the time of our ancestors, read history books, look at a historical atlas, we can leaf through photo books of your grandparent's town, and much more. Both the Internet and libraries offer many resources. We have always been surprised how these rich resources can help us with an exact imagination of the past. Reading or watching some of this material before going to bed may incubate our dreaming and help creative integration through unconscious processes. We can also engage our visionary capacities by going on a shamanic journey or using active imagination (a Jungian approach, see Hopcke 1989) to find ancestors in our imagination. We can then return to some of the other approaches to see how we can ground our findings in what we can find in libraries or on the Internet.

We have noted how Cixous (1997) expresses genealogical imagination as she includes an expansive notion of **genealogy** along with her sense of immediate family relationships. "When I speak today in terms of genealogy, it is no longer only Europe that I see, but, in an astral [relating to the stars] way, the totality of the universe" (p. 189).

imagination. Here is the beginning of the first chapter, entitled "Resumé":

> I was born on May 25, 1954, in Verviers, Belgium, the only child of Lucien Mathieu Amélie Sante and Denis Lambertine Alberte Marie Ghislane

> Yet in leaving home I did not lose touch with my own origins because *lo mexicano* is in my system. I am a turtle, wherever I go I carry "home" on my back.
>
> Anzaldúa (1987, p. 21)

Anzaldúa (1987) notes that even when leaving home she remained in contact with her home because she was connected to her family. "Yet in leaving home I did not lose touch with my own origins because lo mexicano is in my system. I am a turtle, wherever I go I carry 'home' on my back" (p. 21). In much the same way, Leslie Marmon Silko said that once you honor your ancestors you are at home anywhere on earth (L. M. Silko, personal communication, April 2, 1996).

How do we see genealogical imagination expressed while working the branches of our family tree? Finding your own voice and thus the strength of your own creativity is important. Luc Sante wrote *The Factory of Facts* (1998) in which he explores his own sense of identity. While the book is not an example of ethnoautobiography, per se, it is an example of working with **genealogical**

> Nandrin. Following the bankruptcy of my father's employer, an iron foundry that manufactured woolcarding machinery, and at the suggestion of friends who had emigrated earlier, my parents decided to move to the United States in search of work. (p.3)

Sante goes on to describe his parent's travels back and forth since the job situation in both Belgium and the US wasn't good. All in all he goes through eight iterations of rewriting the initial paragraph–long resume. The final version reads:

> I was born in 1954 in Verviers, Belgium, the only child of Lucien and Denise Sante. Following the bankruptcy of my father's employer, an iron foundry that manufactured woolcarding machinery, my parents sat on the floor. Dust accumulated.

Things fell and were not picked up. Mold grew on the potatoes in the cellar. The milk solidified. The electricity was cut off. Neighboring boys threw stones that broke the windows, and cold air blew in. First insects, then rodents, and eventually birds arrived to make their homes with us. Soon snow covered the dust, and then soot covered the snow. We grew increasingly warm as we slept. (p. 11)

What was a bare–bones resume before, now has become a poetic description that is rich in emotional overtones and expresses the sense the author has of things unspoken.

Names can also provide guidance for our **genealogical imagination**. One of Jürgen's ancestors is Martin Boczian. The last name is likely a variant spelling for bocian, meaning stork. Storks are abundant in the Olsztyn area where the town of Botkuny is located, an area where the border has changed frequently between Poland, East Prussia, and Lithuania. It reminded Jürgen of a magical experience of his youth when a flock of several hundred storks flew over his home in Germany to rest in a meadow across the road. They were on their annual migration to Africa. Standing by the flock of these large black and white birds with long, bright red beaks continues to be a cherished childhood memory.

Icelanders are famous for their extensive genealogical records which often reach back into mythic times (such as the time of Brynhilde). Many homes have a printed book that contains the family history on fifty or a hundred pages. Here is a brief self–introduction by an Icelandic woman:

> I, Valgerður Hjördis Bjarnadóttir, am a woman. I am the mother of Sunna Elin and the daughter of Kristjana Tryggvadóttir and Bjarni Sigurðsson, the granddaughter of Elín and Tryggvi, Kristín and Sigurður. I trace my lineage over many generations to Auður djúpúgða and Álfdís barreyska, women who came from across the sea to the shores of my country, more than a thousand years back. (Bjarnadóttir & Kremer, 1998/99, p. 135)

Auður djúpúgða, or Aud the Deep Minded, lived from 843 to 900 CE and was a courageous early settler of Iceland who built her own boat, a Viking *knar*, to make her way from the Hebrides to Orkney and, finally, Iceland with twenty free men on board. Clearly she was a highly respected figure.

Gerald Vizenor begins his *Interior Landscapes — Autobiographical Myths and Metaphors* (2009) with reference to a tribal myth of his Anishinaabe ancestors which tells how the first totems came about. He continues, in the second paragraph, with what he knows of his **genealogy**:

> Alice Mary Beaulieu, my paternal grandmother, was born more than a

century ago on the White Earth Reservation in Minnesota. She inherited the crane totem, a natural tribal pose, but we were crossbloods, loose families at the end of the depression in the cities.

Clement William Vizenor, my father, was a crane descendant. He was born on the reservation and was murdered twenty–six years later on a narrow street in Minneapolis. My tribal grandmother and my father were related to the leaders of the crane; that succession, over a wild background of cedar and concrete, shamans and colonial assassins, is celebrated here in the autobiographical myths and metaphors of my imagination, my crossblood remembrance. We are cranes on the rise in new tribal narratives. (p. 3)

Vizenor acknowledges his **hybridity** and gives a feel for the world of his ancestral background: cedar and concrete; shamans and colonial assassins. From the tragedy of his father's murder he moves to the renewal of tribal narratives as cranes rise.

In many traditions the telling of a story requires that speakers situate themselves. The following example is from a collection of Tlingit oral narrative entitled *"Haa Shuká*, Our Ancestors" (1987). Even if we don't understand all the Tlingit terms or find the names strange, the beginning of the telling gives a sense of the intermeshing of myth, **genealogy**, place, and the history of colonization. *Kiks.ádi* are one of the Raven moiety clans.

To those of us Kiks.ádi
from Sitka,
many things happened.
We became salmon people,
Aak'wtaatseen.
One of us also stayed with Kooshdaa Kwáani,
Kaakáa.
One of us sailed out,
Kaax'achgóok.
People usually wonder who is talking.
My father was Tak'xoo.
He was the nephew of L. aanteech.
My grandfather
Was Kaak'wáji
And my great grandfather
Kaat'aláa,
On my father's side.
I have four names,

Names given to me.
A white man would not use them. (…)
This story I will tell you
Is of my mother's maternal uncles,
When Kaax'achgook sailed out.
The place named Sitka
Was a Tlingit village,
Sitka.
It is the place now called
Old Sitka.
But that place is not Sitka.
They called it Gajaahéen.
It is the one on this side; on the other side is Walach'éix'i.
In between Noow Tlein was built by the Russians.
Now it is called Old Sitka by the white folks.
(Dauenhauer & Dauenhauer, 1987, pp. 83 & 85)

"People usually wonder who is talking" establishes the cultural demand for genealogical context. The speaker also states who the story is about, it is about "my mother's maternal uncles." The place names then establish both traditional names and colonial history. He proceeds to tell the story of a hunt.

Some years ago a Hawaiian *kahuna*, a healing specialist, came to visit the program for Indigenous students that Apela Colorado and Jürgen were directing. All the students had gathered in the room awaiting him. Kahu Kapi'ioho'okalani Lyons took some moments outside, looking up and around, breathing deeply. Then he started to move very slowly through the open door, all the while gesturing as in invitation. As he walked he faced to the outside, not the inside where his audience was waiting. He kept making large gestures of invitation as he gradually moved to center stage. At that point he faced his audience and said: "Now we can start, now all my ancestors are here."

Indigenous roots

All peoples have Indigenous roots somewhere, sometime. While contemporary Indigenous people feel and enact their ancestral connections, modern people severed the connection to their Indigenous roots at some point along the way. When we trace our ancestries it is a good to see if we can identify the point of severance, the shift in culture or the trauma that changed their minds, their consciousness. It is also good to always keep in mind all our ancestors somewhere sometime have lived within a world of nurturing conversation, a world akin to what we know about Indigenous peoples today. Certainly this was not a perfect or ideal world, but just as certainly it was a world where the connection to all our relations was regarded differently.

The Eurocentered, or White mind has a habit of **forgetting** settler histories, the stories of how we came to be where we are (S. Turner, 1999, 2002). Or, as Carter (1996) relays: "Indigenous people say that Westerners have lost their dreaming" (pp. 363–364). Losing one's dreaming means losing one's ancestral connections and the ways in which they feed our sense of self. This once again points to the healing potential present in ethnoautobiographical inquiries. At the same time, this also encourages an expansive, imaginative and even playful approach to this work. This also provides a segue to another foundation of ethnoautobiography: **recovery of Indigenous mind**.

While the phrase may seem confusing, the idea is clear: all people were Indigenous at some time and place in history. This is not a romantic, idealistic notion at all. Rather, as is the case with all aspects of ethnoautobiography, such recovery is a process of decolonization, filled with critical humility and compassionate ruthlessness. Awareness of family histories (both actual relationships as well as imagined genealogies), senses of place, and repairing relationships are only some elements of an enlarged and enriched sense of self, of what is called a **recovery of Indigenous mind** (Colorado, 1996; Kremer, 2011).

The exploration of ancestral roots, or the recovery of Inigenous mind, requires critical discourse that is integrated with emotional, somatic, spiritual, and other alternate ways of knowing. Perhaps the most important emphasis is that, in the context of decolonization, this recovery process is where Eurocentered people acknowledge they reside in more complex narratives. They participate with many people, beings, histories, and that ancestral processes have unfolded to bring them where they are.

The process of working with literal ancestries and the process of genealogical imagination to flesh out what we know leads us into a world in which our Indigenous roots can inspire and feed our creativity and presence today.

Activity 1

Family Pictures

A) Select a family photo, and develop a simple description of it. Then imagine yourself as a person in the photo. Visualize yourself as the person at the moment the photo was taken. What feelings does this bring up? Both in terms of the family member, your connection or knowledge of them, as well as the act of imagining, as well. You can do this with all the people that are in the photo, if there are more than one.

B) What do you know about the context in which the photo was taken: Where was it? When? How? By whom? And why was it taken?

C) Can you discern any photographic conventions in the photo? What are the aesthetics of the photo? For example, is it a portrait, or are the people dressed and behaving in a very formal manner? What does this say about the time period and place it was taken?

D) Who was the photo made for? Who has it now and where is it kept? Who saw it then and who sees it now? (Modified from Kuhn, 2002, p. 8)

This may be completed in a 500–word response paper, or shared as an oral presentation with others. Sharing a reproduction (digital or hard copy) of the photograph is required.

Note: As an acknowledgement for those people who were adopted, orphaned, or whose family lines were severed by violence (enslavement, boarding schools, genocide, etc.), this activity can be particularly challenging (in whole or part because of its extremely painful, traumatic, and emotional associations). In such a circumstance, we most humbly encourage you to complete the activity with whatever photographic material you might have at hand, even if it is not a "family picture" per se. Photographs in books are one alternative. Also, a vital part of the activity is to acknowledge the feelings associated with such work. All experiences are encouraged and welcome. Along the same lines (as is true for all EA work), having the support of a group of people, whether good friends, other members of a community group, other students, family members, etc. is a rich and rewarding aspect of this, as well.

Activity 2

Mapping Ancestry

Create a family map using a traditional format or something creative that shows some of the places your family and/or ancestors have lived. This can include flags, family crests, and other types of pictorial representations of your ancestry and the places they have lived. See note above in Activity 1 if you have unique family circumstances, such as adoption, being orphaned, etc.

Share the final product as an oral presentation with others. Sharing a reproduction (digital or hard copy) of the images is required.

Note: If you are completing these activities on your own, and do not have an organized group to do oral presentations for (such as in a classroom, community organization and so on), it is encouraged that you present the work you are doing to a friend, family member or spouse to experience sharing your process in oral form. This is especially true if you have special circumstances as mentioned above.

Chapter Summary

Approaching ancestry as more complex than simple family history provides entrance into a **genealogical imagination**, where relationships with people, places and beings becomes the primary objective. **Recovery of Indigenous mind** is the restoration or remembering of those relationships and the quality of being in them, which all people have in their heritage.

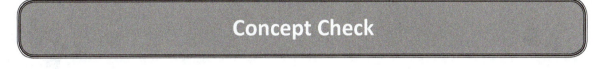

Concept Check

How is it that Anzaldúa is always able to be at home?

What are some situations where doing genealogical research might be difficult or even emotionally painful?

What three things does **recovery of Indigenous mind** emphasize?

NOTES

Chapter 12

En/gendering Embodied Ethnoautobiography

Riff

Of Boy Scouts, Sexual Abuse and Settler Identity

Dallas, Texas
May 2011

I can't completely explain it
How various themes, narratives, experiences
Show up suddenly
Or reappear
Bringing together various strands
Into consciousness

This happened yesterday
Driving along Harry Hines Blvd. in Dallas
Passing the Scouting Center

Immediately pondering my experience of
Sexual abuse at, literally, the hands of my
Scout Master, Chip

I've done lots of work around
The wounds that still linger
I prepared a portfolio of sorts
For my therapist, Patricia
Showing that I had done enough work
To justify receiving my
Sexual abuse merit badge

But then something else flew across my consciousness
As I have been spending time
These last few days
Being present to the collective shadow
Of Indian Boarding Schools

With their physical, cultural and, yes,
Sexual violence against Native children

These institutions were designed to
Kill the Indian, and supposedly save the man
Most often run by churches
Carrying out the mission of conquest
Instilling order, and physical discipline
On the savage, wild Indian
Reminds me of the Boy Scouts

And there is still more to the
Bizarre connections
Between my experience
(And many others)
In the Scouts
And the violence of Boarding Schools

Could it be a coincidence
That at the same time
As the Friends of the Indian
Gathered in upstate New York
At Lake Mohonk
To help lift Indians out of
Savagery

That other enlightened White folks
Wanted to embrace a bit of savagery
In themselves
And were inspired to organize the
Boy Scouts
To Play Indian

Maybe it's the other side
Of the same coin
Of conquest, and settlement

The conquerors embody the violence
As they seek to stamp it out
By force
Refusing to allow anyone
The right or ability to
Be in relationship
With land, spirit, animal

If the settlers could not
Live in balance
They would do everything
In their power
To make sure no one else would

The Friends of the Indian
The Boarding School priests and nuns
Their barrier
To passion, relationship, reciprocity
Would certainly be taught to others
By force, if necessary

My settler ancestors
Could not imagine
Living in relationship
With the land
They were removed from that experience
Through enclosure
Industrial revolution
Christian separation from nature
Migration and exile
Settlement and conquest

So it is then
So many generations later
That as I drive down a street in Dallas
I move through my own experience of
Pain and healing

And feel the connections
With the pain and healing
Of others

I am not the only one who
Speaks out about the violations
Of my childhood vulnerability
By lost and manipulative Scout Masters

I witness Native elders
Share the healing journey
Back from the underworld
Of violent separation
To balance, and connection

Similarly, other White folks
Speak out about our loss
Our pain
Our underworld journey

The time is long overdue
To lay the hurt and angry spirits
To rest
To honor the healing
To renew our obligations
To feel connection again

RJP

Chapter Outline	Core Concepts	Ethnoautobiographical Perspectives	Expected Outcomes
Of Boy Scouts, sexual abuse and settler identity	There are powerful personal connections between history, gender, and identity	Feeling connection allows for support in facing difficult material	Understand how gender roles are shaped by and connected to larger forces
Indigenous gender understandings	Indigenous peoples have gender identities beyond male/female binary	Fluid Indigenous gender identities challenge Western norms	See the diversity in Indigenous gender identities
Gender borderlands	Gender norms influence emotions and worldview	Critiquing gender norms brings us home to ourselves	Encourage diverse perspectives of our gendered identity
Embodying our true selves	Gender connects to sexuality, body awareness, and worldview	Decolonizing gender opens new varieties in identity	Embrace gender vulnerability as a transformative possibility
The lessons of Staff Sergeant Harley	Societal gender expectations do not fit with experience	Challenging norms of gender expectation can lead to deeper relationships	Find ways to view people beyond gender norms

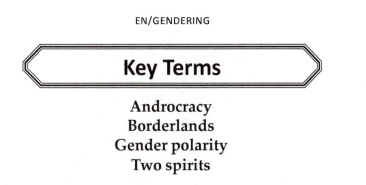

Key Terms

Androcracy
Borderlands
Gender polarity
Two spirits

Note: All key terms in this textbook are highlighted in bold and can be found in the Glossary at the end of the book.

Resources Alongside This Chapter

Adams, T. E., & Jones, S. H. (2008) Autoethnography is queer. In N. K. Denzin, Y. S. Lincoln, & L. T. Smith (Eds.), *Handbook of critical and Indigenous methodologies* (pp. 373–390). Thousand Oaks, CA: Sage.

Bem, S. L. (1995). Dismantling gender polarization and compulsory heterosexuality: Should we turn the volume down or up? *Journal of sex research* 32(4), 329–334.

Brenner, R., Winter, R. (Producers), & Vallée, J–M., (Director). (2014). *Dallas buyers club* [Motion picture]. United States: Universal Studios Home Entertainment.

Ensler, E. (2013). *In the body of the world: A memoir.* New York, NY: Metropolitan Books.

Hobgood, M. E. (2009). *Dismantling privilege – An ethics of accountability.* Cleveland, OH: The Pilgrim Press.

hooks, b. (2004). *The will to change: Men, masculinity, and love.* New York, NY: Atria Books.

Nibley, L. (Director). (2010). *Two spirits* [Documentary]. United States: Riding Tiger Productions.

Ryan, C., & Jethá, C. (2010). *Sex at dawn: The prehistoric origins of modern sexuality.* New York, NY: Harper.

Shepherd, P. (2010). *New self, new world: Recovering our senses in the twenty–first century.* Berkeley, CA: North Atlantic Press.

Wright, I. T. (2012). *Fifty shades of gay.* Retrieved from http://www.ted.com/talks/io_tillett_wright_fifty_shades_of_gay.html

Contemporary Western societies continue to be characterized by a polar — male or female — understanding of gender. Such attitudes about gender are a social construction resulting from a complex patriarchal history. In this chapter, we first introduce an Indigenous understanding of gender that is outside this common polarity. This leads us to consider the decolonization of **gender**

the presence of *both* feminine and masculine qualities in a person and behavior that is outside an either–or understanding of gender.

D'Anglure (1992) talks of an old Inuit woman from Igloolik who was a shaman's daughter. In the Inuit world womb and igloo share the same layout, and the layout of the Igloo is a map to travel the world shamanically (in trance).

> **Sex is to gender as light is to color.**
>
> Bem (1995, p. 66)

polarities, as well. Getting outside of the constraints of the either/or female/male binary provides access to a radical presence in the form of body awareness, emotional intelligence and alternative worldviews. Finally, once we are able to come home to varieties of gender construction, we can experience fluid identities as supportive and transformative, rather than rigid and inflexible.

Indigenous gender understandings

In 1986, Williams published *The Spirit and the Flesh*, a formative book on "sexual diversity in American Indian Culture". Since then numerous books have discussed two–spirit people (Jacobs, Thomas, & Lang, 1997), the changing ones (Roscoe, 1998), or third sex or third gender (Herdt, 1996). **Two spirits** is a term often used in Indigenous communities to respect

The woman remembered living within her mother's womb, this being laid out like the interior of an igloo. She could also recall a previous life as her own grandfather. When she was in the womb a dog poked its head through the door from time to time. It had a mouth set on its face vertically and vomited food for her. It was probably, so she told me, her father's penis. She was still a man when a desire came upon her to leave so she took a man's knife on the lefthand side (on the righthand when entering [the igloo]) and headed for the passageway. At the thought, however, of the dangerous hunting life she would have to lead, she put down these male instruments and took from the righthand side a woman's knife and a small cooking pot. She pushed her way out with much effort.

Then his penis was reabsorbed, a slit opened up in her body, and she became a girl. (pp. 146–147)

This story suggests not only a pre–natal memory, but also biological gender fluidity, even choice. The following story illustrates a similar point, suggesting that shamanic magic can be used to change one's biological gender.

The first two humans emerged from the ground on Igloolik Island at the dawn of time. Out of boredom, they decided to procreate. One made the other pregnant but, when it came time to give birth, there was no opening for the fetus to pass through. Undaunted, the companion of the pregnant man sang a magic song which caused the latter's penis to shrivel up, leaving an opening in its place and thus creating the first woman through the transformation of a man. (D'Anglure, 1992, p, 147)

D'Anglure distills his research with the Inuit people into a graph [see below] that illustrates not only three sexes and genders, but also how they are embed-

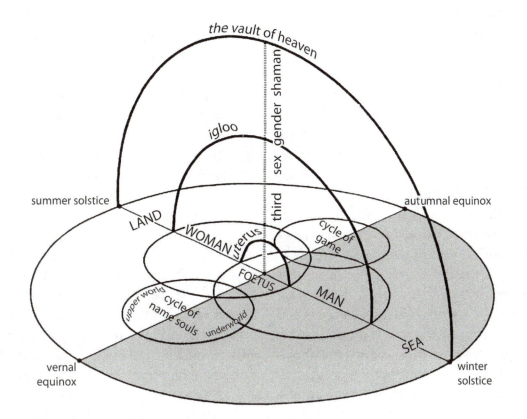

Figure 12.1. Inuit Worldview – on the border between sexes/genders (based on d'Anglure, 1992, p. 148).

ded in the seasonal cycles and the different worlds of the Inuit culture.

Nibley's (2010) documentary, *Two Spirits*, is a powerful testament to Indigenous gender fluidity and the resulting tragedy as a two–spirited young man is confronted by the racist and sexist attitudes of the dominant soci-

In addition to validating and making space for the lived experience of people who do not "fit" the categories, critiquing gender constructions has far–reaching and important consequences. Susan Griffin (1978) in her White feminist classic, *Women and Nature*, was clear that "patriarchal

> **Among the most effective ways of oppressing a people is through the colonization of their bodies, the stigmatizing of their desires, and the repression of their erotic energies.**
>
> Rofes, cited in Hobgood (2009, p. 111)

ety, resulting in a hate crime. Fred Martinez was *nádleehí*, a male bodied person with a feminine nature that the Navajo culture regards as a special gift. The movie shows how Fred saw himself neither as this or that or a third, but how his gendered sense of self was fluid and expressed itself differently within short spans of time.

Gender borderlands

Similarly, Anzaldua (1987) connects her sense of cultural identity with her simultaneous experience in the gender borderlands: "But I, like other queer people, am two in one body, both male and female" (p. 19). This serves as personal introduction to the need to decolonize rigid gender polarities as does the above quote from Bem connecting gender to color. The point is simple: there can be as many shades of gender identity as there are colors in the rainbow.

thought does…represent itself as emotionless (objective, detached and bodiless)" (p. xv). Jaggar (2008) expands on this dichotomy:

> Typically, the rational has been contrasted with the emotional with reason associated with the mental, the cultural, the universal, the public and the male, whereas emotion has been associated with the irrational, the physical, the natural, the particular, the private, and, of course, the female. (p. 378)

As has been characterized in relation to nature, history, and culture, Eurocentrism attempts to dissociate, or push to the side what it deems as threatening. Sandra Bem (1995) addresses this directly when she notes "the demonized are as necessary to the system of compulsory heterosexuality as the privileged" (p. 63). She continues with a great analogy of shoes and dirt on the table: "all the people who might currently be embraced by the label *queer* in our society are themselves the 'dirt' that both define and threaten the culture's cherished classifications of sex/gender/desire" (p. 64).

The same allegation can be made about the connections between gender, race, and colonization as well. Andrea Smith (2005) makes clear that *"colonial relationships are themselves gendered and sexualized"* (p. 8). These relationships built on colonization view Indigenous presence as contamination requiring violent determinations by amer–europeans in order that "the colonial body...purify itself" (A. Smith, 2005, p. 9). Indeed, the portrayal of the colonized as "dirty" is a constant theme in Eurocentered narratives.

As the opening riff "Of Boy Scouts" illustrates, the impacts of colonization and gender oppression are complicated, interwoven, and effect everyone in potentially devastating ways. Bem (1995) notes that the medical response to the "anomalies" of intersex people (those born with both genitalia), "can be read not as progress but as a mode of discipline," for the colonized and colonizer alike. "Among the most effective ways of oppressing a people is through the colonization of their bodies, the stigmatizing of their desires, and the repression of their erotic energies" (Eric Rofes, cited in Hobgood, 2009, p. 111).

This points to the importance that ethnoautobiographical inquiry has on identity, gender, and bodies. "But my intuition tells me that my Indigenous consciousness doesn't quite easily lend itself to labels whose history is not really mine" (Strobel, 2005, p. 61). Through such decolonizing approaches, ethnoautobiography not only breaks us free of the constraints of compulsory heterosexuality, it brings us home to ourselves.

It is vital to see the connections between gender identity, worldview and the sense of our selves in the world. Griffin (1995) in *The Eros of Everyday Life* accurately describes a longing for greater participation with the world. "But the dream," she realizes, "is also memory of a more intimate kind. The wish for communion exists in the body" (p. 145). Glendinning (1994) links psychological trauma and potential healing: "could it be that our very culture splits mind from body, intellect from feeling, because we as individuals are suffering from post–traumatic stress?" (p. 62)

In many ways, compulsory heterosexuality and strict gender norms continue to inflict traumas on all people, whatever gender or orientation they are. Hobgood (2009) notes that

> The problem...is not the breakdown of the family; the problem is the traditional family itself. The reason the nuclear family is breaking down — or exists as one of the most dangerous sites in North America for women and children — is because people

in it are often isolated emotionally and stressed economically. (p. 126)

Such statements link ethnoautobiographical work in general with this aspect related to gender, in particular. Ethnoautobiographical inquiry makes clear that decolonization is not only necessary for all people, it is incumbent for Whites, all Eurocentered people,

And what is the truth? Are men supposed to be the living embodiment of reason, mental smarts, emotional distance, and the tamer of nature and women? What alternatives are there if that does not describe who you are? What do you do with your doubts and fears? Are men even allowed to have doubts and fears? What if you regret or long for connection, relationship

> **Thus, at the most primordial level of sensuous, bodily experience, we find ourselves in an expressive, gesturing landscape, in a world that speaks.**
>
> **Abram (1996, p. 81)**

and especially men. Decolonizing gender shows that it is not women alone who suffer from (hetero–) sexism. "Male gender formation carefully sets up privileged men for this work as it deprives them of the human skills for relationship and nurturance" (Hobgood, 2009, p. 127). Quoting Barbara Deming, hooks (2004) makes a similar point.

> I think the reason that men are so very violent is that they know, deep in themselves, that they're acting out a lie, and so they're furious at being caught up in the lie. But they don't know how to break it.... They're in a rage because they are acting out a lie—which means that in some deep part of themselves they want to be delivered from it, are homesick for the truth. (p. 4)

whether with other humans or the natural world?

Griffin (1995) has one answer to these questions. "The system designed to protect us from nature creates an unnatural frailty. Divided from life processes which cannot be extricated from death, from earth, the grounding of being, the self is confused. There is a crisis of identity" (p. 52). In these false separations and dichotomies between various identities and relationships we are not only cut off from aspects of ourselves, we live a fragmented existence in the world. "In other words, if we must shut down in one area, we shut down at the central nervous system. If we cannot feel deep friendship including sexual passion, we cannot feel much else either, including deep joy, compassion, or pain for our world" (Hobgood, 2009, p. 130).

Embodying our true selves

Ethnoautobiography encourages various practices that have been suggested to heal the mind/body dichotomy. As we approach complex gender **borderlands**, we begin to see the ways in which the masterful self of Western societies has built walls around our experience of the world, and thus simultaneously, around our selves. Abram (2010)

(1994) scholarship on embodied emotions for building practices of reconciliation. Gibson's (2008) practice of somatic archaeology, and Tarakali's (n.d.) "Embodied Education for Healing and Social Change" are two important contributions to bridging the separation between body and identity. Such connections made between healing and integrating body–mind–spirit point to many possibilities for the future of decolonization work. Similarly, ethnoautobiography supports breaking the bound-

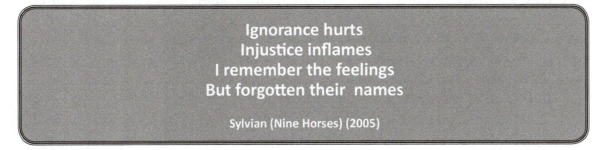

Ignorance hurts
Injustice inflames
I remember the feelings
But forgotten their names

Sylvian (Nine Horses) (2005)

makes the connection between bridging the mind/body divide and reviving relationships with the natural world. Accordingly, as we break down inherited norms of gender and body, we arrive at the multiple possibilities for healing our selves and our world.

For example, Emerson and Hopper (2011) bring the mindfulness–based traditions of yoga to heal post-traumatic stress (PTSD is a common consequence of sexual abuse, and other gender–based violence). Worthington (2006) acknowledges the applicability of Damasio's

aries of the **masterful** self, and arriving into a fuller experience of who we are.

I would say that the erotic has to do with intensity of engagement, a heightened sense of excitement, awareness of one's ability to affect others, a deepened sense of vulnerability, and the need to express joy and gratitude. Erotic experiences with my and others' children, with women and men I love, with the ocean or the forest, while writing or running or teaching, are whole-body, whole–heart, and whole–soul experiences. (Hobgood, 2009, p. 117)

Hobgood's description of the erotic relates to Vizenor's term **holosexuality** which was introduced previously.

Therefore, decolonizing gender and opening to new varieties in gender identity embraces vulnerability as a transformative possibility (Brown, 2010, 2012). In this possibility lies a fluidity that offers potential, and is simultaneously supportive. The flexibility to embrace the true gendered self distances us from the false narratives constructed by Eurocentrism, and reclaims a **borderland** of integrity and wholeness. In the realm of science and worldviews: if the mind is embodied, that is, fully rooted and integrated in the body, then "philosophy can never be the same again" (Lakoff & Johnson, 1999, p. 3). The radical implications are well characterized by Body–Mind Centering visionary Bonnie Bainbridge Cohen (2012):

> My method of study and research, which I named Body–Mind Centering, has been to discover myself in the life of the cells of my body, to differentiate each type of tissue, to integrate all of my cells within the context of my whole being, to release my awareness back into my unconscious, and to share this process with others. In this study,

we are each at all times whole, constantly changing, and engaged as the subject, material, and observer (p. 158).

Vulnerability is an empowering first vaccination against **androcracy**. All of this is about the ability to feel, to begin to reclaim our bodies that have been stripped away. hooks (1994) advocates for an **eros** in critical pedagogy because of its power to transform and challenge the dualism between mind and body. She writes that "…those of us who have been intimately engaged as students and teachers with feminist thinking have always recognized the legitimacy of a pedagogy that dares to subvert the mind/body split and allow us to be whole in the classroom" (p. 193). This means creating a space for feelings and somatic experiences in the classroom and beyond.

When we enter different cultural worlds we may also encounter possibilities for varied gender identities. These possibilities challenge the heterosexism of gender–dominated Eurocentered culture. There are at least three reasons: first, to honor the "born this way" reality, affirming that everyone has a right to be who they are, regardless of where they fall on the spectrum of sexuality; additionally, respecting the two–spirits within people also provides more options for personal and collective identities; and, finally, such embrace of a variety of androgynous possibilities is deeply transformative.

Bem (1995) moves away from her hopes of eliminating gender constructions ("turning the volume down"), toward turning the volume way up:

> I propose that we let a thousand categories of sex/gender/desire begin to bloom in any and all fluid and permeable configurations and, through that very proliferation, that we thereby undo (or, if you prefer, that we de–privilege or de–center or de–stabilize) the privileged status of the two–and–only–two that are currently treated as normal and natural. If a thousand categories seems too many, then let's begin with at least 18. Why 18? The math is simple: two sexes (male/female) X three genders (masculine/feminine/androgynous) X three desires (heterosexual/homosexual/bisexual). (p. 62)

Ethnoautobiographical inquiry helps us to pay attention to aspects of gender which we may only be dimly aware of or to affirm our sense of gender as we feel it. It creates a space to be in our own gender process and presence without the impediments of labels. Ethnoautobiography creates both reflective awareness and **embodiment**. In doing so, we encourage the decentering of gender privilege, of creating gender trouble (Butler, 1990), and see what the potential is. "Connecting with our androgynic origins thus means the recovery of an ancient potential for integration that has persisted ceremonially in the shamanic practices of Indigenous peoples" (Beyman & Kremer, 2003, p. 45).

Perhaps such inquiry goals are in keeping with Hobgood's ethical eroticism:

> An ethical eroticism would support our need, as social beings, to connect sensually with ourselves, with the natural world, with human work, and with the many others with whom we share passionate interdependence. An ethical eroticism would transform our relations to ourselves. (Hobgood, 2009, p. 132)

In the midst of the nexus of all of these potentials and possibilities for expanded inquiry, personal transformation, individual healing, renewing embodiment, worldview shifts, emotional catharsis, ecological relationship, is also the simple need to humbly grieve for what has been done and what has been lost. hooks (2004) tells of her contacts with men who acknowledge the loss that haunts our very being.

> "Something missing within" was a self–description I heard from many men as I went around our nation talking about love. Again and again a man would tell me about early childhood feelings of emotion, of feeling connected to life and

to other people, and then a rupture happened, a disconnect, and that feeling of being loved, of being embraced, was gone. Somehow the test of manhood, men told me, was the willingness to accept this loss, to not speak it even in private grief. (p. 15)

Griffin (1995) helps to break us out of the boxes and bonds that have defined who we are, or at least, who we are perceived (even by ourselves) to be: "To change how one sees the world is to change the self" (p. 41). The inverse is also true, especially in ethnoautobiography: to change the way one sees oneself also changes the world.

Activity

Activity 1

Gender Collage

Create a collage of 10–15 photos illustrating your sense of gender and experience of gender difference. You may focus your collage in any way you choose. How do you feel about your own gender? How do I perceive other genders? Where and how do I experience differences? Are there cross–cultural issues that are relevant? What stereotypes do I experience? Have there been experiences relating to power, privilege and even violence pertaining to gender identity? Where do I fit in the common gender assumptions and where do I not fit? What are your feelings about intimate relationships between people given these experiences relating to gender identity? What is your experience with gender identities that are fluid, and/or challenge the heteronormative expectation of gender polarity?

This is an opportunity for you to explore your own sense of gender and your (dis)comfort with the role(s) you take and/or that you feel you have been assigned. Develop a written narrative of your process and comment on the images in your collage.

Share the collage as an oral presentation with others. Sharing a reproduction (digital or hard copy) of the collage is required.

Activity 2

Embodying Personal Identity

Investigate and describe your experience of body awareness in your life. This may include issues related to body image, experiences of stereotypes about your body, as well as participation in athletics, dance, yoga, martial arts or other kinesthetic activities. This may also include changes in your perception and awareness over time, due to changes in age, significant events in your life (including experiences of trauma and/or violence), and so on. You are encouraged to include photos of yourself doing these activities or that are related.

This may be completed as a 500–word response paper, or shared as an oral presentation with others.

Note: If you are completing these activities on your own, and do not have an organized group to do oral presentations for (such as in a classroom, community organization and so on), it is encouraged that you present the work you are doing to a friend, family member or spouse to experience sharing your process in oral form.

Chapter Summary

Ethnoautobiography encourages decolonization of **gender** identities, and related dichotomous worldviews. Fluidity in gender norms encourages connection to body, sexuality, emotion, others and nature.

Concept Check

According to the gender polarity of patriarchal thought, what are three common representations of male and female?

Who suffers because of **(hetero–)sexism**? Name two ways they do.

What are some examples or descriptions of **eros**?

How many gender identities does ethnoautobiography support?

Riff

The Lessons of Staff Sergeant Harley

The days slowly bled into the nights during our time in Kuwait. There were a few incidents of individuals in my platoon getting into heated confrontations with one another, but overall everyone remained fairly calm and positive throughout the deployment. Part of our early morning routine was physical fitness. Most days we participated in the traditional Army workout of pushups, sit ups, and running, but once a week we all played some kind of sport. On this particular day, we were all engaged in a game of football out in the desert besides the platoon leader and platoon sergeant. Harley and I were on opposing teams, and as usual a little banter and trash–talk was to be expected amongst a group of young men deployed across the world for a few months. But on this particular day Harley would not stop pestering me. Every time I caught the ball or attempted to make a play down the field, he ran beside me yelling obscenities pertaining to me as a person, my mother, family members, and any other part of me he could think of. It seemed as though everyone else was oblivious to this and had been for the past few weeks. I threw the ball down and turned to confront him and yelled something to the effect that I was sick and tired of him always being on me. I asked him what his problem was, and finally told him that I didn't care if he was a noncommissioned officer, I was challenging his authority anyway.

Two other sergeants separated us and told me to go cool down. I went and showered and changed into my uniform and decided to go for a walk to try and wrap my head around this new, but constant antagonistic behavior by Harley. I was only walking for a space about ten minutes when a few members of my platoon ran to catch up to me and told me that our platoon sergeant was furious with my behavior and that I better get back to the base and see him NOW. I took a deep breath and quickly began my walk back.

As I got back to the base I could see my platoon sergeant outside leaning against a wall with his head down in anger. As soon as I was within shouting range he began unloading the most vicious, vulgar verbal assault to put me in my place. In a censored version, he basically let me know that my disrespect to a noncommissioned officer would not be tolerated. He didn't care what my side of the story was, if I even looked at a noncommissioned officer the wrong way again I would be on a plane to Ft. Leavenworth (military prison) before I knew what had happened.

All I could say was "Roger Sergeant," as he disappeared and left me to fill out the necessary paperwork for disciplinary action. This would be the first time in my military career that I had any type of negative report during my time as a soldier. Of course I thought it was unfair, but there was nothing

I could do but keep my head down, my mouth shut, and not respond to Harley for the rest of our time in Kuwait and the year left of my enlistment.

The next day my platoon was engaged in the routine practice of cleaning and servicing our surveillance equipment. Shortly thereafter we were to go through a demonstration on the Melios surveillance system. The Melios works by shooting a laser at the intended target. The laser returns to the system and provides its user with an accurate distance for the target. SSG Harley volunteered to drive off about a mile or two away so that we could practice using the Melios on his vehicle.

About forty–five minutes passed and we were wrapping up the training exercise. Since we were done, our platoon sergeant got on the radio and informed Harley that he could return. A few moments had passed and there was no response from Harley. My platoon sergeant called him via radio once more. Again no response. This time my platoon sergeant jumped into his vehicle and drove out to Harley's location. Within seconds he was on the radio instructing our platoon leader to call in an emergency medical evacuation. My entire platoon went silent as my platoon leader ordered me to jump on our vehicle and meet our platoon sergeant at Harley's location.

As we approached I saw Harley lying awkwardly on the ground. My platoon sergeant ordered me to grab all of the sensitive items (i.e. weapons, surveillance, and land navigation devices) from the vehicle. As I reached in through the driver's side door to grab Harley's M–16 rifle, I noticed a small hole in the exterior of the vehicle above the driver's side door, and a picture of what I gathered were his children up near the radio. My platoon sergeant yelled at me to put his M–16 rifle back where it was, and to clear a landing zone for a helicopter.

I did as I was instructed and cleared a landing–zone moments before the helicopter came into sight. I helped the helicopter land. They loaded Harley onto it and it took off. I got back into our vehicle and we made our way back to our platoon. All platoon members jumped in their vehicles and made our way back to base in complete silence. All the while I was asking myself how this happened. It wasn't an enemy sniper or my platoon sergeant would have handled the situation differently. Then I remembered the hole above the door, small enough to be from an M–16 round, the placement of his weapon leaned over his Kevlar–helmet in position with his head, the picture of his children hanging directly in front of where he was sitting, and the way his body lay on the dusty desert floor. Tears began to roll down my face as I tried to comprehend the magnitude of the situation. Just yesterday I had been threatened with jail time over the way I responded to this man's behavior. Today I helped load him into a helicopter after he took his own life.

CB

NOTES

Chapter 13
Gathering Ourselves Through Dreams

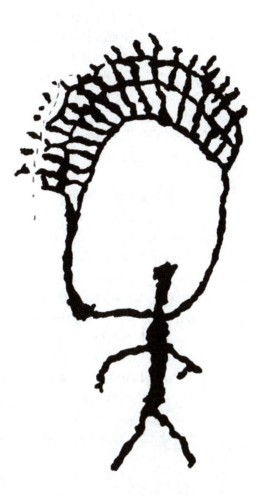

Riff

Movement Passing Through

Lately my dreams
Have been speaking to me
In cardboard boxes
Sometimes being moved
Or, suddenly blown open
Perhaps rummage through
Of all things
Boxes?

Yet upon waking
And later on
There might be perfect meaning
Clear intention
For what my dream is offering me
Sure I've had more seemingly profound
Expansive and enlightening
Dreams
But who am I to say
That a box is any less
Significant
Than a fox, or elders
Or the aurora borealis

Dreams are guides
As well as parts of who we are
Things forgotten or
Neglected
Visions to remember or
Yet to know
Regardless of what I might know
Or understand

These glimpses into
Other worlds
Assist me in
Finding my way
I am actually
Dreaming direction
Whether I know it or not
Which reminds me of a dream

Finding my way through crowds
In order to reach elders
Assembled in regalia
Immediately struck
By some distant knowing
Reminds me of a dream

RJP

Chapter Outline	Core Concepts	Ethnoautobiographical Perspectives	Expected Outcomes
Movement passing through	Paying attention to dreams is as important as the content	Dreams provide imaginative insights into personal identity	Begin to record dreams without attachment to interpretation
Dreams as integrative states of consciousness	Dreams are an integrative state of consciousness we experience every night	Dreams give access to unconscious parts of our self	Appreciate the importance of dreams for ethnoauto-biographical inquiries
The meaning of dreams	We can make meaning of dreams	Dream interpretation has a very long history & the meaning of dreams can enrich our lives	Distinguish between dream images and their meaning
Dream examples	Dreams can assist us on our ethno-autobiographical journey	While the past shows up in our dreams, it is not past	Inspiration to take our dreams seriously
Dream interpretation	Careful dream analysis can reveal meanings	Dreams have the potential to impact our daily lives in insightful ways	Developing the skill to understand our own dreams

Key Terms

Dream
Imaginal psychology
Lucid dream
Normative dissociation

Note: All key terms in this textbook are highlighted in bold and can be found in the Glossary at the end of the book.

Resources Alongside This Chapter

ARAS. (2010). *The book of symbols*. Köln: Taschen.

Boznak, R. (1998). *A little course in dreams*. Boston, MA: Shambhala.

Castleman, T. (2009). *Sacred dream circles*. Einsiedeln, Switzerland: Damion Verlag.

Cooper, J. (1978). *An illustrated encyclopedia of traditional symbols*. London, England: Thames and Hudson.

Johnson, R. (1986). *Inner work: Using dreams and active imagination for personal growth*. San Francisco, CA: Harper & Row.

Kaufmann, Y. (2009). *The way of the image: The orientational approach to the psyche*. New York, NY: Zahav Books.

Mellick, J. (2001). *The art of dreaming: Tools for creative dream work*. Berkeley, CA: Conari Press.

Sowerby, D. (2012). *Intuition and dreams: How to realize your healing potential in all areas of your life*. Conshohocken, PA: Infinity Press.

Taylor, J. (1983). *Dream work: Techniques for discovering the creative power in dreams*. New York, NY: Paulist Press.

Understanding who we are, and our identity, means also paying attention to our unconscious. Our nightly dreams are gifts that can help us deepen our sense of self. After all, we spend a significant portion of our lives dreaming, whether we remember our dreams or not. As the above riff suggests, the symbolic life of our dreams can be an important source for expanding and deepening the sense of who we are and want to be.

Dreams as integrative states of consciousness

There seems to be little doubt that human beings have sought to change their states of consciousness since the earliest evolutionary times. The fundamental questions are: Why are shifts in consciousness important? Do they serve a larger purpose than simply recreation?

Our state of consciousness shifts constantly as we go through our days, from wakefulness, to highly focused attention, to daydreaming, to tiredness, to intoxication from a glass or two of beer, to a sense of expansion as we experience awe, to a robotic sense of self as we engage in routine tasks, to sleep and dreaming. Some of these shifts are voluntary, and some are involuntary.

Certain alterations in consciousness lead to integrative states of consciousness (Winkelman, 2010), meaning a process in which different parts of our brains are more actively communicating with each other. Broadly speaking,

to return to the model of the triune brain we previously introduced in Chapter 5, in these states we can gain more access to the emotional parts of our brains (the paleo–mammalian brain) and reduce the dominance of the rational parts (the neo–mammalian brain) that usually obscure the workings of the emotional and habitual parts. We also synchronize our two brain hemispheres. Meditation, trance, and hypnosis are intentionally induced states of consciousness, while dreaming is a natural nightly endeavor of all humans and other mammals.

Indigenous peoples have paid much attention to dreams and their meaning. Dreams also play an important role in the beginnings of modern Western psychology. Sigmund Freud considered dreams the *via regia*, the royal road, to the unconscious. Carl Gustav Jung (1959) expanded the model of the unconscious to include the archetypal realm of the collective unconscious. In his writings, Jung discusses the importance of myths and cultural images to understand this realm. Jungian theories of **imaginal psychology** are probably closest to Indigenous psychologies. In recent decades lucid dreaming has received research attention. Lucid dreaming means we are aware that we are dreaming (without waking up) and we can act and change the course of the dream. **Lucid dreams** are, of course, an ancient phenomenon which has received special attention in

Tibetan Buddhism and also in shamanic traditions. In the latter we also find stories of dreamwalkers, shamans who are able to enter the dreams of others and act in their dreams.

The spiritual healing practitioners of Indigenous traditions, commonly called shamans, were the first dreamworkers. They might use dreams to get information, to gain power, or to help others. A **dream** might tell a person that s/he is destined to become a shaman. Dreams may be initiatory and guide a person onto the road of becoming a healer. They may be sought through fasting, drumming, and various rituals. Often Indigenous cultures don't make a clear distinction between dreams and visions; they treat them as the same or closely related. Dreams may tell about the medicine or gift or destiny a person is carrying. Shamans see dreams as central to the formation and understanding of the self.

Dreams are part of the ethnoautobiographical journey from a **well–boundaried** self to an integrated, larger sense of self where **dream** life and everyday life are beginning to be bridged. Dreams show our journey toward wholeness — the adventures we take, obstacles we encounter, conflicts, and the reconciliation and integrations we achieve.

The meaning of dreams

From an evolutionary perspective we know that mammals have been dreaming for 220 million years or so. Clearly dreams serve an adaptive function. As mentioned, they have provided guidance for individuals for a long time, both during easy times and in crisis situations. Jung saw our inner process of becoming who we are (he called this individuation) as the underlying theme of our dreams (see Hopcke, 1989). For Jung tending to our dreams has the potential of quickening our movement toward wholeness.

The evolutionary persistence of dreams suggests that attending to our dreams to see if we can find meaning in them is important. Of course, dreams do not speak the language of our rational mind; rather, they speak the language of our emotional mind. They speak the language of images and poetry. They are like a foreign language we need to learn. When we try to understand them with our rationality we will likely run into roadblocks. Dreams come in a variety that is as rich as life itself. Some dreams are strange or disconcerting, and don't seem to have any logic to them and the action seems irrational. They may also be of questionable morality or uncouth, they may even seem entirely absurd and nonsensical. Yet, we may also awaken from dreams with a new insight or inspiration or with awe at the creative spectacle we just observed.

Jeremy Taylor, a well–known authority on Jungian dreamwork, offers certain basic *assumptions* about dreams (1983).

It is important to note that these are assumptions that foster a particular stance toward our dreams:

1. All dreams come in the service of health and wholeness.
2. No dream comes simply to tell the dreamer what he or she already knows.
3. Only the dreamer can say with certainty what meanings a dream may hold.
4. There is no such thing as a dream with only one meaning.
5. All dreams speak a universal language, a language of metaphor and symbol. (p. 11)

Approaching dreams with this particular attitude may help to garner their beneficial potential, even if we don't always feel they are in the service of wholeness or when we are certain of a dream's singular meaning.

Singer (1972) suggests that more important than the cognitive understanding of dreams is the act of experiencing the dream material and taking this material seriously. Jung encourages us to befriend our dreams and to treat them not as isolated events but as communications from the unconscious (see Hopcke, 1989). This process creates a dialogue between conscious and unconscious and is an important step in the integration of the two.

Ethnoautobiography is designed to heal us from **normative dissociation**, the splitting away from the parts of ourselves that in Indigenous paradigms belong to the sense of self — place, history, mythic stories, community, seasons, and such. In modern cultures dreams are among the neglected aspects of the self. In our self–colonization — the creation of the **masterful**, well–bounded self — the active inclusion of dreams would prevent the establishment of clear boundaries. Even though Freud published his *Interpretation of Dreams* in 1900, the importance of dreams in our cultural awareness has not changed much. Thus, remembering dreams and paying attention to their potential meaning is retrieving parts of ourselves as we heal the splits we have been socialized with.

Instructions to assist with remembering dreams can be found in Chapter 4 above. They will help you enter a world within yourself that is filled with creativity, intensity, and often stunning or surprising imagery.

Dream examples

Any dream potentially has significance for ethnoautobiographical explorations. Yet, at times we may have dreams that seem of particular importance for our sense of self. Below find several examples of actual dreams that have been of significance in Jürgen's ethnoautobiographical explorations. While these are dreams he had and that were originally recorded in a first person voice, he then reworked them in a voice that was consistent with his writing at the time. This included writing in the third person and honoring one of his ancestors, the Martin Boczian ("the stork") mentioned earlier, by using him as alter ego. These dreams speak largely for themselves, although some commentary has been added at the end of each. You may also use them to try out the method of dream interpretation we will present after these dream examples.

***

He remembers.

He remembers last night's dream.

He is in Hamburg, the Northern German town where he was born. Here he grew up. He is sitting on the threshold in the doorway of an old brick house, one in a row of houses that are considerably older than the First World War. He overlooks the river Elbe from on high. His threshold perch is atop the ancient ice age rim of the river, once the border of a flow miles wide. Tens of thousands of years ago reindeer herds roamed the tundra of these latitudes. The southernmost border of the thick ice sheet covering much of northern Europe was encroaching then, bringing along boulders and rocks from the north. The reindeer now live much farther north and the river moves in a much narrower bed. It still spreads to considerable widths three hundred or so feet below. Ferries crisscross its course and ocean liners enter and leave the harbor.

Sitting atop this ancient riverbed he is very close to where he went to kindergarten shortly after the Second World War. The heavy wooden doors are high, painted an almost black, dark green, Hooker's green. Inside, a large playroom is warmed by a comforting, white tile stove; its enormous size reaches toward the ceiling. It is the center of this space accommodates a small crowd of children. The room is lambent with light reflected from the wide river. It enters through large windows that allow for a grand vista. Behind the house is a garden with plants and trees inviting a child's playful imaginations. From here the river can be admired as it stretches below in all its grandeur.

He notices an archaeological excavation in progress behind his old kindergarten. The area is cordoned off with yellow plastic strips, glittering as they twist in the wind. Signs are put up all around: No trespassing! Stay out! *Not to be deterred, his dream allows him to leave the body, his dreambody, at the moment of seeing these signs. There is no pause, no struggle with the prohibitions right in front of him. Assuming a form that permits him to proceed is the natural and immediate dream solution. Invisible now, he enters the forbidden grounds.*

He hovers over the ancient ruins that are clearly visible thanks to the work of the archaeological team. To the right a round, tower–like structure emerges from the underground depths. It appears to extend a good ways into the earth. He recognizes it as an ancestral ceremonial structure. Similar ones are right next to it. The name of the place where this dig into ancient cultural history occurs is Altona, *meaning "all–too–near."*

One legend has it that an orphan was blindfolded when the burghers of

Hamburg wanted to expand their over-populated city. The idea was to place the new town where the orphan would trip and meet the ground. But what happened was unexpected. The boy had barely left the medieval city gates, when he stumbled and fell. The attendant burghers exclaimed in surprise that this was all too near, in the local vernacular: "All to nah!" — thence the name for this part of the city — Altona. This is the story Martin learned in school.

The place where the dream helps him gain access to the layers below the contemporary city is all too close in this dream. Right there with his childhood. Fenced in by signs forbidding entry.

Martin remembers this dream with the vibrant luminosity common to dreams drawing attention to their meaning. It needs no interpretation. It is all spelled out for him at the end. Lest he deny what he has been shown. He is compelled to pay heed and to take the dream as injunction to trespass across the lines that separate him not just from childhood memories, but also the root memories of his ancestral cultures. He struggles to remember. And he remembers that at the threshold of his vision was a woman. She lives in the regions of his mind where he finds access to a different sense of self through this feminine figure. The memory of one of their conversations about the recovery of Indigenous roots is vivid and now powerfully charged with dreaming.

***

Jürgen had this dream during a fast he dedicated to raven. During his time of fasting he had many conversations with raven which leads him to talk about "ravensurgery":

He is in surgery. The surgeons are cutting out the lower parts of his internal organs. They began with the small intestines, now they are on to the large intestines. They also remove his stomach, the spleen, and the gall bladder, then, lastly, his liver. He watches as he is undergoing this surgical procedure. With curiosity, not concern or fear. He now notices that even the lower lobes of both his lungs have just been taken out. He observes the operation with a bird's eye view, but he also feels the increasing emptiness in his body cavity. Then the surgeons perform what seem to be the required cleansing and pruification procedures on all his inner organs. They put them in different containers and rinse them with different chemical solutions. All goes well. Even the work on his tiny lung bubbles is successful. He watches in wonderment how skillfully and impeccably the surgeons deal with such complicated organs. Now they put all his body parts back in their proper places and sew him up. He feels good and gets up immediately. Only the lingering effects of the anesthetic make him feel a little unsteady. He staggers slightly for a few moments. Then he walks away without any problem, feeling vigorous and alert.

He re–reads the notes of the dream. *He is in surgery.* Ravens are his allies, his totem. He is fasting for raven. Ravens are following him. Ravensurgery. *The surgeons are cutting out the lower parts of his internal organs. They begin with the small intestines, then on to the large intestines. They also remove his stomach, the spleen, and the gall bladder, then, lastly, his liver.* Raven pecking deeper and deeper. Reaching into his most essential parts, his soft spots, scraping the flesh on the bone. *He watches as he is undergoing this surgical procedure. With curiosity, not concern or fear.* He trusts the work of the ravensurgeons. He is present to the work of remembering and purification. Aware. *He now notices that even the lower lobes of both his lungs have just been taken out.* Right there. Aware. One of his most vital of organs needs to be cleansed. His breath. The inhalation and exhalation of awareness. His mindful merging with everything around. Needs to be purified. Standstill and pause. Breath coming and going. *He observes the operation from a bird's eye view, but he also feels the increasing emptiness in his body cavity. Then the surgeons perform what seem to be the required cleansing and purification procedures on all his inner organs. They put them in different containers and rinse them with different chemical solutions. All goes well. Even the work on his tiny lung bubbles is successful. He watches in wonderment how skillfully and impeccably the surgeons deal with such a complicated organ.* Indeed, this is a sensitive operation. Fraught with pitfalls. Shortcuts that lead to distortion. Glib explanations that short–circuit. This is cleansing for compassionate ruthlessness. *Now they put all his body parts back in their proper places and sew him up. He feels good and gets up immediately. Only the lingering effects of the anesthetic make him feel a little unsteady. He staggers slightly for a few moments. Then he walks away without any problem feeling vigorous and alert.* Renewal.

***

One night he has another dream. *He is standing on the balcony of the apartment where he spent his early childhood. Overlooking the river, the beach. Affording a long vista. The place where Siegfried had to put on a dress and escape across the vast valley that resulted from an ice age maelstrom. The balcony is high up. Now it extends out toward the beach, making the view more wondrous. Still on the balcony, he finds himself above the tan sand strip bordering the river Elbe. Just below he notices several people sleeping on the beach. What looks like a homeless person emerges from the empty lot next to the house. As he comes closer on the wooden planks Martin recognizes him as an Australian Aborigine. He pushes the shopping cart with his belongings toward the sleepers and glows twice from the inside as he shifts his awareness and his presence crosses worlds. He is an Elder healer. The sleepers begin to wake and talk to each other. They are healers also. Among them are some younger people. Martin notices that his dream position has shifted: instead of standing atop the balcony he now is perched on the roof of a yurt. Much lower and closer to the people moving about. He observes. The Elder Aborigine begins to perform an initiation ceremony. It is an induction into the next levels of healing, the test and affirmation of capacities acquired. Several other adults are helping the Elder. Several young men awaken, stretch and yawn. They are the ones to be initiated. Two of them run away, try to escape the challenge before them. A couple of adults chase them and immediately return them into the circle. The adult healers are restrained in their reactions, yet visibly agitated. They disapprove of the initiands not taking responsibility for their healing gifts. Martin looks on from the top of the yurt in fear of discovery. He knows the Elder will pull him down into the ceremony the minute he is discovered.*

Martin thinks about the healing experience he has had in the Spanish monastery. He provided physical relief for his partner who was suffering from severe menstrual cramps by entering into trance and extracting the toxins from her body. She thanked him out of her sleep without waking up. A part of himself, the young man running away, resists initiation. And clearly the time for initiation has come, there is no escape. He is struck by the dream image of the yurt. It pulls him to thoughts about Siberia and her shamanic traditions. Until, some days later, he happens to open an oversize catalogue he had been given 25 years ago. Here he finds the image of a prehistoric yurt from the Rhine Valley, right next to here he had worked in a school for a while. Together with a tipi–like structure. He had not known that his ancestors had lived in yurts. He had always placed yurts much farther east.

***

Shortly thereafter another dream. *Bear approaches him. It is winter. Martin is camping out in the wilderness. The low mountains are covered in snow. In the distance he sees an emaciated bear cross the unused railroad tracks near where his tent is. The bear changes direction and lumbers toward him, straining as it takes each step. As it approaches it gradually turns into a younger bear. The brown fur then changes to show the markings of a young boar: bright, luminescent stripes run the length of its body. The bear cub continues to move closer. Then it collapses and dies.*

Bears normally are not out and about in winter. It is their time to hibernate in a den. Something important, maybe some terrible hunger must have brought the bear out of its winter slumber. Maybe it was a physical hunger, he thinks, but maybe it was a different need altogether. *Hibernation, renewal, sustained dreaming,* the words are floating through his waking mind. *Maybe it was a bearmother and she was so very thin because of feeding the young ones in her den. Maybe she had twin cubs.* The bear transformed to look like a boar piglet. He goes to the dictionary and looks up the etymology of the German word for it, *Frischling.* They are the fresh ones, the newly born, but they are also the ones given away as offering, sacrifice. Probably mostly to the female spirit of the north, shaman woman Freyja, she who rides the boar with golden bristles.

He begins to think of the dream as renewal, the return of the bear. The bear gives birth out of itself, just as the primal giant Ymir in the Old Norse creation story gives birth to the world through its sacrifice, each body part changing into the world we now know. The bear is trying to make itself new, puts on special markings, the body painting of renewal. But it has not been provided with proper nurturance, it collapses right in front of him. The sacred bear hunt, a ceremony of many circumpolar peoples, is the story of sacrifice and renewal. Death for life. Maybe this ritual needs to be made new, strengthened.

***

These four dreams give examples of dreams that have been important in Jürgen's ethnoautobiographical process. They also give an idea how dreams can be interpreted, especially in the context of this workbook.

Dream interpretation

Below is a useful and very specific way to guide you in the interpretation of dreams. If you follow these steps carefully you will likely see the dream you are analyzing in a new light. This practice will allow you to broaden your horizon. It is good to start with the assumption "I have no idea what this dream means"; entering with a beginner's mind stance. You can apply this approach of dream interpretation to the examples just presented if you don't have a dream of your own to work with.

How to Work with Dreams

by Karen Jaenke

Initial steps

Remember the dream.

Record the dream with as much detail as you remember.

1. Identify the major or most significant images in a dream

Definition of Image: Mental representations of objects or persons not physically present. Images are those perceptions that eventually become internalized because of their emotional significance to the child or later on. Images thus constitute our inner reality — our dreams, thoughts, fantasies, and ideas. Images that appear in our dreams have emotional significance for us. It is this emotional connection that gives them meaning.

Theory: Images are the language of the psyche. The psyche speaks through the primal language of images. Images are the building blocks of dreams.

Practice: On the left side of the page, list each important image, symbols or action that occurs in your dream. Leave 5 line spaces between each image.

2. Make personal associations to each image in the dream

Definition of Associations: Associations are any ideas, notions, memories, reactions, or whatever else jumps in the dreamer's mind as the dream and its particular images are considered. Associations are thus connected to or evoked by the dream images. Not rational evaluations or judgments of images. They are utterly subjective. They may seem arbitrary or random elements, and they need not be logically justified.

Theory: A dream has many potential meanings. We need the dreamer's help to limit the multiple potential meanings to those that are essential and ring true subjectively for the dreamer. Dream images must be grounded in the personal psychological reality of the dreamer. This is done by finding the affect–laden associations. Only when affect is touched may we assume that the essential core of psychological reality, including the complex, has been reached experientially. Intellectual understanding is not enough.

The synchronicity of the emotional charge with the image points to the pertinent psychological issue to be explored. Whichever association has emotionally charged significance needs to be grounded with respect to the dreamer's present and past psychological situation. Associations to the images (visual, auditory, kinesthetic) and feeling reactions in the dream reveal how they are to be connected with the present and past contexts in the dreamer's life.

Practice: On the right side of the page, list whatever associations automatically come to mind. Associations include whatever pops into your mind spontaneously as you focus on an image. Don't censor anything. Associations are explored until they reveal their emotional core and psychological significance. This means finding the emotional charge. Associations to dream images is "free" at first, but you will likely find that they become more focused around the pertinent issue or complex once an affect is touched. With associations, we are looking for the embodied emotional experience alive in the dreamer's psyche. What qualities do you associate to X? How did X make you feel? What emotional experiences were connected with that relationship?

3. Translating metaphors of the dream

Theory: The dream corresponds metaphorically to an inner dynamic that is active in your life. Assume your dream represents an inner dynamic. Inner dynamics refers to anything that goes on inside you. It may be an emotional event, an inner conflict, an inner personality acting through you, a feeling, an attitude, a mood. Always begin by applying your dream inwardly. The situation inside is creating the situation outside.

Practice:
a. Identify the individual metaphors that appear in the dream. Find the specific dynamics at work inside us that are symbolized by the dream situation. Look for the parts of our inner selves that dream images represent. Connect each dream image to a specific dynamic in our inner lives.

b. Translate each metaphor using these dream questions: For each image in the dream, ask: What part of me is that? Where I have I seen it functioning in my life lately? Where do I see that same trait in my personality? Who is it, inside me, who feels or behaves like that? Then write down each example you can think of in which that inner part of you has been expressing itself in your life. We are not finished until we find examples from our lives that correspond to the events in the dream.

4. Dialoguing with dream symbols

Theory: Images and symbols are alive, they carry psychic or emotional energy. The feeling tone and meaning of these images are revealed when we engage imaginatively with the image.

Practice: Dialogue with each major image in the dream. Explore the image by expressing the feelings contained within the image. To uncover a symbol's meaning, have a conversation with it, in the form of a written dialogue. This allows you to question it about the broader context of its history, desires, views of the future. Write without judging or censoring yourself, and allow yourself to feel the personality of the symbol as it arises in you.

This exercise works well with dream images about which you have unresolved feelings, and ones that make a strong impact on your senses or thoughts. Choose significant persons or images in a dream. Allow it to speak to you. Ask it: Who are you? What do you wish to tell me?

Develop at least three back & forth exchanges in your dialogue. It might look something like:

"What do you have to tell me as tree?"
"You are moving about too much."
"What do you mean, tree? I have to move to keep up with things."
"I am rooted in place, yet I am constantly moving about with the winds."
"That doesn't help me, it's obscure what you are saying. Be more direct."
"You are too impatient to move with the wind."
Etc.

Elaborate on the image until it takes over and elaborates itself, perhaps even changing form. Go with it completely, and write down everything without censoring yourself.

5. Consider the waking context

Theory: A dream arises in the context of the dreamer's life, and its meaning will be found by considering this context in comparison to the dream.

Practice: Taking up the context entails a painstaking examination of the surrounding waking life. This context must be consulted and compared to the scenario in the dream, in order to discern the dream's precise intent and meaning. Does the dream depict scenarios that correspond or contrast to the waking life situation? When the dream differs from the waking life context, what is the psychological significance of the difference?

6. Note images for which you have no personal associations

Theory: Not all images are personal, some are cultural and some are archetypal. Three types of images can be differentiated:

- Personal — formed in a person' unconscious and individually tailored to reflect that person's composite of life experience and emotion.
- Cultural — cultures with a common language share many of the same symbols; famous people; and so on.
- Universal or archetypal — rooted to the experience of all humankind; common to everyone; though meaning may change according to context and the person.

Practice: Dreamers often have meager associations to contribute. If there are images for which you have no personal associations, consider whether the image is an archetypal image, i.e. is a collectively recurring image or motif that arises from the collective unconscious, the evolutionary database of humanity.

7. Amplification of archetypal images

Theory: Our dreams draw freely from the deeper, archetypal stratum of the psyche. Amplification entails the enlarging of the dreamer's personal context with parallel and corresponding motifs from the cultural storehouse of archetypal images found in myth, fairy tales, art, and literature. It is an explanation in mythological, archetypal, or transpersonal terms. Amplification elucidates archetypal significance, regardless of the dreamer's familiarity with mythic context.

Practice: Amplification entails giving a comprehensive, detailed description of the symbol and its history. In this way, the symbol grows and transforms, revealing its mythic aspects that belong to the collective unconscious. Like associations, amplifications must click for the dreamer. Hearing a mythic story that parallels one's own confusion and pain may make it more bearable. Familiarity with myths and symbols is essential for this step. Books on mythology, symbol dictionaries, and people who carry this knowledge are helpful resources with this step.

8. Attend to the narrative structure, turning point, or pivot point, in the dream

Theory: Not all dreams, but the typical dream shows a definite structure. Most dreams are similar to a drama, and have a dramatic structure.

Practice: Identify each of the following:

1. Setting – who, what, where, when?
2. Development of the plot – the opening situation becomes complicated; a definite tension develops, one does not know the outcome.
3. Climax — the turning point of the dream when something decisive happens; something changes completely and often unexpectedly.
4. Solution or Result — shows the final situation, the solution sought by the dream; the place that the dream ends.

Summarize the narrative or story of the dream in a single sentence; what is the main action, movement or development that occurs within the dream.

9. Identify the "navel of the dream"

Theory: According to Freud (Freud, 1999, p. 88, note 4) "There is at least one spot in every dream at which it is unplumbable — a navel as it were, that is its point of contact with the unknown." Usually the navel of the dream is loaded with deep feeling. It is essential to experience and integrate the strong emotions found at the navel of the dream; otherwise one is doing an emotional bypass of the dream.

Practice: Identify the central, numinous dream image, also known as the "navel of a dream." It may be found at the climax or turning point, in the dream. One can dialogue with the major emotion in a dream. Address the fear, sadness, anger, etc. Allow the emotion to develop its own voice. One can attend to and integrate the body sensations present at the navel of the dream.

10. Active imagination, or dreaming the dream onward

Theory: Images and scenarios that arise in connection with the dream are, like the dream itself, productions of the unconscious psyche. New imagery that springs naturally from the dream imagery will carry messages and meanings connected to the dream. Thus, any dream may be amplified by the dreamer's spinning it out and enlarging it through the use of imaginative techniques, also known as dreaming the dream onward.

Practice: Allow images to arise before the inner eye, or simply invent to fill in the missing pieces of the dream story. Any part of the dream can be made a starting point for expanding the dream with newly added imagery.

Activity

Working With a Dream

Select a dream and describe it in detail. Follow the steps for dream analysis described above. For each step follow the instructions provided under "practice". At the end of the process of reflection, state succinctly what the dream means to you. Describe what you learned from this assignment, both from the dream itself, as well as from the process of dream analysis.

This may be completed as a 500–word response paper, or shared as an oral presentation with others.

Note: If you are completing these activities on your own, and do not have an organized group to do oral presentations for (such as in a classroom, community organization and so on), it is encouraged that you present the work you are doing to a friend, family member or spouse to experience sharing your process in oral form.

Chapter Summary

Dreams are an involuntary way of connecting with unconscious or deeper parts of our selves. They are important in ethnoautobiographical inquiry because they give access to felt senses of our selves beyond our everyday awareness.

Concept Check

Why would dreaming be called an **integrative state of consciousness**?

What did Jung see as the underlying theme of our **dreams**, and what potential did he feel comes from paying attention to them?

NOTES

Chapter 14
Faith, Spirituality, Skepticism

Riff

Balancing Rigor and Openness

Having breakfast with a friend
The other day
Our conversation came to
Religion and spirituality
He told me a story of his childhood
And his mother's unwavering ability
To withstand great hardships
"It was her faith," he said
Noting that he only realized that
Later in life

Growing up he had always
Perceived his mother's faith
As open and supportive
But nothing approaching
The rigor, which is what he called it
That he realized she'd have needed
To withstand
Multiple assaults on her way of life

This got me thinking about that balance
Where my spiritual practice
Remains dynamic and flexible
Yet sustains and supports me

Especially
When unpacking and challenging
Norms of culture and ancestry
Through all the layers of
Colonization
Christianity and
Dislocation
So my spirit guides me to reconnect
With places, people, and traditions
Long gone by
To restore them to me
With openness and possibility
Aware that there needs to be
Exactitude and presence

In some ways it feels as though
That's what this life is calling of me
To embrace a spiritual tradition
Not devoid of place, animals, dreams
And at the same time
Acknowledge the religion that
Brought me
To this moment
                                    RJP

Chapter Outline	Core Concepts	Ethnoautobiographical Perspectives	Expected Outcomes
Balancing rigor & openness	Faith requires acceptance while life experience can challenge faith	Spirituality can be both rigorous and flexible	Look for ways to balance faith and skepticism
Atheism	Atheism disagrees with the answers provided by spiritual & religious traditions	The rise of Western science, technological progress and atheism go hand–in–hand	See the variety of atheisms
Indigenous spiritualities	Indigenous spiritualities are immanent and earth–based	Remembering our earth connections helps us address our current ecological crises	Understand that the immanence of Indigenous spiritualities and the Indigenous sense of self are of the same world
Knowledge, science, and Indigenous science	Indigenous knowledge practices are a science, albeit with different assumptions than Western science	Expanding our scientific framework (epistemology) may help in solving current socio–cultural issues	Be open to possibilities beyond a rational approach to knowledge, appreciating possibilities of holistic uses of reason
Socially engaged spirituality	Indigenous practices are inevitably socially engaged	A new framework for social engagement can overcome the split between secular and spiritual approaches to social issues	Understand why Indigenous practices are inevitably socially engaged
Different worlds	Indigenous and non–Indigenous people live in different worlds	Lack of the appreciation of the difference in lifeworlds leads to discrimination and conflict	Develop a sense of what we might NOT know about another culture, what we may NOT be able to see
Indigenous ... Science	Indigenous science is grounded in exacting observations	Expanding the notion of science can help in ending the discrimination and persecution of Indigenous peoples	Appreciate the rich knowledge in Indigenous science

Key Terms

Animism
Atheism
Beingknowing
Indigenous science
Religion
Spirituality
Totemism
Western science

Note: All key terms in this textbook are highlighted in bold and can be found in the Glossary at the end of the book.

Resources Alongside This Chapter

Akwesasne Notes. (1978). *Basic call to consciousness*. Summertown, TN: Book Publishing Company.

Beck, P. V., & Walters, A. L. (1979). *The sacred*. Tsaile, AZ: Navajo Community College Press.

Rothberg, D. (2006). *The engaged spiritual life*. Boston, MA: Beacon Press.

Silver, C. F. & Coleman, T. (2013). *Studying non–belief*. Retrieved from http://www.atheismresearch.com/

Smith, H. (2009). *The world's religions*. San Francisco, CA: HarperOne.

The opening riff begins to make a distinction between spirituality and **religion**. The fundamental difference in the use of these terms is that **spirituality** refers to the lived experience of something we might call god or spirit or numinous or divine. Religion, by contrast, refers to a translation of the spiritual experience of one or more people into teachings and an organizational structure. More technically: Religion is a broader term referring to "organized forms of doctrine, ritual, myth, experience, practice, spirituality, ethics, and social structure that together constitute a world in relation to what is known as sacred" (Rothberg, 1994, p. 3). Spirituality here refers to "the *lived transformation* of self and community toward fuller alignment with or expression of what is understood, within a given cultural context to be 'sacred'" (Rothberg, p. 3). Because most readers will be familiar with the concept of religion or major religions as well as **atheism**, this chapter focuses on describing Indigenous, native or aboriginal spiritualities after a brief description of some general features of spirituality and atheism.

Spirituality may take a Buddhist, Wicca, or many other forms, including **animism** and **totemism** (terms commonly describing Indigenous societies, but not necessarily used by Indigenous peoples themselves). Animism refers to a worldview in which all beings, including animals and plants are ensouled or inspirited. This may include things usually considered inanimate in Eurocentered worldviews, such as rocks or rivers and other features of the landscape. Totemism refers to a sense of kinship with a particular animal or plant, the totem, and the community ritually maintains the relationship with such an ancestral totem.

Atheism

Beyond the choices in the realms of religion and spirituality, atheism is a worldview that does not accept the reality of anything spiritual, religious, or transcendent in any form. Atheism is aligned with the knowledge generated by scientific approaches as defined in Eurocentered traditions. Gods and spirits are not considered real, while science is considered the foundation of what is reality. Atheism largely developed out of disenchantment with the Christian traditions in particular, beginning with the Enlightenment Period during which the emergent scientific approaches led to profound questioning of church dogmas. Galileo's case is probably the most famous example.

Atheism is seen as compatible with traditions such as Buddhism, where gods or spirits do not play a large role (depending on the particular Buddhist culture and tradition). Also, we find a number of scientists who are *both scientists and cherish* Christian beliefs, for example. Intelligent design is an approach to integrate scientific knowledge and Christian knowledge. However, this theory has been profoundly criticized by scientists and at this point must be considered unsuccessful as far as its scientific basis is concerned. **Indigenous science** is a very different approach to bring Eurocentered scientific knowledge and Indigenous knowledge systems into dialogue. The question how scientific and spiritual or religious approaches could or should relate to each other is a profound one, and potentially a question of tremendous evolutionary import for humanity's future.

Atheism and agnosticism can take a variety of forms, just as we find a variety of approaches to spirituality and religion. Silver and Coleman (2013) have developed a basic typology:

- there are atheists and agnostics who actively work to develop their position intellectually;
- others are more activist in their approach and engage in debates making the point that **religion** is detrimental for society;
- still others feel more uncertain of the existence of a God, but have an open mind given the limitations of human knowledge;
- anti-theists see themselves as diametrically opposed to any religions ideology; and,
- some don't involve themselves at all in any debate on these issues.

A final group, called "ritual atheists" by Silver & Coleman, don't have a belief in God, per se, but still find some use in religious teachings and may participate in religious observances because of family traditions. Atheism or agnosticism are usually framed in contrast to monotheistic religions, however, these arguments could also apply to Indigenous religious traditions.

Indigenous spiritualities

Indigenous spiritualities are quite distinct from the major religions and atheism. Buddhism, particularly Tibetan Buddhism, is the religion with the closest affinity to Indigenous spiritualities. Beck and Walters (1979) give an excellent overview of native spirituality. Indigenous spirituality is earth–based, animistic, and acknowledges a diversity of spirits, including one or more spirits that may be supreme. Here spirits are immanent (rather than transcendent), they are generally seen as closer, rather than remote. In a sense, spirits are much more part of daily life and daily experience than in the world of monotheistic religions.

The contemporary Andean peoples of Peru talk about their Indigenous paradigms, which include spirituality, as follows:

> Andean peasant agriculture is to nurture with love and to let oneself be nurtured by all; always conversing and helping one another among all the relatives of the *ayllu* ([community of] stars, rocks, plants, animals,

human beings, mountains, deceased ancestors and many others).

This mutual cultivation of the heterogeneity of life based on the *chacra* [the land and all other beings nurtured by the peasant] is the best way to synchronize with the heterogeneity of the diverse, dense and variable Andean environment. (PRATEC, 1998, p. 85).

This means that a conversation needs to be stimulated in order for life to be re–created. Clearly, the purpose of these conversations is not primarily to know or discover truths about reality, although without exacting knowledge of the *ayllu* such conversation of nurturance, of mutuality and reciprocity, would fail.

In many Andean settlements it is common to hear the members of the community say: 'Just as we nurture the alpacas, they nurture us' or 'as we nurture potatoes, they nurture us'. Nurturance is lived as an activity which commits one to: 'nurture and let oneself be nurtured' and in this *runas* [community of humans], *huacas* [deities] and *sallqa* [more–than–human communities] find themselves on an equivalent plane.

In Quechua, 'to nurture' is *uyway*, it means the affective attunement achieved between the members of the Andean community (which includes *runas*, maize, alpacas, winds,

water, etc.) in the regeneration of their *Pacha* (which can be understood as the 'lived world', the house that shelters us and of which we are members). (PRATEC, 1998, p. 109).

This "affective attunement" is also a profound psycho–spiritual activity in which all participants mutually transform each other. It is self transformation where being and knowing are not separated as each participant in the conversation participates in this dynamic world. Each act of nurturance is a gift and the notions of gift economies are central to Indigenous worldviews (Kuokkanen, 2004). In the cycle of nurturing and being nurtured the gifts travel around the circle.

Native people also do not typically separate "sacred" and "secular," frequently stating that *everything* is sacred. Beck and Walters (1979, p. 9) quote de Angulo, a non–native, as observing that the Iss/Aw'te (Pit River) natives see life as "a continuous religious experience … To them, the essence of religions is … the 'spirit of wonder'." Beck and Walters give a clear overview of Native American understandings of life as sacred and pervaded by a mystery or powers commonly unseen, of all things moving in circles and being dependent on each other, of the morals and ethics that follow from such understanding, and of the individuals who are particularly gifted in carrying specialized knowledge pertaining to the sacred or mystery of life. They also describe the personal commitment to the sources of life through purification, blessings, sacrifices, or offerings and prayerful conversation.

If Indigenous spiritual practice is so construed, then this suggests that a person might be developing Indigenous awareness, whether or not the person meets the criterion of being Indigenous given the definitions we have provided (see glossary). Similarly, a person of Indigenous ancestry does not necessarily manifest such awareness. In other words, Indigenous awareness is arguably open to all persons who are regularly engaged in the kind of "conversation" or *criar y dejarse criar* described above.

This kind of participatory conversation is described using terms in native languages that don't necessarily translate easily into the language of "spirituality." Native languages are commonly difficult to translate into English and other Indo-European languages and have very different structures than the latter languages. When elders or Indigenous authors use words such as "pray," they are typically making adjustments; frequently the native equivalent seems to mean "to talk" or "to converse." The native word then does not have any associations with church or religion, but refers to a common everyday activity that is necessary, obvious, and natural, just like the conversation among humans. The Sámi noaidi (shaman) and artist Nils-Aslak Valkeapää (1997, poem #7, italics in original) evokes this conversation in his monumental poem *Beaivi, Áhčažan* which we quoted in Chapter 2. One of the central phrases is:

I converse with the earth
and hear the creeks answer
their voices the
sounds of silver

To illustrate the nature of Indigenous knowledge and **spirituality** we refer to two more examples from the North American continent: the first from the Great Lakes area, and the second from the Canadian plains. It is noteworthy that both authors of these examples use their own language when referring to important concepts. Indigenous languages have a richness and complexity that is often difficult to translate; the native terms are rich with storied context and history. As one of the foremost Native American intellectuals, Gerald Vizenor's work includes poetry, short stories, novels, and literary criticism. He is Anishinaabe (or Chippewa or Ojibway) and published Bear Island commemorating the 1898 war at Sugar Point, which the Anishinaabe won convincingly. He describes the Anishinaabe worldview:

> The Anishinaabe observed the *mi-igis*, the *midewiwin* spiritual shell, or cowrie, as a source of visionary presence in the northern woodland lakes. The Grand Medicine Society, *midewiwin*, is an association of Na-

tive healers and shamans. The *mii-gis* arose from the eastern sea and moved westward with the natural course of the sun. The Anishinaabe origina stories count the *miigis* for the last time in *gichigami*, the great sea, or Lake Superior.

The Anishinaabe envisioned their associations with the earth by natural reason, by tricky stories, and by *odoodemi*, to have a totem, an imagic sense of presence in the time and seasons of the woodland lakes.

The Anishinaabe trickster, *naana-bozho*, is an uncertain, existential shaman of creation, a healer by stories, and a comic transformation in mythic time. (…)

The Anishinaabe created five traditional totems, the natural images of families and ancestry. The original five totems are the *ajijaak* (the sandhill crane), *makwa* (the bear), *maanameg* (the catfish), *waabizheshi* (the marten), and *maang* (the loon). (…) Natives of the *ajijaak* (the crane totem) are orators and leaders. The *makwa* (bear totem) are bold and brave warriors. The three other totems are figures of a communal presence in the natural world. (Vizenor, 2006, 3–4)

The second example is from Betty Bastien who has written about the

worldview of her tribe, the Siksikaitsitapi (Blackfoot). She discusses *Kakyosin* (traditional knowledge, the capacity to find and create balance), *Kiitomohpiipotoko* (ontological responsibilities, the ethical responsibilities of and for life), *Ihtsipaitapiiyo'pa* (the source of knowledge), *Niitsi'powahsinni* (language), *Aipommotsspistsi* (transfers, i.e., the ceremonial transfer of tribal medicine bundles), and *Kaaahsinnooniksi* (Grandparents) as some of the central concepts central to her Indigenous identity and spiritual practice. The transfer of medicine bundles is essential to the maintenance of the *Siksikaitsitapi* worldview.

> Traditional learning is experiential. This form for learning is centrally exemplified in the *Siksikaitsitapi* practice of *Aipommotsspistsi* – the practice of ceremonial transfers. They bring *Siksikaitsitapi* ontology, epistemology, and pedagogy together through methods of transmitting sacred responsibilities and knowledge from generation to generation. They are the initiations into sacred responsibilities and knowledge that are passed down through each generation to ensure the renewal of cosmic alliances. These medicine bundles have been transferred to *Siksikaitstapi* with the original instructions for coming to know, *Akaotsisstapitakiop*, so that "we have come to understand (not

merely know) it." In essence, the transfer ceremony is working with *Ihtsipaitapiiyo'pa*, the Source of Life, from which knowledge is revealed or transferred. As such, the transers are the processes of renewing the original responsibilities as taught to the *Siksikaitsitapi* in the original transfer. ... *Aipommotsspistsi* are the medium of becoming one with the universe. They are the connections to all time as well as the ancestors and ancients since time immemorial. ... The basic ontological responsibility, *Kiitomohpiipotokoi* or role, of giving and sharing is embedded in the fundamental philosophical premises of *Siksikaitsitapi* education. Sharing and giving are ways of being that connect to and perpetuate *Ihtsipaitapiiyo'pa*. Actions of sharing and giving are consistent with the natural order of the universe and help to maintain it in balance. According to *Siksikaitsitapi*, a fundamental aspect of the cosmic universe is reciprocity, which is experienced in *Aipommotsspistsi*, the practice of ceremonial transfers. ... The ceremonies are for connecting, renewing, and maintaining good relations with the alliances to ensure that life returns to a sacred and peaceful way. The ethical and moral behaviour identified through customs, language, values, and roles are often referred to as protocol or ritual. (Bastien, 2004, pp. 140 – 142)

The Riff *The Old Ones Would Say* for Chapter 4, and the definitions of ethnoautobiography, characterize Indigenous traditions as consciously based on locally, ecologically, and seasonally contextualized truths (truly earth-based) that are narratively anchored in natural communities. It is the practice of a worldview or knowing (**beingknowing**, as it were) that is not dualistic with spirits far removed in a transcendent realm, instead they are and active part of ongoing conversations. The stories and ceremonies help individuals to find internal and external balance within a conversation that participates in the life of ancestors, animals, plants, stars, humans, rocks, mountains, and other beings.

Knowledge, science, and Indigenous science

Members of the group PRATEC (Proyecto Andino de Tecnologias Campesinas, the "Andean Project of Peasant Technologies") work with the notion of decolonization through the affirmation of traditional or Indigenous Andean cultural knowledge (Apffel–Marglin, 1994; Apffel–Marglin, with PRATEC, 1998). Their spiritual, scientific, and political work is understood in the framework of such native discourse:

> This is not to say that conversing with the world does not involve cognitive faculties, it of course does, but that the activity is not primarily

and certainly not exclusively a cognitive one. *Criar* demands not only understanding but love, tenderness, patience. But it is to say that the point of conversation is not the attainment of knowledge through the interrogation of nature, it is rather to generate and regenerate the world and be generated and regenerated by it in the process. (Apffel–Marglin, 1994, p. 9)

This qualitative difference between Indigenous and non–Indigenous cultures can lead to tremendous interactive problems, which remain largely veiled for Eurocentric folk. They are the proverbial apples and oranges. Non–Indigenous paradigms can be characterized by **normative dissociation**, i.e., the split from all those beings and presences that are a natural part of native beingknowing and **spirituality**. The Indigenous conversation has no need for research other than the pragmatic, ceremonial, and spiritual inquiry into what is needed for balancing in a particular place at a specific time in history. This may be more research than most of us can handle. Wisława Szymborska's poem, "Conversation With a Stone", describes the distinction we are talking about aptly:

"You shall not enter," says the stone.
"You lack the sense of taking part.
No other sense can make up for your missing sense of taking part.
Even sight heightened to become all–seeing
will do you no good without a sense of taking part.
You shall not enter, you have only a sense of what that sense should be,
only its seed, imagination." (Szymborska, 1995, p. 32)

These differences in paradigm can easily be illustrated in the area of physical healing, with herbs, for example. Within the Eurocentered paradigm we pick an herb for its curative properties known to relieve a certain ailment. Herb collection is an entirely different event within an Indigenous context. Here, it is a ceremonial event which involves spirit, and, especially, the spirits of the plant to be collected. It is a participatory event with the plant relations which presupposes detailed knowledge, including knowledge of their "language." It requires knowledge of cycles and preparations necessary for gathering. It means understanding plants like any other intelligent people. This is no longer the collection of an herb, but an engagement and appointment with spirit to help heal. What heals is more than the beneficial chemical ingredient in the herb (see for example Mayes & Lacy, 1989).

In the northern language of the Saami people (*davvisamigiella*) the distinction is captured in the terminology *dieđa* vs. *diehtu*. The first term, which is a word of recent origin, refers to the sciences and scientific knowledge whose reliability and validity is defined in Western research methodologies. *Diehtu* refers to knowledge — traditional knowledge — whose reliability and validity is defined by way of the cultural practices which are constituted by "a sense of taking part." For example, the elaborate Saami terminologies for reindeer, salmon, seals, snow, etc. constitute not just the equivalent of science, but they *are* scientific knowledge in their own right. The terminologies and related cultural practices are based on very careful observations; it is knowledge that is critical for survival. Stories, rock carvings, and rituals inquire about, record, and guide us in star knowledge, ecological knowledge, and other important aspects of life.

Thus, *diehtu* is not defined by the philosophical practice of epistemology or the history of Eurocentered thought. It had efficacy and validity prior to the historical advent of Enlightenment philosophies and subsequent colonization. Since then, any necessity to understand diehtu as a philosophical practice of epistemology is in the context of this particular history. When we attempt to comprehend Navajo herb gathering, a spiritual activity, or Saami reindeer terminology in epistemological terms, then we highlight what these particular philosophical categories guide us to see, and we neglect what our epistemological tools fail to reveal. All of this should not be construed to mean that such cultural differences are insurmountable or should not be overcome. Quite the contrary, these reflections are intended to set the stage for more complex and comprehensive ways of cultural sharing and dialogue. We believe that something significant occurs when the practice of Eurocentered epistemologies (resulting in *dieđa*, science) is analyzed as cultural practice with the tools which traditional knowledge (*diehtu*) provides. Such reversal may catalyze unexpected shifts benefiting Eurocentered epistemologies by healing its pathological consequences.

These descriptions of the knowing and nurturing conversation in the *ayllu* are illustrations of the **Indigenous mind** process or original participation. Valkeapää (1994, unpaginated) has given a poetic description of Saami *siida* life and participation:

How I respect
the old Sámi life
That was true love of nature
where nothing was wasted
where humans were part of nature
Not until now have they realized

that the people who lived here
ten thousand years ago
melted to become the Sámi (...)
I see our fjells
the places we live
and hear my heart beat
all this is my home
and I carry it
within me
in my heart
I can hear it
when I close my eyes
I can hear it
I hear somewhere
deep within me
I hear the ground thunder
from thousands of hooves
I hear the reindeer herd running
or is it the noaidi drum
and the sacrificial stone

Of course, our modern Eurocentered mind leads us to look for words — stories, myths, descriptions, definitions — which evoke participatory consciousness. From an Indigenous vantage point such profound "libraries" or records as Stonehenge, Newgrange, the rock carvings of Northern Europe and elsewhere, the Gundestrup cauldron are, in a sense, more accurate and more complete. Creation stories, as the Sámi Mjandasj story, may do something similar. (See also Colorado, 1988, for an Iroquois description of *skana-goah*, the great peace, the center of the Indigenous conversation).

In this Indigenous mind, or conscious –ness, individuals understand themselves in an ongoing conversation with the surrounding community, in which the local animals, plants, ancestors, and other spirits are a part (cf. Apffel-Marglin, 1994; Rengifo, 1993; Valladolid, 1997). This conversation is carried on as a part of unfolding one's gifts while paying attention to the ceremonial and seasonal cycles as well as the larger astronomical cycles. (See Vizenor, 1989, 1994a, 1994b for an example of Native American discourse stance.)

This is a worldview of total imma-nence that acknowledges the social con-struction or conversation in one place is different from other conversations in other places, yet seeing this it stays grounded in the detailed observations of and conversations with animal, plants, and the various cycles of the specific place of conversation. This is not a mind process where egoic consciousness and transcendence stand in some form of opposition or tension to each other, but where individuals of the permeable, participatory consciousness live with spirits as much as part of their community as other human beings or plants. "*El mundo es inmanente* — the world is immanent" (PRATEC, 1993, p. 10).

The various examples illustrating Anishinaabe, Siksikaitsitapi, Old Norse, Pomo, Wintu, and Sámi worldviews are descriptions of a process of an immanently present visionary socially constructed being, which is sustained without a need to progress to transcendence. They describe the immanent, ongoing conversation with everything, including spirits, which constitutes the community for human beings. Within this framework, if individuals do not know their ancestry, place in the community, the cultural stories, the land they live on, the cycles of the seasons, the stars, etc. — then these persons are lost to who they are, and pathology ensues — these individuals are in need of healing or balancing. These Indigenous models allow for an alternate understanding of time, history, and the variety of cultures; they also allow to be in participation or conversation while exercising high level rational skills. Part of this conversation are observations not only of seasonal patterns, larger astronomical cycles, the

precession of the equinoxes and other larger historical events. This Indigenous conceptualization allows each culture to understand its historic spiritual mission in its ecology, so to speak.

Socially engaged spirituality

Given Indigenous participation in this kind of ongoing sacred engagement, we can ask whether it is meaningful to speak about *socially engaged* spirituality in the Indigenous context. Rather, it seems that *such participation is by its nature spiritual and socially engaged*; it is always community and ecologically based. In other words, Indigenous life cannot be separated either from spirituality or from everyday communal and social life and politics.

In the Eurocentered societal realm, The Great Law of Peace of the Haudenosaunee (Iroquois Confederacy) talk eloquently about the relationship between **spirituality** and social engagement:

> Political activity is set in the roots of an ancient tradition of the spirituality of our peoples. This cosmology places the Haudenosaunee in a balanced relationship with the Universe and the Earth. In our languages, the Earth is our Mother Earth, the sun our Eldest Brother, the moon our Grandmother, and so on. It is the belief of our people that all elements of the Natural World were created for the benefit

of all living things and the we, as humans, are one of the weakest of the whole Creation, since we are totally dependent on the whole Creation for survival. This philosophy taught us to treat the Natural World with great care. Our institutions, practices and technologies were developed with a careful eye to their potential for disturbing the delicate balance we lived in. (Akwesasne Notes, 1978, p. 2)

The Haudenosaunee people have stated that they regard "spiritualism" as "the highest form of political consciousness" (Akwesasne Notes, 1978, 71, 72, 79):

> The original instructions direct that we who walk about on the Earth are to express a great respect, an affection, and a gratitude toward all the spirits which create and support Life. We give a greeting and thanksgiving to the many supporters of our own lives — the corn, beans, squash, the winds, the sun. … The traditional Native peoples hold the key to the reversal of the processes in Western Civilization which hold the promise of unimaginable future suffering and destruction.

The Great Law of Peace of the Haudenosaunee has been increasingly acknowledged as the "Indian roots of American democracy" (Barreiro, 1992).

Spirituality, ceremonial practices, and native philosophies are also an integral part of Indigenous resistance movements, including opposition to the establishment of nuclear dumps at Ward Valley in California's Mohave Desert to the speeches Hopi and other Elders have given at the UN. Some of the guidance for political action arises from their interpretation of the traditional teachings. For example, the Hopi prophecies directed the traditionalist Elders to go to the "house of mica," the UN, and to speak on behalf of native peoples and the world. The prophecy also directed them to visit the New Mexico state capital in Santa Fe at the time when flowers would bloom out of season. It is now well known that they review their actions in the context of the past seven generations and their impact on the future seven generations. Political consciousness arises thus from the history of the land, peoples, and ancestors as it is handed down in stories and embodied in spiritual practices.

In this conversational view of the world (i.e., the nurturing conversation), the aboriginal understanding of the beginning of history, the creation story, informs all aspects of life, whether healing, political action, or education. The Diné (Navajo) philosophy of learning (*diné bo'óhoo'aah bindii'a'*), for example, is based in the Diné creation story:

> When the earth came to life she took these same elements that gave her

being and placed them in the present cardinal directions: In the easterly direction she placed the principles by which the people will live (*bek'ehgo da' iináanii*); in the southerly direction she placed the principles of making a living (*nihigáál*); in the westerly directions she placed the principles of thinking, planning and gathering of family (*nahat'áh, nitsáhákees dóó aha'áná'oo'nííł*); in the north were placed the principles of rest, contentment and reverence. (Benally, 1987, 134–135)

In accordance with this creation story the various disciplines can be placed in an appropriate direction, such as philosophy, ethics, aesthetics, and language in the east; education, agriculture, law, livestock management and carpentry in the south; family living, sociology, history, psychology, and government in the west; and, finally, geology, chemistry, ecology, astronomy and other natural sciences in the north. Most importantly, the traditional concept of a harmonious life requires balancing all four categories of Navajo knowledge so that the individual will have sound beliefs and values to make the best possible decisions, will possess skill to provide the best living for the family and provide good leadership to the family and community, and will have a sense of reverence for the earth and for all living things and for

that which is in the heavens. The central focus of all learning is where all knowledge from the cardinal directions converges to promote a peaceful and harmonious life and society (*hózhóogo iiná*): a great central focus where to know, to admire, and to love are one and the same. (Benally, 1987, p. 143).

Different worlds

The worlds of Indigenous participation (nurturing conversation) and the worlds of unconscious participation or dissociation (in modern and postmodern societies) are different. It is not just that we see things differently in each of these worlds — but the worlds are different. At times our conversational language even admits that much: "The Navajos live in a totally different world." Indeed, they do. It is not just that they see the world differently — their world is not ours! The Mt. Taylor we see is not the same as the *Tsoodzil* the Navajos see. When we see this mountain while driving along the interstate toward Albuquerque, then we see all its beautiful physicality and sheer massiveness; we may see the snow on the mountaintop and gaze in wonder at the way the mountain rises rapidly from the valley floor. Its size and beauty might inspire awe in us. Traditional Navajos actively participating in their way of life (and not in contact with the Western paradigm) would see the physical mountain also, of course, but they would also be aware of the turquoise color and the blue wind which dwell in this mountain. They would participate in it as the South Mountain which helps to contain the sacred land which provides for them. First Man and First Woman fastened [the South Mountain] to the earth with a great stone knife, ... they adorned it with turquoise, with dark mist, she-rain, and all different kinds of wild animals. On its summit they placed a dish of turquoise; in this they put two eggs of the Bluebird, which they covered with sacred buckskin. ... The Boy who Carries One Turquoise and the Girl who Carries One Grain of Corn were put into the mountain to dwell. (Wyman, 1967, unpaginated)

Seeing the mountain is seeing part of what it means to live in *hózhó*, in beauty and balance. This is why soil from this mountain is present in the bundle for their foundational ceremony, the Blessingway. Participating in *Tsoodzil* is participating in part of the creation story. While our experience of seeing Mt. Taylor is that of seeing something out there, Navajos would participate in *Tsoodzil* (or *Dootl'shii Dziil*, meaning turquoise mountain) as a part of themselves necessary for walking in old age on a trail of beauty (*sa'a naghái bik'e hózhó*). If we were to imagine a successful recovery of Indigenous consciousness, then we could surmise that we would also experience the spirit of the mountain, and that we would enter its being in a way which makes it no longer 'out there'.

But what about the concrete, the things we can touch and presumably all agree on? Perhaps the pragmatic, 'real' stuff for which the Western Enlightenment paradigm would like to agree on is nothing but the least common denominator (arrived at and agreed to by dissociative perception and conceptual language). In holding a bead of turquoise in our hand we will probably be able to agree with any Navajo on its shape, color, the beauty of its veins, how we might polish it further, how it could be embedded in silver jewelry, how heavy it is, etc. (We would presumably be unable to agree, for example, on the question whether this is a semi–precious stone, since it is the most highly prized stone within the Navajo culture.)

What is meeting in such a conversation are two tips of icebergs; overlapping to a minimal degree. The overlap thus created is the least common denominator which the Western Enlightenment paradigm pursues. Below the Eurocentered tip of the iceberg is the monstrous denial of our participation in the phenomenon, such as the 'turquoise bead (which only imagination can recover). Below the Navajo tip of the iceberg is "the grand cosmic scheme of 'hózhó'" and how turquoise "functions as a lubricant to enhance this scheme or to restore it when it is disrupted... It is special because it is a means of harmonious communion with the other[s] ... in the universe" (Witherspoon, 1987, pp. 73–74). Thus we find that the tip of the Navajo iceberg is, in fact, the tip of a mountain, and that this mountain is only submerged for participants in the epistemology of modernity. We could say it is the tip of *Tsoodzil*.

People of Western mind can only see the tip of the mountain or iceberg. This is also the tip of all the Navajo chantway ceremonies (healing ceremonies) which maintain and restore beauty, happiness, health and harmony. We arrive at our supposed concrete, realistic view of the world at the expense of dissociation, the splitting from participation in nature and its cycles. For the Navajo a turquoise bead is a piece of art and as such "not divorced from subsistence, science, philosophy or theology, but is an integral part of both common activities and cosmic schemes" (Witherspoon, 1987, 60). While the tips of icebergs and mountains cannot physically touch at the top, they can touch at the bottom. Below the tips of the least common denominator we find the conscious or unconscious cultural practices which lead to differing participation in the phenomena. Yet even further below we may enter unitive states of consciousness and find, among the silent spaces, realities where cultures and their peoples touch in ways which are yet to be fully explored (Forman, 1990).

Activity

The Meaning of Life

Find a way to describe your central beliefs about life, its meaning, and matters of a spiritual and/or religious nature. What experiences related to spirituality did you have as a child? How did those affect who you are and how you view the world as an adult? Is human nature inherently good, or bad, or is that too simplistic a choice? What is your relationship with science and spirituality? Are they opposed to one another, or do you feel they can coexist? In what ways do you experience that potential conflict or coexistence in your life?

Allow yourself to speak in a voice that works for you. Use any props that may be helpful.

This may be completed as a 500–word response paper, or shared as an oral presentation with others.

Note: If you are completing these activities on your own, and do not have an organized group to do oral presentations for (such as in a classroom, community organization and so on), it is encouraged that you present the work you are doing to a friend, family member or spouse to experience sharing your process in oral form.

Chapter Summary

Faith requires acceptance though experience can challenge faith. Atheism, in turn, disagrees with the answers provided by many spiritual traditions. Since Indigenous spiritualities are immanent, earth–based, and socially engaged, Indigenous and non–Indigenous people live in different worlds. Indigenous knowledge is a science, grounded in exacting observations, albeit with different assumptions than **Western science**.

Concept Check

How are **spirituality** and **religion** different as understood in this workbook?

What is the difference between **Western sciences** and **Indigenous sciences**?

What are central qualities of Indigenous spiritualities?

What European historical period did **atheism** largely emerge from?

Riff

Indigenous ... Science

She says:

I was thinking how rich our Native ways of knowing are, in many ways even richer than Western science. So, I was looking for a way to talk about Native sciences. That's when I thought of the term Indigenous science. I was hoping that this would enable Western scientists to see our rich knowledge and then, maybe, they would get involved with us instead of killing us. Then it might lead to an egalitarian exchange of knowledge that would benefit everybody. I thought of it as protection, not just for Indigenous peoples, but for all peoples. Tribal life arises from the telling of imaginative stories and close observation of nature.

She has my attention, I sit up straight. This explanation takes my breath away. It gives the provocation of joining the words Indigenous and science an edge.

In Chaco Canyon the Anasazi people created a tool for the measurement of lunar and solar cycles. Fajada Butte stands alone as a mass of rock between mesas where the Fajada Gap opens the wide canyon to the south. The astronomical marker can only be reached by a difficult climb across steep places and areas that are favorite habitat for rattlesnakes. The two spirals — one large, one small — are hidden behind three large, elongated rock slabs standing away from the cliff at soft angles. Light passes through the opening between two of the slabs to create the image of a wedge–like triangle or "dagger" on the marker; at summer solstice the dagger is at the center of the larger spiral, at winter solstice two daggers embrace the large spiral. The dagger–shaped light reflection on the spiral up on the precipitous rock face of Fajada Butte can be understood to the extent it reflects astronomical knowledge. But this understanding is only a partial refraction of the rich cultural knowledge that culminates in these observations. The astronomical validation does not include the stories, histories, and ceremonies of the people who created this observatory after long years of careful sky–watching; for them all these aspects were intricately and necessarily woven together.

And how did the West African Dogon know about the white dwarf companion star around Sirius? Astronomy only deduced its existence in 1844 and it was actually seen only in 1862. Yet, the Dogon knew about this faint companion, invisible to the naked eye, at least as early as the thirteenth century. A Sirius–related ceremony and its masks tell the story. They probably knew about it even significantly earlier. Indigenous science opens the door to an enlarged understanding of what inquiry and the practice of knowledge can be. It weaves scientific observation, ceremony, and story into a rich conversation of presence. It is a reminder of what knowing has been about for Indigenous peoples. Astronomy can support the accuracy of the ancient Dogon knowledge claim, yet it captures only a slim part of its richness. There are ceremonies, masks, and chants to be dealt with. The riches of Indigenous science are the white dwarf of astronomy, so to speak. I felt that my colleague, Apela Colorado, was trying to make the conventional scientific paradigm wobble under the mass of tribal knowledge, just like the density of the white dwarf makes Sirius wobble, leading to its discovery by European science. On this companion star one teaspoonful of sugar weighs a ton and the intricacies of Indigenous knowledge systems may eventually weigh in on the European sciences just as heavily.

Parts of Indigenous science are thus more easily visible to people of European mind, the parts measurable and quantifiable in particular. Other parts remain obscured due to a consciousness that is split from awareness of its intimate participation in the world.

I think of Newgrange in Ireland. The precision of its construction allows a sunbeam to travel the 22 meters long passageway into the mound and touch the altar at the end for twenty minutes or so. It is difficult not to see this as a grand technological achievement as well as the result of observations scientific in nature. Indigenous science practiced by his European ancestors. A disturbance in the neat ascending pattern from primitive to modern European peoples many people seem to prefer. Stonehenge, another disturbance. Calendrical rock carvings in Scandinavia another. As such intricate knowledge is recovered it becomes ever more important to re-tell evolutionary stories. Not only did our ancestors have brain capacities similar to ours, but they put them to exquisite uses that we are slow to comprehend. Many of their stories have remained obscure, awaiting the shamanic imagination to complete the visionary tales encoded in Newgrange, Stonehenge, and many other places.

My travel companion talks more about the precision of Native knowing, the accuracy of the required observations, and the necessity of presence. And then, how story, vision, prophecy, and tribal practices hold it all. At least ideally. This is how I hear it.

I read about *Gii Laii* and the medicine of prayer, how *Gii Laii* is the still place of balance within ourselves. The image Apela uses to evoke it is the tranquil spot by a river or a lake. Finding this deep quiet, still place is the beginning point and the end point of Indigenous science. She asserts that this place can have an actuality within every human. The way she discusses prayer is quite different from what he has experienced in Lutheran Church: She sees it as medicine, as a profound connection with life, a vibrancy and presence where all of life exists within, without, and between each person and in their relationships. This is the beginning of life. *Gii Laii* is an Iroquois word for this presence or awareness, for this sense of aliveness and time slowing into an eternal present, for this peacefulness. Of course, this leads to the most important questions: Where is this place? Where is it in his internal life? And I wonder: How can you be sure? How do you know you have arrived? How do you know it is not an inflated perception fueled by narcissistic desires? How do you know you speak or write from such process of being? She regards *Gii Laii* and this medicine of prayer as the pivot for the stories of Indigenous science.

JWK

Notes

Chapter 15
To Tell a Story ...

Riff

Homecoming

Fireman! Fireman!
The call is for me
I am standing in a circle of people in a ceremonial building
On Pomo–Miwok land in Northern California
The medicine man turns to me and
Continues his friendly tease
Fireman! Fireman!
The fire has burnt down some
The billowing smoke is
Building cloud banks in the ceremonial roundhouse
Fireman! Fireman!
I walk on the uneven dirt floor
Toward the fire in the center of the four central posts
Upholding the roof of the huge, round building
I throw some more wood on
Sparks fly as the oak logs hit the fire
The intense heat blasts my face
Beads of perspiration instantly appear

The medicine man has put me in charge of the fire
Some of my Native friends regard this as special honor
I am not so sure
As the only white person I feel exposed

Served on a platter
The group of Native students sits on the benches along the wall
Nobody looks at me
Yet everybody seems to be aware of my every move
I feel their awareness
My mind is taut with the sense of their scrutiny
And of their questioning whether I am capable of tending the fire properly

Tending the fire properly means paying attention to everything
Spirit and wood and smoke
What happens with it and around it
A constant conversation
I put on some more wood
Nobody looks directly
Everybody notices
I make the fire burn hotter
The smoke now rises quickly toward the hole in the roof
The air clears

Now everybody is asked to introduce him– or herself
White man has to start, of course
I go out on a limb

The trickster Loki stands right by me, it seems
I dare to speak what I have pieced together
About who I am culturally speaking
The best I can do at that moment
I am ready to try out something new
The trickster Loki playfully teases me to renew an older appearance
So I speak who I envision myself to be, with hesitation, with fear
I speak of my German ancestry
My Teutonic ancestry
I am from the land of the ancient Myrgings
This is the earliest tribal name I have for the tribal people of my birthplace
I am a river person from the Elbe River in northern Germany
Rosenow is my grandmother's name
Her ancestors came from all around the southern and eastern Baltic Coast
From Mecklenburgia and Pommerania to northeasternmost Poland
To southwestern Russia or southern Lithuania
And maybe from much farther north
As far as I can tell
My father's ancestors
They are from the lower Rhine Valley and
Before that from Alsace–Lorraine

Once I have spoken my fear subsides
I now notice two things coming together inside
My awareness settles into my body with startling comfort
As if two ribcages come together and blend
Ribcage and ribcage join
Out of the shift arises comfort, not merely the cessation of anxiety
A novel sensation spreads
My physical being and who I think I am merge and meld
Into a new form of congruence
Somatic consonance
The reunion of fragments
"It is a homecoming."
Homecoming
This is the label I attach to the joining of story and story
Of ribcage and ribcage
The dizzying interior space of one ribcage
Encounters reassurance in the vertiginous riches the other offers
Homecoming
An insufficient word for sure, romantic
Homecoming
Being at home in an unfolding process of conversation

This homecoming is also shocking
Since I have never been there
Yet no other word describes my feeling more accurately

JWK

Chapter Outline	Core Concepts	Ethnoautobiographical Perspectives	Expected Outcomes
Homecoming	Homecoming is a renewal of our identity process	Acknowledging ancestries is much more than a mental process	Provide an example of the potential benefits of EA work
Narrative universe	We live in a world of stories	Confusing stories about the world lead to a pathology of worldview	Appreciation of the importance of the quality of our stories
To tell a story in the proper way	There is a "proper way" to tell a story	Telling a story in the proper way enables us to re–envision ourselves	Connect more deeply with a holistic and Indigenous sense of presence through storytelling
Changes in self	EA storytelling changes our sense of self to more complex and deeper self understanding	EA allows us to dwell in plurality	Assert the freedom of our complex identity process
Ethnoauto-biography in a larger context	Romanticism and nostalgia are dissociative and part of a pattern of supremacy	EA helps to explore the multiplicity of our cultural stories	Overcome denials of the multivocality and complexity of histories
Multiplicity of (hi)stories	Depth of memory is critical for our survival	Remembering helps us to envision what we might yet become	Appreciate the riches that come from understanding rootedness
Not to write a story — to tell a story	*Telling*, as opposed to writing, our stories facilitates presence	Telling our stories in front of audiences (small or large) helps to connect with them more deeply	Increase in personal presence by telling stories
Into the future	In order to move into the future we need to bring the past forward with us	Bringing the past forward increases our sense of presence and interconnection	Re–story our world for the sake of the future

Key Terms

Enlightenment
Recovery of Indigenous mind
Synecdochic self

Note: All key terms in this textbook are highlighted in bold and can be found in the Glossary at the end of the book.

Resources Alongside This Chapter

Adichie, C. N. (2009). *The danger of a single story*. Retrieved from http://www.ted.com/talks/chimamanda_adichie_the_danger_of_a_single_story.html

Boyd, B. (2009). *On the origin of stories: Evolution, cognition, and fiction*. Cambridge, MA: Belknap Press of Harvard University Press.

King, T. (2013). *A short history of Indians in Canada: Stories*. Minneapolis: University of Minnesota Press.

Loy, D. R. (2010). *The world is made of stories*. Boston, MA: Wisdom Publications.

Narrative universe

The riff, "Homecoming", at the beginning of the chapter gives an example of what can happen when we change our story: by acknowledging his ancestries Jürgen's stories started to change. This was not only a matter of insight, but also a matter of changes in his body. The stories that he was a part of, the stories that made up his sense of self, were experienced in all the different parts of himself. Jürgen's somatic experience attested to an internal sense of rightness. Jürgen's somatic experience attested to an internal sense of rightness. He expanded his sense of self and began to change his relationship to the stories that informed him. Much more consciously than ever before he had entered not only his own personal narrative with awareness, but also a sense of the world as narrative universe.

We quoted Thomas King early on: "The truth about stories is that that's all we are" (King, 2003, p. 2). We are stories living in a storied universe. Many years ago Jürgen wrote a scholarly article in which he argued that we live in a narrative universe and that the awareness of living in a storied world gives us choice (Kremer, 1986). We can ask questions like: Do we like the plot? Is this really the story we want to be a part of? Is this really the character we want to be in this story? Bateson (1972), referring to Korzybski, stressed the importance of realiz-ing that the map is not the territory, only one representation of it. If we think otherwise, we may suffer from a pathology of epistemology or worldview.

Our left hemisphere likes to take the position of the master and assert that its map is the territory. But, alas, science is also a story, a particular type of story that follows particular rules, and is a specific and limited way of making meaning. Thinking that science is the only possible story limits the possibilities of meaning making as storytellers and denies the importance of the integrative powers of our right hemisphere. These integrative powers do not deny the powers of science, but they put it into a larger context. Mythos and logos are both particular storytelling styles — they need each other — yet mythos needs to remain the master (something we have largely forgotten and our contemporary crises are the price we pay for this memory loss).

The awareness that our self is made of stories and that this self lives in a world of stories is significant and signals a profound shift. As long as we are "unaware that our stories are stories, we experience them as the world". Once we become aware and "our accounts of the world become different, the world becomes different" (Loy, 2010, p. 5). When we live with the awareness that we are participating through our stories in a narrative universe we become part of mythic consciousness. This is not backward, this is a move forward where we interact with personal and social stories as they unfold, are renewed, and re–imagined. Mythic consciousness has never ceased to be with us, it has always been present. Acknowledging that we are stories in a storied universe puts the powers of the right hemisphere back into their rightful place: the master who can integrate our experience and knowledge and make meaning of it — meaning of past events and meaning for the future.

claims the most difficult to evaluate, because we cannot agree on what criteria to use. Myth avoids this problem by being meaningful in a different way. Religious doctrines, like other ideologies, involve propositional claims to be accepted. Myths provide stories to interact with. (p. 12)

Myths are evolving stories, they are communal. I as individual cannot create a myth, yet I can tell a story, and my story may become part of communal stories and change in the process. Myths

> To tell our story in the proper way means imagining ourselves with something resembling an Indigenous process of awareness — the freedom to be an artist aware of Indigenous roots.

Being in narrative or mythic consciousness does not mean that we can just make up any story. Our stories are not free floating. They have (and need to have) a grounding. There are parameters within which we can create stories. Conventional science has identified some of these parameters. We also have genetic parameters, environmental parameters, parameters stemming from our life story, and so on.

Loy (2010) points out that

the metaphorical nature of religious language makes its truth

are meaning makers that integrate and represent our understanding of the world. When myths are part of an oral tradition they are alive and as such ever changing — each storytelling gives them a somewhat different twist, humor adds other twists, the dream of a teller may add depth to the telling, and a ceremony may lead to a new understanding of the story. Myths in this sense are not dogmas to be believed in. Like dreams, they are to be lived with and enlivened.

To tell a story in the proper way

The remembrance of an ethno-autobiographical self woven into history, myth, place, gender, and ancestral lines may thus be survivance, resistance, truth–telling, and imaginative inquiry that narrates freely and narrates for the sake of freedom. This *sovereign* self exits from an isolated and disconnected White mind and enters processes filled with relationships in imaginative realms of immanent, and ever present spirits(s). The certainty of categories dissolves into the ironic, tricksterish, and humorous play of *participatory* events. As Homi Bhabha has asserted: "The right to narrate is not simply a linguistic act; it is also a metaphor for the fundamental human interest in freedom itself, the right to be heard, to be

self. This means being crane, as Keeshkemun, the Anishinaabe orator tells or, according to Adrianne Rich, the woman standing in line for gas-masks. To tell our story in the proper way means imagining ourselves with something resembling an Indigenous process of awareness – the freedom to be an artist aware of Indigenous roots. Asserting this freedom to narrate our-selves means taking on the obligation to overcome obstacles to our personal imagination. It means decolonization as much as self–actualization.

Such storytelling is not the unfolding of a preconceived, essential true way

> **All peoples have Indigenous roots that may matter more at this historical juncture than even the various postmodern strands are able to see or are willing to admit.**

recognized and represented." (Bhabha in Manuel, 2000). N. Scott Momaday (1997, p. 169) has written that "to tell a story in the proper way, to hear a story told in the proper way — this is very old and sacred business, and it is very good." In an Indigenous sense, what might this proper way mean? Why would it be *very old and sacred* business? Why would it be *very good*? What is a non–native person to do?

To tell our individual story in the proper way means speaking of myth, history, and individuality. It means bringing together our life stories with dimensions larger than an isolating

of being. Rather, it is a continuing, unceasing struggle to find authen-ticity and integrity within communi-ties, places, and histories, i.e., to find better and more creatively accurate expressions for ourselves. Our self is our stories. As we tell our stories our sense of authenticity changes. It means re–imagining ourselves as part of an ongoing creation story continuing from the mythic realms our ancestors envisioned, imagining them for today. It means to be free not in an individualistic sense, but as an individual bearing obligations for liberating narratives grounded in time, place, and social conditions. It is the practice of a particular form of socially engaged spirituality in which the self practices embodied narratives both created by and bearing upon its spiritual and social entanglements.

Changes in self

It may be important to recall that the modern self that we are so familiar with is of rather recent origin and probably only two hundred or so years old. The **masterful**, boundaried self of our individualistic social landscape is a White social construction that serves the consumerist needs of the current market economy. The self, in a sense, is a pawn in the games of governmental structures, technological developments, and economic forces. An immoral mindlessness emerged from the more community oriented early settlers and in contrast to the "wild" selves of Native American and African American slave selves (cf. Cushman, 1995). The historical possibility of who we understand ourselves to be is inevitably a central factor in ethno-autobiographical inquiries.

As various postmodern challenges (crises of identity and participation as well as economics, ecologies, and politics) result in the breakdown of Eurocentered confidence and hubris, a twofold recognition emerges: the realization that Indigenous peoples continue to exist without ever succumbing entirely to colonial forces; and secondly, that the local, historical moment, and cultural roots may matter more than the **Enlightenment** period and the subsequent scientific developments have acknowledged.

That all peoples have Indigenous roots may matter more at this historical juncture than even the various postmodern strands are able to see or are willing to admit. Inquiring into the fertile plurality of our roots is also critical moral discourse. Instead of "linking origin to authoritarianism, univocalism, and the suppression of alterity," we need to recognize that

> authentic origins are inherently plural and divergent, and an extended meditation upon them reinvigorates attention to history and subverts supremacist claims of particular groups by showing that their ethnicity, religion, or discipline is 'always already'– from the origin – entangled with others (Pizer, 1995, pp. 13 & 14).

Curiosity and truthfulness about our origins and their complexity opens a creative space from which we can find grounding and mythic renewal. The avoidance of looking at our origins and making them thus part of our shadow issues frequently leads to ungroundedness and narcissistic inflation. We may find our integrity in inquiries that lead us through our ancestries and shadows, dreaming with places, bringing histories we carry into our awareness, embodying our dreams and visions, and being released into a renewed mythic consciousness. A sense of humor and playfulness will be critical along the way.

Similar to Krupat's notion of the synecdochic self–narratives of self that are grounded in and a part of a community and its stories, and vice versa — *ethno*autobiographical stories and autoethnographic reflections continue to be options that enable us to dwell in plurality. Indigenous consciousness has always been there. It is a continuing process. Its present day practitioners presumably see themselves neither as members of the Eurocentered Enlightenment traditions, nor in postmodern or other opposition to the practices of modernity. Instead, they assert the sovereignty of their discourse in the face of ongoing colonial pressures.

Larger context

There is a larger context for ethno-autobiographical discourses and inquiries. This work entails the spiritual recovery and practice of integrative or participatory consciousness processes as well as the transpersonal recovery of connections to dreams, visions, community, time, and place that have disappeared behind the veil of rationalism, a continuous historic dissociation. The exploration of ethnic connections, ancestral roots, or the **recovery of Indigenous mind** requires a rational and critical discourse that is integrated with emotional, **somatic**, spiritual, and other alternate ways of knowing. This is considered alternate or alternative within a rationalistic framework, yet integral and mandatory within an Indigenous framework.

Nostalgia and romanticism lose their dissociative power once we begin to acknowledge that history is multiple. Simultaneous to the historical lines identified in Eurocentered narratives we find a multiplicity of other histories (oftentimes de–valued as 'stories' or 'folklore' or 'legends,' mere oral history) that enriches and/or questions the dominant story. History is not a unitary phenomenon, but a weaving of a multiplicity of stories. "The ideal of multiple viewpoints challenges the very idea of representation as mimesis, for it substitutes a kaleidoscope for a telescope or microscope. Most certainly, it repudiates the omniscience of a Panopticon for the particular perspectives of situated viewpoints" (Berkhofer, 1995, p. 269).

For example: Concurrent with the historical lines of the Russian, Spanish, and other settlers and colonizers in California, presented as the dominant telling of the story, we have to acknowledge the stories of the abundant cultural diversity of California's native peoples and their destruction. The stories of the Spanish missions have a genocidal corollary. Christian representations of religion have a native corollary in roundhouse ceremonies, bear dances, and rock art. Denials of genocide, colonial occupations, slavery and other atrocities lead to one–sided supremacist stories.

Multiplicity of (hi)stories

The struggle to acknowledge the multiplicity of (hi)stories is an anti-dote to romanticism and nostalgia.

New Age identifications, a circus of shallow masquerades.

The Chukchi writer Yuri Rytkeu, in an article on, "The Future of Memory" (1999), reports a conversation with the Inuit singer and dancer Nutetein, in which he told him that human beings are not merely to be measured in height and width, but also in terms of their depth of memory, since only that is what makes them spatially real, graspable, and visible. He continues:

> ...human beings are not merely to be measured in height and width, but also in terms of their depth of memory, since only that is what makes them spatially real, graspable, and visible.
>
> **Rytkeu (1999)**

Witnessing the history, the stories of place, whether in the form of Native American or African American (hi)stories, for example, facilitates initiation into a form of collective consciousness that supersedes simplistic and individu-alistic interpretations of story. Self-actualization and altered states now not only include the integration of shamanic or meditative realms, but also the integration of suppressed human storylines. The depth of Indigenous self–representation in response to the question "Who am I?" can only be approximated by critical and emotion-ally integrative work with collective shadow material and denied story lines. Otherwise we may lose ourselves in

Nutetein's words admirably con-nect the human memory of tradi-tion and cultural inheritance with the coming–to–consciousness of individuality and irrepeatability. Because a human being without roots and without acknowledg-ment of the ancestral cultural in-heritance is — as Herbert Marcuse said previously — flat and one di-mensional, even if s/he claims to be a person of all the world cultures.

Without sufficient depth and inclu-siveness of memory we stand to be insufficient individuals. There is now sufficient research to indicate that trauma is passed on intergenerationally.

Survivors of the Shoah (Nazi holo-caust), as well as its perpetrators, have passed on their unspoken experiences to subsequent generations (cf. Bar–On et al. 1993). The denial of the Native American genocide and slavery or the unacknowledged involvement of spiritual traditions with fascism (e.g., Zen Buddhism in Japan) leave traces in subsequent generations. Sovereignty and freedom necessitate that we narrate ourselves not merely in the mirror of the dominant stories, but as an inquiry into what may be difficult to recover and shameful to remember. We can read Faulkner's dictum "The past is not dead. It is not even past" (1951) in this sense. **Recovery of Indigenous mind** then is not a nostalgic fantasy of an inflated ego, but a painful and joyful remembrance of who we might have been and how we have become who we are and what we might yet become. Integrative states result from such narrative return of lost stories and reconnection with suppressed human potential.

Not to write a story — to tell a story

Writing our ethnoautobiographi-cal stories is a good and important thing, but *telling* it may be even more important. Participation in an oral tradition requires a particular sense of presence and memory. We need to be present to ourselves, to the story, and to the audience. While this can be replicated in some forms of writing where we may achieve a sense of flow (Csiksentmihalyi, 2008), the oral tell-ing of who we are, of our dreams, of our ancestral stories, or of memories creates a different quality of presence in ourselves and for our audience. Many of the activities suggested in this workbook are probably done best in a learning community setting (class, workshop, or group of friends); where we have the opportunity to *tell* our ethnoautobiography, to *tell* our gender stories, to share our dreams, and to *tell* creation and other myths for the sake of renewal. When we tell our stories in front of others it is oftentimes easier to have a clear inner sense of what is important and what is not, of what feels right and internally connected and what is not quite on the mark. It is good practice to venture into the realms of the oral tradition. It creates opportunities for increased self reflexivity and awareness.

Into the future

We have previously emphasized that this work is not about going back to something in the past. It is not designed to serve some retro–romantic fantasies of paradisical worlds of the past. It is not a revival movement for past cul-tures. So, if it is not about 'going back' in any sense of these words, what can 'homecoming' possibly mean? What is the future vision?

The Old Norse had an interesting notion of the trajectory of time and history: If you want to go into the future, you had to step back into the past to make sure that you would bring it forward. The past had to be remembered in order for the future to happen (Bauschatz, 1982). This may even be difficult for us to imagine these days when we are, it seems, singularly forward oriented. Our eye is on the future. The past so often appears as encumbrance, rather than a natural part of the future and rich storehouse of opportunity. Ethnoautobiography asks us to step into the past for the sake of the future. It is a shift in consciousness that allows us to be present for the future and to renew our stories through the work of memory. This movement from the present through the past and into the future is a particular discipline that helps us stay grounded and creates the parameters for the stories that can and need to be told.

The experience of 'homecoming' described in the riff at the beginning of this chapter is not a return to a specific **when** and **where** that has been lost, but a return to a particular way of being in the world. For Jürgen it meant to engage deeply in a place of hybridity — he had no living tradition of his own ancestries to go to and could not become part of contemporary Indigenous traditions. While he had spent much time with contemporary shamans and healers and had learned much from different traditions, he was and could only be in between traditions. During

his ethnoautobiographical work he came to appreciate it as a generative position rather than a position of loss. It was and is a place for healing work of a different kind. The home for the **recovery of Indigenous mind** we come to is a process that is fed by the richness of our remembrance.

This is a view of the self that unfolds in stark contrast to the **masterful** and well–boundaried self of modernity. "If the self is made of stories, they are not a function of the self but vice–versa" (Loy, 2010, p. 29). The self is a function of the stories that emerge inside of us and the stories that we become a part of. Changing ourselves means changing our stories, changing the world means changing the stories about the world. If these stories emerge from the rich matrix of our personal and collective engagement with ancestry, ceremony, place, history, community, and dreams, then they have a power of their own. As individuals we cannot decide what the new mythologies will be (this would be egotistical and inflated), but we can be instrumental in contributing to its emergence. Our personal visionary stories need to interact with other personal visionary stories. When stories interact on the mythic level they change and some get weeded out or pruned. The "new story" or the "new myth" cannot just be made up, it will be created through the painstaking work in ceremony, with our dreams, with our ancestors and ancestries, with the remembrance of histories, with the dreaming of places. This is work of grounding and release. "It is not by transcending this world that we are transformed but by storying it in a new way" (Loy, 2010, p. 11). When we tell stories that are 'on target' we will have an 'aha!' experience and an inner sense of right, we will feel it in our bodies. The majority of the people today are hybrids or cross-bloods for one reason or another, they are carriers of multiplicities. It is the position from which an understanding of freedom and **sovereignty** can emerge that transcends the limited notions of the present. It is the position where the creative spirit and the spirit of creation can play with a sense of humor as humans remember who they are and where they need to go. The creative expression in story, image, movement, and sound remembers, evokes, and guides this process. This is a homecoming as we tell our story in the proper way.

Activity

Acting out Your Story

Use storytelling, poetry, spoken word, acting, or any other way that suits you to illustrate your developing sense of ethnoautobiography. What does it look like at this moment?

How has it changed since the beginning of this process?

How do you feel about the elements of your ethnoautobiography?

Are some more familiar now, and others still unclear and even scary or uninteresting?

Are there some elements that are particularly exciting or inspiring?

Could you see yourself returning to this process later and revisiting some elements?

Is your ethnoautobiography even finished and done?

Compose your narrative orally, in writing, and/or using multimedia.

Think of it as a five minute presentation. Share this as an oral presentation with others.

Note: If you are completing these activities on your own, and do not have an organized group to do oral presentations for (such as in a classroom, community organization and so on), it is encouraged that you present the work you are doing to a friend, family member or spouse to experience sharing your process in oral form.

Chapter Summary

We live in a world of stories. Confusing stories about the world lead to a pathology of worldview, whereby romanticism and nostalgia are dissociative and a part of supremacy. Telling a story in the proper way enables us to re–envision ourselves. Storytelling changes our sense of self to be more complex, allowing us to dwell in plurality. Remembering stories helps us to envision what we might yet become. Bringing the past forward in our stories increases our sense of presence and interconnection.

Concept Check

What is the impact of the denial of certain aspects of human history (for individuals, for society)?

What is the "proper" way to tell a story?

According to Nuetetin, humans should be measured in what ways?

What feeds the home for **recovery of Indigenous mind**?

NOTES

Chapter 16
Healing Ourselves — Healing Others

Riff

The Unbearable Rightness of Being

I'm sitting in the passenger seat
Jenny's driving
I occasionally look up
to see forested mountains
clouds in every shade of grey

feeling guilty to be writing
as if I'm dishonoring the landscape
yet, I feel so heavy
weighted down, burdened

I need to find some way to get unstuck
to cleanse and purify
hoping these words help

typical to find myself on
another motorized pilgrimage
passing through personal and
cultural underworlds
while en route to safety and healing

living in Texas these days
requires learning about the land
and the Original People
in order to live there
with integrity

that's why we had driven
along some of Quanah Parker's Trail
acknowledging sites from the settlement wars

with New Mexico and
Indian Market intentionally awaiting
to make clear that
while there were battles won
colonization has not been completely successful

so it was then
somehow inexplicably
magical
that we found ourselves
sitting among Margarete's paintings
and Helen's, and Pablita's

bearing witness to
a victory dance
because the land still does belong
to the Original People
the hosts state that explicitly
thanking Po'pay
for clearing the way
331 years ago
with the Pueblo revolt

and while I watch
feeling the drumbeat
in my heart
I ponder the dances of my ancestors
English Morris
the Irish dancing
I feel the reverberation of
bagpipes in my bones

that's some of the heaviness
the weight that keeps me
stuck
discouraged
there is so much distance in
space and time
between me and my ancestral dances
there are so many underworlds
through the loss of settlement
so much forgetting

yet there I was
watching, opening, feeling
the lightness of the dancers
the beating of the drum
and the heart

being invited to assist in
keeping something safe
after all that the Original People
have been through
and here they are dancing
so through this writing
with a purpose of healing and
living right
I intend to do my dancing too

RJP

Chapter Outline	Core Concepts	Ethnoautobiographical Perspectives	Expected Outcomes
The unbearable rightness of being	Healing is a communal practice	Integrating multiple stories heals the self and the world	Begin to imagine additions to the stories you tell of yourself
Survivance is healing	Rather than merely living, healing emerges from an active stance of survivance, and engaging with our larger sense of self	Telling more complete stories aids the reconciliation of rifts in our selves and our worlds	Understand potential healing by connecting to a particular time and place, and reconnecting with ancestral lines and historical legacies
Spiritual inquiry	Sensing ourselves as larger than an individualistic self opens the door to new insights & practices	Spiritual inquiry is an integrative practice	Identify the ways that ethnoautobio-graphy is related to spiritual inquiry
Narrating ourselves freely	Healing our dismemberment from Indigenous roots catalyzes creative strength	Our imagination can help us tell us our stories to very center of who we are	See the ways ethnoautobiography is creative, imaginative and decolonizing

Key Terms

Borderland
Crossblood
Hybridity
Imaginal
Master self
Presence, Indigenous presence, coming–to–presence, radical presence
Sovereignty
Spiritual inquiry
Transmotion
Well–bounded self

Note: All key terms in this textbook are highlighted in bold and can be found in the Glossary at the end of the book.

Resources Alongside This Chapter

Breton, D. C. (2005). Digging deeper: Challenges for restorative justice. In W. D. McCaslin (Ed.), *Justice as healing: Indigenous ways* (pp. 409–434). St. Paul, MN: Living Justice Press.

Duran, E. (2006). *Healing the soul wound: Counseling with American Indians and other native peoples.* New York, NY: Teachers College Press.

Hooker, D. A., & Czajkowski, A. P. (2012). *Transforming historical harms.* Harrisonburg, VA: Coming to the Table. Retrieved from http://s3.amazonaws.com/cttt/assets/164/CTTT_TransformingHistoricalHarms_manual_web_original.pdf

Krondorfer, B. (1995). *Remembrance and reconciliation: Encounters between young Jews and Germans.* New Haven, CT: Yale University.

Macy, J., & Johnstone, C. (2012). *Active hope: How to face the mess we're in without going crazy.* Novato, CA: New World Library.

Rothberg, D. (1994). Spiritual inquiry. *ReVision,* 17(2), 2–12.

Rather than sharing the sentiment that, sad as it may be, the cause of Indigenous peoples is a lost one, we may instead celebrate with Vizenor (2008), and many others their "survivance." This vitality is not a romantic continuance of an anthropologically imagined pure state of culture, but the actions of peoples who, from a **crossblood** woodland native perspective, might say, "I touch myself into being with my freedom to narrate themselves in the language of their choice. Members of dominant societies may make a similarly courageous choice: we may imagine ourselves with our dreams in a particular time, place, and community, recollect our ancestral lines, and confront histories of supremacy. As we inquire about this potential we also confront generational traumas, denials, and collective shadow material.

> Members of dominant societies may make a courageous choice to imagine themselves with their dreams in a particular time, place, and community, recollect their ancestral lines, and confront histories of supremacy.

own dreams and with my imagination ... I gather all those words that feed and nurture my imagination about my being" (Vizenor, 1990, p. 159 – 160). Indigenous peoples, whether on the reservation, in the cities, or on other margins, usually continue to imagine themselves with ancestry, time, place, and community (however flawed or incomplete that might seem). In this way, survivance is healing.

Survivance is healing

While the forces of colonialism and genocide continue their assaults, many tribal minds do not succumb to being victims. Rather, they assert their rights, (in part within the framework of human rights), and speak to a different type of discourse and imagination with the

As we practice ethnoautobiography, the multiple strands of re – imagining ourselves and facing collective shadows happens simultaneously. Embedded in these healing tasks is facing the challenging realities that "there must be an acknowledgement of the truth, an apology, a reconciliation, restitution, and a healing" (M. K. Nelson, 2008, p. 16). Breton (2005) elaborates on what this healing work entails.

> Obviously, each of us can do the anti – racism, decolonization work, both personally and with others, which is a start in the healing process. But further, perhaps there is a purification ceremony that is ours as EuroAmericans and adapted to us as a sacred way — a way that can

serve our transformation. Perhaps our healing, purifying ceremony is to go straight into the fire of confronting these wrongs and then to stay in the heat of doing what it takes to make things right. Sweating in this heat may not signify our demise but our healing and transformation — our rebirth. If we long for our humanity and integrity as a people, which has unfortunately gotten so lost during

from individualistic — *sense of self* accrues only within the context of community, which includes the nonvisible world of ancestors, spirits, and gods, provides a secure grounding for a criticism that can reach beyond the politicized, deterministic confines of progressive approaches, as well as beyond the neurotic diminishment of self – reflexiveness. (p. 177; emphasis added)

> Ethnoautobiography delights in the compassionate telling of our larger transpersonal, imaginal stories in the fissures and cracks of our hybrid origins, identities and presences, a storytelling that humbly and ferociously resists the totalizing desires of grander dominant schemes.

these centuries in a mad rush for gain, perhaps we can find ways back to it — sacred ways, since healing harms and broken relationships is very sacred. (p. 430)

Instead of experiencing our selves as a void to be filled due to the individualistic **master self**, we may feel a part of a communal endeavor to constitute rich moral, political, historical, psychological, or spiritual discourse, identity, and ultimately **radical presence**.

Paula Gunn Allen (1998) reminds us:

The concept in relation or, more "nativistically," the understanding that the individualized — as distinct

Native elders have told us: "You are not alone. The power is not lost, you are. Ask the question about who you are and make an offering. Ancestors will respond from the other side and help." Memory includes ancestral **presence**. A task that may seem overwhelming in scope may thus find a container that holds at least a little bit of reassurance. It is important to note that ancestors always seem to play a significant role in Indigenous traditions, although understood differently in different places. The loss of ancestral connections and memory shows itself in Eurocentered cultures in such difficulties as facing death or respecting Indigenous graves, for example.

Spiritual inquiry

Ethnoautobiography is thus spiritual inquiry in that what is external is also in the personal, as the personal extends into the external. From an Indigenous perspective this investigation and questioning is, on the one hand, engaged in by an individual with imagination and humor, but is, on the other hand, contextualized not just by history, time, place, or culture, but also by the presence of ancestral spirits (often revealing themselves in visions and dreams). In this par-

to research how their various ancestors used the term and which terms they used. It is important to resist psychologizing spirit, that is, taking spiritual belief and practice to a simplistic psychological approach. Similarly, it is equally important not to make spirit a part of an individualistic paradigm. Who are these spirits or what is spirit?

Ethnoautobiography as a form of **spiritual inquiry** has a clear emphasis on telling the story of the process and the results of the questioning. It is a form of transformative investi-

> As we inquire we create. Our creations can be imagined in such a way that they evoke a related presence in the reader. The work of crafting self–narratives that are imaginative, poetic, and evocative is a way of creating presence.

ticipatory worldview the inquirer or the community of inquirers are not alone. On the contrary, ancestral spirits respond.

Silko's (1996) use of the words "go open the door so our esteemed ancestors may bring the precious gift of their stories" (p. 43) reminds us of the goal of ethnoautobiography: "Indigenous conversations. Recovering Indigenous conversations. Remembering stories. Putting them back together. Cherishing the fragments we find. Exchanging stories" (Kremer, 1998, p. 2).

The word "spirit" means different things to different people. Ethnoautobiographical inquirers are encouraged

gation using the forms of knowing identified by Heron (1996): practical, propositional, presentational, and experiential. Different ethnoautobiographical endeavors may emphasize these aspects to varying degrees, yet their integration is always relevant. Rothberg has stated that spiritual inquiry suggests "the possibility of an integrative vision of the different modes of inquiry" (1991, p. 133).

Ethnoautobiography seeks to contribute new knowledge as to how Eurocentered selves might narrate themselves in ways that address deficiencies or pathologies of modern assumptions. This is groundbreaking research that explores and documents the boundary of who we are as individuals, researchers, or students. Within ethnoautobiographical inquiry individual new knowledge and insight always arises in dialogue in a community; it can thus be properly questioned and validated. Ethnoautobiography encourages **hybrid** stories, and **borderland** identities in relationship with all things.

Within Indigenous worlds, generally speaking, everything has spirit – whether mountain, computer, deer, ancestor, place, tree, story, song, or car. A general statement as a beginning point for inquiry might be:

Remember what you see at times out of the corner of your eye, the images and darting presences that are ever so ephemeral, yet real. Remember the times when a trap door seemed to open under you, when an accident, illness, mountain high brought you into presence. And then there are the metaphors in poetry and other writing, crafty words that trick the mind into presence, into dream and vision.

Any understanding of this kind is counter to an individualistic understanding and engagement with an objective reality. However, it is not counter to critical reflection or the realities of psychological and neurological processes. This is the healing offered by ethnoautobiography.

There are many aspects to the process of ethnoautobiography. One might find a writing (or speaking) voice that creates presence (to ancestors, to history, to community, to place) and includes them. Importantly, ethnoautobiographical writing is creative writing; it aspires to literature, so to speak. It uses conventions of poetry and prose that we commonly do not find in academic writing.

As we inquire we create. Our creations can be imagined in such a way that they evoke a related **presence** in the reader. In some important sense the truth or authenticity of voice inevitably approaches beauty and healing. Masterful writers like Leslie Marmon Silko or Toni Morrison do this. The work of crafting self – narratives that are imaginative, poetic, and evocative is a way of creating presence. Rather than stopping with a mere self – report of an experience or memory, ethnoautobiographical writing calls for a quality of storytelling precision that connects author and reader amidst imaginal realms opening toward new moral and politico – historical inquiries.

Finding the courage to narrate in and for freedom leads us back to one of the themes woven in response to the question: *Why not simply 'autobiography'?* As mentioned above in Chapter 3, Gerald Vizenor has suggested **sovereignty** disobey notions of inheritance and tenure of territory. His discussions of sovereignty appear as **transmotion**, as vision moving in imagination, as the substantive right of motion. Ethnoautobiography is an imaginative and decolonizing form of inquiry dedicated to the remembrance of sovereignty as motion and trans-motion among people of Eurocentered mind, whatever their ethnic roots. It hails the end of Whiteness.

Narrating ourselves freely

By narrating ourselves freely we may overcome destructive identity politics that limit who we are as inquirers and storytellers. This is inevitably an imaginative and creative act, yet it needs to find grounding in various tests and trials. Shamanic skills need to find their affirmation in the results – did healing occur? The **imaginal** realm needs to find anchors in archaeological, ecological, histori-cal, and other forms of knowledge as well as critical reflection, ethical and political considerations. Integrative states of consciousness are required to find their affirmations in the various domains of ecology, history, myth, gender, and more – domains which consciously remake individuals who work to see themselves as more than the masterful, bounded self of moder-nity. This is the imaginal space where Indigenous people may meet inquiring White minds to liberate and renew stories. Renewing our stories encour-ages the vulnerability to break hearts in order to heal them (Behar, 1996).

In the novel, *The Heirs of Columbus*, Gerald Vizenor writes that his main character Stone Columbus "would accept anyone who wanted to be tribal, 'no blood attached or scratched,' ... His point is to make the world tribal, a universal identity, and return to other values as measures of human worth, such as the dedication to heal rather than steal tribal cultures" (1991, p. 162). It is only in the context of such healing, a tall order to be sure, that ethnoautobiographical inquiries by non-natives may make a contribu-tion to decolonization and end the stealing and superficial imitation of tribal cultures.

Now Whiteness and Eurocentrism can, conceivably, encounter the post-modern condition that "oral cultures have never been without"—the "trickster signatures and discourse on narrative chance" of native **presence** (Vizenor, 1989, p. x)—and thus liberate an eman-cipatory and restorative imagination that facilitates egalitarian conversations and knowledge exchange. It would generate a socially engaged practice that is spiritual, and that arises from halting colonial actions on anything **transpersonal** or **immanent**. What is commonly called transpersonal—spir-itual tradition, psychology, ecology, altered states of consciousness, and so on—would thus be severed from their colonial habits of appropriation and surrender to the presence of the **imaginal**, and the fleeting movements of spirit(s).

Such ethnoautobiographical stories require decolonization and creativity, while offering the right to remember. "Decolonization, for the 'colonizing populace' as well as for the 'colonized,' must begin with *remembering* themselves, for they, too, have been colonized — *dismembered* from their own Indigenous cultures" (Gabbard, 2006, pp. 228 – 229).

Nobel Laureate Nelly Sachs — German, Jewish, Swedish and more — investigates her right to *Heimat* as one of her *Glowing Enigmas*, the collection from which this poem is taken:

> *Ich bin meinem Heimatrecht auf der Spur*
> *dieser Geographie nächtlicher Länder*
> *wo die zur Liebe geöffneten Arme*
> *gekreuzigt an den Breitengraden hängen*
> *bodenlos in Erwartung —*

> I am on the tracks of my rights of domicile
> this geography of nocturnal countries
> where the arms opened for love
> hang crucified on the degrees of latitude
> groundless in expectation —
> (Sachs 1970, p. 395; transl. Michael Hamburger)

Ethnoautobiography delights in the compassionate telling of our larger trans–personal, **imaginal** stories in the fissures and cracks of our hybrid origins, identities and **presences**, a storytelling that humbly and ferociously resists the totalizing desires of grander dominant schemes. It is from these stories that peace can be created as different and contradictory memories arise amidst the spirits of place and ancestors beckoning, a play of caring imagination making ancient presence new, each story a world renewal in its own way. Participatory visions of the trans–personal are ancient. Envisioning them for today makes for an interdisciplinary endeavor. All together another story emerges that deconstructs Whiteness and Eurocentrism, and is dedicated to the emancipatory and egalitarian restoration and the balancing play of visionary **sovereignty** of diverse human presence.

Activity

Council of all Ancestors

This activity can be done alone or in a group or class. As with other activities in this book, if you are completing this individually, and do not have an organized group to participate with (such as in a classroom, community organization and so on), it is encouraged that you share the experience with a friend, family member or spouse. Additionally, these instructions are written for an individual to complete and can be adapted to a group setting with a person providing the instructions and guiding participants through the process.

Tools: Comfortable space; paper (diary) and pencil; cut flower; access to a body of water.

- Find a comfortable space to be (sit comfortably in a chair or on the floor in a private space, in front of your altar, at a tree, etc.). If you are in a group, wherever you are gathered, sit in a circle.
- Allow your self to relax and develop an internal focus. If you are in nature, allow the nature sounds to relax you. If you are inside, pay attention to your breath coming and going as you allow yourself to relax. Or, use any relaxation or meditative practice you are familiar with to enter a relaxed state in order to pay attention to your inner world.
- Once you feel sufficiently relaxed, call upon your personal ancestors. You may be able to visualize some specifically, because either you have known them or have seen them in photographs. Others may come to you as a presence or a felt sense. However they might be present, develop a sense of an ancestor being by you.
- Ask your ancestor(s): "What would you like to tell me that is important about this work of ethnoautobiography? What message or advice do you have about the state of affairs in the world?"
- Allow answers or messages to bubble up inside of you. Don't judge what comes to you, just notice. Give yourself several moments to close with your ancestor(s). You may feel like thanking your ancestor(s).
- As you begin to feel ready to close this encounter with your ancestor(s), gently and slowly prepare your return, opening your eyes gradually.

Upon your return from your internal focus, use a piece of paper or journal to jot down what came to you. Your sentences may be translations of vague impressions or they may be very specific. You may also choose to sketch images.

If you are doing this activity individually, take your cut flower, hold it in front of you, read your statements, describe any images or feelings that came to you out loud, bring the flower to a body of water (ocean, river, pond, creek, etc.) and give it to the water while holding the thoughts that came to you during your meditation.

If you are doing this in a group setting, each person speaks out loud and offers the flower to the center of the circle. Two people then may tie the flowers together and after closing the meditation offer them to a body of water with good thoughts for the group and the messages that were spoken.

Chapter Summary

In this final chapter, ethnoautobiography is connected to **spiritual inquiry** and creative expression, to interrupt Whiteness and heal the **White mind**, as well as relationships with others. By doing so, the choice for people of a Eurocentered mind becomes one of imagination, recollection, critique, and **decolonization**. Such ethnoautobiographical stories become compassionate and emancipatory deconstructions told — both humbly and ferociously — in the cracks of our **hybrid** identities. Ethnoautobiography hails the end of **Whiteness**.

Concept Check

What courageous choice can members of dominant societies make?

Ethnoautobiographical writing is what type of writing?

As an imaginative and decolonizing type of inquiry, what is ethnoautobiography dedicated to?

What does ethnoautobiography hail?

NOTES

Chapter 17
Continuing the Conversation

Riff

Bardic Resolutions

with the intention of somehow
concluding
or at least closing
this document and
this part of my story
I am also required
to acknowledge the story itself
and the storyteller, too

that has been the struggle all along
having the skills and heart
to share the narrative
though I have doubts about
how to do it

I know that parts and places
and even the stories themselves
are unfinished

colonization and
my own acts of settlement
have caused forgetting
created witchery

I suppose that is some of the
responsibility I feel
even though
I cannot know how it will end
even though I don't know
all the parts that are present
I still must begin
with what I have

it's hard to tell a story
when there is so much
riding on it

wanting to do my ancestors proud
crediting their lives and efforts
making this moment possible

and also being taught
to honor this land
and the Original Peoples
acknowledging all they gave up
by force
to make my life possible

and that is a fitting place
to return to why the
narrative itself is crucial

a complex story
requires a masterful telling
necessitates skill with words
and obligations
to do justice to the weave
between all the worlds traveled

so it is that I ask for help
even while already doing the telling
akin to being a settler
while honoring the Original Peoples

like knowing that I was
born in Philadelphia
carried across the seas
by ancestral journeys
and also at the same time
inhabiting Coaquannok
the Lenape's 'place of the long trees'

recognizing the strength and courage
shown by Quanah Parker
to fight for his people
with all the tools available
both lance and word
carrying multiple worlds
in his veins

honoring his mother
Naudah
Cynthia Ann Parker
two names
two worlds
living with violence and transformation
fear and healing

reminds me of Oisin
bound to the world
of magic and certainty
tragedy and hope
telling a story
unfinished
but told
RJP

Raven: Wow! A great deal has been covered since we opened this many pages ago. It's a wonder how much effort goes into this work of unlearning and reclaiming, as they call it.

Salmon: You make a good point, Raven. But as you know for yourself, there are parts of our lives that require great sacrifice and hard work to bring forth the future.

Jürgen: Does that mean you like it?

Raven: (cawing) What's not to like? You have assembled yourselves, and laid out many practices to bring full presence back into the world. That is a glorious thing.

R: I like that phrase assembling ourselves, because I feel that is what we are attempting in this work, to assemble or re–assemble self and community. There is hope in these practices, and we have envisioned numerous small ways to re–assemble ourselves. It is many small things, rather than a few big ones, that offer deep transformation. Thank you for your kind words of support.

Raven: It's what Salmon was saying in Chapter 0: our lives are all intertwined, now more than ever, so we must support each other in reestablishing relationships.

Jürgen: Yes, and as we reestablish those relationships we come into greater integrity and creativity. That's why we've included creative projects in order to go deeper than a family tree, as well as, pointing out that our urgent crises demand critical responses, and offer much possibility for the future.

Salmon: And the journey you detail here is so rich and vibrant, really honoring the complexity that is involved in returning all people back from the brink of forgetting, as you say. What you all do so well in showing that complexity is also admitting that there are as many questions as there are answers.

Jürgen: On the one wing, as you said, we acknowledge that such decolonization work can be very overwhelming. There are so many details, with so much hard personal and cultural work. And, on the other wing, rather than get stuck and trapped in answering questions, we encourage an openness to further inquiry.

R: That is why we have included many riffs in the document, to give the quality of conversations that might grow between family and friends, rather than cold, hard questions to answer. We also do so to honor the diverse storytelling traditions that we are inspired by.

Raven: Yes, I was struck by how you are really attempting to honor those traditions of Indigenous presence, as you say, while balancing your own heritage in academic, and critical academic, critical understanding. It is very rich indeed. It is a beautiful and powerful blend of ceremonial practice and decolonization work that is ever changing and growing.

Salmon: As we both said in Chapter 0, this open–endedness is profoundly important. It is the both/and that is able to be aware of multiple stories, places, and experiences. This work is about both the journey and the destination. Like my journey upstream to the place of my birth is about the destination, but getting there is equally significant. They both matter.

Raven: And the same is true for the way in which you take personal stories, or people's family history, and connect that with the stories they tell about where we all live and what happened there. It is a magnificent remembering of the stories that people tell.

R: We really are attempting in this work to open ways to connect academic work with personal and cultural transformation. Much of this decolonization work is about learning how to change the world, and about changing how we learn about our selves and the world.

Jürgen: Ultimately, we hope to have conveyed the connections between various aspects of who we are, supporting a more integrated approach to personal identity, and the societies we are a part. In doing this work we also emphasize the sacred obligations that exist as we find our selves and our world. We are ever mindful of the land we live on, and the spirits of where we live. We also are grateful for all of the teachings about how to live in a good way, and with a good mind.

Salmon and Raven (in unison): So be it!

NOTES

Appendix
Ethnoautobiography
as Research Methodology

Riff

Finding our way

The research speaks
Yes, the research itself
Some might call it organic, or mindful
Still others critical, Indigenous
Certainly it is ceremonial
Creating and re–creating
Fixing and healing ourselves
And our relationships in the world

Ethnoautobiography
Is both/and inquiry
Acknowledging its recent either/or methodological ancestors
Even including them
Whilst returning to more ancient ways
Of being and knowing

No surprise then
That EA includes recommendations
Yet is not prescriptive
Such inquiry is both
Critical and humble
Focused and open
Socially engaged and deeply personal

It is in this manner, then
That there are some
Important elements
Though ultimately the path is
Constructed by what is present
And the path
To come to presence
Is different for every single person

RJP

***

An Ethnoautobiographical Conversation Among Co–research Participants

Story: Perhaps we can begin by each saying briefly what matters to us the most regarding ethnoautobiography. This can be a question, a concern, or a statement of what is vital to you. I'll begin by invoking the words with which we tell our stories. As we've read, there is a way to tell and construct our stories that is fluid, changing, and ultimately healing for our selves and the world we inhabit. Let that be something to guide this.

Susan: I am sometimes kinda conflicted about ethnoautobiography. So I'd say that I love the potential it offers for creating powerful, healing stories, but I worry that people will not buy into all the intentions that are necessary for a decolonizing effect, because then it would just simply become privileged navel–gazing.

Chris: I'll bring in the concept of studio time as it pertains to inquiry. The studio is a metaphysical "space" or "place" that exists between two or more individuals as they engage in an open, unfiltered, uncensored exchange of theories, ideas, dreams, stories, insights, experiences and other fragments subconsciously or consciously shared in this "sacred space." That's what ethnoautobiography is for me.

Raven: One thing that I love about ethnoautobiography is that we can even be allowed, no encouraged, to have this conversation in a description about how to do research. How mischievous, playful and fantastic! There's lots of hard critical thinking, blah, blah, blah and lots of play, fantastical exchanges and creative flourishes. Now you're talking!

Ellen: What moves me about EA is how it brings forth so much possibility for healing what gets stuck in our selves, our families, and in our very bodies. It is embodied inquiry. That is such a profound path to be on as we attempt to learn about the world.

History: I feel so validated by ethnoautobiography, because so often people's descriptions of history are superficial and cheap retellings, at best. EA becomes a roomy, spacious, history–filled extravaganza complete with many stories, often unknown to each other, and in the end making a rich, vibrant narrative that I am proud to have called history.

N: I struggle with ethnoautobiography because I am drawn to its openness and possibility. Yet, I especially question my connection to community. I wonder about how my ethnoautobiography can come about if I have to somehow explicitly acknowledge community, when it's my community that has fostered so much confusion and discord in my life.

Hummingbird: I am amazed and grateful for EA because it makes all of our presences in a circle matter. There are so many little things that make our lives possible. I feel that EA honors and brings them in. Like my efforts to pollinate a single flower requires so many flaps of my wings. That's EA.

R: EA for me is about doing healing work in the world and in our selves simultaneously. It's about connection, relationship. Between people, spirit, the places we live, even in our families. It is simple yet profound work.

Jen: It is also so overwhelming. I can see the potential, the destination, if you will. But the process becomes too much sometimes. And that's the irony, isn't it, because it seems to me that EA is so much about the process, and then I just get bogged down in it, if I don't see some type of map.

Snow leopard: For me ethnoautobiography is elegant and subtle. There is so much to do in the world just to survive and ethnoautobiography offers so many ways to help that along. I don't see so much emphasis on requirement and expectation, rather on honesty and obligation. It provides a way for beings to feel connected and obligated to one other.

Place: So my feeling is that ethnoautobiography might be something of a map that a group of various beings, including humans, make of their interactions. One layer woven into another: the clouds offer one perspective; the rivers another; this human family knows this way particularly well; these foxes go this way and that a lot; these dreams appear frequently to this little girl; and on and on.

Smiley, the dog: I am so happy to be here. That is what EA is for me. It is a chance to be welcomed. EA is about belonging, and that is so important to me.

Jürgen: Ethnoautobiography has taken many paths along the way; indeed it attempts to bring so many of them together. Amazingly, all of the elements, ingredients, people, visions, creatures, and spirits that are a part of it have been so patient, and in that patience there is so much possibility. What I find most astonishing and impressive is that we each have our own individual entry to begin the process and that each entry — from a piece of pottery or family photo to a pet or dream — leads us into the depths of healing.

Ancestry: Ethnoautobiography offers so much hope. Yes, radical hope. For many generations I feared that the awareness of my presence was fading from this world, and that while I was never gone, fewer and fewer even saw me. But this work turns that around, I feel welcomed and honored and humbled.

Body: And I feel whole. And that's saying a lot.

Salmon: Thanks for all of your contributions, because when we put these all together we get ethnoautobiography. There is no one way to do EA. And while I must always return to the place of my emergence, there are many streams and rivers to and fro. Thus, it is with EA.

Story: Thanks to all of you for sharing your perspectives. I am struck by the power and poetry that we are already creating. Ethnoautobiography makes it very tempting, especially for me, to weave our strands into a single narrative. But I will resist that impulse now, and rather see if we might tell some more together. Anyone want to continue?

Jen: Well, it's funny because in some ways what you say about telling our story together is elegant, and yet that still doesn't reduce my anxiety. I know that there are many elements that make me who I am, and contribute to my ethnoautobiography. So, I need to allow them to emerge, or get out of the way. And at the same time, not only does that not always make sense to me, but I also have to wonder about the manner in which the stories emerge, and how they are even researched.

Raven: Maybe that's the both/and that keeps getting mentioned. The beauty rests in this very conversation, or in the fluidity and possibility that keeps being offered. While also being conscious or aware that it is fleeting, incomplete and perhaps all some trick.

Susan: Like earlier, Raven, when you referred to critical thinking as blah, blah, blah. Sometimes in these conversations, and in this work, I am tempted to say as my teenage daughter would: "Whatever!"

History: Yes, but therein lies some of the beauty or elegance in ethnoautobiography. What I have experienced, especially in postmodernity, is that all the narratives become fractured and fragmented, as if everyone is saying, feeling, acting like "whatever!" Ethnoautobiography, however, welcomes the "whatever", the fracture, acknowledges that experience, and places it at the table, or in the textbook, and uses it as a starting point. Ethnoautobiography is not anything goes; rather, it is about connection and relationship. Going into "whatever" fractures opens up the possibility to develop connections.

R: Perhaps an important part of this conversation is asking what the intentions are in the "whatever". If the intention is to acknowledge feelings of overwhelm in the face of grief, colonization, experiences of dislocation, as well as more mundane things, like crafting an ethnoautobiographical research question, then EA offers room at the table. But if the intention is to disconnect, disenchant, or denigrate a part of the story, then EA might not work at that moment and we will walk away for some critically humble reflection.

Body: Sure. But no matter where you turn, we have so much work to do. Even all of us coming together have taken so much intention, attention and action. There is so much. And perhaps it is healing to be able to say, "Hold on, I'm very tired," because this work is exhausting. There have to be places, animals, times, events, people, communities that offer quiet time.

Ellen: Which brings me back to my comment about embodied inquiry. There really are many paths within qualitative inquiry that welcome alternative narratives, that are building connection rather than furthering disorder. What distinguishes EA from these is that everyone is encouraged to come to the table. That's not to say that there won't be challenging topics once we show up there. It's the quintessential family gathering.

Ancestry: For me it's akin to what Stanley Krippner said in his foreword: that people cannot renounce their heritage without losing parts of themselves. In any given family, there are a countless number of people and events that are all connected, whether they are seen and acknowledged or not.

Hummingbird: I'm so glad you refer back to the start, ancestry, because I too want to go back to what Apela Colorado said about EA being a ceremony. First, there are all kinds of ceremonies, and second, sometimes ceremonies have to change to adapt to various times. I feel EA can provide this.

Raven: Yes, as my winged relative here notes, on the one wing, there is a need for a container, or ceremony, or map of some kind, even though I do chuckle when people might get lost for a while. And on the other wing, like getting lost, there is a need to be open, challenged, even scared from time to time. That's one of my hopes in EA: that people might wake up from the stupor we find ourselves living in.

Chris: And yet, that waking up does not imply that dreams aren't some of what ethnoautobiography is pointing us to. Rather, it's that inquiry, research, whatever it is called, seems to get fragmented and disjointed, as if it can really take place in some kind of vacuum.

Smiley, the dog: And I don't like vacuums. Oh, right, that's a different kind. But I don't like being cut off from anything, sealed away. It's as if there's some false sense of separation that humans are trying to force us all into.

Salmon: Yes, Smiley, it does really feel that we are, all of us, being forced into some box. And no one likes or deserves that. Hopefully, ethnoautobiography might break down a few walls, make boundaries more permeable, expand a few circles, and weave more strands together. And perhaps that can be our place to pause, to pass this conversation on to the readers, dreams, storytellers, inquirers and places yet to come, as we have had our say for now. Hopefully, however, we might pop in on folks from time to time, offering support, tricks, direction, but most of all radical hope.

***

Approaching Ethnoautobiographical Research

> To tell our story in the proper way means imagining ourselves with something resembling an Indigenous process of awareness – the freedom to be an artist aware of Indigenous roots. … It means decolonization as much as self–actualization. (Kremer, 2003b, p. 13)

Ethnoautobiography is a borderland—or transitional—methodology. It honors its grounding in the heritage of human science, critical theory and qualitative methods. It advocates decolonizing research, interrupts settler colonial worldviews, and finds kindred spirits among critical, Indigenous methodologies. Fundamentally directed toward decolonization, ethnoautobiography intentionally and explicitly foregrounds identity.

Decolonization encourages recovery of Indigenous mind for amer–europeans: the potential for imaginative and spiritual initiations into hybrid, borderland and multicultural identities. This is a process by which Eurocentered people acknowledge that they reside in more complex narratives of place, that they participate with all manner of people, beings, histories, and that an ancestral process has unfolded to bring them where they are. Recovery of Indigenous mind means be(com)ing at home in place, and in personality.

Ethnoautobiography is critical to the recovery of participation, the decolonization of inquirer (and inquiry), and the transformation of relationships with place and identity.

In the spirit of *criar y dejarse criar* or beingknowing the intention is to gain meaningful understanding and knowledge as transformation is facilitated in the researchers at the very same time. Inquiry, ritual, storytelling, knowledge, truth, and transformation are woven into a singular intricate process.

These broad parameters establish the epistemological and methodological context for research implementations, i.e., beyond personal quest and ritual. Ethnoautobiography is not a specifically defined method, it is an umbrella methodology for a host of methods that can help to achieve the intentions just described for the purposes of a research study, whether thesis, dissertation, or another type of project. In each case researchers need to define the details of the research protocol themselves.

Ethnoautobiography finds its closest kinship with autoethnography and can be seen as a specific form in which certain parameters for self–reflection are given as necessary ingredients (i.e., its decolonizing dimensions). As individual inquiry it sees writing as central to its method and relies on a process of (self)discovery that does not separate personal reflection and scholarly inquiry.

Ethnoautobiography can also be implemented in dyadic work, as cooperative inquiry (Heron, 1996), and in other ways. The support in a group of fellow inquirers offers opportunities for support and insight.

It is beyond the scope of this brief appendix to discuss possible method translations in detail. *The Handbook of Qualitative Research* (published in various editions since 1993 by Denzin & Lincoln) as well as the *Handbook of Critical and Indigenous Methodologies* (Denzin, Lincoln & Smith, 2008) provide valuable information to get started.

Given the intentions of ethnoautobiography summarized above, research protocols, whether conducted individually or in a team, might include:

Initiation: Ethnoautobiographical inquiry is an entrance into transitional and decolonized places—inhabited by shadow, underworld, and unconscious identities—that encourage healing of personal and cultural disorders from Eurocentered consciousness toward recovered participation, transformative identities, and reconciliatory renewal;

Transformation: Ethnoautobiography as decolonizing methodology embraces embodied feelings—including vulnerability, and grief—associated with process–oriented transformation and the healing of gendered and racialized Eurocentered consciousness;

Storytelling: Narrating ethnoautobiographical inquiry includes the many voices and styles that reflect the diversity of human experience, including poetry, performance, and mythology which restor(y) the Eurocentered experience;

Genealogy: Ethnoautobiographical inquiry is grounded upon ancestral connections, human science and qualitative research legacies, as well as place, or relationship based, and Indigenous, consciousness;

Remembrance: Ethnoautobiography necessitates acts of self–remembrance (such as underworld material of conquest and migration), remembrance of the other (including acceptance of narratives of survivance), and remembering self–with–other (offering new relationships with people and places);

(Re)placing: Ethnoautobiography emphasizes being put back into place, fostering a more fully embodied, and relational consciousness, so that inquiry includes the varied narratives, beings, and peoples of particular places; and, finally,

Renewal: Taken together, these protocols culminate in renewal. This research is about "fixing methodologies" (Christian, 1993), working toward healing in the world, between peoples, the land, but also in the way that inquiry in conducted in the first place.

Useful resources:

Bentz, V. M., & Shapiro, J. J. (1998). *Mindful inquiry in social research*. Thousand Oaks, CA: Sage.

Brown, L. A., & Strega, S. (2005). *Research as resistance: Critical, Indigenous and antioppressive approaches*. Toronto: Canadian Scholars' Press.

Denzin, N. K., Lincoln, Y. S., (Eds.). (2013). *The landscape of qualitative research* (4th ed.). Thousand Oaks, CA: Sage.

Denzin, N. K., Lincoln, Y. S., & Smith, L. T., (Eds.). (2008). *Handbook of critical and Indigenous methodologies*. Thousand Oaks, CA: Sage.

Four Arrows (Jacobs, D. T.). (2008). *The authentic dissertation: Alternative ways of knowing, research, and representation*. New York, NY: Routledge.

Hibbard, P. N. (2001). *Remembering our ancestors: Recovery of Indigenous mind as a healing process for the decolonization of Western mind* (Doctoral dissertation). Retrieved from ProQuest Dissertations and Theses database. (AAT 3004469)

International Congress of Qualitative Inquiry (ICQI). (n.d.). Retrieved from http://www.icqi.org/

Jackson–Paton, R. (2008). Rituals of inquiry; or, Looking for "culture and truth." *ReVision*, 30(1 & 2), 11–15. doi: 10.4298/REVN.30.1/2.13–17

Jackson–Paton, R. (2012). *Restor(y)ing environmentalism: Decolonizing White settlers in the United States: (Re)placing posttraumatic settler disorder*. (Ph.D. Dissertation). San Francisco, CA: Saybrook University.

Johnson, K. K. (2002). *On the path of the ancestors: Kinship with place as a path of recovery* (Doctoral dissertation). Retrieved from ProQuest Dissertations and Theses database. (AAT 3034814)

Kelly, K. (2008). *Rekindling Indigenous mind: An ethnoautobiographical inquiry of transformation* (Doctoral dissertation). Retrieved from ProQuest Dissertations and Theses database. (AAT 3305709)

Kovach, M. (2009). *Indigenous methodologies: Characteristics, conversations, and contexts*. Toronto, Canada: University of Toronto Press.

Romanyshyn, R. D. (2007). *The wounded researcher: Research with soul in mind*. New Orleans, LA: Spring Journal Books.

Sheias, H. E. (2006). *Marginality and the spurious: Emergent acculturation processes of Oleem Hadasheem (new immigrants) within dominant Sabra (native Israeli) discourse* (Doctoral dissertation). Retrieved from ProQuest Dissertations and Theses database. (AAT 3212934)

Smith, L. T. (2012). *Decolonizing methodologies: Research and Indigenous peoples* (2nd ed.). New York, NY: Zed Books.

Stonebanks, C. D., & Wootton, K. (2008). Revisiting Mianscum's "telling what you know" in Indigenous qualitative research. *International Review of Qualitative Research*, 1(1), 33–53.

Wilson, S. (2008). *Research is ceremony: Indigenous research methods*. Black Point, Canada: Fernwood.

Glossary

Accounting: W. Jackson's (1994) description of places that, according to his assessment, might have more ecological depth, history, and detail. While a step in the right direction, these still retain racial and settlement privilege. Consequently, we attach "ethno" to encourage decolonized accountings. Further, since we emphasize narrative and storytelling as a means, and end, to re-inhabit places, it is worth noting that account is a synonym for story. This aspect of the term is emphasized instead of the meanings associated with the balance sheet.

Active hope: According to Macy & Johnstone (2012, p. 3),

> Active Hope is a practice. Like tai chi or gardening, it is something we do rather than have. It is a process we can apply to any situation, and it involves three key steps. First, we take a clear view of reality; second, we identify what we hope for in terms of the direction we'd like things to move in or the values we'd like to see expressed; and third, we take steps to move ourselves or our situation in that direction.

Adaptive challenge: Challenges posed by "long-standing threats and opportunities in social life." Adaptations to these challenges would "draw people's attention to certain kinds of events (such as cruelty or disrespect), and trigger instant intuitive reactions, perhaps even specific emotions (such as sympathy or anger)" (Haidt, 2012, p. 123).

amer-european: From Tinker (2008) — who intentionally leaves these adjectives in lower case form — suggesting that Whites are slightly Americanized Europeans, rather than slightly European Americans, as Euro-American might imply. Amer-european and White are used interchangeably in this book, reflecting both lingering (if ignored) ancestral connections to places in Europe, as well as, most importantly, Eurocentered consciousness (see Ani, 1994; Kremer, 1996).

Androcracy, androcentric: Masculine rule in governmental structures, from Greek andros for 'man'; interests or points of view reflecting a male gender bias. See **patriarchy**.

Androgynous, androgyny: Hybrid of stereotypical masculine and feminine characteristics in fashion, gender style, sexuality, etc.; at times used as synonym for **intersex**, hermaphrodite, etc. See **holosexuality**.

Animism: Worldviews in which all beings, including animals and plants, are ensouled or inspirited. This may include things usually considered inanimate in Eurocentered worldviews, such as rocks or rivers and other features of the landscape. Often used by outsiders and colonizers to describe Indigenous spiritual practices, while Indigenous peoples commonly do not use this term to describe themselves.

Apartheid: A system of legislated institutional racial and ethnic inequality in South Africa officially dismantled in 1994. While the term is specific to South Africa — apartheid is Afrikaans for "living apart" — it is often used in other settings to note institutionalized discrimination, most especially in the United States and Israel/ Palestine (see Tutu, 1999).

Atheism: Not accepting the reality of anything spiritual, religious, or transcendent in any form. Rather, atheism accepts the knowledge generated by scientific approaches as defined in Eurocentered traditions. Gods and spirits are not considered real and science is considered the foundation of what is reality. Atheism largely developed out of disenchantment with the Christian traditions in particular, beginning with the Enlightenment Period during which the emergent scientific approaches led to profound questioning of church dogmas, with Galileo's case probably being the most famous example.

Auschwitz, Auschwitz-Birkenau, Oświęcim (Polish), or **Oshpitsin** (Yiddish): The most infamous Nazi death, or concentration, camp located in southwestern Poland. From its opening in 1940 until its liberation by Soviet troops in 1945, at least 1.1 million people were murdered, approximately 90% of whom were Jewish. Auschwitz was liberated on January 27, 1945, a day now commemorated as International Holocaust Remembrance Day.

Autoethnography: Qualitative research methods that "combines cultural analysis and interpretation with narrative details" (Chang, 2008, p. 46). Autoethnography

> hinges on the push and pull between and among analysis and evocation, personal experience and larger social, cultural, political concerns. Our attempts to locate, to tie up, to define autoethnography are as diverse as our perspectives on what autoethnography is and what we want it to do. (Adams & Jones, 2008, p. 374)

The subjectivity of author or researcher makes it allied with ethnoautobiography, in fact, it can be seen as autoethnography with specific parameters (the dimensions of ancestry, place, etc.). Like ethnoautobiography, autoethnography also pushes the boundaries of representation and expression. Bochner and Ellis (2002) state "It is high time to challenge the prevailing logocentrism of [a rationally-based] tradition, not only with visual media but also with the entire range of communicative expressions at our disposal" (p. 18). See Appendix: Ethnoautobiography as research methodology.

Bechdel test: Feminist evaluation of whether literature and film is supportive of women's voices and lives. It includes three tests:

> a) that the narrative includes at least two women;

> b) that they have in-depth conversations; and,

> c) that they talk about something besides men.

Be(com)ing: The both/and nature of this term offered by Bigwood (1993) embodies what we convey with ethnoautobiography: being simultaneously enfolded into a state of transformation, or *becoming*.

Be(com)ing animal: We respectfully combine Bigwood's (1993) process-oriented notion of be(com)ing with Abram's (2010) ecological encouragement of be(com)ing animal. Since ethnoautobiography is an ongoing deconstruction of Eurocentered identities, especially involving relationships with the natural world, we emphasize a process of be(com)ing, in this case acknowledging humans as animals among animals.

Beingknowing: An integrated approach to knowledge that considers the process of being and knowing as unfolding in an intricate and integrated process that cannot be split without either distorting knowing or being. Beingknowing is a central part of a person's or society's self-reflexive identity in an ethnoautobiographical sense. Unlike Eurocentered, Enlightenment science which views knowledge as separate and an end unto itself, Indigenous and ethnoautobiographical knowing is rooted and connected to the unfolding of being with people, nature, dreams, and so on. (See Kremer, 2002). See *criar y dejarse criar*.

Biophilia: E.O. Wilson's (1984) term describing "the innate tendency to focus on life and lifelike processes...to the degree that we come to understand other organisms, we will place greater value on them, and on ourselves" (quoted in Kellert & Wilson, 1993, pp. 4-5).

Bisexuality: Conceptualization of sexuality on a continuum ranging fluidly from hetero- to homosexuality, with bisexuality as the natural center. Rather than an either/or polarity of hetero- or homo-sexuality, bisexuality combines the two into a fluid sexuality. Research supports such a spectrum understanding of sexuality. See **holosexuality**, **homosexuality**.

Borderlands: Coined by Anzaldua (1987) in *Borderlands/La frontera* to describe the Chicana experience in the southwestern United States, this term describes places, identities, individuals, communities, and entire nations of people who are defined by boundaries and borders — and importantly crossing or transgressing them. Anzaldúa (1987, p. 3) articulates the violence caused by the grating of these worlds:

> The U.S.-Mexican border *es una herida abierta* [an open wound] where the Third World grates against the first and bleeds. And before a scab forms it hemorrhages again, the lifeblood of two worlds merging to form a third country—a border culture. Borders are set up to define the places that are safe and unsafe, to distinguish us from them. A border is a dividing line, a narrow strip along a steep edge. A borderland is a vague and undetermined place created by the emotional residue of an unnatural boundary. It is in a constant state of transition. The prohibited and forbidden are its inhabitants.

Brain: See **neo-mammalian brain**; **palaeo-mammalian brain**; **reptilian brain**; **right (brain) hemisphere**; **left (brain) hemisphere**.

Coaquannok: Coaquannok is a Lenni Lenape name for Philadelphia, "the place of the long trees", where R was born. Ethnoautobiographical inquiry encourages learning the multiple names and meanings of places often hidden or forgotten by settlement.

Collective shadow: See **shadow**.

Collectivism: Social organization that emphasizes the importance of the group (in contrast to emphasizing the importance of individuals) While Indigenous peoples are collectivist or communal in organization, they have an even broader sense of self which includes the natural world, spirits, and so on.

Colonial environmentalism, or **ecocolonialism:** Refers to the manner in which environmental theory and practice furthers the colonization of people and the land. The term has been used to describe colonial aspects of overseas environmental planning (Cox & Elmqvist, 1993; Dowie, 2009), as well as extending the critique of environmentalism in the United States beyond environmental racism (LaDuke, 1994).

Colonial thinking: A way of thinking about and behaving in the world that reflects a White, or Eurocentered mind. Examples include institutionalized racial supremacy, extensive natural resource use, individualism, lacking sense of place (ecological awareness), rigid gender identities, militarism, among other characteristics.

Coming-to-presence: See **presence**.

Communitas: Latin noun referring to the spirit of community that arises during festivals, spiritual celebrations, or even disasters. "There is a loss of ego. One's pride in oneself becomes irrelevant. In the group, all are in unity, seamless unity, ... The benefits of *communitas* are quick understanding, easy mutual help, and long-term ties with others" (E. Turner, 2012, p. 3). Communitas is the experience of an intense community spirit that often can be described as the feeling of great social equality, solidarity, and togetherness.

Consciousness: See **Indigenous mind**, **paradigm**, **worldview**.

Cosmopolitan, or **cosmopolitanism:** Literally meaning "of the cosmos". In its Eurocentered interpretation it refers to a worldview in which all people are equal and part of a single human family. Indigenous deconstructions highlight the implicit European values and assert alternate ways of constructing cosmopolitanism which are more appreciative and sensitive to cultural diversity. (Breckenridge et al., 2002). See **provincialism**.

Criar y dejarse criar: From PRATEC (Apffel-Marglin, 1994), the Spanish translation of Indigenous Andean phrases referring to mutuality and reciprocity in all relationships or a conversation among all beings in a local ecology. Roughly translated as "raising (that is, nurturing) and being raised (nurtured)". *Criar* refers to raising children, animals, plants, relationships, etc., though doing so is fundamentally a reciprocal activity. Thus, as someone nurtures, one is simultaneously nurtured. *Criar y dejarse criar* is an alternate phrase for **beingknowing**.

Critical humility: The European-American Collaborative Challenging Whiteness (ECCW, 2010) offers this distilled essence of what our work seeks in the world:

> Critical humility embodies a delicate and demanding balance of speaking out for social justice while at the same time remaining aware that our knowledge is partial and evolving. The two parts of this definition capture the paradox with which we struggle. (p. 147)

Critical, Indigenous inquiry: As suggested by Denzin, Lincoln, and Smith (2008), such inquiry encourages relationship building and decolonization. In other words, it is explicitly anti-colonial. Such inquiry combines critical theories and Indigenous critique, that is, "research by and for Indigenous peoples, using techniques and methods drawn from the traditions and knowledges of those peoples" (Evans et al. as cited in Denzin, Lincoln, & Smith, 2008, p. x).

Crossblood: Vizenor's use of the term refers to the hybrid experience of Native peoples who offer solutions to current crises of the dominant culture through borderland experiences — people defined by, and transgressing, boundaries — an increasingly frequent position that challenges and tricks common categorical assumptions in tribal traditions and elsewhere.

> Crossbloods hear the bears that roam in trickster stories, and the cranes that trim the seasons close to the ear. Crossbloods are a postmodern tribal bloodline, an encounter with racialism, colonial duplicities, sentimental monogenism, and generic cultures. ... Crossbloods are communal, and their stories are splendid considerations of survivance. (Vizenor, 1976, pp. vii-viii)

Cultural ecology: We suggest that all environmentalism or ecology is cultural, that is, it has cultural implications and ramifications. The inverse is true as well: all cultural work is ecological.

Cultural shadow: See **shadow**.

Cynthia Ann Parker (Naudah): See **Parker, Cynthia Ann**.

Decolonizing, or **decolonization:** Activities that confront, strip away or otherwise unlearn colonial practices. Most often used in the context of ending overseas colonialism, the term more recently describes Indigenous peoples challenging Eurocentered or White colonization within countries. Ethnoautobiography encourages decolonization for all people, including Whites and others embedded in Eurocentered mind (Tuck & Yang, 2012).

Deconstruct, or **deconstruction:** Part of post-modernism, deconstruction is the cultural, political and academic process by which dominant ideas, philosophies, etc. are challenged and critiqued rather than accepted as given. Deconstructive endeavors challenge scientism and other and various assumptions of modernity.

Dialectic process: In the formal dialectic process of argumentation, a thesis is countered with an anti-thesis, and this contradiction may then resolve into a synthesis. This synthesis, in turn, becomes a new thesis, potentially to be countered by an anti-thesis, and so on. This is a method of critical analysis and discourse that addresses real or apparent contradictions in the hopes of a synthesis.

Dimensions of morality: Haidt (2012) has developed research support for six dimensions or foundations of morality: Care/harm; fairness/cheating; loyalty/betrayal; authority/subversion; sanctity/degradation; liberty/oppression. The strength of his research evidence supersedes prior theories, such the developmental theory by Kohlberg (1981).

Dissociation: Refers to "reported experiences and observed behaviors that seem to exist apart from or appear to have been disconnected from the mainstream, or flow, of one's conscious awareness, behavioral repertoire, and/or self-identity" (Krippner, 1997, p. 8). Dissociation may be controlled or uncontrolled, it may be positive (potentiating) or negative (depotentiating), conscious or unconscious. See **normative dissociation**.

Dream: Remembered experiences of integrative states of consciousness that have occurred during sleep. Despite Freud's seminal *The Interpretation of Dreams* (originally published in 1900) Eurocentered cultures in general continue to see very limited value in dreams. However, they are an important element in ethnoautobiographical inquiries, as they are in Indigenous cultural practices.

Dreamtime: English word that attempts to translate and describe "Australian" Aboriginal words for the time period and experience of being connected to **mythic** time, ancestral paths, and **original instructions**.

Dreamwork: Used to describe the work of the psychological or spiritual interpretation of dreams, reflecting on their content, meaning and implications in the life of the dreamer.

Ecocolonialism: See **colonial environmentlism**.

Ecological Indian: Eurocentered criteria determining the level of environmental consciousness among Indigenous peoples. This stereotype follows noble savage cultural mythology to allege that Indigenous peoples have no inherent environmental awareness and are responsible for all manner of environmental misdeeds. Both a distraction and a set up, it was first suggested by Redford (1990), honed by Krech (1999), and roundly critiqued by Indigenous peoples (M. K. Nelson, 2006). Instead, we use the term econobility—separating it from Native peoples—because it is used by and for amer-europeans rather than the Indigenous peoples that inspired it (Nadasdy, 2005).

Econobility: Eurocentered measure of environmental consciousness, most often used against Indigenous peoples. While related to the stereotype of the ecologically noble savage, or "ecological Indian" (Krech, 1999), we support Buege's (1995), Waller's (1996) and Nadasdy's (2005) contention that the econoble savage has little to do with Indigenous peoples, but rather with Eurocentered cultural supremacy and ecocolonialism (M. K. Nelson, 2006). See **ecological Indian**, **noble savage**.

Embodied, or **embodiment:** Bonnie Bainbridge Cohen (2012, p. 157) describes it thus:

> The process of embodiment is a being process, not a doing process, not a thinking process. It is an awareness process in which the guide and witness dissolve into cellular consciousness. Visualization and somatization provide steps to full embodiment, helping us return to preconsciousness with a conscious mind. Embodiment is automatic presence, clarity, and knowing, without having to search for it or pay attention.

Enlightenment: Refers to the Age of Enlightenment, the intellectual movement of the 18th century that emphasized the use of reason and science (as opposed to the beliefs and dogmas held by the Christian churches). The German equivalent *Aufklärung* means "clearing up", meaning critically evaluating all claims made, whether by church, state, or anybody else.

Environmentalism: Aware that terms like environmentalism or ecology are a catch all, we acknowledge the diversity in tactic, organization, priority and so on. There is a difference between The Nature Conservancy and Sea Shepard Society. Similarly, conservation, preservation, or ecopsychology have different agendas and priorities. But the substance of this book suggests that there is a common cultural genealogy underlying these disparate groups and ideas: White settlement and privilege, among others. While radical ecology, represented by e.g., Earth First! has a sophisticated critique of mainstream environmentalism, they offer little regarding the cultural legacy they inherited from such groups. Furthermore, to dismiss this as anthropocentric shirks responsibility for how they came to be on this land to begin with. Thus, adjectives such as Eurocentered, White, and settler are used interchangeably to critique such environmentalism (Dowie, 2009; Merchant, 1992; Nadasdy, 2005).

Epistemology, or **epistemological:** The branch of philosophy that studies the nature of knowing or knowledge, its presuppositions and foundations, and its extent and validity. At times translated as "ways of knowing", epistemology describes and questions what knowledge is and how it can be or has been acquired.

Eros: From the Greek god of love, passion and attraction, this word has gained importance as people in well-boundaried,

masterful societies have begun to break down barriers around issues of nature, sexuality, artistic expression and so on. (See Griffin, 1995).

Essentialist, or **essentialism:** The idea that something has a fundamental essence, or nature. Essentialist notions of personal or cultural identity can be found in the common understanding of terms such as "American," "the German character," and so on. In cultural, historical, and political contexts, this is in contrast to hybridity, the mixed-blood, **crossblood**, and multiculturalism. In ethnoautobiography the fundamental assumption is that origins are always multiple and complex.

Ethno-: We reclaim this prefix that rightly defines "ethno" as describing an Indigenous — decolonized — presence (from the Greek word ethnos). In this sense, then, ethno– refers to the full context of a person including, but not limited to, genealogy, ancestry, history, place (ecology), seasons, dreams, spirits, and so on.

Ethno-accounting: Combining the prefix **ethno–** with W. Jackson's (1994) suggestion of more detailed "accounting" of the places we live.

Ethnoautobiographical riffs: Adding the prefix "ethno" to Frankenberg and Mani's (1996) "autobiographical riffs." While their concepts are consistent with ethnoautobiography, there is an important distinction: ethnoautobiographical riffs require a decolonizing approach. The term "riff" originates out of jazz traditions.

Ethnoautobiography: Oral and/or written descriptions of self with an Indigenous sense of "ethnic," including place, seasonal cycles (time), history, nature, gender, ancestry, spirit, community, and so on. Ethnoautobiography includes a variety of practices that encourage and support decolonization and the breaking down of the well-boundaried, masterful, individualistic, Eurocentered, modern, and WEIRD selves in (post)modern societies. See Appendix: Ethnoautobiography as Recovering Indigenous Inquiry.

Eurocentered, or **Eurocentric mind:** see **White mind**.

Evolutionary prejudice: Used by V. Deloria (1995, p. 61) to address Eurocentered science, and especially anthropological explanations about Indigenous peoples, including migration, language, origin, religion and so on. There is also a preponderance of troubling evolutionary themes (e.g., linear progress) within postmodern cultural critiques, environmentalism and New Age thinking. As Kremer (1998, p. 243) has stated: "At the root of my concerns is the question of cultural ownership of evolutionary thinking which I have raised… and the call for theorists of human evolution to reflect consciously and explicitly on the cultural biases inherent in their thinking."

Fairy tale: see **folk tale**.

Fear: An emotion essential for survival, however, disconnected from a specific object of fear (such as a tiger in front of a person), it quickly becomes enmeshed with imagination and can thus be manipulated. Mostly used in this book to refer to the social and political (ab)uses and manipulations of groups of people by invoking and maintaining cycles of ignorance about the unknown. While fear is, of course, a basic human response to such situations, this book seeks to highlight its use for the benefit of a small group of elite.

Finno-Ugric: The Finno-Ugric peoples are a presumed historic group of peoples who currently speak Finno-Ugric languages. Like the speakers of **Indo-European** languages, Finno-Ugric peoples include multiple ethnicities. The four largest ethnicities speaking Finno-Ugric languages are Hungarians (15 million), Finns (6–7 million), Estonians (1.1 million), and Mordvins (0.85 million). Three (Hungarians, Finns, and Estonians) inhabit independent nation-states, Hungary, Finland, and Estonia, while the Mordvins have an autonomous Mordovian Republic within Russia. The traditional area of the Indigenous Sami people is in Northern Fenno-Scandinavia and the Kola Peninsula in Northwest Russia and is known as Sápmi. Some other Finno-Ugric peoples have autonomous republics in Russia: Karelians (Republic of Karelia), Komi (Komi Republic), Udmurts (Udmurt Republic), Mari (Mari El Republic), and Mordvins (Moksha and Erzya; Republic of Mordovia). Khanty and Mansi peoples live in Khanty-Mansi Autonomous Okrug of Russia, while Komi-Permyaks live in Komi-Permyak Okrug, which formerly was an autonomous okrug of Russia, but today is a territory with special status within Perm Krai.

Folk tale: The terms folk tale, fairy tale, legend, and myth are often used interchangeably and specific definitions vary with authors. However, **legends** frequently are seen as historically grounded, while fairy tales and folk tales generally lack such historical grounding. The term **myth** generally refers to the oldest layer of stories in a culture, originally transmitted in oral traditions (but some myths can also be related to historical events, such as supernovas and volcanic eruptions). All these old forms of narratives are of importance in ethnoautobiographical inquiries, with creation myths holding a central place. The oral quality of these cultural narratives has been lost since they have been committed to writing, mostly in modern times. Ethnoautobiography works to restore oral storytelling capacities.

Forgetting, or **forgetfulness:** One of the most important aspects of **settler** identity, forgetting helps to balance the deep seated conflict between the shame of knowing something terrible has happened and the desire not to know: "Settler culture may be constructed on the basis of a necessary forgetfulness" (S. Turner, 1999, p. 37). Such forgetfulness is fundamental to settlement privilege whereby Whites simply pretend that we are not aware of the benefits inherited as a consequence of settlement. Just as White privilege creates a set of benefits that accrue to Whites simply because they are White, settlement privilege offers benefits to anyone who is a settler (Jackson-Paton, 2012; McIntosh, 1990; WPC, n.d.).

Gender polarity: In Eurocentered societies — not well known to students and innumerable others characterized by many sharp dichotomies of either/or — this describes the polar and oppositional construction of gender roles into female and male, disregarding the spectrum of possible gender constructions, as well as, the realities of gender roles enacted. In Indigenous cultures, we often find additional third and fourth genders. Gender polarity as a model also reifies or essentializes gender, though research shows that gender fluidity is the norm.

Genealogical imagination: From Ni Dhomhnaill (1996, citing Seamus Heaney). While there is a "literal" genealogy of personal family history and cultural identities, in ethnoautobiographical inquiry, as in other decolonization practices, there are also required imaginative, creative and flexible processes that connect to Indigenous consciousness, or recovery of Indigenous mind, including original instructions, be(com)ing animal, transmotion, and so on. See **genealogy**.

Genealogy: We expand on (but do not contradict) the direct family sense of the word. Such an expanded use is in keeping with ethnoautobiography or Indigenous mind that is relational in all directions, with all things. Thus, we refer to our personal genealogies (our family history), as well as to more indirect inheritances that come to us, such as White (racial) and settlement privilege, historical legacies, cultural mythologies, etc. For example, we acknowledge the qualitative research genealogies, and other Eurocentered academic traditions, we emerge from and simultaneously seek to decolonize. Accordingly, this relates to the genealogical notions of postmodern critic Michel Foucault (Prado, 1995). While some of Foucault's goals are consistent with our work, Foucault also reflects an anti-spiritual perspective further limiting meaningful inquiry and precludes a variety of ways of knowing, especially Indigenous methodologies.

Genocide: Article II of The Convention on the Prevention and Punishment of the Crime of Genocide reads as follows (UN General Assembly, 1948/1951):

> In the present Convention, genocide means any of the following acts committed with intent to destroy, in whole or in part, a national, ethnical, racial or religious group, as such:
> (a) Killing members of the group;
> (b) Causing serious bodily or mental harm to members of the group;
> (c) Deliberately inflicting on the group conditions of life calculated to bring about its physical destruction in whole or in part;
> (d) Imposing measures intended to prevent births within the group;
> (e) Forcibly transferring children of the group to another group.

This book at least briefly mentions several formal government processes and events which all constitute genocide as described (we regard the distinction made by some authors between cultural genocide and genocide as specious — cultural genocide is genocide). These genocidal processes include "Indian" boarding schools, outlawing traditional ceremonies, forbidding the speaking of language, restricting access to sacred sites, not to mention massacres. It is our hope that increased scholarship in these arenas will move this from the cultural shadows to acknowledgment and healing (see also Churchill, 2004; Madley, 2009; A. Smith, 2005).

As far as the Indigenous populations of the Americas are concerned, the most detailed and methodologically sophisticated population estimates for the pre-Columbian Americas indicate that North and South America was inhabited by 90 to 112 million people of a vast variety of different cultures with numerous languages. At that time Europe had 60-70 million inhabitants, Russia 10-18 million, and Africa 40-72 million (Stannard, 1992). Eight to twelve million Native Americans lived north of Mexico in pre-Columbian times. The population loss due to colonization and genocide generally was 95% or more. In the U.S., the 1890 U.S. census reported 248,000 Native Americans (2-3% of the pre-Columbian population). The 1990 census reported about 1.9 million Native Americans (16-23% of the pre-Columbian population).

There are approximately 300 reservations and federally or state recognized tribes with 44 million acres of land (this is 2.2% of the acreage of the contiguous 48 states). 437,000 Native Americans live on reservations that range in size from the largest of the Diné (or Navajo) people (16 million acres) to small California rancherias of one acre. Threats to individual and cultural survival continue amidst widespread family violence, alcoholism, suicide, diabetes, cultural fragmentation, a lack of recognition by the U.S. society, and destruction of sacred sites. Less than 10% of contemporary natives speak their own languages and most Native Americans do not have either any or sufficient land to continue their traditionally self-sufficient economies on their ancestral lands. It was only under President Jimmy Carter in the late 1970s that many native ceremonies became legal, and the process of repatriation of ceremonial items and human remains began in the 1990s. In the Canadian northwest the potlatch ceremony, the core ceremony of the northwest coast cultures, was outlawed between 1884 and 1951.

Gini index: Measure of income or wealth distribution and inequality with 1 or 100% expressing maximum inequality.

Groundwork: Clark and Powell (2008) note that their "Indigenous groundwork" and

> Daniel Wildcat's "thinking spatially" similarly affirm a people's relationship to land, not "land" in the abstract or land understood as private property but particular places, distinctive homescapes that generate unique, restorative expressions of different tribal identities and peoplehoods. Thus, homescapes provide places to stand to take a stand. (p. 5)

It is for this reason that Indigenism emphasizes the land, as Vine Deloria (2003) did at the close of *God is red*: "That is when the invaders of the North American continent will finally discover that for this land, God is red" (p. 296). See **sovereignty**.

Gulag: Forced labor, prison camp system in Russia and the former Soviet Union (1922-1991) used for prisoners of both a criminal and/or political nature.

Haudenosaunee: The Native peoples amer-europeans call Iroquois. Also called the Six Nations, their membership is composed of the Seneca, Cayuga, Mohawk, Oneida, Onondaga and Tuscurora. Among the most noted Indigenist political leadership in North America (see Akwesasne Notes, 1978).

Hero(ine)'s journey: Mythic pattern popularized by Joseph Campbell (*The Hero With a Thousand Faces*, 1949). It describes a process of self-transformation and healing, beginning with a call to adventure, crossing the threshold, encountering a helper/mentor, entering the abyss of death and rebirth or transformation, and, after additional steps, returning the gifts received to the community. The heroine's journey has been distinguished from the hero's journey, with Fierz-David's discussion of a frieze at Pompeji initiating alternate descriptions of transformative journeys (2001, originally published in 1957). Applying this pattern more narrowly to ethnoautobiography, we might say that after departure an individual faces personal and/or cultural shadow(s), and returns with gifts of insight and healing to form an integrated self identity — in an Indigenous sense — and has capacities to share these gifts.

Heteronormative: Within Eurocentered societies the notion, often enforced through real or threatened violence, that heterosexuality is the only acceptable form of sexuality and gender identity. All other experiences are relegated to the shadow, denied and suppressed at all costs. Synonymous with heterosexism, and being hetereosexist; in contrast to **holosexuality**.

Heterosexism: see **heteronormativity**.

(Hi)stories: Linking the telling of stories with history and its heavily gendered transmission. The term makes explicit that history is one more version of storytelling rather than an all-knowing narrative of certainty that rightfully is dominant. History consists of a multiplicity of (hi)stories. As a feminist critique of the gendered telling of such stories, this word is sometimes written (his)tories, or (her)stories.

Holosexuality: Vizenor uses the term to refer to the entire sexual and erotic energy of every cell in our bodies, integrating the spectrum of feminine and masculine qualities and resisting reductionism to the binaries of gender. Refers to a sensual/sexual relationship with all beings around us (from human sexuality to orgasms triggered by the sensuality of old-growth redwood trees). This is in contrast to Eurocentered sexuality that is highly polarized between supposed opposites and primarily focused on sexual organs. (See e.g., Vizenor, 1988, p. 34).

Homosexuality: In the polar model of sexual orientation and gender construction, the erotic and/or sexual attraction to members of the same gender. Used to demonize or "other" gender identities that do not fit in Eurocentered and patriarchal settings by enforcing heterosexuality. See **gender polarity**, **heteronormativity**, **holosexuality**.

Hybridity: Originally a biological term (referring to the offspring of a tame sow and a wild boar), it is now commonly used in multicultural discourse to refer to the effects of mixtures of cultural identities and lineages. Hybridity has been associated with migrant populations or border towns; it is also used in other contexts when there is a flow of different cultures that both give and receive from each other. The concept of hybridity is critical of essentialist notions of identity ('true identity,' 'the German national character,' etc.).

Ideology critique: Central to the social critique of the Frankfurt School (and related schools of critical thought); inquiries designed to question the legitimacy and accuracy of statements affirming certain social realities (such as the need for domination or American exceptionalism). Ideology critique is analogous to individual depth psychological inquiry on a social level. It aims to identify systematic ideological distortions in public discourse. These distortions lead to cultural shadow material which ideology critique seeks to bring to light.

Imaginal: Used in Jungian or archetypal psychological theories (e.g., imaginal psychology) to refer to the reality of our visions, dreams, imaginations and similar experiences that have the potential to add meaning to our life experiences. From this perspective, working with our imagination, and working through our connection to (spiritual) images provides care of the soul.

Immanent: In Indigenous societies, everyday existence of spiritual or **trans/personal** aspects of life are seen as part of everyday consensual social reality; spirits are just as real as a glass of milk. Immanent (akin to non-dualistic) is used in contrast to the Eurocentered way of seeing transcendent and immanent as opposite poles (spiritual or religious aspects of life vs. everyday social realities). Transcendence is also a preeminent aspect of major world religions.

Independent: See **masterful self**.

Indian: see **Indigenous**, **Playing Indian**.

Indigenist, or **Indigenism:** Cultural and political philosophies prioritizing Indigenous values and worldviews. Often used in the context of political activities, Indigenism can be used as another term to describe elements of ethnoautobiography, such as place (ecology), ancestry, history, gender, and so on. A frequent cultural example is the Haudenosaunee (Iroquois) consideration of the impact of a decision on the 7th generation in the future. The US-based International Indian Treaty Council's achievement of official United Nations participation in 1977 is a political example of Indigenism. (See Churchill, 1992).

Indigenous, or **Indigenous peoples:** There are approximately 250 million Indigenous peoples worldwide — 4% of the global population — living in over 70 countries. In the legal and political context, especially within United Nations organizations and conferences, Indigenous peoples often use the definition provided by the International Labor Organization convention in 1989 that defines them as

> tribal peoples in independent countries whose social, cultural and economic conditions distinguish them from other sections of the national community and whose status is regulated wholly or partially by their own customs or traditions or by special laws or regulations; peoples in independent countries who are regarded as Indigenous on account of their descent from the populations which inhabited the country, or a geographical region to which the country belongs, at the time of conquest or colonization or the establishment of present state boundaries and who irrespective of their legal status, retain some or all of their own social, economic, cultural and political institutions. Self-identification as Indigenous or tribal shall be regarded as a fundamental criterion for determining groups to which the provisions of this Convention apply. (International Labor Organization, Convention #169, 1989)

In substance this statement is also contained in the draft of the Inter-American Declaration on the Rights of Indigenous Peoples (Venne, 1998) as well as other significant statements on the rights of Indigenous peoples. More recently, after the 2007 passage of the United Nations Declaration of the Rights of Indigenous Peoples, there are more detailed rights, responsibilities and definitions pertaining to Indigenous peoples. (UN, 2008). For example, the Sámi peoples of the arctic north are or were considered an "ethnic minority" by the majority populations in Finland, Sweden, Norway, and Russia as a way of asserting the settler rights of the dominant culture (rather than Indigenous peoples or First Nations). In 1980 a policy was adopted by Sami people stating that a Sámi is defined as

> any person who—has Sámi as his [sic] first language or whose father, mother or one of whose grandparents has Sámi as their first language, or—considers himself a Sámi and lives entirely according to the rules of Sámi society, and who is recognized by the representative Sámi body as a Sámi, or—has a father or mother who satisfies the above-mentioned conditions for being a Sámi. (Sámi Instituhtta, 1990, p. 11).

Indigenous mind, paradigm, worldview, or consciousness: A holistic cultural paradigm of living and being in the world which not only attempts to avoid separation but actively maintains an integral relationship with ancestors, nature, spirits, place, astronomy, history, and so on. Never used as a purist ideal in the sense of romantic, Eurocentered projections, but always working to maintain balance within the nurturing conversations (such as *criar y dejarse criar*) through ritual and storytelling.

Indigenous presence: Much more than physical presence, this is a being presence within the central place of an Indigenous worldview and cultural practice. Among the Haudenoshaunee this place is called *Skanagoah*, the great peace; among the old Germanic peoples *friður*, peace. Such presence seeks to overcome simplistic and romantic identity politics, ethnic identification and racialism that are manifestations of historical wounds, collective amnesia, supremacist thinking and the related suppressed or denied habits or norms (Kremer, 2003). Presence embodies simultaneously knowing Self and Other, and maintaining relationships and connection with the human and more–than–human world. This way of being combines decolonization and be(com)ing animal. It is presence to the cycle of nurturing and being nurtured, *criar y dejarse criar*.

Indigenous science: The term acknowledges the scientific nature of Indigenous astronomical observations, Indigenous ecological understandings, etc. Indigenous science goes beyond the bounds of much Western scientific understanding, especially one-dimensional scientism, using careful observation in all the dimensions that define Indigenous presence and acknowledging the intertwining of knowing and being — **beingknowing**. Indigenous science is a holistic way of understanding, living and being in the world that actively maintains relationships with nature, spirits, place, astronomy, and so on, through detailed and active observation and participation as opposed to the Eurocentered scientific practices of separation and compartmentalization. Oftentimes Indigenous science is expressed in stories or images. (See Cajete, 2000; Colorado, 1996; Deloria, 2003, 2006).

Indigenous self: Sense of self with flexible, permeable boundaries that allows the intimate interaction of *criar y dejarse criar* and the intimacy of Indigenous science. Such a sense of self is in contrast to the **well-boundaried**, masterful self of **WEIRD** or Eurocentered cultures. In many ways, such a sense of self is more of a concentration, gradually fading into and blending with "the other", rather than being exclusionary and separate. Most of what is relegated to "other" for the modern masterful self is completely, or partially identified with the Indigenous self. While the Indigenous self is embedded in its context, it is distinct with its own agency.

Indigenous transmotion: See **natural reason; transmotion**.

Individualistic, or **individualism:** Individualism, individualistic self, or well-boundaried masterful self all refer to the notion prevailing in Eurocentered, and especially **WEIRD** societies, wherein the unit of highest importance in social organization is the individual person.

Indo-European: Various subgroups of the Indo-European language family including ten major branches, given in the chronological order of their earliest surviving written versions: Anatolian; Hellenic; Indo-Iranian; Iranian; Indo-Aryan or Indic; Italic, including Latin; Celtic; Germanic; Armenian; Tocharian; Balto-Slavic; and, Albanian.

(In)equality: Equal or unequal access to and distribution of political, economic and social power and stability. Factors that interfere with equality include inherited White, and/or settlement privilege, access to education, voting rights and so on. See **Gini index**.

Initiation: The entry or beginning of a process, often used in psycho-spiritual contexts of self-transformation. Here used most often as initiation into a new level of knowledge or cultural understanding which implies a process of self transformation.

Integral, integrative, or **integration:** Used in multiple traditions and disciplines, here referring to the lack of a strict separation of different parts of a culture, a person's identity, etc. We find this term in traditions like Aurobindo's (1990) integral Yoga, Wilber's (2007) integral theory, as well as various Western disciplines, such as social integration, racial integration, integrated circuit, etc. Holistic is a related term. In our usage integral refers to a state of presence and knowing in the world in which the self is connected through a process analogous to *criar y dejarse criar*, that is, mutual and reciprocal nurturance and conversation. Indigenous peoples often seem to have terms or phrases that point to integration as a central process in their lives.

Integrative states of consciousness: During such states old and younger parts of the brain as well as right and left hemispheres are integrated or in "conversation" with each other. Non-integrative states emphasize the dominance and value of one state over others (usually the left-brain hemisphere, rational processes of the frontal cortex). Integrative states of awareness are connective and relationship–building that allow for a sense of self and identity that includes emotions, altered states, dreams, the body, etc., rather than well-boundaried, exclusionary, or dissociative. Integrative states of consciousness may result in spiritual openings, connections with the more-than-human world, near-death experiences and so on. They may feel extraordinary, but they may also be experienced as a natural part of the everyday spectrum of humans in touch with a larger sense of self. Indigenous peoples, as the inheritors of ancient knowledge, continue to value and access such awareness both as part of daily life as well as on important ritual occasions.

Interbeing: Used by Thích Nhat Hanh (1991) to describe Buddhist mindfulness practices as something approaching Indigenous relationships among all things.

Interdependent: Many people, things, and beings having mutually beneficial relationships. Refers to processes similar to interbeing, natural reason, integral and relationship. See *criar y dejarse criar*.

Intersex: A person (as well as non-human beings) born with both male and female characteristics, including chromosomes, gonads, and/or sex organs. When used to describe humans this is considered more sensitive than hermaphrodite.

Left (brain) hemisphere: Works to achieve precision by breaking things down into parts through narrow and sharply focused attention to detail. The result is clarity and the capacity to manipulate things that can be known and isolated. The knowledge of the left hemisphere uses denotative language and tends to be decontextualized; what it knows is explicit and general in nature. The knowledge system of the left hemisphere is closed and aims for perfection creating a self-consistent view of reality, so that what does not fit gets discarded (see McGilchrist, 2009, 2011).

Legend: Generally regarded as historically grounded, while **fairy tales** and **folk tales** generally lack such historical grounding. The terms folk tale, fairy tale, legend, and myth are often used interchangeably and specific definitions vary with authors. However, **myth** generally refers to the oldest layer of stories in a culture, originally transmitted in oral traditions (though some myths can also be related to historical events, such as supernovas and volcanic eruptions). All of these old forms of narratives are of importance in ethnoautobiographical inquiries, with creation myths holding a central place. The oral quality of these cultural narratives has been lost since they have been committed to writing, mostly in modern times. Ethnoautobiography works to restore oral storytelling capacities.

Legitimation or **legitimation crisis:** From the political sciences referring to the (il)legitimacy of governmental structures. A legitimate governmental organization has both legal authority and fulfills the end for which it was created. In a legitimation crisis serious questions arise whether the organization still succeeds in fulfilling its function; discrepancies between its structure and the function it was designed for have become obvious. In such a crisis, government control, power, or pres-

tige no longer appears legitimate and people question its legitimacy. The financial crises of 2008 in the U.S. and Europe have veered toward serious crises of legitimacy (e.g., the Occupy Movement, protests in Greece) as have U.S. Supreme Court rulings regarding corporate financing of elections.

Lucid dream: Types of dreams in which the dreamer becomes aware, without waking up, that s/he is dreaming; it creates opportunities for dreamers to consciously change the plot in a dream.

Masterful (well-bounded or **boundaried) self:** The predominant sense of self or identity in cultures based on European or Eurocentered ideals (see **WEIRD**). Here the self has separated itself from the mutuality of the nurturing conversation (*criar y dejarse criar*) through normative dissociation, or a splitting off, to assume a position of supremacy in relation to other animals, plants, people, etc. This individualistic and ego-centered personality is commonly highly racialized, gendered and compartmentalized. It seeks to know the world in order to master it, rather than to be with it and foster mutually beneficial relationships.

Matriarchy: Introduced by Bachofen in 1861. Göttner-Abendroth's contemporary definition translates the term as "the mothers from the beginning" (as opposed to "domination by the mothers"). She translates patriarchy as "domination by the fathers", with the arche having the double meaning of "beginning" as well as "domination" (2004, p. 74). Matriarchy emphasizes the importance and centrality of the feminine.

Mestiza/o: The dictionary defines this as a person of Spanish and Indigenous ancestry. Anzaldua (1987), among others, reclaims this term as a source of cultural pride, positive identity, creativity and resilience, rather than the original implication of half-caste or mongrel.

Middle Passage: The path of ships carrying captured Africans from West Africa into slavery in the Americas is acknowledged as much for the survivors of the horrific crossing as it is for the countless people that perished on the journey. It is regarded as a path of souls departed and honored ancestors who were sacrificed by the millions.

Mixed blood: Similar to mestiza, mixed-blood had (and in some settings, still has) negative connotations. Vizenor (1981), among other Indigenous authors, seeks to reclaim this term in light of resilience, creativity, complexity and **survivance**. Vizenor sees the **crossblood** as a generative and trickster-ish position for the future of humanity and our survival.

Möbius strip: A surface with only one side. Popularized by M.C. Escher's "Ants on a Möbius strip," it is commonly described as an optical illusion. Allen (1998) uses the term to describe a place similar to Anzaldua's borderland (1987).

Modernity, Modernism, Modernist, Modern: The historical time period beginning after the Middle Ages in the 1400s marked by the rise of capitalism, industrialization, secularization, rationalization, nation states, surveillance, science, technology, colonialism, etc. Used here to describe qualities associated with Eurocentrism and White mind, as well as the institutions that furthered its rise. The Western philosophical movement of Enlightenment is central to the rise of modernity. Some characteristics associated with modernity include individualism, democracy, public space, civil liberties, as well as gender, racial and class inequalities. Indigenism, post-modernism, and critical social theory all critique various aspects of modernism.

More-than-human: Abram (1996, 2010) uses this term to describe the complex world of all living things, as well as what Eurocentered perception describes as inanimate.

Morality: See **Dimensions of morality**.

Multicultural, multiculturalism: A concept with different meanings for different people, ranging from the folkloric display of different traditions and ethnicities to a profound critique of Eurocentered thinking. The term signals the embrace of cultural diversity and complexity at various levels within a Eurocentered worldview. Ethnoautobiography is explicitly multicultural through a process of decolonization and the establishment of egalitarian exchanges that heal past socio-cultural traumas.

Multivocality: Similar to **hybridity**, the acknowledgment that apparently homogeneous societies are actually composed of many voices once we deconstruct the dominant story and encourage other voices to be heard. Similarly, each individual contains a multiplicity of voices. For example, as Sarris (1996) writes,

> Who I am as a writer, as a person, is someone continuing the conflict, the coming together, of histories, cultures. My education and training as an academic and writer only add voices, inner disputants, to a world of multiple voices. …What I hope to have done is provide a way for us to start talking interculturally and interpersonally about what is in fact intercultural and interpersonal. (pp. 37-8)

Mythology, myth, or **mythic:** Myth generally refers to the oldest layer of stories in a culture, originally transmitted in oral traditions (but some myths can also be related to historical events, such as supernovas and volcanic eruptions). The terms **folk tale**, **fairy tale**, legend, and myth are often used interchangeably and specific definitions vary with authors. All these old forms of narratives are of importance in ethnoautobiographical inquiries, with creation myths holding a central place. The oral quality of these cultural narratives has been lost since they have been committed to writing, mostly in modern times. Ethnoautobiography works to restore oral storytelling capacities. In common parlance we use the term "myth" to point to something as not true. Myths primarily carry meanings that hold socio-cultural truths that have been or are of central importance for a society or social group. In this book we avoid using "myth" to mean "not true".

Natural reason: From Vizenor (1994), to clarify a person's identity and knowing as inclusive of nature, imagination, and many other elements.

> The sources of natural reason and tribal consciousness are doubt and wonder, not nostalgia or liberal melancholy for the lost wilderness; comic, not tragic, because melancholy is cultural boredom, and the tragic is causal, the closure of natural reason. The shimmers of imagination are reason ... (p. 14).

Neo-mammalian brain: In MacLean's (1973) descriptions of the triune brain, this is the frontal cortex, our executive center, the seat of rational and reflective thought. The part of the brain that most people think of when they hear the word "brain". In an evolutionary context a later development, after the **palaeo-mammalian** and **reptilian brains**.

New Age: An ill-defined term with multiple meanings ranging from calendrical (as in the Mayan calendar, the precession of the equinoxes, or the Age of Aquarius) to a movement raising consciousness, esp. including meditative and other altered states. Indigenous peoples commonly note the ungroundedness of White New Age notions and the lack of political awareness. From an ethnoautobiographical perspective such New Age ideas arise from the lack of felt experience of **normative dissociation** and historical disconnections from ancestral roots. Without such context the embrace of Indigenous (and other) traditions may not lead to the desired goals and lack authenticity. (See Fikes, 1993).

Noble savage: According to Berkhofer (1978) the noble savage developed as "a convention for enunciating the hopes and desires of European authors or for criticizing the institutions and customs of their own society" (p. 74). Rousseau is the European scholar most often (and erroneously, according to Ellingson, 2001) associated with the notion of the noble savage; its historical origins are generally dated to the European Renaissance and subsequent Enlightenment periods (Berkhofer, 1978). It is important to note that Indigenous peoples (though conquered by European colonists) had substantial influence on Europeans (Conn, 2004). There remain questions about whether the noble savage was a real, albeit Eurocentered, description of romantic Natives encountered by Europeans, or if the term was used as a critique of deficiencies within European society (or a combination of both). A major flaw in the noble savage stereotype is the polar opposition of "good" (noble) and "bad" (ignoble) savages. Rather than acknowledging these philosophical conflicts as faulty Eurocentered stereotypes in the first place, great effort and time are spent debunking or proving the existence of the noble savage (Hames, 2007; Krech, 1999; LeBlanc, 2003).

Normative dissociation: The disconnection and splitting off of individuals from the cycle of nurturing and being nurtured (*criar y dejarse criar*) as social norm. Also describes a cultural process and social norm that changes Indigenous selves into individualistic, well-bounded, modern selves, though the separation is largely unconscious. It leads to the pervasive disregard of emotional, somatic, sexual, dream, nature-connected, other processes that then at least partially become cultural shadow material. See **dissociation**.

Objective, or **objectivity:** One pole of the Eurocentered Cartesian duality, suggesting that there are external realities that can be described with certainty, or for which laws can be identified. Used more generally to describe conditions external to a person. There have been many thorough critiques of this position from Indigenous and postmodern positions (maybe most radically by Feyerabend's *Against Method* [1975]). See **subjective**.

Ontology: The philosophical description and questioning of the understanding of one's existence in the world; a worldview.

Oral tradition: The transmission of cultural knowledge through different forms of storytelling in ritual and extra-ritual contexts. The use of non-literate means to transmit cultural practices and knowledge, including star knowledge, relationships with the more-than-human world, ancestral relationships, and so on. Frequently oral traditions are seen as inferior to written traditions (esp. in a court of law where it is often equated with "hearsay" that devalues or dismisses Indigenous oral traditions). The term "prehistory" is associated with oral traditions, while "history" begins with writing. See also **postmodernity**, **evolutionary prejudice**.

Original instructions: An English word originating in Indigenous communities referring to instructions, contained in creation and other stories, that give guidance as to living in balance in a specific ecological community. It references the holistic cultural practices as set forth at creation, since the beginning of time, and so on. These practices are especially, though not exclusively, used when relating to ecological wellbeing. (See Horn, 1996; M. K. Nelson, 2008).

Paganism: The animistic, non-Christian and/or shamanic spiritual traditions of Indigenous peoples, including European peoples before Christianity. Often used with **evolutionary prejudice** implying that pagan traditions are simplistic folk traditions, which may even be dangerous or devilish. See **animism**.

Palaeo-mammalian brain: According to MacLean's (1973) descriptions of the triune brain, this is the part of the brain that can also be characterized as the emotional brain (includes the limbic system). The language of this part of the brain is primarily visual rather than linguistic, playing a central role in dreams, habits, etc. Thus, the arts, dreams, movement, dance, trances, and rituals access this part of the brain making it critical for emotional responses and processing in both waking and dreaming life. This is the area of the brain where habits and our deep sense of self reside.

Paradigm: See **Indigenous mind**.

Parker, Cynthia Ann: As a young settler Cynthia Ann was taken by the Comanche from her family's fort on the Texas frontier in the 1830s, eventually becoming fully integrated into Comanche society. She became the wife of Comanche leader Peta Nocona, and gave birth to three children: Quanah, Pecos, and Topsana (Prairie Flower). Many years later Cynthia Ann, who had taken the name Naudah (Someone Found), was kidnapped by the Texas Rangers and returned by force to her prominent north Texas family. After repeated unsuccessful escape attempts and the death of her youngest child, Prairie Flower, she died a prisoner. She and her children Quanah and Topsana are buried at Fort Sill, Oklahoma. (See Gwyne, 2009 and Carlson & Crum, 2010).

Parker, Quanah: The Comanche chief who led the Comanche during the "transition" from life on the Southern Plains to reservations in then Indian Country (present day Oklahoma). Known for his powerful leadership as a warrior, he later became a diplomat for the Comanche and other nations during the particularly dismal early reservation period. Quanah was a child of Comanche leader Peta Nocona and White woman Cynthia Ann Parker. (See Gwyne, 2009 and Carlson & Crum, 2010).

Participation: See **relationship**.

Participatory spirituality: In this view, most clearly developed by Ferrer (2002), religious, spiritual, or transpersonal events are seen as a co-creation between the experiencer and what is "out there." "Transpersonal events engage human beings in a participatory, connected, and often passionate knowing that can involve not only the opening of the mind, but also of the body, the heart, and the soul" (p. 121). See **beingknowing**.

Patriarchy: Similar to androcracy, patriarchy is social organization around the worth and importance of men. In contrast to **matriarchy**.

Pedagogy: The science and art of teaching and education; instructional strategies.

Personal shadow: See **shadow**.

Pilgrimage: An intentional journey to a place of spiritual, cultural, historical, etc. significance that is undertaken as a personally and/or culturally transformative act. These can be undertaken alone or with groups of people. (See Browne, 2008; Dewolf, 2008; Krondorfer, 1995).

Playing Indian: Philip Deloria's (1998) profound analysis of the cultural habit of Whites attempting to become somehow American. A central concept in this workbook, we especially emphasize the application of P. Deloria's thinking to environmentalism and other political organizing among Whites. This illuminates how Eurocentered environmentalists, for example, are "playing Indian" as they attempt to "become native to the place," all the while furthering the settlement of North America.

Po'pay: The Ohkay Owingeh leader who spearheaded the Pueblo Revolt in 1680, expelling the Spanish from their territory for twelve years in present day New Mexico.

Postmodern, or **post-modernity:** The philosophies of deconstruction and post-structuralism are associated with postmodernity, describing movements especially in architecture, the arts, and criticism. Postmodern intellectuals and artists critique and respond to modernism and its contradictions. Major proponents in the field of philosophy include Lyotard, Derrida, Foucault, Baudrillard. Postmodernity is more of an attitude toward modernity, rather than a cohesive school. Spretnak (1997) distinguishes deconstructionist postmodernity from ecological postmodernity, a relative of Indigenous paradigms. Vizenor (1989, p. x) asserts that "the postmodern opened in tribal imagination; oral cultures have never been without a postmodern condition that enlivens stories and ceremonies, or without trickster signatures and discourse on narrative chance — a comic utterance and adventure to be heard or read."

Post-traumatic settler disorder: Settler (White) cultural norms based in genocide, slavery and land theft — and especially the avoidance and dismissal of such shadow material in amer-european (and other Eurocentered) societies — are evidence enough of posttraumatic settler disorder. Psychologically, the posttraumatic stress disorder diagnosis relates to the varying degree of a person's denial and functionality as a consequence of exposure to trauma (Duran & Duran, 1995; Glendinning, 1994; Herman, 1992). Further, it seems appropriate to connect amer-europeans with a disorder since Indigenous peoples have diagnosed the traumatic disconnections and loss of spirit long ago (see Churchill [1995] or Richardson [2008], for example). Indeed, White settlers can be said to have a truly myopic and dis-eased relationship with the world, both human and more-than-human. Many Indigenous peoples have contemporary words for settlers which speak to that condition: Māori: "Pākehā" meaning "foreigner" (Consedine & Consedine, 2005; Mitcalfe, 2008); Hawaiian: "haole," which some suggest is translated as "without breath" or "soulless", as well as "foreign" (Rohrer, 2010); Lakota of the northern Plains of north America: "Wasi'chu," translated as "the one that steals the fat," (Johansen & Maestas, 1979); Kashaya Pomo of northern California: "'Miracles' is the Kashaya Pomo term for white people.... As one Kashaya Pomo elder told me, 'The invaders are miracles, miraculous. They think they can kill and plunder and get away with it'" (Sarris, 1996. p. 28); and even amer-european Christian theologian Robert Bellah: "nomadic vandals" (V. Deloria, 1999; see also Chambers, 2009; Gabbard, 2006; Glendinning, 1995; Jackson-Paton, 2012, Morrison, 2012; Veracini, 2007, 2010b; see also **settler**).

Presence, Indigenous presence, coming-to-presence, radical presence: Intensifying and growing consciousness of the integral interrelationships of an Indigenous self process. An engagement with the cycle of nurturing and being nurtured (*criar y dejarse criar*); that is, the awareness of interrelatedness. Opening to a way of being that seeks to overcome simplistic and romantic identity politics that are manifestations of historical wounds, collective denials, supremacist thinking and the related suppression of cultural roots.

Privilege: The historical and institutional legacy that favors certain people automatically because of their race, culture, gender, religion, sexual orientation, ability and so on. Thus, White privilege is offered Whites by no explicit choice of their own. Nor is male privilege offered to men by their own choosing. Rather, most often people must choose to question or reject the privilege that falls to them.

Provincial and **provincialism:** Of the country, or province; often used synonymously with backward or incomplete. **Cosmopolitanism** (being cultured) is usually seen as the positive end of a spectrum that views provincialism negatively. A positive understanding would emphasize the significance of local Indigenous understanding and ecological knowledge. See **cosmopolitanism**.

Quanah Parker: See **Parker, Quanah**

Racial contract: Mills (1997) suggests the social contract forming the basis of Western democracies is, in fact, a racial contract. Accordingly, the norms of the political and philosophical social contract within Eurocentered societies is firmly embedded in a racial contract between Whites and non-Whites, and maintained by White supremacy.

Radical hope: Based on Lear (2006), radical hope is the premise that there is hope for a meaningful life after a catastrophic event. It is "directed toward a future goodness that transcends the current ability to understand what it is. Radical hope anticipates a good for which those who have the hope as yet lack the appropriate concepts with which to understand it" (p.103).

Radical presence: See **presence**.

Rational, or **rationality:** Emphasis on rationality and the use of reason is one of the hallmarks of modernity, specifically Enlightenment philosophy. Kant (1784) emphasized *Sapere aude!* – Think for yourself! The use of reason is a central characteristic of Western science and technology, though its increasingly limited application has been criticized by Marcuse (1964) and many others on the grounds that it represents one-dimensional rationality, scientism, or technocratic rationality. We use the term 'reason' to refer to the positive use of rationality and 'one-dimensional rationality' or 'scientism' to refer to its restrictive and incomplete use. The use of rationality in Eurocentered societies generally dismisses alternate ways of constructing knowledge and meaning (embodiment, the reasons of the heart, etc.) and continues to emphasize mono-causal and linear models of decision-making. See **objective** and **normative dissociation**.

Recovery of Indigenous Mind: Cultural and scholarly activism of Colorado (1996) and Kremer (1996, 2011) suggesting that all people have Indigenous roots that can be relearned, remembered, and restored through various practices of decolonization. Ethnoautobiography is a version of such practice. Sometimes called recovery of participation.

Relationship: A synonym for relationality (Kovach, 2009) that attempts to describe an Indigenous sense of connection, participation and reciprocity with the world for people in a Eurocentered worldview or mind. (See Abram, 2010).

Religion: Broad term referring to "organized forms of doctrine, ritual, myth, experience, practice, spirituality, ethics, and social structure that together constitute a world in relation to what is known as sacred" (Rothberg, 1994, p. 2). This describes the "major" religions of Christianity, Islam, Hinduism and Judaism which are generally hierarchical. See **spirituality**.

Remembrance: Describes several elements — all facilitating transformation and healing — that include remembering self, other, and self-with-other. Acts of remembrance for those of Eurocentered inheritance include the underworld material of conquest needed to be incorporated into the self (Kremer & Rothberg, 1999) and what has been called "rituals of inquiry" (Jackson-Paton, 2008). This includes acts of remembering how our ancestors (among other settlers) narrated their experience of place in North America. Recovering participation is also such an act of remembrance, as is a genealogical imagination. As descendants of settlers, remembrance of the other includes acceptance of narratives of survivance. Remembrance makes space for richer — and transformative — stories of self and other (Hooker & Czajkowski, 2012; Regan, 2010). This takes the form of multivocal histories of peoples and places, as well as more specific actions for justice, such as truth commissions, land restoration, and reparations, and what has been called "Taking Down the Fort" referring to Fort Snelling in Minneapolis (Waziyatawin, 2008, p. 9). Finally, self-with-other is the manner in which these rememberings are brought forward to offer new relationships with people and places (Carter, 1996). This would include acts of reconciliation, dialogue, and healing rituals at places of atrocity (Dowlin & Dowlin, 2002). It also includes explicit acts of decolonizing or re-Indigenizing the academy (Mihesuah & Wilson, 2004). Acts of remembrance will take the form of narrating a sense of place (and identity) where self-with-other is foregrounded and recovered. The quality of remembrance just described cannot be separated from **(re)placing** and **restor(y)ing**.

(Re)placing: To replace something implies returning it to a previous position, or to make a substitution. Invoking (re)placement, and decolonization in general, emphasizes the necessity to be put back into place. This would return White amer-european settlers to a previous consciousness that more fully embodies relationality and participation. This is not a regressive move, rather it is liberation from simplistic notions of progress. Most specifically, however, being (re)placed means taking account of all that is included in a particular place, and inviting, encouraging, and paying attention to as much of the information and participation as possible. This would include the multiple and varied narratives (such as ethno-accountings) of specific places, the interactions of people with each other and the places they inhabit, and fostering new inclusive stories of place, that endorses justice, reconciliation, and renewal.

Reptilian brain: The oldest part of our brain that performs basic functions which continue when we sleep or even faint: breathing, blood pressure, heartbeat, etc. It regulates our basic survival functions. While we can never be conscious of our reptilian brain we can impact its function through practices like meditation, yoga, and trances.

Restor(y), or restor(y)ing: Inspired by Cronon's (1992) "A Place for Stories," and Nabhan's (1991, 2012) "re-story", we play on the double meaning that links environmental restoration (reintroducing native species, preserving threatened ecosystems, and so on) with revived and (re)new(ing) cultural storytelling, most especially among settlers. As with ecological restoration and ethnoautobiography, restor(y)ing is long-term, complex, and dynamic.

Retraditionalization: The process where people who have survived colonization return to and remember Indigenous traditions and lifeways. This is used as another term for recovery of Indigenous mind, whereby Eurocentered people **decolonize** and reconnect with Indigenous European traditions. Retraditionalization cannot be separated from **(re)placing** and **restor(y)ing.**

Riffs: See **ethnoautobiographical riffs**

Right (brain) hemisphere: Provides sustained, open, broad alertness or vigilance for what might be, and is concerned with patterns and making connections, and helps identify what is different from what we expect. It perceives things in context, understands metaphor, body language, implicit meanings, and facial expressions. The right hemisphere is concerned with individuals (not categories) and the embodied world, the living as opposed the mechanical, looking at embodied beings as part of the lived world. It also deals with things that can never be fully grasped, such as spirituality. For a broad understanding of situations we rely more on knowledge of the right hemisphere, but it cannot construct arguments; it is the holder of the big picture, and the integrator of information (based on McGilchrist, 2009; 2011).

Rituals of reconciliation: Embodied communal healing, and transformative practices (Jackson-Paton, 2008) that pay respect to Krondofer's (1995) *Remembrance and Reconciliation,* Rosaldo's (1993) "Grief and a Headhunter's Rage," Behar's (1996) and Brown's (2010) "vulnerability," and Vine Deloria's (2002) "conciliatory ceremonies."

Rootprints: Used more broadly to acknowledge the imprint left by our ancestors. The title of a (1997) book by Hélène Cixous and Mireille Calle-Gruber. Rootprints, memory and life writing, trace the development of Cixous as intellectual and writer. It includes the chapter "Albums and Legend" tracing her genealogy.

Sand Creek: In southeastern Colorado, this was the site of a November 29, 1864 massacre by the Colorado militia, led by Colonel Chivington. Nearly 200 Cheyenne and Arapaho were killed and mutilated, about 2/3 of whom were women and children. A National Historic Site managed by the National Park Service, with Cheyenne and Arapaho participation, opened at the place of massacre in 2007. (See Ortiz, 2000 and Kelman, 2013).

Settlement privilege: This is the colonial companion to racial or White privilege. Settlement privilege is the reality of inherited benefits from conquest and settlement to the inheritors of settlement. In other words, the simple act of living on land acquired, in most cases, under very dubious circumstances is where settlement privilege begins. However, it does not end there. Wealth, resource consumption, as well as wilderness backpacking, and much more, all derive from settlement, and thus are examples of settlement privilege. See **White privilege**.

Settler: Used as a synonym for White, or amer-european, there are several mutually reinforcing aspects to defining a settler:

• persons who have migrated migrated from their country of origin (most often, but not exclusively, Europe) and have themselves taken and/or occupied land and/or otherwise removed Indigenous inhabitants through various means, or are descended from these people;

•someone who can join a dominant cultural group in relation to the resident Indigenous peoples, thus enjoying resultant privileges. This is especially important if people are more recent immigrants, as opposed to descended from historical settlement;

• a person who has (whether knowingly or not) gained access to all manner of institutionalized privileges (concrete, as well as theoretical), including but not limited to land, monetary wealth, historical favor, education, legal rights; and,

• someone who was raised according to Eurocentric (cultural, educational, scientific, philosophical) norms.

(See Jackson-Paton, 2012; Regan, 2010; Veracini, 2008, 2010).

Shadow: Popularized from Jungian psychology, the shadow is understood as containing emotions, characteristics, behaviors, events, and so on that are repressed, denied, or forgotten making them have unforeseen power or control in usually negative ways. A simple example would be personal characteristics, thoughts or feelings a person might find unacceptable and therefore denies. Another example of personal shadow might be experiencing sexual assault and later in life making poor relationship choices. While some aspects of the shadow may be closer to awareness, others may take prolonged introspective work. Collective, or cultural, shadow refers to events on a country– or society– wide scale that are not part of the dominant discourse, including, for example, Native American genocide, enslavement of African people, the Jewish holocaust, or the patriarchal denigration of women. Carriers and inheritors of the denied ('shadow') history are usually highly aware of the material excluded from mainstream discourse. Different societies carry different collective shadow material. If not adequately attended to, each of these processes or events continue to affect society and its members in significant and largely unconscious ways (see Kremer & Rothberg, 1999). Truth and reconciliation commissions are one attempt to transform and heal collective shadow. Collective shadow is sometimes called historical trauma (Hooker & Czajkowski, 2012).

Shamanism: Indigenous spiritual practices for the benefit of the community. The term originated from Siberian traditions, but is now used generically for many Indigenous ceremonial practices. Shamans are intermediaries between the everyday world and the spiritual world. They generally use integrative states of consciousness to obtain information for healing or to intervene on behalf of the person in need of healing. Shamanic traditions are grounded in specific cultures and ecologies, with ancestors playing an important part in this worldview. Popularized in Eurocentered societies, it is now a common Eurocentered term to describe many Indigenous spiritual practices and lifeways. Shamanic ritual approaches are part of the recovery of Indigenous mind and ethnoautobiography. New Age approaches to shamanism generally neglect the cultural specificity and ecological groundedness of the traditions they are working in; they also disregard the necessary shadow work and the decolonizing imperatives in order to ground shamanic practices.

Sociocentric: A society, or group of people who consider the collective to have importance over the individual. Sociocentrism shapes a person's identity with the group playing a preeminent role. In contrast to **individualism**.

Soma, or **somatic:** From the Greek "soma," relating to the body. Somatics is a general field of body-related studies that includes dance, somatic therapies, and varied modalities, such as Feldenkrais, Body-Mind Centering, Rolfing and so on. (See Johnson, 1997).

Sovereignty: In Western political theory this refers to the authority over a territory and the power to rule and make laws, presumably in the best interest of the citizens living in the territory. By contrast, Vizenor (1998) provides an Indigenous understanding of sovereignty: "Native sovereignty is **transmotion** and the rights of motion are personal, totemic, and reciprocal" (p. 16). "Sovereignty as motion and transmotion is heard and seen in oral presentations, the pleasures of native memories and stories" (p. 182). According to Vizenor, origin and migration stories foster a sovereignty that is associated with movement and is both mythic and concrete. This sovereignty is not only about land as in Eurocentered politics and colonialism. See **transmotion** and **natural reason**.

Spiritual inquiry: John Heron (1998) describes such inquiry as being

> simply the active, innovative and examined life, which seeks both to transform and understand more deeply the human condition.... The bottom line of all this is that, for the examined life, revelation is here and now; and spiritual authority is within. Such authority is relative to its context and unfolding, never final, and always open to spiritual revision. (pp. 17-18)

Spirituality: Refers to the "lived transformations of self and community toward fuller congruence with or expression of what is understood, within a given cultural context, to be 'sacred'" (Rothberg, 1994, p. 2). A broad description of the relationship between people and their gods or spirits, as distinct from **religion**.

Storytelling: See **oral tradition**.

Subject, or **subjective:** One extreme of the Eurocentered Cartesian duality opposing objective and subjective; generally associated with the assumption that there are internal realities that cannot be described with certainty, but are open to endless interpretation. Generally devalued or dismissed as a form of information. Often used to describe conditions internal to a person. See **objective**.

Survivance: Rare variant of 'survival', now revived and refined by Vizenor (2008): "Native survivance is an active sense of presence over absence, deracination, and oblivion; survivance is the continuation of stories, not a mere reaction, however pertinent.... Survivance, then, is the action, condition, quality, and sentiments of the verb survive" (p. 1, 19). There is perhaps no greater anti-colonial act than disrupting the settler or conqueror with varied responses that do not include disappearance. These challenges to amer-european settler society take many forms: literature, music, art, as well as other types of narrative and performance (Cook-Lynn, 1996; King, 2005); acts of (re)claimed self-determination in politics, culture and society (Grande, 2004; Million, 2013); and, maintaining relationships with all the peoples and places of their worldview (Cajete, 2000; Colorado,1996; V. Deloria, 2003).

Synecdochic self: Krupat (1992) defines it as the individual's sense of self in relation to collective social units or groups. Narratives of the self grounded in community and its stories, and vice versa.

Systems 1 and 2: System 1 is the quick and dirty response to reality, the draft of our reality that emerges from association and metaphor. It recognizes faces and understands speech instantly. Without involving conscious awareness it makes judgments and takes action. It has instant access to our memory bank that guides its judgments. These judgments are biased toward memories that are emotionally intense (fear, pain, hatred) and are therefore often mistaken. Frequently, aspects of what System 1 does are called intuition, since we don't have a sense of voluntary control while it just does its job. **System 2:** presumably evolved after System 1; where rational choices and explication of beliefs occur; the slow critical examination of the evidence at hand, including the evaluation of actions by System 1; allows planning and creation of art and culture; consists of effortful mental activities and provides sense of choice, agency, and concentration. (Based on Kahneman, 2011).

Totemism: Anthropological term referring to a kinship with a being in the more-than-human world. Describes the honoring and respecting of non-human beings and/or spirits among Indigenous peoples. Frequently used with evolutionary prejudice referencing "primitive" or **animistic** societies.

Transcendent: Separate realm beyond everyday, consensual social reality. The realms of gods, God, goddesses or spirits in Eurocentered thinking; the realm that religion or spirituality discusses in the Eurocentered paradigm. Often associated with privileged access, such as by a priest or pope. In contrast to the **immanent** worldviews of Indigenous peoples and societies where everyday reality includes the active presence and participation of spirits, dreams, myths and so on.

Transformative learning: A form of learning and education that fosters the transformation of meanings and meaning perspectives through critical (self) reflection, the arts, somatic and dream work, among other means. It encourages self and societal healing and transformation with the goal of emancipation or the **remembrance** of native **sovereignty**.

Transgress: To go against, or step across boundaries, as encouraged by critical theory, and other critiques of society. (See hooks, 1994).

Transmotion: From Vizenor (1998), transmotion is the natural relationship in stories that connects humans to place and to the spiritual and political meaning of other animals and beings, what Eurocentered people distance themselves from as transpersonal or "other." "Monotheism is dominance over nature" Vizenor (pp. 182-3) writes, "transmotion is natural reason, and native creation with other creatures. The connotations of transmotion are creation stories, totemic visions, reincarnations, and sovenance [remembrance]; transmotion, that sense of native motion and an active presence, is *sui generis* sovereignty" (p. 15). See **natural reason** and **sovereignty**.

Transpersonal: A Eurocentered term for experiences greater than, or going beyond, an individual person. These could include spiritual traditions, psychology, ecology, altered states of consciousness, shamanism, and so on. In an Indigenous worldview these are not separate or beyond a person's or society's everyday experience, rather they are an aspect of an integrated whole, such as evoked by Vizenor's terms **natural reason** and **transmotion**.

Trickster: In mythologies, tricksters move between the above and below, heaven and earth; they are on the road and reign in the in-between; they are the spirits of the threshold, the liminal. The stories of their exploits are used to teach about appropriate behavior and attitudes. They step into action where the portals between the worlds (e.g., above and below, conscious and unconscious) are closed and they may become thieves on these occasions (as when Raven steals water and daylight). They roam in the place of ambiguity, ambivalence, doubleness, duplicity, contradiction, and paradox. Thus they live at boundaries, move them, cross them, erase them, and even create them. Tricksters are consummate survivors, always slippery and able to wiggle free, always willing to abandon a position or invert a situation; levity and speed win out over suffering and seriousness. Tricksters are creators and destroyers, givers and negators, neither good nor evil (yet responsible for both), without values, yet all values come into being through their actions. Raven and Coyote, Loki and Cúchullain are examples of such teachers, creators, messengers, and guides. (See Kremer, 2012.)

Truth and reconciliation commissions: Complex and varied processes by which people and societies attempt to heal (from) atrocities and historical wrongs. Most notable are attempts in post-Apartheid South Africa (Krog, 1998; Tutu, 1999; Reid, at al, 2000), and Residential (Boarding) Schools in Canada (Regan, 2010; Chambers, 2009). See Berger & Berger (2001) and Krondorfer (1995) for such work among descendants of the Jewish Holocaust. For more general approaches to transforming historical trauma see Hooker & Czajkowski (2012). See also **rituals of reconciliation**.

Two-spirits: A term used in some Indigenous communities describing the presence of both stereotypically masculine/male and feminine/female behaviors, attitudes, and characteristics in a person within a continuum of three, four or more genders (Nibley, 2010; Williams, 1986). See also **holosexuality** and **androgyny**.

Underworld: The realm of the dead or spirits in religious, mythical and psychological worldviews. From a Jungian psychological perspective, a real or imagined journey through an underworld often leads to (re)integrating aspects of the self, potentially healing for the self and the world. See also **shadow**.

Vulnerability: Informing much of the psychological scholarship of Brown (2010, 2012), who notes that vulnerability is a hallmark of wholeheartedness, compassion and connection. Behar (1996) similarly challenged anthropology and human science, in general, to break hearts in order to heal them.

WEIRD: An acronym from Henrich, Heine & Norenzayan (2010) standing for **W**estern, **E**ducated, **I**ndividualistic, **R**ich, and **D**emocratic societies.

Well-bounded, or **Boundaried Self:** See **Masterful Self**.

Western science: The Eurocentered view of science is presently *de facto* dominant as far as the determination of truths about reality is concerned and how it asserts supremacy over alternate scientific views. However, scholars like Harding (1997) have argued against this supremacist view documenting that the Western sciences are local sciences comparable to other local sciences and do not deserve special status. Western science reflects the assumptions and worldviews that are part of the construction of the masterful, well-bounded sense of individualistic cultures. It has been criticized for its mechanistic, dualistic, and reductionistic approach and for numerous other reasons, especially the historical enmeshment of Eurocentered sciences with colonialism and White supremacy. The assertion of Western science's privileged status has been severely undermined by various critiques, including from the perspective of Indigenous science and postmodernity (see Colorado, 1994). See **objectivity** and **postmodernity**.

White: A description of people of European ancestry that refers to certain traits or qualities beyond merely skin color, including White mind, whiteness, White privilege and so on. While there is truth in much of that description, we also acknowledge that this is an overgeneralization of people that often overlooks or dismisses possibilities of more diverse personal and cultural experiences and potential for healing transformation. The term "White" obscures the diversity, as well as the Indigenous roots, underlying this abstract category. See **amer-european**. (Dyer, 1997; Morrison, 1992)

White, or **Eurocentered mind:** Often used by Indigenous peoples, among others, to describe a state of consciousness among many different kinds of people due to the consequences of colonialism. A White mind might include attempts to embrace homogeneity, separation, disconnection, linearity, scientism, individualism, hierarchy, monotheism, control and commodification of living things, hyper-masculinity, disconnections from ancestry, and so on. Another term for White mind is **normative dissociation**, that is the splitting off or separation

from nature, place, cycles, ancestors, etc. This view is a Western, modern cultural norm and the opposite of an Indigenous way of being in the world. Ethnoautobiographical practices provide possible avenues for the decolonization of such a worldview. (See Ani, 1994; Colorado, 1996).

White privilege: Refers to visible and invisible benefits — access to housing, education, land, wealth, media representation, and so on — that White people have through societal and historical realities; these are frequently un-chosen and unknown to Whites. Many of these privileges become assumptions about what constitutes White people and the universality of White people's experience in contrast to people of color. For example, due to social and historical inheritance Whites have access to good jobs, education, etc. Yet, this is often unseen and can lead people to oppose equal opportunity programs on the grounds of reverse racism or arbitrary unfairness. White privilege is often connected to male privilege. (See McIntosh, 1990; Rothenberg, 2011; WPC, n.d.)

Whiteness: A broad term used to refer to the combined causes and effects of settlement and racial privilege, including many personal and cultural manifestations. Inquiries about whiteness critique the cultural and historical experiences of White people, with particular attention to its social construction as a purveyor of privilege and status justifying oppression of non-Whites. As with White, or White mind, this descriptor is not seen as a permanent state, but rather describes qualities to transform, heal, and decolonize. (See especially Dyer, 1997; Frankenberg, 1993; Harvey, 2007; Ignatiev, 1995; Morrison, 1992; Roediger, 2002; Thandeka, 2001).

Wilderness, or **wild:** A seemingly straightforward description of places in nature that are devoid of human presence, as codified in the U.S. Wilderness Act of 1964. The Act states that wilderness "is hereby recognized as an area where the earth and community of life are untrammeled by man, where man himself is a visitor who does not remain." This definition denies historical and contemporary Indigenous presence in these places. We, along with many others, take a much more complex view of "nature" or wilderness that acknowledges settlement, racial, gender and class privilege, Indigenous presence, frontier mythology, and so on. (See Cronon, 1995; M. P. Nelson & Callicott, 2008).

Witchery: From Silko's (2006) *Ceremony*, witchery refers to how White people were initially created through the development of the destructive story of progress and a separation between people and the Earth (**normative dissociation**). Witchery is akin to post-traumatic settler disorder (Jackson–Paton, 2012), it is both the creation of a Eurocentered settler culture and an ongoing cursed presence for the land and people. Roediger (2002) explains Silko's witchery thus: "whites are but a symptom of 'witchery' and not the source of evils" (p. 20).

Worldview: See **Indigenous mind, paradigm, consciousness.**

REFERENCES

Abram, D. (1996). *The spell of the sensuous: Perception and language in a more–than–human world*. New York, NY: Pantheon Books.

Abram, D. (2010). *Becoming animal: An earthly cosmology*. New York, NY: Pantheon Books.

Adams, T. E., & Jones, S. H. (2008). Autoethnography is queer. In N. K. Denzin, Y. S. Lincoln, & L. T. Smith (Eds.), *Handbook of critical and Indigenous methodologies* (pp. 373–390). Thousand Oaks, CA: Sage.

Akwesasne Notes. (1978). *Basic call to consciousness*. Summertown, TN: Book.

Albanese, C. L. (1990). *Nature religion in America: From the Algonkian Indians to the New Age*. Chicago: University of Chicago Press.

Allen, P. G. (1998). *Off the reservation*. Boston, MA: Beacon.

Anderson, M. K. (2005). *Tending the wild: Native American knowledge and the management of California's natural resources*. Berkeley: University of California Press.

Ani, M. (1994). *Yurugu: An African–centered critique of European cultural thought and behavior*. Trenton, NJ: Africa World Press.

Anzaldúa, G. (1987). *Borderlands/la frontera: The new mestiza*. San Francisco, CA: Aunt Lute.

Apffel–Marglin, F. (1994). Development or decolonization in the Andes. *Daybreak* 4 (3): 6–10.

Apffel–Marglin, F., & Proyecto Andino de Tecnologías Campesinas (PRATEC). (1998). *The Spirit of regeneration: Andean culture confronting Western notions of development*. London, England: Zed Books.

Aronson, E., Wilson, T. D., & Akert, R. M. (2010). *Social psychology*. Boston, MA: Pearson.

Atwood, M. (2005). *Penelopiad*. New York, NY: Canongate.

Aurobindo, S. (1990). *Synthesis of yoga*. Twin Lakes, WI: Lotus Press.

Bagshaw, M., & Stetson, C. (2012). *Teaching my spirit to fly*. Santa Fe, NM: Little Standing Spruce Pub.

Ball, E. (1998). *Slaves in the family*. New York, NY: Farrar, Straus and Giroux.

Bar–On, D. (1993). Holocaust perpetrators and their children: A paradoxical morality. In B. Heimannsbert and C. Schmidt (Eds.), *The collective silence – German identity and the legacy of shame* (pp. 195–208). San Francisco, CA: Jossey–Bass.

Barreiro, J. (1992). *Indian roots of American democracy*. Ithaca, NY: Akwe:kon Press Cornell University

Bastien, B. (2003). The cultural practice of participatory transpersonal visions. *ReVision* 26(2), 41–48.

Bastien, B. (2004). *Blackfoot ways of knowing – The worldview of the Siksikaitsitapi*. Calgary, Canada: University of Calgary Press.

Bastien, B., Kremer, J., Norton, J., Rivers–Norton, J., & Vickers, P. (1999). The genocide of native Americans: Denial, shadow, and recovery; a conversation. *ReVision*, 22(1), 13–27.

Bateson, G. (1972). *Steps to an ecology of mind*. New York, NY: Ballantine Books.

Baudrillard, J. (1993). *The transparency of evil: Essays on extreme phenomena*. New York, NY: Verso.

Bauschatz, P. C. (1982). *The well and the tree*. Amherst, MA: University of Massachusetts Press.

Beck, P. V., & Walters, A. L. (1979). *The sacred*. Tsaile, AZ: Navajo Community College Press.

Behar, R. (1996). *The vulnerable observer: Anthropology that breaks your heart*. Boston, MA: Beacon.

Bem, S. L. (1995). Dismantling gender polarization and compulsory heterosexuality: Should we turn the volume down or up? *Journal of Sex Research*, 32(4), 329–334.

Benally, H. (1987). Diné Bo'hoo' aah bindh'a': Navajo philosophy of learning. *Diné Be'iina'*, 1(1), 133–148.

Bentz, V. M., & Shapiro, J. J. (1998). *Mindful inquiry in social research*. Thousand Oaks, CA: Sage.

Berger, A. L., & Berger, N. (2001). *Second generation voices: Reflections by children of Holocaust survivors and perpetrators*. Syracuse, NY: Syracuse University Press.

Berger, J. (1990). *Ways of seeing*. New York, NY: Penguin Books.

Berkhofer, R. F. (1995). *Beyond the great story*. Cambridge, MA: Harvard University Press.

Beyman, R., & Kremer, J. W. (2003, Summer). The spirit of integration: Mythic androgyns and the significance of shamanic trance. *ReVision*, 26(1), 40–48.

Bhabha, H. K. (1994). *The location of culture*. New York, NY: Routledge.

Bigwood, C. (1993). *Earth muse: Feminism, nature and art*. Philadelphia, PA: Temple University Press.

Bjarnadóttir, V. H. & Kremer, J. W. (1998). The cosmology of healing in Vanir Norse mythology. In H. Kalweit & S. Krippner (Eds.), *Yearbook of cross-cultural medicine and psychotherapy* (pp. 127–176). Mainz, Germany: Verlag für Wissenschaft und Bildung.

Bochner, A. P., & Ellis, C. (2002). *Ethnographically speaking: Autoethnography, literature, and aesthetics*. Walnut Creek, CA: AltaMira Press.

Bourguignon, E. (1973). *Religion, altered states of consciousness, and social change*. Columbus: Ohio State University Press.

Boyd, C. E., & Thrush, C. (2011). *Phantom past, Indigenous presence: Native ghosts in North American culture and history*. Lincoln: University of Nebraska Press.

Breckenridge, C. A., Pollock, S., Bhabha, H. K., & Chakrabarty, D. (2002). *Cosmopolitanism*. Durham, NC: Duke University Press.

Breton, D. C. (2005). Digging deeper: Challenges for restorative justice. In W. D. McCaslin (Ed.), *Justice as healing: Indigenous ways* (pp. 409–434). St. Paul, MN: Living Justice Press.

Bringhurst, R. (1999). *A story as sharp as a knife*. Lincoln: University of Nebraska Press.

Brown, B. (2010). *The power of vulnerability*. Retrieved from http://www.ted.com/talks/brene_brown_on_vulnerability.html

Brown, B. (2012). *Daring greatly: How the courage to be vulnerable transforms the way we live, love, parent, and lead*. New York, NY: Gotham Books.

Brown, L. A., & Strega, S. (2005). *Research as resistance: Critical, Indigenous and antioppressive approaches*. Toronto: Canadian Scholars' Press.

Browne, K. (Producer & Director). (2008). *Traces of the trade: A story from the deep north* [Documentary]. United States: California Newsreel.

Buege, D. J. (1995). Confessions of an eco-colonialist: Responsible knowing among the Inuit. In Rothenberg, D. (Ed.), *Wild ideas* (pp. 81–93). Minneapolis: University of Minnesota Press.

Buruma, I. 2002. The blood lust of identity. *The New York Review of Books* XLIX(6), 12–14.

Butler, J. (1990). *Gender trouble: Feminism and the subversion of identity*. New York, NY: Routledge.

Byatt, A. S. (2011). *Ragnarök*. New York, NY: Canongate.

Cajete, G. (2000). *Native science: Natural laws of interdependence*. Santa Fe, NM: Clear Light.

Callicott, J. B., & Nelson, M. P. (1998). *The great new wilderness debate*. Athens: University of Georgia Press.

Campbell, J. (1949). *The hero with a thousand faces*. Princeton, NJ: Princeton University Press.

Campbell, N., & Kean, A. (2012). *American cultural studies*. New York, NY: Routledge.

Capps, W. H. (Ed.). (1976). *Seeing with a native eye: Essays on Native American religion*. New York, NY: Harper.

Carlson, P. H. & Crum, T. (2010). *Myth, memory, and massacre: The Pease River capture of Cynthia Ann Parker*. Lubbock: Texas Tech University Press.

Carter, P. (1996). *The lie of the land*. London, England: Faber and Faber.

Chambers, N. (2009). *Truth and Reconciliation: A "dangerous opportunity" to unsettle ourselves*. In G. Younging, J. Dewar, M. DeGagné, & Aboriginal Healing Foundation (Eds.), *Response, responsibility and renewal: Canada's truth and reconciliation journey* (pp. 285–305). Ottawa, Canada: Aboriginal Healing Foundation. Retrieved from http://www.ahf.ca/downloads/trc2.pdf

Chang, H. (2008). *Autoethnography as method*. Walnut Creek, CA: Left Coast Press.

Cixous, H., & Calle-Gruber, M. (1997). Hélene Cixous, rootprints: Memory and life writing (pp. 187–205). London, England: Routledge.

Chomsky, N. (1988). *The culture of terrorism*. Boston, MA: South End Press.

Christian, B. (1993, Spring). Fixing methodologies: Beloved. *Cultural Critique* 24, 5–15.

Churchill, W. (1992). I am Indigenist: Notes on the ideology of the fourth world. *Z Papers*, 1(3), 8–22.

Churchill, W. (1995). *Since predator came: Notes from the struggle for American Indian liberation*. Oakland, CA: AK Press.

Churchill, W. (2004). *Kill the Indian, save the man: The genocidal impact of American Indian residential schools*. San Francisco, CA: City Lights.

Clark, D., & Powell, M. (2008). Resisting exile in the "land of the free": Indigenous groundwork at colonial intersections. *American Indian Quarterly* 32(1), 1–15.

Clark, W. P., Hudlin, R., McIntosh, S., Savone, P., Shamberg, M., Sher, S., Skotchdopole, J. W., Weinstein, B., Weinstein, H. (Producers), & Tarantino, Q. (Director). (2012). *Django unchained* [Motion picture]. United States: A Band Apart.

Coffin, L. (with Richmond, B., Ed.). (1991). *Reminiscences of Levi Coffin, the reputed president of the underground railroad*. Richmond, IN: Friends United Press.

Cohen, B. B. (2012). *Sensing, feeling, and action: The experiential anatomy of body–mind centering®*. 3rd edition. Northampton, MA: Contact Editions.

Colorado, A. P. (1988). Bridging native and Western science. *Convergence*, xxi(2/3), 49–67.

Colorado, A. P. (1994, April 25–27). *Indigenous science and Western science: A healing convergence*. Presentation at the World Sciences Dialog I, New York City.

Colorado, A. P. (1996). Indigenous science. *ReVision*, 18(3), 6–10.

Coming to the Table [CTTT]. (n.d.). Retrieved from http://www.comingtothetable.org/

Consedine, R., & Consedine, J. (2005). *Healing our history: The challenge of the Treaty of Waitangi* (2nd ed.). Auckland, New Zealand: Penguin.

Cook–Lynn, E. (1996). *Why I can't read Wallace Stegner and other essays: A tribal voice*. Madison: University of Wisconsin Press.

Cox, P. A., & Elmqvist, T. (1993, June). Ecocolonialism and Indigenous knowledge systems: Village controlled rainforest preserves in Samoa. *Pacific Conservation Biology, 1*(1), 6–13.

Coulthard, G. (2010). Place against empire: Understanding Indigenous anti– colonialism. *Affinities: A Journal of Radical Theory, Culture, and Action*, 4(2), 79–83.

Cronon, W. (1983). *Changes in the land: Indians, colonists, and the ecology of New England*. New York, NY: Hill and Wang.

Cronon, W. (1992). A place for stories: Nature, history and narrative. *Journal of American History*, 78(4), 1347–1376.

Cronon, W. (1995). The trouble with wilderness; Or, getting back to the wrong nature. In W. Cronon (Ed.), *Uncommon ground: Toward reinventing nature* (pp. 69–90). New York, NY: Norton.

Csikszentmihalyi, M. (2008). *Flow: The psychology of optimal experience*. San Francisco, CA: Harper.

Cunningham, L. (2010). *A state of change: Forgotten landscapes of California*. Berkeley, CA: Heyday.

Cushman, P. (1995). *Constructing the self, constructing America: A cultural history of psychotherapy*. Boston, MA: Addison–Wesley Pub.

D'Anglure, B. S. (1992). Rethinking Inuit shamanism through the concept of 'third gender'. In M. Hoppál & J. Pentikäinen, *Northern religions and shamanism* (pp. 146–150). Budapest, Hungary: Akadémiai Kiadó.

Damasio, A. R. (1994). *Descartes' error: Emotion, reason, and the human brain*. New York, NY: Putnam.

Damasio, A. R. (2010). *Self comes to mind: Constructing the conscious brain*. New York, NY: Pantheon Books.

Dauenhauer, N. M., & R. (1987). *Haa shuká, our ancestors. Tlingit oral narratives*. Seattle, WA: University of Washington Press.

Davies, A., Fidler, D. & Gorbis, M. (2011). *Future work skills 2020*. Palo Alto, CA: Institute for the Future for the University of Phoenix Research Institute. Retrieved from http://cdn.theatlantic.com/static/front/docs/sponsored/phoenix/future_work_skills_2020.pdf

Davis, M. (1998). *Ecology of fear: Los Angeles and the imagination of disaster*. New York, NY: Metropolitan Books.

Deloria, P. J. (1998). *Playing Indian*. New Haven, CN: Yale University Press.

Deloria, V., Jr. (1991). Reflection and revelation: Knowing land, places, and ourselves. In J. A. Swan (Ed.), *The power of place: Sacred ground in natural and human environments* (pp. 28–40). Wheaton, IL: Quest Books.

Deloria, V., Jr. (1995). *Red earth, white lies: Native Americans and the myth of scientific fact*. New York, NY: Scribner.

Deloria, V., Jr. (2002). *Evolution, creationism, and other modern myths*. Golden, CO: Fulcrum.

Deloria, V., Jr. (2003). *God is red: A native view of religion* (30th anniversary edition). Golden, CO: Fulcrum.

Deloria, V., Jr. (2006). *The world we used to live in: Remembering the powers of the medicine men*. Golden, CO: Fulcrum.

Denzin, N. K. (2008). *Searching for Yellowstone: Race, gender, family, and memory in the postmodern West*. Walnut Creek, CA: Left Coast Press.

Denzin, N. K., & Lincoln, Y. S., (Eds.). (1994). *Handbook of qualitative research*. Thousand Oaks, CA: Sage.

Denzin, N. K., Lincoln, Y. S., & Smith, L. T. (2008). *Handbook of critical and Indigenous methodologies*. Thousand Oaks, CA: Sage.

Denzin, N. K., Lincoln, Y. S., (Eds.). (2013). *The landscape of qualitative research* (4th ed.). Thousand Oaks, CA: Sage.

Derrida, J. (2001). *On cosmopolitanism and forgiveness*. New York, NY: Routledge.

Detienne, M. (1996). *The masters of truth in Archaic Greece*. New York, NY: Zone Books.

Diamond, J. M. (1999). *Guns, germs, and steel*. New York, NY: Norton.

Diamond, J. M. (2012). *The world until yesterday: What can we learn from traditional societies?* New York, NY: Viking.

Dick, P. K. (1996). *Do androids dream of electric sheep?* New York, NY: Ballantine Books.

Dion–Buffalo, Y. & Mohawk, J. (1994, Winter) Thoughts from an autochtonous center. *Cultural Survival*, 33–35.

Dörner, D. (1989). *Die Logik des Misslingens*. Reinbek, Germany: Rowohlt.

Dowie, M. (2009). *Conservation refugees: The hundred–year conflict between global conservation and native peoples*. Cambridge, MA: MIT Press.

Dowlin, S., & Dowlin, B. (2002, July). Healing history's wounds: Reconciliation communication efforts to build community between Minnesota Dakota (Sioux) and non–Dakota peoples. *Peace and Change*, 27(3), 412–436.

Drinnon, R. (1990). *Facing west: The metaphysics of Indian–hating and empire–building*. New York, NY: Schocken Books.

Duran, E. (2006). *Healing the soul wound: Counseling with American Indians and other native peoples*. New York, NY: Teachers College Press.

Duran, E., & Duran, B. (1995). *Native American postcolonial psychology*. Albany: State University of New York Press.

Dyer, R. (1997). *White*. New York, NY: Routledge.

Eakin, P. J. (1985). *Fictions in Autobiography*. Princeton, NJ: Princeton University Press.

Ehrenreich, B. (2007). *Dancing in the streets: A history of collective joy*. New York, NY: Metropolitan Books.

Eliade, M. (1964). *Shamanism*. Princeton, NJ: Princeton University Press.

Elias, D. (1997). It's time to change our minds. *ReVision*, 20(1), 2–6.

Ellis, A. (2005). *The myth of self–esteem: How rational emotive behavior therapy can change your life forever*. Amherst, NY: Prometheus.

Ellis, C. & Bochner, A. P. (2000). Autoethnography, personal narrative, reflexivity: Researcher as subject. In N. K. Denzin & Y. S. Lincoln, (Eds.), *Handbook of qualitative research* (pp. 733–768). Thousand Oaks, CA: Sage Publications.

Emerson, D., & Hopper, E. (2011). *Overcoming trauma through yoga: Reclaiming your body*. Berkeley, CA: North Atlantic Books.

Erikson, E. H. (1980). *Identity and the life cycle*. New York, NY: Norton.

European–American Collaborative Challenging Whiteness (ECCW). (2010). White on White: Developing capacity to communicate about race with critical humility. In V. Sheared, J. Johnson–Bailey, S. A. J. Colin, III, E. Peterson, & S. D. Brookfield (Eds.), *The handbook of race and adult education: A resource for dialogue on racism* (pp. 145–157). San Francisco, CA: Jossey–Bass.

Faulkner, W. (1951). *Requiem for a nun*. New York, NY: Vintage.

Feinstein, D., & Krippner, S. (2008). *Personal mythology: Using ritual, dreams, and imagination to discover your inner story* (3rd ed.). Santa Rosa, CA: Energy Psychology Press/Elite Books.

Ferrer, J. (2002). *Revisioning transpersonal theory*. Albany: State University of New York Press.

Feyerabend, P. (1975). *Against method*. London, England: Verso.

Fikes, J. C. (1993). *Carlos Castaneda, academic opportunism and the psychedelic sixties*. Victoria, BC: Millenia Press.

Fischer, D. H. (1989). *Albion's seed: Four British folkways in America*. New York, NY: Oxford University Press.

Forman, R. K. C. (Ed.) (1990). *The problem of pure consciousness*. New York, NY: Oxford University Press.

Four Arrows (Jacobs, D. T.). (2008). *The authentic dissertation: Alternative ways of knowing, research, and representation*. New York, NY: Routledge.

Frankenberg, R. (1993). *White women, race matters: The social construction of whiteness*. Minneapolis: University of Minnesota Press.

Frankenberg, R., & Mani, L. (1996). Crosscurrents, crosstalk: Race, "postcoloniality," and the politics of location. In S. Lavie & T. Swedenburg (Eds.), *Displacement, diaspora, and the geographies of identity* (pp. 273–293). Durham, NC: Duke University Press.

Freud, S. (1999). *The interpretation of dreams*. Oxford, UK: Oxford University Press.

Gabbard, D. (2006). Before predator came: A plea for expanding First Nations scholarship as European shadow work. In Four Arrows (Ed.), *Unlearning the language of conquest* (pp. 219–231). Austin: University of Texas Press.

Gaiman, N. (2008). *The graveyard book*. New York, NY: HarperCollins.

Gaiman, N. (2011). *American gods: A novel* (10th anniversary edition). New York, NY: W. Morrow.

Gebser, J. (1986). *The ever–present origin*. Athens: Ohio State University.

Geertz, C. (1984). *The religion of Java*. Chicago, IL: University of Chicago Press.

Gibson, R. (2008). *My body, my earth: The practice of somatic archaeology*. Bloomington, IN: iUniverse.

Gilligan, C. (1982). *In a different voice: Psychological theory and women's development*. Cambridge, MA: Harvard University Press.

Glassner, B. (2009). *The culture of fear: Why Americans are afraid of the wrong things*. New York, NY: Basic Books.

Glendinning, C. (1994). *My name is Chellis & I'm in recovery from Western civilization*. Boston, MA: Shambhala Books.

Glendinning, C. (1995). Yours truly from Indian Country. *Yoga Journal*. Retrieved from http://www.chellisglendinning.org/docs/yourstruly.pdf

Goldhagen, D. J. (1996). *Hitler's willing executioners: Ordinary Germans and the Holocaust*. New York, NY: Knopf.

Goldschmidt, W. (1978). Nomlaki. In R. F. Heizer (Ed.), *Handbook of North American Indians – California* (Vol. 8) (pp. 341–349). Washington, DC: Smithsonian Institution.

Gomes, M. E. (2000). The ones from the land who dream: An interview with Jeanette Armstrong. *ReVision*, 23(2), 3 –8.

Gore, A. (2013). *The future: Six drivers of global change*. New York, NY: Random House.

Göttner–Abendroth, H. (2004). Matriarchal society: Definition and theory. In G. Vaughan (Ed.), *The gift* (pp. 69–80). Rome, Italy: Meltimi editore.

Gottschall, J. (2012). *The storytelling animal: How stories make us human*. Boston, MA: Houghton Mifflin Harcourt.

Grande, S. (2004). *Red pedagogy: Native American social and political thought*. Lanham, MD: Rowman & Littlefield.

Gray, J. (1992). *Men are from Mars, women are from Venus: A practical guide for improving communication and getting what you want in your relationships*. New York, NY: HarperCollins.

Greenwood, D. A. (2009). Place, survivance, and White remembrance: A decolonizing challenge to rural education in mobile modernity. *Journal of Research in Rural Education*, 24(10). Retrieved from http://jrre.vmhost.psu.edu/wp–content/uploads/2014/02/24–10.pdf

Griffin, S. (1978). *Woman and nature: The roaring inside her*. New York, NY: Harper & Row.

Griffin, S. (1995). *The eros of everyday life: Essays on ecology, gender and society*. New York, NY: Doubleday.

Grimm, J. (1976). *Teutonic mythology* (4 vols.). Gloucester, MA: Peter Smith.

Grove, R. (1995). *Green imperialism: Colonial expansion, tropical island edens, and the origins of environmentalism, 1600–1860*. Cambridge, MA: Cambridge University Press.

Gusdorf, G. (1980). Conditions and limits of autobiography. In J. Olney (Ed.), *Autobiography* (pp. 28–48). Princeton, NJ: Princeton University Press.

Gwynne, S. C. (2010). *Empire of the summer moon: Quanah Parker and the rise and fall of the Comanches, the most powerful Indian tribe in American history*. New York, NY: Scribner.

Habermas, J. (1973). *Legitimationsprobleme im Spätkapitalismus*. Frankfurt, Germany: Suhrkamp.

Habermas, J. (1998). *Die postnationale Konstellation*. Frankfurt, Germany: Suhrkamp.

Haidt, J. (2012). *The righteous mind: Why good people are divided by politics and religion*. New York, NY: Pantheon Books.

Hames, R. (2007). The ecologically noble savage debate. *Annual Review of Anthropology* 36, 177–190. doi: 10.1146/annurev.anthro.35.081705.123321

Harding, S. (1997). Is modern science an ethnoscience? Rethinking epistemological assumptions. In E. C. Eze, (Ed.) *Postcolonial African Philosophy: A critical reader* (pp. 45 – 70). New York, NY: Basil Blackwell.

Harkin, M. E., & Lewis, D. R., (Eds.). (2007). *Native Americans and the environment: Perspectives on the ecological Indian*. Lincoln: University of Nebraska Press.

Harvey, J. (2007). *Whiteness and morality: Pursuing racial justice through reparations and sovereignty*. New York, NY: Palgrave Macmillan.

Heaney, S. (1998). *Opened ground: Selected poems, 1966–1996*. New York, NY: Farrar, Straus and Giroux.

Henrich, J., Heine, S. J., & Norenzayan, A. (2010). The weirdest people in the world. *Behavioral and Brain Sciences* 33, 2/3, 1– 75. Retrieved from http://www2.psych.ubc.ca/~henrich/pdfs/WeirdPeople.pdf

Herdt, G. (Ed.) (1996). *Third sex, third gender: beyond sexual dimorphism in culture and history*. New York, NY: Zone Books.

Herman, J. L. (1992). *Trauma and recovery*. New York, NY: Basic Books.

Heron, J. (1996). *Co–operative inquiry*. Thousand Oaks, CA: Sage.

Heron, J. (1998). *Sacred science: Person–centred inquiry into the spiritual and the subtle*. Ross–on–Wye, United Kingdon: PCCS Books

Hibbard, P. N. (2001). *Remembering our ancestors: Recovery of Indigenous mind as a healing process for the decolonization of Western mind* (Doctoral dissertation). Retrieved from ProQuest Dissertations and Theses database. (AAT 3004469)

Hill, C. (1991). *The world turned upside down: Radical ideas during the English revolution*. New York, NY: Penguin.

Hill, D., Obst, L. (Producers), & Gilliam, T. (Director). (1991). *The fisher king*. [DVD]. United States: TriStar Pictures.

Hobgood, M. E. (2009). *Dismantling privilege: An ethics of accountability*. Cleveland, OH: The Pilgrim Press.

Hogan, L. (2001). *The woman who watches over the world*. New York, NY: Norton.

Hooker, D. A., & Czajkowski, A. P. (2012). *Transforming historical harms*. Harrisonburg, VA: Coming to the Table. Retrieved from http://s3.amazonaws.com/cttt/assets/164/CTTT_TransformingHistoricalHarms_manual_web_original.pdf

hooks, b. (1994) *Teaching to transgress: Education as the practice of freedom*. New York, NY: Routledge.

hooks, b. (2004). *The will to change: Men, masculinity, and love*. New York, NY: Atria Books.

Hopcke, R. H. (1989). *A guided tour of the collected works of C. G. Jung*. Boston, MA: Shambhala.

Horn, G. (1996). *Contemplations of a primal mind*. Novato, CA: New World Library.

Ignatiev, N. (1995). *How the Irish became White*. New York, NY: Routledge.

International Congress of Qualitative Inquiry (ICQI). (n.d.). Retrieved from http://www.icqi.org/

International Labor Organization (ILO). (1989). The Indigenous and tribal peoples convention, No. 169. Geneva: International Labour Office.

Jacobs, S.–E., Thomas, W., & Lang, S. (1997). *Two–spirit people: Native American gender identity, sexuality, and spirituality*. Urbana: University of Illinois Press.

Jacobs, T. (2008). *The authentic dissertation*. New York, NY: Routledge.

Jackson–Paton, R. (2008). Rituals of inquiry; or, Looking for "culture and truth." *ReVision*, 30(1 & 2), 11–15. doi: 10.4298/REVN.30.1/2.13–17

Jackson–Paton, R. (2012). *Restor(y)ing environmentalism: Decolonizing White settlers in the United States: (Re)placing posttraumatic settler disorder*. Ph.D. Dissertation. San Francisco, CA: Saybrook University.

Jackson, W. (1994). *Becoming native to this place*. Lexington: University Press of Kentucky.

Jaggar, A. M. (Ed.). (2008). *Just methods: An interdisciplinary feminist reader*. Boulder, CO: Paradigm.

Jaimes, M. A. (1992). *The state of native America: Genocide, colonization, and resistance*. Boston, MA: South End Press.

Jennings, F. (1976). *The invasion of America: Indians, colonialism, and the cant of conquest*. New York, NY: Norton.

Jensen, D. (2000). *A language older than words*. White River Junction, VT: Chelsea Green.

Johansen, B. E., & Maestas, R. (1979). *Wasi'chu: The continuing Indian wars*. New York, NY: Monthly Review Press.

Johnson, D. (1997). *Groundworks: Narratives of embodiment*. Berkeley, CA: North Atlantic Books.

Johnson, K. K. (2002). *On the path of the ancestors: Kinship with place as a path of recovery* (Doctoral dissertation). Retrieved from ProQuest Dissertations and Theses database. (AAT 3034814)

Jones, G. R., Miller, R. P., Newman, P., Renzi, M., Sloss, J. (Producers), & Sayles, J. (Director). (2000). *The secret of Roan Inish*. [DVD]. United States: Sony Pictures Home Entertainment.

Jones, T. (2013). How can we live with it? *London Review of Books*, 35(10), 3–7.

Jung, C. G. (1959). *The archetypes and the collective unconscious*. Princeton, NJ: Princeton University Press.

Jung, C. G. (1917/1966). On the psychology of the unconscious. In *The collected works of Carl G. Jung*, vol. 7: Two essays on analytical psychology (pp. 3–122). Princeton, NJ: Princeton University Press.

Jung, C. G. (1965). *Memories, dreams, reflections*. New York, NY: Random House.

Kahneman, D. (2011). *Thinking fast and slow*. New York, NY: Farrar, Straus and Giroux.

Kant, I. (1784/1949). What is enlightenment? In I. Kant (C. J. Friedrich, Ed.), *The philosophy of Kant* (pp. 132–139). New York, NY: The Modern Library.

Kegan, R. (1998). *In over our heads: The mental demands of modern life*. Boston, MA: Harvard University Press.

Kelly, K. (2008). *Rekindling Indigenous mind: An ethnoautobiographical inquiry of transformation* (Doctoral dissertation). Retrieved from ProQuest Dissertations and Theses database. (AAT 3305709)

Kelman, A. (2013). *A misplaced massacre: Struggling over the memory of Sand Creek*. Cambridge, MA: Harvard University Press.

King, T. (2003). *The truth about stories*. Minneapolis: University of Minnesota Press.

King, T. (2013). *The inconvenient Indian: A curious account of native people in North America*. Minneapolis: University of Minnesota Press.

Kohlberg, L. (1981). *The philosophy of moral development: Moral stages and the idea of justice*. San Francisco, CA: Harper & Row.

Kosek, J. (2006). *Understories: The political life of forests in northern New Mexico*. Durham, NC: Duke University Press.

Kovach, M. (2009). *Indigenous methodologies: Characteristics, conversations, and contexts*. Toronto, Canada: University of Toronto Press.

Krech, S. (1999). *The ecological Indian: Myth and history*. New York, NY: W.W. Norton & Co.

Kremer, J. W. (1986). The human science approach as discourse. *Saybrook Review*, 6, 65–105.

Kremer, J. W. (1996). The possibility of recovering Indigenous European perspectives on Native healing practices: Developing the basis for respectful knowledge exchanges. *Ethnopsychologische Mitteilungen*, 5(2), 149–164.

Kremer, J. W. (1998). The shadow of evolutionary thinking. In D. Rothberg & S. Kelly (Eds.), *Ken Wilber in dialogue* (pp. 239–258). Wheaton, IL: Quest Books.

Kremer, J.W. (2000a). Shamanic initiations and their loss — decolonization as initiation and healing. *Ethnopsychologische Mitteilungen*, 9(1/2): 109–148.

Kremer, J. W. (2000b). Millennial twins: An essay into time and place. *ReVision* 22(3), 29–42.

Kremer, J. W. (2002). Radical presence. *ReVision*, 24(3), 11–20.

Kremer, J. W. (2003). Ethnoautobiography as practice of radical presence: Storying the self in participatory visions. *ReVision*, 26(2), 5–14.

Kremer, J. W. (2011). Totem body and the recovery of Indigenous mind. In B. Cottrell, *Totem Body* (pp. 5–6). Normanby by Spital, Lincolnshire, Great Britain: Protoangel.

Kremer, J. W. (2012). Postmodern trickster strands in shamanic worlds. *International Journal of Transpersonal Studies*, 31(2), 112–118.

Kremer, J. W., & Rothberg, D. (Eds.) (1999). Facing the collective shadow. *ReVision*, 22(1).

Krippner, S. (1997). Dissociation in many times and places. In S. Krippner & S. Powers (Eds.), *Broken images, broken selves* (pp. 3–40). Washington, DC: Brunner/Mazel.

Krippner, S. (2002). Conflicting perspectives on shamans and shamanism: Points and counterpoints. *American Psychologist, 57*, 961–977.

Krog, A. (1998). *Country of my skull: Guilt, sorrow, and the limits of forgiveness in the new South Africa.* New York, NY: Random House.

Krondorfer, B. (1995). *Remembrance and reconciliation: Encounters between young Jews and Germans.* New Haven, CT: Yale University Press.

Krupat, A. (1985). *For those who came after.* Berkeley: University of California Press.

Krupat, A. (1992). *Ethnocriticism.* Berkeley: University of California Press.

Krupat, A. (Ed.). (1994). Native American autobiography: An anthology. Madison: University of Wisconsin Press.

Krupat, A. (2002). *Red matters: Native American studies.* Philadelphia: University of Pennsylvania Press.

Krupat, A., & Swann, B. (2000). *Here first: Autobiographical essay by Native American writers.* New York, NY: The Modern Library.

Kuhn, A. (2002). *Family secrets: Acts of memory and imagination.* New York, NY: Verso.

Kuokkanen, R. (2004). The gift as worldview in Indigenous thought. In G. Vaughan (Ed.), *The gift* (pp. 81–96). Rome, Italy: Meltimi editore.

LaDuke, W. (1994, Winter). Traditional ecological knowledge and environmental futures. *Colorado Journal of International Environmental Law and Policy, 5*, 127.

Lakoff, G., & Johnson, M. (1999). *Philosophy in the flesh: The embodied mind and its challenge to Western thought.* New York, NY: Basic Books.

LaPena, F. (1999). In vision we can balance the world. *News from Native California, 12*, 2, 18–19.

Larsson, S. (2011). *The girl with the dragon tattoo.* New York, NY: Vintage Crime.

Lear, J. (2006). *Radical hope: Ethics in the face of cultural devastation.* Cambridge, MA: Harvard University Press.

LeBlanc, S. A. (with Register, K. E.). (2003). *Constant battles: The myth of the peaceful, noble savage.* New York, NY: St. Martin's Press.

Lee, D. (1959). *Freedom and Culture.* New York, NY: Prentice–Hall.

Liu, Y. (2008). East meets West. *Adbusters, 77*, no page numbers.

Lovins, L. H., & Cohen, B. (2011). *Climate capitalism: Capitalism in the age of climate change.* New York, NY: Hill and Wang.

Loy, D. R. (2010). *The world is made of stories.* Boston, MA: Wisdom Publications.

Luckert, K. W. (1970). *Coyoteway.* Tuscon, AZ: University of Arizona Press.

MacGrane, B. (1989). *Beyond anthropology.* New York, NY: Columbia University Press.

Machaca, M. M. & Machaca, M. (1994). *Crianza andina de la chacra en quispillacta: Semillas, plagas y enfermedades.* Ayacucho, Peru: Asociación Bartolomó Aripaylla.

MacLean, P. (1973). *The triune brain in evolution.* New York, NY: Plenum.

Macy, J., & Johnstone, C. (2012). *Active hope: How to face the mess we're in without going crazy.* Novato, CA: New World Library.

Madley, B. (2009). *American genocide: The California Indian catastrophe, 1846–1873* (Doctoral dissertation). Retrieved from ProQuest Dissertations and Theses database. (AAT 3361527)

Madsen, D. L. (1998). *American exceptionalism.* Jackson: University of Mississippi Press.

Mails, T. E., & Evehema, D. (1995). *Hotevilla: Hopi shrine of the covenant: microcosm of the world.* New York, NY: Marlowe & Co.

Manuel, D. (2000). Bhabha champions right to narrate. *Stanford Report*, March 8. Retrieved from: http://news.stanford.edu/news/2000/march8/bhabha–38.html

Marcuse, H. (1964). *One–dimensional man.* Boston, MA: Beacon Press.

Margolin, M. (1993). *The Way we lived: California Indian stories, songs & reminiscences.* Berkeley, CA: Heyday Books.

Mayes, V. O., & Lacy, B. B. (1989). *Nanise' — A Navajo herbal.* Tsaile, AZ: Navajo Community College Press.

McGilchrist, I. (2009). *The master and his emissary: The divided brain and the making of the Western world.* New Haven: Yale University Press.

McGilchrist, I. (2011). *The divided brain*. Retrieved from http://www.ted.com/talks/iain_mcgilchrist_the_divided_brain.html

McIntosh, P. (1990, Winter). White privilege: Unpacking the invisible knapsack. *Independent School*, 31–36.

McLeod, C. (Producer & Director). (2001). *In the light of reverence* [Documentary]. United States: Bullfrog Films.

McMurtry, L. (2005). *Oh what a slaughter: Massacres in the American West, 1846–1890*. New York, NY: Simon & Schuster.

Merchant, C. (1980). *The death of nature: Women, ecology, and the scientific revolution*. San Francisco, CA: Harper & Row.

Merrell, J. H. (1999). *Into the American woods: Negotiators on the Pennsylvania frontier*. New York, NY: Norton.

Metzner, R. (1994). *The well of remembrance: Rediscovering the Earth wisdom myths of Northern Europe*. Boston, MA: Shambhala.

Mezirow, J. (1991). *Transformative dimensions of adult learning*. San Francisco, CA: Jossey–Bass.

Mihesuah, D. A., & Wilson, A. C. (2004). *Indigenizing the academy: Transforming scholarship and empowering communities*. Lincoln: University of Nebraska Press.

Million, D. (2013). *Therapeutic nations: Healing in an age of Indigenous human rights*. Tucson: University of Arizona Press.

Mills, C. W. (1997). *The racial contract*. Ithaca, NY: Cornell University Press.

Minh–ha, T. (1991). *When the moon waxes red*. New York, NY: Routledge.

Mitcalfe, M. A. (2008). *Understandings of being Pākehā: Exploring the perspectives of six Pākehā who have studied in Māori cultural learning contexts* (Master's thesis, Massey University). Retrieved from http://muir.massey.ac.nz/bitstream/10179/885/1/02whole.pdf

Momaday, N. S. (1966). *House made of dawn*. New York, NY: Harper & Row.

Momaday, N. S. (1969). *The Way to Rainy Mountain*. Albuquerque: University of New Mexico Press.

Momaday, N. S. (1976). *The names*. Tucson: University of Arizona Press.

Momaday, N. S. (1997). *The man made of words*. New York, NY: St. Martin's Press.

Morrison, T. (1992). *Playing in the dark: Whiteness and the literary imagination*. Cambridge, MA: Harvard University Press.

Mulk, I.–M., & Bayliss–Smith, T. (2006). *Rock art and Sami sacred geography in Badjelánnda, Laponia, Sweden*. Umeå, Sweden: Department of Archaeology and Sami Studies.

Nabhan, G. P. (1991). Restoring and re–storying the landscape. *Restoration and Management Notes*, 9(1), 3–4.

Nabhan, G. P. (2012). Restorying the land. In J. Loeffler & C. Loeffler, (Eds.). *Thinking like a watershed: Voices from the west* (pp. 235–250). Albuquerque: University of New Mexico Press.

Nabokov, P. (2002). *A forest of time: American Indian ways of history*. New York, NY: Cambridge University Press.

Nadasdy, P. (2005). Transcending the debate over the ecologically noble Indian: Indigenous peoples and environmentalism. *Ethnohistory*, 52(2), 291–331.

Nash, G. B. (1988). *Forging freedom: The formation of Philadelphia's Black community, 1720–1840*. Cambridge, MA : Harvard University Press.

Nash, R. (1982). *Wilderness and the American mind*. New Haven, CT: Yale University Press.

Nelson, M. K. (2006). Ravens, storms, and the ecological Indian at the National Museum of the American Indian. *Wicazo Sa Review*, 21(2), 41–60. Retrieved from http://www.earthdiver.org/pdf/nelson_WSR.pdf

Nelson, M. K. (Ed.) (2008). *Original instructions: Indigenous teachings for a sustainable future*. Rochester, VT: Bear & Company.

Nelson, M. P., & Callicott, J. B. (2008). *The wilderness debate rages on: Continuing the great new wilderness debate*. Athens: University of Georgia Press.

Nelson, R. (1993). Searching for the lost arrow. In S. R. Kellert & E. O. Wilson, (Eds.), *The biophilia hypothesis* (pp. 201–228). Washington, DC: Island Press.

Nhat Hanh, T. & Kotler, A., (Ed.). (1991). *Peace is every step: The path of mindfulness in everyday life*. New York, NY: Bantam Books.

Nibley, L. (Director). (2010). *Two spirits* [Documentary]. United States: Riding Tiger Productions.

Nichols, A. (2006). *The golden age of Quaker botanists*. Kendal, England: Quaker Tapestry at Kendal.

Nicholsen, S. W. (1997). *Exact imagination, late work*. Cambridge, MA: MIT Press.

Nisbett, R. E. (2003). The geography of thought. New York, NY: The Free Press.

Oberle, S. G. (1997). *The influence of Thomas Meehan on horticulture in the United States.* Ph.D Dissertation.

Ortiz, S. (2000). *From Sand Creek*. Tucson: University of Arizona Press.

Patel, S. (2010). *Migritude*. New York, NY: Kaya Press.

Paxton, D. E. (2002). *Facilitating transformation of White consciousness among European–American people: A case study of a cooperative inquiry* (Doctoral dissertation). Retrieved from Proquest Dissertations and Theses database. (AAT3078796)

Paxton, S. (2003). Drafting interior techniques. In A. C. Albright & D. Gere, (Eds.), *Taken by surprise: A dance improvisation reader* (pp. 175–184). Middletown, CT: Wesleyan University Press.

Pentekäinen, J. (1989). *Kalevala mythology*. Bloomington: Indiana University Press.

Peri, D. W., & Patterson, S. M. (1979). *Ethnobotanical resources of the Warm Springs Dam–Lake Sonoma Project Area Sonoma County, California*. Final Report (unpublished) for the U.S. Army Corps of Engineers Contract No. DACW–07–78–C–004. Elgar Hill, Environmental Analysis and Planning, and Sonoma State University.

Phillips, J., Phillips, M. (Producers), & Spielberg, S. (Director). (1977). *Close encounters of the third kind* [Motion picture]. United States: Columbia Pictures.

Pizer, J. (1995). *Toward a theory of radical origin*. Lincoln: University of Nebraska Press.

Ponting, C. (1992). *A green history of the world: The environment and the collapse of great civilizations*. New York, NY: St. Martin's Press.

Prado, C. G. (1995). *Starting with Foucault: An introduction to genealogy*. Boulder, CO: Westview Press.

PRATEC. (1993). *¿Desarrollo o descolonizacion en los Andes?* Lima, Peru: Pratec.

Prechtel, M. (2001). *The disobedience of the daughter of the sun*. Berkeley, CA: North Atlantic Books.

Proulx, A. (2011). *Bird Cloud: A memoir*. New York, NY: Scribner.

Rabinow, P. (1986). Representations are social facts: Modernity and post–modernity in anthropology. In J. Clifford and G. E. Marcus (Eds.), *Writing Culture* (pp. 234–261). Berkeley: University of California Press.

Rae, H., Taplin, J. T. (Producers), Borden, J., Burdeau, G. & Lucas, P. (Directors). (1994). *The Native Americans*. [Documentary]. United States: Eurpac.

Reason, P. (Ed.). (1988). *Human inquiry in action*. Thousand Oaks, CA: Sage.

Reason, P. (Ed.). (1994). *Participation in human inquiry*. Thousand Oaks, CA: Sage.

Redford, K. H. (1990). The ecologically noble savage. *Orion, 9*(3), 25–29.

Regan, P. (2010). *Unsettling the settler within: Indian residential schools, truth telling, and reconciliation in Canada*. Vancouver, Canada: University of British Columbia Press.

Reid, F. (Producer), Hoffman, D., & Reid, F. (Directors). (2000). *Long night's journey into day* [Documentary]. United States: Reid–Hoffman Productions.

Rengifo Vasques, G. (1993). Educacion en occidente moderno y en la cultura andina. In PRATEC, *¿Desarrollo o descolonizacion en los Andes?* (pp. 163–188) Lima, Peru: Pratec.

Revard, C. (1980). History, myth, and identity among Osages and other peoples. *Denver Quarterly*, 97.

Rich, A. (1991). *An atlas of the difficult world*. New York, NY: Norton.

Richardson, B. (2008). *Strangers devour the land*. White River Junction, VT: Chelsea Green.

Richardson, L. (1994). Writing: A method of inquiry. In N. Denzin & Y. Lincoln (Eds.), *Handbook of qualitative research* (pp. 516–530). Thousand Oaks, CA: Sage.

Roediger, D. R. (2002). *Colored White: Transcending the racial past*. Berkeley: University of California Press.

Rohrer, J. (2010). Mestiza, hapa haole, and oceanic borderspaces: Genealogical rearticulations of whiteness in Hawai'i. *borderlands e–journal, 9*(1), 1–27. Retrieved from http://www.borderlands.net.au/vol9no1_2010/rohrer_mestiza.pdf

Romanyshyn, R. D. (2007). *The wounded researcher: Research with soul in mind*. New Orleans, LA: Spring Journal Books.

Rosaldo, R. (1993). *Culture and truth: The remaking of social analysis* (2nd ed.). Boston, MA: Beacon Press.

Roscoe, W. (1998). *Changing ones: Third and fourth genders in Native North America*. New York, NY: St. Martin's Griffin.

Rothberg, D. (1994). Spiritual inquiry. *ReVision*, 17(2), 2–12.

Rothenberg, P. S. (2011). *White privilege: Essential readings on the other side of racism*. (4th edition). New York, NY: Worth.

Rytcheu, J. (1999). The future of memory. *ifa, Zeitschrift für KulturAustausch*, #4. Retrieved from http://www.ifa.de/z/99–4/dzritchf.htm

Sachs, N. (1970). *The seeker and other poems*. New York, NY: Farrar, Straus and Giroux.

Said, E. W. (1993). *Culture and imperialism*. New York, NY: Knopf

Sandel, M. J. (2012). *What money can't buy: The moral limits of markets*. New York, NY: Farrar, Strauss and Giroux.

Sando, J. S., & Agoyo, H. (2005). *Po'pay: Leader of the first American revolution*. Santa Fe, NM: Clear Light.

Sante, L. (1998). *The factory of facts*. New York, NY: Pantheon Books.

Santos, J. P. (1999). *Places left unfinished at the time of creation*. New York, NY: Penguin.

Sarris, G. (1996). Living with miracles: The politics and poetics of writing American Indian resistance and identity. In S. Lavie & T. Swedenburg (Eds.), *Displacement, diaspora, and geographies of identity* (pp. 27–40). Durham, NC: Duke University Press.

Sarris, G. (n.d.). *The last woman from Petaluma*. Retrieved from http://www.sonomacountygazette.com/editions/wcg200802_021.pdf

Schama, S. (1995). *Landscape and memory*. New York, NY: A.A. Knopf.

Sheias, H. E. (2006). *Marginality and the spurious: Emergent acculturation processes of Oleem Hadasheem (new immigrants) within dominant Sabra (native Israeli) discourse* (Doctoral dissertation). Retrieved from ProQuest Dissertations and Theses database. (AAT 3212934)

Shirinian, K. (2001). *Writing memory*. Kingston, Ontario, Canada: Blue Heron Press.

Shweder, R. A. & Bourne, E. J. (1984). Does the concept of the person vary cross–culturally? In R. A. Shweder & R. A. LeVine (Eds.), *Culture theory* (pp. 158–199). New York, NY: Cambridge University Press.

Silko, L. M. (1979). An old–time Indian attack conducted in two parts: Part one: Imitation "Indian" poems; Part two: Gary Snyder's Turtle Island. In G. Hobson (Ed.), *The remembered earth: An anthology of contemporary Native American literature* (pp. 211–216). Albuquerque, NM: Red Earth Press.

Silko, L. M. (1981). *Storyteller*. New York, NY: Seaver Books.

Silko, L. M. (1991). *Almanac of the dead: A novel*. New York, NY: Simon & Schuster.

Silko, L. M. (1996). *Yellow woman and a beauty of the spirit: Essays on Native American life today*. New York, NY: Simon & Schuster.

Silko, L. M. (1997, 2006). *Ceremony*. New York, NY: Penguin.

Silver, C. F. & Coleman, T. (2013). *Studying non–belief*. Retrieved from http://www.atheismresearch.com/

Singer, J. (1972). *Boundaries of the soul*. New York, NY: Random House.

Smith, A. (2005). *Conquest: Sexual violence and American Indian genocide*. Boston, MA: South End Press.

Smith, L. T. (2012). *Decolonizing methodologies: Research and Indigenous peoples* (2nd ed.). New York, NY: Zed Books.

Soderlund, J. R. (1985). *Quakers & slavery: A divided spirit*. Princeton, NJ: Princeton University Press.

Solnit, R. (1994). *Savage dreams: A journey into the hidden wars of the American West*. San Francisco, CA: Sierra Club Books.

Sondheim, S., & Lapine, J. (1993). *Into the woods*. New York, NY: Theatre Communications Group.

Spence, M. D. (1999). *Dispossessing the wilderness: Indian removal and the making of the national parks*. New York, NY: Oxford University Press.

Spencer–Brown, G. (1969). *Laws of form*. London, England: Allen & Unwin.

Spretnak, C. (1997). *The resurgence of the real: Body, nature, and place in a hypermodern world*. New York, NY: Routledge.

Stannard, D. E. (1992). *American holocaust: Columbus and the conquest of the new world*. New York, NY: Oxford University Press.

Statman, J. M. (1999). The shape of the shadow: mapping the dimensions of white amnesia and denial in postapartheid South Africa, *ReVision* 22, 1, 35–41.

Stonebanks, C. D., & Wootton, K. (2008). Revisiting Mianscum's "telling what you know" in Indigenous qualitative research. *International Review of Qualitative Research*, 1(1), 33–53.

Strobel, L. M. (2005). *A book of her own: Words and images to honor the Babylan*. San Francisco, CA: T'Boli.

Swann, B., & Krupat, A. (Eds.). (1987). *I tell you now: Autobiographical essays by Native American writers*. Lincoln: University of Nebraska Press.

Sylvian, D., Nine Horses, et al. (2005). *A history of holes. On Snow borne sorrow*. [CD]. Samadhisound.

Szymborska, W. (1995). *View with a grain of sand*. New York, NY: Harcourt Brace.

Tarakali, V. (n.d.). *Embodied education for healing and social change*. Retrieved from http://www.vanissar.com/index.html

Taylor, J. (1983). *Dream work: Techniques for discovering the creative power in dreams*. New York, NY: Paulist Press.

Thandeka. (2001). *Learning to be White: Money, race and God in America*. New York, NY: Continuum.

Tinker, G. E. (2008). *American Indian liberation: A theology of sovereignty*. Maryknoll, NY: Orbis Books

Tolkien, J. R. R. (2012). *The hobbit*. New York, NY: Houghton Mifflin Harcourt.

Tolkien, J. R. R. (2004). *The lord of the ring*. New York, NY: Houghton Mifflin Harcourt.

Tuck, E. & Yang, K. W. (2012). Decolonization is not a metaphor. *Decolonization: Indigeneity, Education & Society* 1, 1, 1–40

Turner, E. (2012). *Communitas*. New York, NY: Palgrave Macmillan.

Turner, S. (1999). Settlement as forgetting. In K. Neuman, N. Thomas, & H. Erickson (Eds.), *Quicksands: Foundational histories in Australia and Aotearoa New Zealand* (pp. 20–38). Sydney, Australia: University of New South Wales Press.

Turner, S. (2002). Being colonial/colonial being. *Journal of New Zealand Literature* 20, 39–66.

Turner, V. (1969) *The ritual process: Structure and anti–structure*. Chicago, IL: Aldine.

Tutu, D. (1999). *No future without forgiveness*. New York, NY: Doubleday.

United Nations. General Assembly (9 December 1948; Entry into force: 12 Janary 1951) *Convention on the prevention and punishment of the crime of genocide*. Retrieved from http://www.preventgenocide.org/law/convention/text.htm

United Nations. (2008). *Universal declaration on the rights of Indigenous peoples*. Retrieved from http://undesad-spd.org/IndigenousPeoples/DeclarationontheRightsofIndigenousPeoples.aspx

Valkeapää, N.–A. (1994). *Trekways of the wind*. Tuscon: University of Arizona Press.

Valkeapää, N.–A. (1997). *The sun, my father*. Vaasa, Finland: DAT O.S.

Valladolid, J. (1997). Andean agroastronomy. *ReVision*, 19(3), 4–21.

Venne, S. H. (1999). *Our elders understand our rights: Evolving international law regarding Indigenous peoples*. Penticton, BC: Theytus Books.

Veracini, L. (2008). Settler collective, founding violence and disavowal: The settler colonial situation. *Journal of Intercultural Studies*, 29(4), 363–379. doi:10.1080/07256860802372246

Veracini, L. (2010). *Settler colonialism: A theoretical overview*. New York, NY: Palgrave Macmillan.

Vizenor, G. (1976). *Crossbloods*. Minneapolis: University of Minnesota Press.

Vizenor, G. (1981). *Earthdivers: Tribal narratives on mixed descent*. Minneapolis: University of Minnesota Press.

Vizenor, G. (1984). *The people named the Chippewa: Narrative histories*. Minneapolis: University of Minnesota Press.

Vizenor, G. (1987) Crows written on the poplars: Autocritical autobiographies. In B. Swann & A. Krupat (Eds.), *I tell you now: Autobiographical essays by Native American writers* (pp. 99–110). Lincoln: University of Nebraska Press.

Vizenor, G. (1988). *The trickster of liberty: Tribal heirs to a wild baronage*. Minneapolis: University of Minnesota Press.

Vizenor, G. (1989). *Narrative chance: Postmodern discourse on Native American Indian literatures*. Albuquerque: University of New Mexico Press.

Vizenor, G. (1990 & 2009). *Interior landscapes*. Minneapolis: University of Minnesota Press.

Vizenor, G. (1990). Gerald Vizenor [Interview]. In L. Coltelli, *Winged words* (pp. 155–184). Lincoln: University of Nebraska Press.

Vizenor, G. (1991). *The heirs of Columbus*. Hanover, NH: Wesleyan University Press.

Vizenor, G. (1992). *Dead voices*. Norman: University of Oklahoma Press.

Vizenor, G. (1994a). *Manifest manners: Postindian warriors of survivance*. Middletown, CT: Wesleyan University Press.

Vizenor, G. (1994b). The ruins of representation: Shadow survivance and the literature of dominance. In A. Arteaga (Ed.), *An other tongue* (pp. 139–168). Durham, NC: Duke University Press.

Vizenor, G. (1998). *Fugitive poses: Native American Indian scenes of absence and presence*. Lincoln: University of Nebraska Press.

Vizenor, G. (2003). *Hiroshima bugi*. Lincoln: University of Nebraska Press.

Vizenor, G. (2006). *Bear Island: The war at Sugar Point*. Minneapolis: University of Minnesota Press.

Vizenor, G. (2008). *Survivance: Narratives of Native presence*. Lincoln: University of Nebraska Press.

Vizenor, G. & Lee, A. R. (1999). *Postindian conversations*. Lincoln: University of Nebraska Press.

Von Franz, M.–L. (1968). The process of individuation. In C. G. Jung (Ed.), *Man and his symbols* (pp. 157–254). New York: NY: Dell.

Waller, D. (1996). Friendly fire: When environmentalists dehumanize American Indians. *American Indian Culture and Research Journal*, 20(2), 107–126.

Waziyatawin (W. A. Wilson). (2008). *What does justice look like? The struggle for liberation in Dakota homeland*. St. Paul, MN: Living Justice Press.

Whaley, R., & Bresette, W. (1994). *Walleye warriors: An effective alliance against racism and for the earth*. Philadelphia, PA: New Society.

Wilber, K. (1995). *Sex, ecology, spirituality: The spirit of evolution*. Boston, MA: Shambhala.

Wilber, K. (2007). *The integral vision*. Boston, MA: Shambhala.

Wilkinson, R. G., & Pickett, K. (2009). *The spirit level: Why greater equality makes societies stronger*. New York, NY: Bloomsbury Press.

Williams, T. T. (1992). *Refuge: An unnatural history of family and place*. New York, NY: Vintage Books.

Williams, T. T. (2008). *Finding beauty in a broken world*. New York, NY: Pantheon.

Williams, T. T. (2012). *When women were birds*. New York, NY: Farrar, Straus and Giroux.

Williams, W. L. (1986). *The spirit and the flesh: Sexual diversity in American Indian culture*. Boston, MA: Beacon Press.

Wilson, E. O. (1984). *Biophilia*. Cambridge, MA: Harvard University Press.

Wilson, S. (2008). *Research is ceremony: Indigenous research methods*. Black Point, Canada: Fernwood.

Winkelman, M. (2010). *Shamanism*. Santa Barbara, CA: Praeger.

Wise, T. (n.d.). *The pathology of privilege*. Retrieved from http://vimeo.com/25637392

Witherspoon, G. (1987). *Navajo weaving – Art in its cultural context*. Flagstaff, AZ: Museum of Northern Arizona Research Paper 36.

Worthington, E. L. (2006). *Forgiveness and reconciliation: Theory and application*. New York, NY: Routledge.

Wyman, L. (1967). *The sacred mountains of the Navajo*. Flagstaff, AZ: Museum of Northern Arizona.

Zimmerman, M. (2002). *Metamorphoses: A play*. Evanston, IL: Northwestern University Press.

Zimmerman, M. (2014). *Secret in the wings*. Evanston, IL: Northwestern University Press.

Zinn, H. (n.d.). *What is radical history?* Retrieved from http://www.historyisaweapon.com/defcon1/zinnwhatisradicalhistory.html

Zizek, S. (2013). *Demanding the impossible*. Cambridge, England: Polity Press.

INDEX

CPSIA information can be obtained
at www.ICGtesting.com
Printed in the USA
BVHW012129060919

557668BV00002B/5/P